D0085885

Table of Contents

Preface

The growth of managed care is an attempt by private employers and the federal government to gain some control on both the cost and the quality of medical care. The field of case management has grown parallel with the growth of the managed care field. Case Managers are on the front line of managed care and clinical care, providing information, support, and counseling. Case management has been shown to improve clinical outcomes and to both increase the efficiency and decrease the costs associated with complex medical care. Insurers, employers, providers, and patients all are utilizing the Case Manager's skills and, as such, the demand for qualified Case Managers grows every year. Case management is a very information-intensive field. The amount of medical, psychological, legal, and technological information a Case Manager needs at his or her fingertips is staggering. Further, this information is cosseted in hundreds of different books, articles, newsletters, and government publications.

The current practitioners of case management come from many disciplines, including nursing, social work, psychological counseling, etc. Although these varied backgrounds add depth and complexity to a Case Manager's skills, the knowledge base of any individual Case Manager may be incomplete. Case management certification is aimed at ensuring a uniform knowledge base for all Case Managers. This study guide was developed to support that goal by providing the following:

- a source of clear, concise information on case management for those in the health care industry
- a quick reference resource to Case Managers working in the field
- a study tool for those preparing for case management certification

This book does not represent a compendium of all information needed to pass the Certified Case Manager (CCM) exam. It is hoped that this book will provide a basis from which the readers may expand their studies in case management. The authors refer the readers to the many excellent texts available in case management and related fields to "flesh out" their understanding of the various topics. In addition, the interactive CD-ROM enclosed facilitates practice test taking. The CD-ROM enables the user to select questions randomly or by subject area or take a timed practice exam. The application displays the test score, test time, number of questions attempted, and number and percentage of questions answered correctly.

HOW TO USE THIS STUDY GUIDE

While the book may be read from beginning to end, it has been written so that each chapter comprises information on each of the major testing areas in the CCM exam. The questions have been written in the formats favored by the CCM and are included as a tool to help focus your study sessions. Due to the comprehensive nature of the exam, there are questions included in the book and CD-ROM that have not been covered in the text. Therefore, we highly recommend that you read the books in the reading list provided by the Commission for Case Management Certification in their Certificate Guide. We have included it in Appendix H.

The authors recommend the following approach to using this book and CD-ROM.

- Take a practice test.
- Assess your strengths and weaknesses in each area.
- Note those areas in which you need the most work.
- Study those areas.
- Re-test.

Continue this process until you are proficient in all the subject areas.

1) **Of the following, which are common causes of malpractice litigation?**

1. Discourteous behavior by the professional
2. Provider/patient miscommunication
3. Lack of patient understanding
4. Failure to inform a patient's family of pertinent issues
   A. 1, 3
   B. 2, 4
   C. 1, 2, 3
   D. All of the above
   E. None of the above

2) **Case Managers may decrease the legal liability associated with patient discharges through which of the following activities?**

1. Reviewing the case with the treating physician
2. Confirming the integrity of the patient's support network
3. Reviewing the complete medical record
4. Confirming the adequacy of follow-up outpatient care
   A. 1, 3
   B. 2, 4
   C. 1, 2, 3
   D. All of the above
   E. None of the above

3) **Disclosure of confidential information is mandatory when:**

A. It is pursuant to judicial proceedings
B. It is government mandated
C. A professional has a duty to warn a third party about the illness of a patient
D. All of the above
E. None of the above

4) **The court case of *Wickline v. State of California* found:**

1. Medical doctors have a duty to protest adverse determinations by payers.
2. Medical doctors can shift their liability to payers if they do protest adverse determinations.
3. Payers of health care can be held accountable if their adverse decisions are arbitrary, for cost containment and are not based on acceptable medical standards of practice in the community.
4. Case Managers are not liable for their roles in adverse determinations.
   A. 1, 2, 3
   B. 2, 3, 4
   C. 1, 2, 3
   D. None of the above

5) **Which of the following statements best defines ethics, as they relate to case management?**

1. The rules of conduct that govern a person, or members of a profession
2. The thoughts that govern a person's conduct
3. A society's ideal for a person's conduct
4. The minimal acceptable standards for a person's conduct
   A. 1, 3
   B. 2, 4
   C. 1, 2, 3
   D. All of the above
   E. None of the above

6) **Of the following, which activity(s) is (are) associated with a decreased risk of allegations of breach of patient confidentiality?**

1. Understanding applicable federal and state regulations on the disclosure of medical information
2. Quickly transferring information to any and all parties who request it, without bothering to notify patient, attorneys, etc.
3. Informing the patient of his or her right to refuse the disclosure of medical information to any or all parties.
4. Transferring patient information concerning abortions or venereal and psychiatric diseases to third parties, without discussing first with the patient and/or attorneys
   A. 1, 3
   B. 2, 4
   C. 1, 2, 3
   D. All of the above
   E. None of the above

7) **A request by an insured or a provider to re-review a denial of a utilization review organization's decision is also known as:**

1. An appeal
2. A reconsideration
3. An expedited appeal
4. An IME
   A. 1, 2
   B. 1, 3
   C. 1, 4
   D. All of the above
   E. None of the above

8) **During a case management interview, in a Workers' Compensation case, the patient confides to the Case Manager that he is a recovering alcoholic and has been alcohol free for 5 years. The Case Manager should:**

A. Include the information in the psychosocial section of her insurance company report.
B. Immediately notify the patient's attending physician.
C. Make no comment verbally or in writing as it has no current bearing on a work-related injury.
D. Close the case.

9) **A Case Manager is frustrated by her inability to get her patient to agree to occupational therapy. The patient was involved in a high-speed motor vehicle accident and suffered severe head injuries. When encouraged to attend therapy sessions the patient refuses, becomes verbally abusive and hangs up. Likely reason(s) for this patient's reaction is (are):**

A. Head injuries can result in emotional instability.
B. Head injuries can result in cognitive impairments.
C. Head injuries can result in prolonged head pain and mood depression.
D. All of the above
E. None of the above

10) **Which of the following diagnoses should trigger an inquiry for potential Case Management services?**

1. Blepharitis
2. Spinal cord injury
3. Coryza
4. Non–Hodgkin's lymphoma
    A. 1, 3
    B. 2, 4
    C. 1, 2, 3
    D. All of the above
    E. None of the above

11) **Of the following, which are "sentinel procedures" that should prompt inquires for Case Management services?**

1. Brain biopsy
2. Bone marrow biopsy
3. Endocardiac biopsy
4. Skin biopsy
    A. 1, 3
    B. 2, 4
    C. 1, 2, 3
    D. All of the above
    E. None of the above

12) **Of the following, which utilization figure for an individual's medical claims would make an appropriate financial threshold for Case Management evaluations?**

A. Claims exceeding $500 per year
B. Claims exceeding $1,000 per year
C. Claims exceeding $10,000 per year
D. Claims exceeding $100,000 per year
E. Claims exceeding $1,000,000 per year

13) **Which of the following is needed in order for the Case Manager to ensure an accurate assessment of the impact an injury will have on a patient and his ability to return to work?**

A. The physical requirements of the patient's position
B. The coworkers'/employer's opinion of the patient's ability
C. A history of childhood diseases
D. All of the above
E. None of the above

14) **Which of the following statements are true regarding the clinical consequences of head injuries?**

1. A patient may become depressed.
2. A patient's cognitive ability may be impaired.
3. Emotional lability is common.
4. Chronic headaches may be result.
    A. 1, 3
    B. 1, 2, 4
    C. 1, 2, 3
    D. All of the above
    E. None of the above

15) **Of the following methodologies, which are common means that insurers and Case Managers use for identifying potential patients for Case Management services?**

1. Selecting cases with catastrophic diagnoses, such as head or spine injury
2. Selecting cases with "sentinel procedures," such as bone marrow biopsy or brain biopsy
3. Selecting cases with claims costs over $10,000 a year
4. Selecting cases at random, and investigating for potential problems
   A. 1, 3
   B. 2, 4
   C. 1, 2, 3
   D. All of the above
   E. None of the above

16) **A variety of cognitive techniques may be utilized for pain control. The following are examples of some of these techniques.**

1. Distraction
2. Pain medication
3. Relaxation training
4. Biofeedback
   A. 3, 4
   B. 1, 2, 3
   C. 1, 3, 4
   D. All of the above
   E. None of the above

17) **The Case Manager can expect which of the following after ACL reconstruction surgery?**

A. Jogging by the twelfth postoperative week
B. Full weight bearing and range of motion by the fourth postoperative week
C. Bent knee raises and isometric exercises on the affected leg for the first postoperative week while immobilized in a hinged-type brace
D. All of the above

18) **_____ is the paralysis of all four limbs.**

A. Hemiplegia
B. Paraplegia
C. Quadriplegia
D. Quadripara

19) **_____ is the inability or difficulty in swallowing.**

A. Dysphasia
B. Aphasia
C. Apraxia
D. Dysphagia

20) **The Case Manager with a patient who is paraplegic because of a spinal cord injury recognizes that a major early problem will be:**

A. Use of ambulation aids
B. Patient education
C. Bladder control
D. All of the above
E. None of the above

21) **Which of the following organizations are exempt from the mandates of the Americans With Disabilities Act?**

1. Small businesses with fewer than 15 employees
2. The federal government
3. Native American tribes
4. Software manufacturers

A. 1, 3
B. 2, 4
C. 1, 2, 3
D. All of the above
E. None of the above

22) Under the proscriptions of the Americans With Disabilities Act, which of the following are *not* considered "reasonable accommodations" by the employer?

1. Making the disabled "typist" a receptionist who only answers phones
2. Modifying equipment to accommodate disabled employees
3. Making the paralyzed "ballet dancer" into a "theatrical director" of the ballet company
4. Providing qualified interpreters for the hearing impaired
    A. 1, 3
    B. 2, 4
    C. 1, 2, 3
    D. All of the above
    E. None of the above

23) Which of the following statements are true, regarding the Women's Health and Cancer Rights Act?

1. It is a new law, enacted as part of the Omnibus Appropriations Bill.
2. It assures coverage for surgery of the contralateral breast to provide a symmetrical appearance after mastectomy.
3. It amended ERISA to require both health plans and self-insured plans to provide coverage for mastectomies and certain reconstructive surgeries.
4. It assures coverage for breast prostheses after mastectomy.
    A. 1, 3
    B. 2, 4
    C. 1, 2, 3
    D. All of the above
    E. None of the above

24) Which of the following statements are true regarding unemployment insurance?

1. Financing of unemployment benefits are uniform from state to state.
2. Unemployment compensation benefits guarantee a replacement of 50% of salary.
3. Benefits are never extended past the usual maximum length of benefit.
4. All states pay a minimum of 46 weeks of unemployment benefits.
    A. 1, 3
    B. 2, 4
    C. 1, 2, 3
    D. All of the above
    E. None of the above

25) Which of the following is (are) true regarding Workers' Compensation insurance?

1. The scope of coverage varies from state to state.
2. Benefits generally include the cost of legal bills only.
3. Employees are entitled to the level of benefit mandated by the state.
4. Self-funded health insurance programs are exempt from the mandates of Workers' Compensation regulations.
    A. 1, 3
    B. 2, 4
    C. 1, 2, 3
    D. All of the above
    E. None of the above

26) **Which of the following statements about indemnity Health Insurance Plans is (are) *not* true?**

   1. It is a legal entity.
   2. It is licensed by the federal Department of the Interior.
   3. It exists to provide health insurance to enrollees.
   4. It reimburses enrollees for the cost of any health care they desire.
      A. 1, 3
      B. 2, 4
      C. 1, 2, 3
      D. All of the above
      E. None of the above

27) **Which of the following does not determine minimum policy limits of PIP automobile insurance?**

   1. State insurance department
   2. Accident rate in local community
   3. State insurance commissioner
   4. Driver's record of accidents
      A. 1, 3
      B. 2, 4
      C. 1, 2, 3
      D. All of the above
      E. None of the above

28) **A 35-year-old male engineer, who is wheelchair bound secondary to a spinal injury, applies for a job in a large engineering firm. The job advertisement calls for candidates with a PhD in engineering, yet he only has a master's degree. The applicant reasons that under the proscriptions of the ADA, the employer must make "reasonable accommodations" to the disabled, and therefore his master's degree should be good enough to get the job. The employer is justified (under the ADA) in denying this applicant employment because:**

   A. The candidate cannot perform the "essential functions" of the job, because he is wheel-chair bound and therefore cannot use the existing computer equipment.
   B. The candidate is not "qualified" for the job, because he does not have the requirements requested in the written job advertisement.
   C. The candidate cannot enter the building because it lacks a ramp.
   D. The candidate cannot perform the job adequately because it requires adherence to a strict time schedule, and his disability requires advance notice for his transportation.
   E. The candidate cannot work in the building because it lacks appropriate bathroom facilities.

29) **Which of the following benefits are usually *included* under the terms of the Pregnancy Discrimination Act?**

   1. Home health care
   2. Abortions
   3. Home physical therapy care
   4. Mandatory maternity leave
      A. 1, 3
      B. 2, 4
      C. 1, 2, 3
      D. All of the above
      E. None of the above

30) **Which of the following mental health benefit limitations are not allowable under the tenets of the Mental Health Parity Act?**

   1. Annual dollar limit for mental health care
   2. Limited number of annual outpatient visits
   3. Lifetime dollar limit on mental health care
   4. Limited number of inpatient days annually
      A. 1, 3
      B. 2, 4
      C. 1, 2, 3
      D. All of the above
      E. None of the above

31) **Case Management is defined by the CMSA as a process that includes which of the following?**

   1. Managed care
   2. Assessing, planning, and monitoring
   3. Collaboration, coordination, and communication
   4. Implementation and evaluation
      A. All of the above
      B. None of the above
      C. 1, 2, 3
      D. 2, 3, 4

32) **Which of the following answers are not included in the Five Core Areas of Case Management?**

   A. The return to work process
   B. Benefit systems and cost benefit analysis
   C. Case Management concepts
   D. Community resources

33) **Case finding, gathering and assessing information and problem identification are all part of:**

   A. Patient advocacy
   B. The return to work assessment
   C. The Case Management process
   D. The precertification process

34) **Diagnosis, high costs, and multiple admissions or treatments are red flags for:**

   A. Pre-existing HMO exclusions
   B. Utilization management review
   C. Case Management evaluation
   D. Disability hearings

35) **The Case Manager never contacts:**

   A. The patient
   B. The caregivers
   C. The employer
   D. The patient's coworkers

36) **A Case Management consent agreement provides for which of the following?**

   1. Release of clinical information to the Case Manager
   2. Claims payment
   3. Permission to review the case information with the parties involved in the care of the patient or the payment of services
   4. Provision of durable medical equipment

A. 1, 2
B. 2, 3
C. 1, 3
D. 3, 4

37) **In the Case Management process the stage of "obtaining approval" refers to:**

A. Permission from the patient to implement Case Management
B. Permission from the payer to implement a care plan
C. Permission from claims to negotiate fees
D. None of the above

38) **Case Managers perform their function in the following four areas: medical, financial, vocational and _____:**

A. Workers' Compensation
B. Social
C. Legal
D. Behavioral/motivational

39) **Continual assessment of the care plan is part of which process(es)?**

A. Initial evaluation
B. Goal setting
C. Implementation
D. Monitoring and evaluation

40) **The CMSA states that nationally the typical savings for every dollar spent on Case Management services are:**

A. $1–$5
B. $5–$7
C. $5–$11
D. $11–$15

41) **Which of the following is true regarding the purpose of an orthosis?**

1. It can be used to support body parts.
2. It can be used to position body parts.
3. It can be used to immobilize body parts.
4. It can be used modify muscle tone.
   A. 1, 3
   B. 2, 4
   C. 1, 2, 3
   D. All of the above
   E. None of the above

42) **Which of the following is true regarding a prosthesis?**

1. It may restore or replace all or part of a missing body part.
2. It may improve a person's sense of wholeness or body image.
3. It has as its goals increased function and cosmesis.
4. It may result in injury or illness if improperly fitted.
   A. 1, 3
   B. 2, 4
   C. 1, 2, 3
   D. All of the above
   E. None of the above

43) **Which of the following is true regarding assistive devices?**

1. They are products that substitute for an impaired function.
2. They are a substitute for rehabilitation services.
3. They allow an individual to perform an activity more independently.
4. When prescribing one, little input is needed from the patient or the patient's family.
   A. 1, 3
   B. 2, 4
   C. 1, 2, 3
   D. All of the above
   E. None of the above

44) **Which of the following factors may influence the rate of prosthesis replacement?**

1. Activity level
2. Age of user
3. Type of prosthesis
4. Impact resistance of materials used
   A. 1, 3
   B. 2, 4
   C. 1, 2, 3
   D. All of the above
   E. None of the above

45) **Which of the following are (is) considered an assistive device?**

1. Text to speech synthesizer
2. Phone receiver volume control
3. Quad cane
4. Grab bars in the tub
   A. 1, 3
   B. 2, 4
   C. 1, 2, 3
   D. All of the above
   E. None of the above

46) **The three basic goals of a patient interview is to:**

1. Provide information.
2. Establish rapport.
3. Provide a care plan.
4. Collect information.
5. Formulate a care plan.
   A. 1, 2, 3
   B. 2, 3, 4
   C. 1, 4, 5
   D. 2, 4, 5

47) **When the Case Manager is arranging for discharge to a traumatic brain injury (TBI) rehabilitation facility she should:**

1. Confirm that the facility can provide the therapies, by credentialed providers, that the patient requires.
2. Verify that there is a board certified medical director at the facility.
3. Ensure that the facility is accredited by the Joint Commission on Accreditation of Health-care Organizations (Joint Commission or JCAHO) and CARF.
4. Certify an unlimited length of stay to ensure the patient gets the care he needs.
   A. 1, 2, 3
   B. 2, 3 , 4
   C. All of the above
   D. None of the above

48) **The Case Manager will find which of the following services difficult to arrange at home?**

A. Homemaker services
B. Durable medical equipment
C. Personal care
D. All of the above
E. None of the above

49) **When conducting an interview it is important that the Case Manager ask about the medical history of the patient. In order to get the most from the interview, questions should be of what type?**

A. Open-ended
B. Who, what, where, when, why and how
C. Direct
D. Leading

50) **Case Managers should follow up on arrangements they have made for durable medical equipment to:**

A. Determine if it is being used.
B. Determine if it was delivered.
C. Determine if the patient and caregiver are satisfied with the equipment.
D. Determine if it meets the current need of the patient.
E. All of the above

1) **Answer: D**

Discourteous behaviors, communications failures, lack of patient understanding and lack of family understanding are the most common causes of malpractice litigation. Malpractice litigation stems more commonly from poor relationships with patients than from negligent medical care.

2) **Answer: D**

The Case Manager has an obligation of "reasonable care" to the patient. Failing to assure that the discharge is "safe" would be negligent on the part of the Case Manager.

3) **Answer: D**

4) **Answer: C**

Case Managers are liable for damages if their referral of patients to providers is negligently performed and harm comes to the patient as a direct result of that referral.

5) **Answer: A**

Ethics are the rules or standards that govern the conduct of a person or members of a profession. Ethical rules describe a society's ideal of how a person or professional should conduct him- or herself.

6) **Answer: A**

A Case Manager can decrease the risk of allegations of breach of confidentiality by fully understanding the following: the implications of federal and state regulations on the disclosure of medical information; that venereal diseases, abortion, mental illness, and substance abuse are very sensitive topics, and transferring such information should be done only after discussion with the patient and attorney; and that a patient has the right to refuse all information release.

7) **Answer: A**

An appeal or reconsideration. An expedited appeal may be requested if an urgent need exists for a particular service or treatment. An IME is an independent medical exam and is most often used in Workers' Compensation or Disability cases.

8) **Answer: C**

According to the Code of Professional Ethics, it is the responsibility of the Case Manager to safeguard the patient's confidentiality unless there is a legal requirement to disclose the information.

9) **Answer: D**

10) **Answer: B**

Both spinal cord injuries and lymphomas are complex, high-cost and life-threatening illnesses that may potentially benefit from Case Management. Coryza is a common cold, and blepharitis is a minor infection of the eyelid.

11) **Answer: C**

Although biopsies of the endocardium, the brain and bone marrow involve high risk, and are done infrequently, biopsies of the skin are low risk, are commonly performed and require Case Management services in a small minority of cases.

12) **Answer: C**

Screening all patients with claims over $500 and $1,000 per year would yield too many claims and too few catastrophic illnesses. Those patients with claims of $100,000 and over would no doubt be well known to the insurers and Case Managers long before the patients hit those thresholds. Thresholds of $5,000 to $10,000 are most commonly seen in the industry.

13) **Answer: A**

In order to make an accurate determination in regard to a patient's ability to return to work, the Case Manager and the team involved in the care of the patient must know the physical requirements of the patient's job.

14) **Answer: B**

15) **Answer: C**

Common methodologies include screening claims of catastrophic diagnoses, sentinel procedures, high claims cost, and direct case referral from community physicians.

16) **Answer: C**

Pain medication is not a cognitive technique.

17) **Answer: C**

Postoperatively, the knee is immobilized in a hinged brace in a flexed position.

18) **Answer: C**

19) **Answer: D**

20) **Answer: C**

The micturation reflex center is located in the sacral region of the spinal cord. As a result bladder function may be impaired with a lower spinal cord injury.

21) **Answer: C**

The exceptions to the ADA are:

- Religious organizations, or private membership clubs, except when these organizations sponsor a public event
- The federal government or corporations owned by the federal government
- Native American tribes
- Compliance with this Act can prove a hardship for small employers. Therefore, if an employer has fewer than 15 employees, he is exempt. (Note: Because an accommodation is expensive for an employer, it does not automatically make it a "hardship.")

22) **Answer: A**

The employer is obligated to make "reasonable accommodations" to an individual's disability that allow the employee to perform his job. Reasonable accommodations in employment may include:

- Making existing facilities readily accessible to, and usable by an individual with disabilities
- Job restructuring, part-time or modified work schedules, reassignment to a vacant position
- Acquisition or modification of equipment or devices
- Appropriate adjustment or modification of examinations, training materials or policies
- Provision of qualified readers or interpreters, and other similar accommodations for individuals with disabilities

In the examples above, the individual hired as a typist must be able to type, similarly, a ballet dancer must be able to dance; changing the essential job function, while laudatory, is not mandated by the ADA.

23) **Answer: D**

The Women's Health and Cancer Rights Act is a new law that was enacted as part of an Omnibus Appropriation Bill, and became effective for plan years beginning on or after October 21, 1998. This Act amended ERISA to require group health plans, including self-insured plans that provide coverage for mastectomies, to provide certain reconstructive and related services following mastectomies. The services mandated by the Act include:
- Reconstruction of the breast upon which the mastectomy has been performed
- Surgery and reconstruction of the other breast to produce a symmetrical appearance
- Prosthesis and treatment for physical complications attendant to the mastectomy, for example, lymphedema

24) **Answer: E**

State financing and benefit laws vary widely. In general, unemployment compensation benefits under state laws are intended to replace about 50% of an average worker's previous wages. Maximum weekly benefits provisions, however, result in benefits of less than 50% for most higher-earning workers. All states pay benefits to some unemployed persons for 26 weeks. In some states, the duration of benefits depends on the amount earned and the number of weeks worked in a previous year. In others, all recipients are entitled to benefits for the same length of time. During periods of heavy unemployment, federal law authorizes extended benefits, in some cases up to 39 weeks; in 1975 extended benefits were payable for up to 65 weeks. Extended benefits are financed in part by federal employer taxes.

25) **Answer: A**

The scope of coverage for Workers' Compensation benefits varies by state, with respect to benefits payable in case of death, total disability, and of partial disability owing to specific injuries or continuing during specified periods. Although they vary among states, these benefits generally include the cost of medical bills attendant to treating the illness or injury, as well as some percentage of lost wages. The compensation benefits, set forth by the state, take precedence over the funding source. Employees are entitled to the level of benefits mandated by the state without regard to the financial status or desires of the employer. Therefore, even if the employer is self-funded or self-administered, he is required to offer the full level of benefits required by the state's Workers' Compensation Commission. Self-funded group health insurance plans may be exempt from mandated benefits under ERISA guidelines, but are not exempt under Worker's Compensation regulations.

26) **Answer: B**

An indemnity health insurance plan is a legal entity licensed by the state insurance department. It exists to provide health insurance to its enrollees. An indemnity health insurer "indemnifies" or reimburses the enrollee for the costs of health care claims that are medically necessary and appropriate for his care. Indemnity insurers historically had not spent money or time on utilization or quality management. Now, because of savings demonstrated by the managed care companies, some indemnity companies have adopted these cost-saving approaches.

27) **Answer: B**

Each state determines what the minimum level of liability insurance will be for drivers in that state. While the costs of car insurance premium may vary by the cost of the automobile, the community accident experience, or the driving record of the owner, the minimum policy limits for personal injury protection don't.

28) **Answer: B**

The ADA offers protection for "qualified disabled" individuals. In this case the candidate for the job is not qualified for the job. The ADA does not consider a change in the essential functions of the job to be a "reasonable accommodation."

29) **Answer: A**

Although its scope is large, the Pregnancy Discrimination Act does exclude some benefits. Those benefits are abortions and mandatory maternity leave. When home health and home physical therapy are allowed under medical benefits, they are included under maternity benefits also.

30) **Answer: A**

Although annual or lifetime dollar limits cannot be set under the provisions of the Mental Health Parity Act, other limits are allowed. Examples of other allowable limits are:
- Limited number of annual outpatient visits
- Limited number of inpatient days annually
- A per-visit fee limit
- Higher deductibles and copayments are allowed in mental health benefits under MHPA, without parity in medical and surgical benefits

If an employer does not offer medical benefits, he does not have to offer mental health benefits; said differently, if an employer chooses not to offer mental health benefits, he must also choose not to offer medical benefits.

31) **Answer: D**

32) **Answer: A**

The return to work process (RTW) is part of Workers' Compensation Case Management, not a core component of Case Management. The five core areas consist of B, C, and D, physical and psychological factors and coordination and service delivery.

33) **Answer: C**

The Case Management process, which also includes planning, reporting, obtaining approval, coordination, follow-up, monitoring and evaluation.

34) **Answer: C**

These are the three criteria for Case Management referrals.

35) **Answer: D**

The first three choices are involved in the patient's care or benefit payment. The caregivers are contacted for the assessment of the patient and his progress. The employer is contacted for approval of benefit plans or return to work information. The patient is contacted to collaborate with the Case Manager on his care plan.

36) **Answer: C**

37) **Answer: B**

38) **Answer: D**

39) **Answer: D**

40) **Answer: C**

41) **Answer: D**

An orthosis is a device that is added to a person's body to achieve one or more of the following ends: support, position, immobilize, correct deformities, assist weak muscles, restore muscle function, and modify muscle tone. The term *orthosis* generally encompasses such devices as slings, braces, and splints. Orthoses are used to support or aid in the functioning of the upper and lower extremities, hands and feet, as well as the trunk and spine. These devices can be relatively simple affairs, made of cotton belts and plastic splints, or they can be complex electromechanical appliances replete with steel alloys, cantilevered joints, and servomotors.

42) **Answer: D**

A prosthesis is a device that restores or replaces all or part of a missing body part. The science of prosthetics addresses the mechanical, physiologic and cosmetic functions of restorations. While the orthoses are aimed at *assisting* the body to restore function, prostheses restore or *replace* those parts of the human body that are absent or no longer function. The need for replacement and cosmesis rather than a simple increase in functionality stems from a person's need for "wholeness" and a "positive body image." With this in mind, the professional prosthetist has as his goals, increasing both functionality and cosmesis. Poorly fitted prostheses can cause injury or illness.

43) Answer: A

Assistive or adaptive devices are products that substitute for an impaired function, and allow the individual to perform an activity more independently. Adaptive devices should be used only if other methods of performing the task are not available or cannot be learned. A reasonable effort should be made to teach the patient a method of performing the task in question, before an adaptive device is suggested. Mastery of a task, for example walking, allows the patient greater independence and flexibility in that he does not need a wheelchair to move around and is not limited by lack of ramps, etc. The device may serve as a useful supplement, however, or permit a function to be performed if the adapted method cannot be learned or requires too much effort. The type of assistive device is determined by the needs of the individual patient, his abilities and functional limitations, and his environment.

44) Answer: D

Many factors influence replacement frequency. For example, lower extremity prostheses bear weight, sustain high impact and are exposed to the elements. Damage to the prostheses acquired by these activities demands maintenance, repair and replacement. Replacement frequency depends on the activity level of the patient and the demands he puts on the prosthesis as well as the complexity of the prosthesis and the properties of the materials used. Further, an individual's prosthetic needs may change. For example, a sedentary individual may become more active, requiring a new prosthesis with more features and flexibility. Conversely, an active individual, with advancing age or disease may become more sedentary, requiring a replacement prosthesis that is lighter and more stable. Finally, the younger patient will require successively larger prostheses to compensate for growth.

45) Answer: D

46) Answer: D

Providing information is not one of the basic goals of the interview. Providing a care plan does not allow the patient to be an active participant in the care planning process.

47) Answer: A

Certifications should be time limited and progress reports should be evaluated prior to extending lengths of stay. Verifying the credentials of the facility and providers is important in choosing an appropriate facility for the patient.

48) Answer: E

49) Answer: A

Open-ended. All the other answers do not leave room for the patient to introduce new information, nor do they leave the door open for free communication.

50) Answer: E

Chapter 2

Legal Aspects of Case Management

Case Managers today assume responsibilities in all care settings, from critical care and mental health to workers' compensation and health maintenance organizations (HMOs). Though the Case Manager's role involves patient and family education, aiding communication, seeking new health care resources and improving outcomes, it is a sad truth, but even an involvement that is this positive projects legal liability. A Case Manager's autonomy and responsibility put the Case Manager at higher risk for malpractice litigation.

Common causes in malpractice litigation are:

- Discourteous behavior
- Communication failures
- Lack of patient understanding
- Lack of information given to the patient family[1]

For some, it is surprising that the terms "bad clinical outcome" and "negligence" are absent from this list. Investigations into the cause of malpractice litigations[2,3] reveal the following surprising facts:[4]

- In the course of standard medical management there is a *substantial amount of injury to patients*.
- Many of these injuries are the *result of substandard care*.
- Malpractice litigation *infrequently* compensates patients injured by medical negligence.
- Malpractice litigation *rarely identifies* or holds providers accountable for their substandard care.

Put alternatively, malpractice suits don't occur necessarily because of negligence or even a bad outcome but because of bad relationships between providers and patients. One study documented that "poor relationships with providers before the injury"[4(p792)] were responsible for 53% of calls to plaintiff attorney's offices. Other important causes for calling an attorney mentioned in this article were explicit recommendations by health care providers to seek legal counsel, and the impression, held by the patient, of not being kept informed by providers.

Managing the patient relationship, keeping the patient and family informed, and using prudence and circumspection when discussing litigation with patients are all areas in which the Case Manager exerts considerable control. Through this control, a Case Manager can prevent litigation.

LIABILITY ISSUES IN CASE MANAGEMENT

When one examines instances of professional liability, several areas are noted for their high risk of litigation. They are premature discharge, bad faith claims denials, negligent patient assessment, negligent referral, invasion of privacy, breech of confidentiality, and lack of informed consent. These high-risk occurrences are explained in more detail in the following paragraphs.

Premature Discharge

When a Case Manager encourages the discharge of a patient or refuses to approve payment for continued stay in a health care facility, he or she undertakes a grave responsibility. Discharging a patient before the patient is ready, or discharging the patient to an outpatient setting inappropriate to meet that patient's needs, can have disastrous results. In the case of *Wickline v. State of California*, Lois Wickline's physician requested additional hospitalization for his patient. MediCal, the insurer in this case, refused. Medical complications, which may have been avoided if Ms. Wickline was hospitalized, necessitated the amputation of her leg. Ms. Wickline successfully sued MediCal. This settlement was later overturned. Some lessons derived from this case are that Case Managers and their employers can be held responsible for bad outcomes, and that Case Manager's input can affect medical judgment of providers. (Further discussion of this can be found in Chapter 5.) Therefore, Case Managers should aggressively seek all data necessary to make an informed decision, and then exercise their influence with restraint and in the best interests of the patient. In the case of *Wilson v. Blue Cross of Southern California, Blue Cross/Blue Shield of Alabama, and Western Medical Review*, a depressed patient was discharged from a psychiatric hospital against the recommendations of the treating physician. The patient subsequently committed suicide. The estate sued the insurer and the utilization management company for wrongful death. During the trial it was revealed that the medical director had not adequately reviewed the medical record before denying continued hospitalization. The medical director of the insurer claimed it was the treating physician's responsibility to make him aware of all information necessary to substantiate continued stay in the hospital. Though the courts found that Mr. Wilson's suicide could not be causally related to his early discharge, the case has been interpreted to support the position that insurers exercise "reasonable care" when denying coverage for services, even if the attending physician does not appeal the decision. A Case Manager may decrease the risk associated with patient discharges by doing the following:

- reviewing the patient's complete medical record
- discussing the intention to discharge the patient with the treating physician
- confirming the adequacy of follow-up medical care for the patient
- confirming the integrity of the patient's social support network.

Bad Faith

Bad faith claims are often the result of the plaintiff's perception of an inappropriate denial of benefits. The insurer and its agents are contractually obligated to act in "good faith and fair dealing" in the administration of claims. Bad faith occurs when any of the following criteria are met:

- There is no reasonable basis for the denial of benefits. This often occurs because no procedure for determining medical necessity or appropriateness of proposed care exists.
- The insurer is aware that claims are denied without a reasonable basis but does nothing about it.
- An insurer's impenetrable bureaucracy, complicated or unnecessary procedures, or frank ineptitude in claims processing results in dangerous delays in approval. The courts view these inappropriate delays as *de facto* denials.

A landmark case that demonstrates bad faith on the part of the insurer is *Fox v. Healthnet*.[5] In *Fox v. Healthnet* the courts awarded the estate of Nelene Fox $89.3 million based on the insurer's refusal to pay for a bone marrow transplant. Though Ms. Fox had met all benefit provisions for treatment of her metastatic breast cancer, Healthnet refused to pay. The managers in Healthnet even went so far as to coerce her treating physician to reverse his recommendation for the procedure. Ms. Fox was able to raise money and received her transplant after a delay of two months. Ms. Fox did not go into remission and died 8 months later. The final nail in Healthnet's coffin was hammered in when the jury was notified that bonuses were paid to the utilization executives based on the total dollars in medical care denied during the year. Healthnet evidenced bad faith because it placed earnings before the interests of its subscribers and actively conspired to deny appropriate medical care.

Case Managers can decrease their risk of bad faith litigation by observing the following suggestions.[6]

- *Medical director:* Only the medical director should issue claims denials.
- *Documentation:* The medical director and the Case Manager should extensively document denials and their rationale.
- *Review medical records:* Medical records may contain mitigating circumstances that could change a claims denial to an approval. Information gleaned from medical records should be communicated to the medical director. A Case Manager should record the time, date, and findings of his or her chart review and any discussion with attending physicians in notes.
- *Review benefit allowance and exclusions:* A full understanding of the benefit contract will obviate many discussions of medical necessity and appropriateness. Consultation with legal counsel or medical experts may be necessary in some cases.
- *Determination of medical necessity:* Many claims for services may be denied for lack of medical necessity. This decision is the province of the medical director and should be the product of a well described and documented procedure.
- *Awareness of timelines:* Be aware of regulatory and contractual turnaround times for case review. These may range from a few days to more than a month. In emergent situations, subscribers have the right to an expedited review, usually completed in 48 hours. If evaluation of the case will take longer than the time allowed, the subscriber should be informed of the delay and given the reasons, as well as the expected date of completion.
- *Appeals process:* In most instances, a subscriber is entitled to appeal adverse decisions made by the insurer. The courts have held that failure to inform the patient of his or her right to appeal is a violation of good faith. The prudent Case Manager should include information regarding a patient's right to appeal the adverse decision in the letter of denial. This information should include the name, address or phone number of the ap-

peals coordinator, the appropriate methods of appealing (phone, letter, through provider, etc.), timelines for appeal, and when a response can be expected.

Negligent Patient Assessment

A Case Manager is expected to make recommendations based on an intimate understanding of the patient's condition and individual care needs. That is, a Case Manager has a duty of care to provide a comprehensive assessment of a case. This comprehensive assessment should include an appreciation of not only the patient's medical condition but also intellectual, educational, psychological, social, religious, and financial conditions as well. Without this information, a Case Manager's recommendations may lead to disastrous outcomes because of unrecognized barriers to care. For example, the patient is precluded from a treatment because it violates a cultural or religious law, or a minor may not receive appropriate care because one or both of his parents are intellectually incapable of following a complex care plan. With these caveats in mind, a skillful patient assessment should include the following:

- chief complaint
- current diagnoses
- current treatments (including medications) and treatment plan
- past medical history
- social history (including educational achievements, available family and community support system, sexual history and orientation, history of substance abuse)
- religious affiliations and involvement
- insurance eligibility for private and federal programs and their benefits packages
  – expected outcomes

Careful attention to the above should limit a Case Manager's exposure to malpractice litigation.

Negligent Referral

In his or her role as a gatekeeper, a Case Manager often makes referrals to specific providers for a patient's care. Under the legal theory of *ostensible agency*, that provider becomes an "agent" of the Case Manager. The Case Manager may be held responsible for negligent actions taken by the provider within the scope of his practice. The Case Manager has an affirmative duty to assure that the care being provided is of the highest quality available. It is imperative, therefore, that the Case Manager be knowledgeable about the providers he or she recommends. This knowledge should include the status of the provider's licensure, accreditation, certifications, and relevant clinical experience, as well as any history of patient complaints, negligence, malpractice, or criminal activity. Much of this information is available through the credentialing process of insurers and managed care organizations. The Case Manager should follow up with the patients, to review their experience with referred providers. Incidents of dissatisfaction, negligence, or misconduct should be reported to appropriate agencies. A Case Manager can decrease risk of malpractice litigation by observing the following rules:

- Be aware of the criteria for credentialing providers in your network.
- Make no personal recommendations concerning a provider; refer only to the credentialing criteria.

- When possible, do not recommend a single provider, but provide the patient with a list of providers in the appropriate specialty. Allow the patient to choose the provider.
- Notify appropriate authorities immediately of any suspicion of irregular, dangerous, unethical, or illegal behavior in providers.

Breach of Confidentiality (also invasion of privacy)

This is the purposeful or negligent release of the content of a privileged communication (e.g., doctor/patient) where the publication of such information causes injury to the patient. Both professional ethics and statutory law require that medical information be kept confidential. Therefore, disclosing confidential information to another, without the consent of the patient, puts the Case Manager at risk for litigation. The following are suggestions a Case Manager can use to limit the risk of breech of confidentiality litigation:

- The Case Manager should be conversant with the applicable federal and state regulations on the disclosure of medical information.
- Medical information that pertains to human immunodeficiency virus and acquired immunodeficiency syndrome (HIV/AIDS), venereal diseases, abortion, mental illness, or substance abuse is particularly sensitive. All requests for this information should be discussed first with the patient and legal counsel before disclosure. Documentation of these discussions is essential for avoiding liability. Be aware that this information may require that its own specific consent form be signed before disclosure.
- Patients should be informed that their medical information might be shared with others in order to provide appropriate medical care. A record of this discussion, including the patient's views, should be memorialized in the Case Manager's record.
- Patients should be informed that they have the right to refuse the disclosure of information, but also that this refusal may affect the ability of providers to render effective medical treatment.

Lack of Informed Consent

A person's agreement to allow something to happen (such as surgery) should be based on a full disclosure of the facts needed to make the decision intelligently. In medicine, as in most other venues, every individual of adult years and sound mind has the right to determine what shall be done with his or her own body and to control the course of his or her own medical treatment.[7]

REQUIREMENTS OF FULL DISCLOSURE

When obtaining consent for a procedure, treatment, or medical, surgical, or psychological intervention, the provider should disclose the following:

- the projected or desired outcomes of the proposed treatment and the likelihood of success
- reasonably foreseeable risks or hazards inherent in the proposed treatment or care (done in manner that the patient can understand)
- alternatives to proposed care or treatment plan
- consequences of foregoing the treatment

Informed consent is required by law and is derived from the theory that performing a procedure or treatment on a patient without full disclosure of risks and benefits and without the patient's informed consent constitutes assault and battery.

The following criteria[8] for obtaining informed consent have been developed for Case Managers and should be observed.

- The patient must consent voluntarily.
- The patient must have the capacity to give consent.
- The patient must be an adult (under existing state law).
- In the event that the patient is a minor or adult without capacity to consent, parents, attorneys, or legal guardians may give consent.
- The patient must have a full understanding of the scope of activities of the Case Manager, with all its attendant risks, benefits, and alternatives.
- The Case Manager must obtain informed consent prior to the beginning of the professional relationship.
  - The Case Manager must document the consent. (A signed consent agreement is adequate.)

LEGAL TERMS WITH WHICH A CASE MANAGER SHOULD BE FAMILIAR

Agency: Agency is defined as the relationship between two or more persons by which one (the principal) consents that the other(s) (the agent[s]) shall act on his behalf. A principal/agent relationship exists between the Case Manager and his/her employer. Agency implies an agent's legal obligations to the principal, among which are:

- using care and skill
- acting in good faith
- staying within the limits of the agent's authority
- obeying the principal and carrying out all reasonable instructions
- advancing the interests of the principal
- acting solely for the principal's benefit

One may notice that these duties of agency imply a conflict of interest between the Case Manager's duties to the employer and the professional duties owed the patient. This conflict is largely unresolved and has become an ethical sticking point for most Case Managers.

Apparent authority (see also Ostensible agency): When a principal has taken such actions that would indicate to third parties that someone is his agent, the principal is held to have given "apparent authority" to the agent and will be held responsible for his actions. Apparent authority is seen when providers' names are placed in HMO network brochures or on hospital staffs, even though there is no employer/employee relationship.

Abandonment The termination of a professional relationship (physician/patient, Case Manager/patient) without reasonable notice to the patient and without an opportunity for the patient to acquire alternative care or services, thereby resulting in injury to the patient.

Bad faith (claims denial): Bad faith implies either an attempt to mislead or deceive another, or a neglect or refusal to fulfill some duty or some contractual obligation. Bad faith is not simply bad judgment or even negligence, but rather it implies a conscious doing of a wrong. Insurance companies, managed care organizations, and their agents owe a duty of "good faith and fair dealing" to their subscribers. This implies acting in the subscriber's best interest, within the limits of the insurance contract. A failure to follow through on this duty, especially when denying medical care, can result in a bad faith claim. This failure to act in good faith is usually manifest in insurance companies by a frivolous or unfounded refusal to pay proceeds of a policy.

A "bad faith claims denial" has three components:

1. The absence of a reasonable basis for the denial of benefits,
2. The insurer's (or its agent's) knowledge or reckless disregard of the lack of reasonable basis for denying a claim, and
3. Misfeasance or maladministration in processing of claims for benefits.

Bill of particulars: An amplification of a complaint that supplies more information and detail, thereby giving the defendant a more specific picture of the claim(s) against him or her.

Breech of confidentiality: A failure of a fiduciary duty or refusing to hold secret a privileged communication entrusted by one party to another.

Claim: A report by the insured to the insurance company, based on notification by a patient or the patient's attorney, of an event out of which malpractice has been alleged.

Comparative negligence: A method of measuring negligence among the participants in a suit, both defense and plaintiff, in terms of percentages of culpability. Damages are then diminished in proportion to the amount of negligence attributable to the complaining party.

Complaint: The document by which the plaintiff gives the court and the defendant notice of the transactions, occurrences, or series of transactions or occurrences intended to be proved and the material elements of each cause of action or defense.

Confidentiality: The state or quality of being confidential; treated as private and not for publication.

Corporate negligence: A term that encompasses the legal grounds for managed care organizations' liability based on the corporate activities of the managed care organization itself, rather than on the care-related activities of participating health care professionals. Negligent credentialing and negligent supervision are examples of corporate negligence.

Corporate practice of medicine: A legal doctrine that prohibits corporations from engaging in the practice of medicine, that is, the treatment of injuries as well as the discovery of the cause and nature of disease, as well as the administration of remedies or the prescribing of treatment. In states that recognize this doctrine, corporations, including hospitals, cannot employ physicians.

Damages: A pecuniary compensation recovered by the courts for acts of tort. These recoveries or compensations are for both tangible injuries or torts (medical expenses, lost earnings) and intangible injuries (pain and suffering).

Discovery: The ascertainment of what is not previously known; generally, the pre-trial stage of a lawsuit beginning with the service of summons and complaint and concluding with the filing of a "note of issue." During this time period, all evidence that is material and necessary in the prosecution or defense of action is produced and exchanged by the parties or as ordered by the court.

Event (incident): A situation that is reported by the insured provider to his or her insurance company that may lead to a formal claim or malpractice suit.

Examination-before-trial (EBT): A method of obtaining disclosure of information that is material and necessary to the underlying lawsuit by way of sworn oral testimony. This usually occurs during the discovery phase of litigation.

False Claims Act: The False Claims Act is a federal act providing for civil and criminal penalties against individuals who knowingly present false claims to the government. The criminal False Claims Act makes it illegal to present a claim upon or against the United States that the claimant knows to be false, fictitious, or fraudulent. The civil False Claims Act says that any person who knowingly presents or causes to be presented, to the United States government, a false or fraudulent claim for payment approval or who knowingly makes, uses, or causes to be made or used a false record or statement to get a false or fraudulent claim paid or approved by the government by getting a false or fraudulent claim allowed or paid violates the Act. The penalties for violation include substantial fines and imprisonment.

Hold-harmless provision: A contractual arrangement between the insurer and the provider of service that is typically contained in a managed care contract. This provision specifies that the provider assumes the liability for covered services and cannot sue or assert any claims against enrollees for those covered services, even if the managed care organization becomes insolvent.

Informed consent: A person's agreement to allow something to happen (such as surgery) that is based on a full disclosure of the facts needed to make the decision intelligently. In medicine, as in most other venues, every individual of adult years and sound mind has the right to determine what shall be done with his or her own body and to control the course of his or her own medical treatment.[7] As such, providers are required to disclose to the patient the following:

- the projected or desired outcomes of the proposed treatment and the likelihood of success
- reasonably foreseeable risks or hazards inherent in the proposed treatment or care (done in manner that the patient can understand)
- alternatives to proposed care or treatment plan
- consequences of foregoing the treatment

Informed consent is required by law and is derived from the theory that performing a procedure or treatment on a patient without full disclosure of risks and benefits and the patient's informed consent constitutes assault and battery.

Inherent risk: A complication that is commonly associated with a procedure but is not the result of the negligence of the operator (physician, nurse, or other provider performing the procedure or treatment).

Invasion of privacy: An unwarranted appropriation or exploitation of another's private affairs with which the public has no legitimate concern; a wrongful intrusion into one's private activities in such a manner as to cause mental suffering, shame, or humiliation to a person of ordinary sensibilities. Such an invasion by an individual or government may constitute an actionable tort.

Liability: A debt, responsibility, or obligation.

Liability, joint and several: Joint and several liability is an obligation of a group and its individual members. The party that has been harmed is able to sue all of the liable parties as a group or any one of them individually. He may not, however, recover more compensation by suing each of them individually than by suing them as a group.

Liability limits: Liability limits refer to a restriction or upper boundary on the amount of money an insurance company will pay in order to satisfy a claim against an insured. A claim for a sum beyond this limit is not protected by the insurance policy.

Liable: Bound by law or fairness; responsible; accountable.

Malpractice: A professional negligence with two components: (1) negligence, which is a deviation from the approved and accepted standards of care, as defined within a given specialty, and (2) injury, which is damage to the patient as a result of the stated negligence or deviation from the standard of care.

Most-Favored-Nation (MFN) Clause: A contractual arrangement between a purchaser and provider. In this arrangement the provider is obligated to render products or services to the purchaser at the same rate as his most-favored customer.

Negligence: A failure to use the degree of care a reasonably prudent and careful person would use under similar circumstances. Either acts of omission, commission, or both may constitute negligence.

Negligent referral: A failure to use such care in making a referral as a reasonable professional would use under similar circumstances. Referring a patient to a provider who does not possess the skills, experience, licensure, or certifications to care for that patient would constitute a negligent referral.

Negligent credentialing: A failure on the part of the managed care organization to exercise reasonable care in screening and selection of providers. Negligent credentialing can occur when a managed care organization selects a provider who negligently injures a patient, is found to have a history of doing the same, or is found not to have the appropriate training, experience, skills, or licensure to care for the patient.

Ombudsman: A person whose occupation consists of investigating customer complaints against his or her employer. These employees are often found in the appeals and grievance section of the quality management departments of HMOs.

Ostensible agency (see also Apparent authority): An implied or presumptive agency, which exists where one, either intentionally or from want of ordinary care, induces another to believe that a third person is his agent, though he never in fact employed him. In these cases, the "principal" is responsible for the acts of his "agent" when he has given actual authority for that agent to act. Further, when a principal has taken such actions as would indicate to third parties that someone is his agent, the principal is held to have given "apparent authority" to the agent and will be liable for his acts. Case Managers can be real or ostensible agents of the insurer, physician, hospital, or health care facility. A Case Manager's actions can become the liability of the employer or principal.

Out of court settlement: An agreement or transaction between litigants to settle the matter privately, without being referred to the judge for authorization or approval, before the court has rendered its decision.

Privacy: The quality or condition of being secluded from the presence or view of others; the state of being free from unsanctioned intrusion: *a person's right to privacy;* the state of being concealed; secrecy.

Privileged communications: Information that a person authorized to practice medicine, registered nursing, etc., acquires in attending to a patient in a professional capacity, and that is necessary to enable him or her to act in that capacity. Such information shall not be disclosed unless the patient waives that privilege. Disclosure of such information may constitute an invasion of privacy, which is an actionable tort.

Res ipsa loquitor (from the Latin: "The thing speaks for itself"): A doctrine of law with reference to cases where mere proof that an occurrence took place is sufficient under the circumstances to shift the burden of proof upon the defendant to prove that it was not due to his or her negligence. Implied in this doctrine is that the instrumentality causing injury was in the defendant's exclusive control, and that the accident was one that ordinarily does not happen in the absence of negligence. An example of *res ipsa loquitor* would be when a patient is found to have a surgical instrument left in his abdomen after an appendectomy (assuming there was only one surgeon involved).

Respondeat superior (from the Latin "Let the master answer"): A master is liable, in certain cases, for the wrongful acts of his servant (likewise, a principal for those of his agent). A master/servant or principal/agent relationship exists where one person, for pay or other valuable consideration, enters into the service of another and devotes his or her personal labor for an agreed period, for example, employee/employer.

Statute of limitations: The period of time in which a plaintiff may bring lawsuit after an incident has occurred.

Subpoena (from the Latin "under penalty"): A judicial process (or writ) requiring a witness to give relevant information or testimony "under penalty" of contempt for disobedience.

Summons: A document issued by the plaintiff's attorney that when properly delivered, commences a legal action.

Vicarious liability: Legal liability that a person may have for the action of someone else. For instance, in the employer/employee relationship, an insurer could be vicariously liable for the action of the Case Managers employed in its plan.

Tort (from the Latin "to twist," implying injury): A damage, injury, or a wrongful act done willfully, negligently, or in circumstances involving strict liability; a legal wrong committed upon the person or property independent of contract. A tort may be:

- a direct invasion of some legal right of the individual
- the infraction of some public duty by which special damage accrues to the individual or
- the violation of some private obligation by which like damage accrues to the individual

MEDICAL RECORDS AND CONFIDENTIALITY

Why Case Managers Need To Record and Manage Medical Records

Case Managers record patient information for many reasons. These include:

- To provide the rationale for the actions taken by Case Managers
- To form the basis of case management costs and savings reports
- To allow supervisors or coworkers to assume management of a case in the absence of the original reviewer
- To provide a longitudinal perspective on long and complex cases
- To provide the foundation of a legal defense when questions of propriety of the care are raised.

A medical record documents the privileged conversations between a patient and provider. Communications with a patient fall within the *patient-provider privilege* and (with limitations) are protected from disclosure. This confidentiality is a right held by the patient and may be waived by the (fully informed) patient but not by the provider. Generally speaking, the patient's medical records are private, and it is the responsibility of medical professionals to ensure that they remain private, unless otherwise directed by the patient or the courts.

Who Usually Has Access to a Patient's Medical Records?

While it is assumed that only the patient's primary health care provider has access to confidential medical information, a surprising number of others have regular and legal access to it. These others include:

- *Professional colleagues*: partners in a medical group, who may care for the patient in the primary provider's absence.
- *Clinical experts and consultants*: may aid the primary provider with determining the diagnosis or treatment of the patient.
- *Hospitals:* especially when the spread of communicable diseases may endanger other patients, for billing purposes, or when discussions of the quality improvement committee require an examination of disease states, treatments, etc.
- *Insurance companies and managed care companies*: who have an obligation to pay only for medically necessary care.
- *Third party administrators and utilization management agents:* who examine medical records for compliance with allowable benefits, medical necessity, and medical appropriateness.
- *Pharmacy benefits administrators:* who are responsible for adjudicating pharmaceutical claims and drug benefits, as an agent of the insurer.
- *Specialty management organizations:* specialty management or "carve out" organizations adjudicate claims in specialized areas of care for insurers and HMOs. Services provided by these organizations range from optometry and podiatry to cancer and HIV care.
- *Government agencies*: such as the Centers for Disease Control and Prevention, the National Institutes of Health, and the National Cancer Institute, who are engaged in research and providing for the public health.
- *The Medical Information Bureau:* The MIB is a central medical information database. It is sponsored by insurance companies and exists to collect, analyze, and distribute information about life insurance policy applicants.
- *Pharmaceutical companies*: who are in charge of collecting information concerning adverse reactions to drugs produced.

Despite the fact that medical information is shared regularly with all these agents and organizations, *there are currently no comprehensive laws regarding medical record privacy.* This apparent legal informality should not be construed by the Case Manager as an appropriate approach to a patient's privacy, but rather should instill a heightened vigilance when handling, transmitting, or releasing patient information. It is the Case Manager's responsibility to his or her patient to protect the patient's privacy.

Circumstances Where a Case Manager May Release Confidential Patient Information

There are special circumstances when a Case Manager may release patient information. These include:

- after receiving a written authorization or waiver from the patient
- when required by law (civil, criminal, or public health law). Licensed practitioners in most states have an affirmative duty to report the following and are not required to seek the permission of the patient before doing so:
  – suspected child abuse, neglect, or exploitation

- suspected elder abuse, neglect, or exploitation
- abuse, neglect, or exploitation of a resident of a long-term care facility
- information regarding treatment of patients with physical injury that has been inflicted by nonaccidental means (e.g., gunshot wounds, stab wounds, etc.)
- births
- unusual or suspicious deaths
- specific diseases, required by public health laws in some states such as animal bites, sexually transmitted diseases including HIV/AIDS, tuberculosis, head or spine injuries, meningitis, etc.
- upon receipt of court order or subpoena

When releasing information pursuant to the above, the Case Manager is usually held harmless from liabilities to the patient or other persons. However, when a request for "sensitive" information is received, the prudent Case Manager will review the case with his or her corporate counsel before releasing it. Sensitive information includes, but is not restricted to, the following topics: mental health, substance abuse, sexually transmitted diseases, cancer, and HIV/AIDS.

What Medical Information Should Not Be Regularly Released?

Communications between a psychiatrist and patient are absolutely privileged. A psychiatrist cannot be compelled to reveal those communications, even by a subpoena. Case Managers should not release this information without signed consent forms from the patient and explicit direction from their corporation's legal counsel.

CASE MANAGERS SHOULD MANAGE MEDICAL RECORD SECURITY

The first step to be taken in the management of the confidentiality of medical records is to set the expectations for the staff. This includes:

- developing confidentiality policies
- distributing confidentiality policies to all staff
- reviewing the policies. Staff should then sign statements affirming that they have read and understood the corporation's confidentiality policies, the corporation's expectations regarding handling of confidential material, and what penalties exist for violation of these policies.

Development of Confidentiality Policies

These policies should include, but are not limited to, the security of electronic records, paper records, and the release and transmittal of patient information.

Security of Electronic Records

Access to electronic records should be limited to those who "need to know." This can be accomplished by restricting access to Case Managers' computers, which should be placed in separate work areas that have locking doors, and to Case Managers' electronic files, by using passwords known only to the Case Managers. Case Managers should be aware of all areas where electronic information is stored and take appropriate precautions to secure it (e.g., voice mail, faxes, recorded conversations, e-mail, tapes, floppy disks, CDs with medical information, etc.). Electronic storage mediums, such as computer tapes, floppy disks, and CDs containing sensitive information should be secured in a locked cabinet when not in use.

When possible, computerized medical information should be recorded in "encrypted files." A secure audit trail built into the computer should record all those who access the medical files, and it should record any alteration of data.

Computer files containing medical records that are no longer useful should be erased, not just deleted. Deleted documents can easily be "undeleted" by the computer savvy. Use of names and other identifying data should be limited to situations where they are necessary. Utilization of telecommunication "firewalls" that prevent unauthorized parties, especially those outside the organization, from gaining electronic access to medical information systems, should be part of the electronic system's software package.

Security of Paper Records

Limit the use of paper records when possible. Know where all paper records are generated, and stored (e.g., mail, faxes, memos, clinical notes, etc.). Take proper precautions to secure them. Limit the use of patient and provider names on paper records when possible (use of file numbers and/or provider and patient code numbers is helpful).

Case Managers should personally destroy (not simply discard) paper records when they are no longer needed. (Paper-shredders should be available in the case management area.) Access should be limited to the area where paper records are stored. Only those that "need to know" should have this access. The area where paper records are stored should be locked when not in use. Paper records in the possession of Case Managers should be stored when not being used. Filing cabinets and desks drawers containing sensitive records should be locked when they are unattended.

Security of Information Release and Transmittal

Before releasing any patient information to a third party, a prudent Case Manager should do the following:

- Check that a "release" or "waiver" signed by the patient has been received, and filed.
- Assure that the information being released is explicitly requested in the release. No other information should be released.
- When particularly "sensitive" information is requested, such as information concerning sexually transmitted diseases, HIV/AIDS, substance abuse or cancer, the organization's corporate counsel should be consulted before release.

What Should Be Done When a Patient Has Been Discriminated Against Due to Violation of Medical Privacy?

The Case Manager can suggest the patient seek redress under the following laws: According to the Americans with Disability Act of 1990,[9] in workplaces with more than 25 employees, employers may not ask job applicants about medical information or require a physical examination prior to offering employment. Similarly, after employment is offered, an employer can only ask for a medical examination if it is required of all employees holding similar jobs.

Applicants can only be denied a job based on the results of a physical examination if this examination reveals that the applicant is physically unable to perform the "essential functions" that the job requires (for example, poor eyesight, even with corrective lenses, in an applicant for a position as commercial pilot).

Under the Equal Employment Opportunity law, you cannot be discharged from employment, fired, or made to retire solely because of age, race, sex, or disability. Complaints or charges can be filed with the Equal Employment Opportunity Commission (EEOC). The EEOC is the federal agency with the power to investigate, mediate, and file lawsuits to end employment discrimination.

ETHICAL ISSUES IN CASE MANAGEMENT

Ethics are the rules or standards governing the conduct of a person or members of a profession. The word ethics comes from a Greek root *ethos,* and means "character" or that combination of positive qualities or values that distinguishes one person from another.

Ethical and legal principles are closely related as both are based on what a given society values as an appropriate standard of conduct. Legal duties are what a society describes as the minimum acceptable standards of conduct. A legal duty usually carries a punishment for those whose conduct falls below its standards. Ethical duties, on the other hand, represent a society's version of ideal conduct for an individual or a profession. Lapses in ethical behavior, to the extent that the behavior also is not illegal, is usually not punishable outside of a professional society. In general, the demands of ethical duties usually exceed those of legal duties. It is held by the American Medical Association (AMA), that in the rare instances when legal duties and ethical duties are in conflict, a professional's ethical duties should supersede his legal duties.[10]

Five Ethical Principles of Case Management

In order to aid the Case Manager in making decisions, a code of ethics has been promulgated by the Case Management Society of America. In this code there are five principles that should be adhered to.*

1. Autonomy: The Case Manager should encourage the client to make his or her own well-informed decisions. The patient's freedom to choose or act on his or her own behalf is one of the fundamental liberties that a Case Manager should secure for the client. Education and empowerment are the tools with which the Case Manager promotes the development of informed self-advocacy. Prejudice and discrimination (on the part of the Case Manager) are the enemies of self-advocacy and are to be avoided at all costs.

2. Beneficence: The state or quality of being kind, charitable or beneficent. This implies that the Case Manager has an obligation to "do good" for the patient, rather than for himself or herself, for the provider, or for the insurer.

3. Nonmaleficence: Nonmaleficence is an amplification of the Case Manager's obligation of *beneficence.* Nonmaleficence implies that a Case Manager has an obligation not just to do good by doing "a good job," but to actively seek to prevent harm from coming to the patient. Therefore, the Case Manager cannot abnegate the responsibility of beneficence by stating that the patient has made his own choice and therefore what injuries that come to him as a result of his decision are "his fault." Predictable harm that could come to the patient should be prevented through education and counseling.

4. Justice: The quality of being just or fair. Justice is the upholding of what is just, in accordance with honor, standards, or law. Justice is derived from the Case Manager's sense of

---

*Courtesy of Case Management Society of America, Little Rock, Arkansas.

moral rightness and is manifest by ensuring equity of treatment for one's patients. Often in case management, this means balancing what is just for one's patient versus what is just for the larger society. The following question is illustrative of this point: Should extraordinary measures (and resources) be taken to preserve a single patient in a vegetative state rather than spending the resources on preventative care for thousands?

5. Veracity: An adherence to the truth. It is the obligation for the Case Manager to conform, in dealings with patients and families, to fact or truth, to accuracy and precision. Without veracity in dealings with the patient, a trusting relationship will never develop between the Case Manager and the patient. As a result, the goal of patient self-advocacy can never be attained. A lack of truth and fair dealing not only undermines the raison d'être of the Case Manager but may be a source of legal liability.

In a situation where two or more equally desirable outcomes are in conflict, an ethical dilemma exists. For example, protecting a patient's confidentiality is a desirable outcome, while notifying the spouse of the risk of contracting the patient's potentially lethal venereal disease is another desirable outcome. The resulting conflict is an ethical dilemma.

When an ethical dilemma is identified, the Case Manager has the obligation to act in the best interest of the patient, the payer, and society at large. Balancing these sometimes competing obligations is one of the great challenges in the field of case management.

Laws of Ethical Decision Making

Ethical dilemmas by their nature have no easy answer, and no answers are provided in this section. As stated above, ethical dilemmas occur in a situation where two or more equally desirable outcomes are in conflict, and where only one outcome is possible. This brings us to the four ineluctable laws of ethical decision making:

1. Case Managers must make decisions as to which one of the equally desirable outcomes will occur.
2. Choosing one outcome logically implies that the other desirable outcomes will not occur.
3. Those that stood to benefit from the outcomes that were not chosen will be displeased and may feel alienated or betrayed by the Case Manager.
4. Effective ethical decision makers must be content with the realization that the decision made was the most fair and circumspect decision that the situation allowed.

Common Ethical Dilemmas in Case Management

The following examples are the three most common dilemmas encountered in case management.

1. **Focus of advocacy:** For whom is the Case Manager an advocate? For the patient? For the patient's family? For the insurer she works for? For society at large? The answer to all these questions should be yes. But the best interests of each of these parties are not always harmonious and may be in conflict. For example, the insurance company wants to limit its medical expenditures, the patient may need more benefits than he or she is entitled to under the strict limits of the policy, the family may be impoverished funding futile care for a dying patient, and as unrestricted medical spending raises the cost of medical care beyond the reach of some members of society, where should medical spending be restricted and by whom? Experienced Case Managers have encountered all these scenarios, sometimes in the same case.

2. **Supremacy of values:** Values may be defined as a set of behaviors or characteristics held in high esteem by a person or group of people. Values are derived from personal experiences, cultural expectations or norms, and religious or social laws. What a Case Manager values will affect decisions. A Case Manager will naturally tend to make decisions that are harmonious with his or her values. What occurs when the values of the patient are in conflict with those of the Case Manager? Some decisions made by the Case Manager will require him or her to violate the patient's values or her values. Should they? Whose values have supremacy? Whose should have? The patient's? The family's? The insurer's? Should a Case Manager surrender her values just to accommodate a paying client (or anyone)? Should she run roughshod over the values of the patient because they don't agree with the values she holds dear? There is no right answer.

3. **Conflict of duties:** A Case Manager has a positive duty to put the best interests of the client first. What should the Case Manager do, when the best interests of the client cause harm to another? Can a Case Manager ethically act in a way that will cause harm to the patient? Does a Case Manager's duty to the patient supersede duties to others? What is the Case Manager's duty to others? Some common examples of this dilemma of conflict of duties involve the issue of the confidentiality of the patient's medical record and the privacy of information gained during medical interviews. For example, should a Case Manager inform a parent that her child (a minor) is in a physically abusive relationship or that her child is addicted to illegal drugs? Should a Case Manager inform the husband of her client that his wife has contracted HIV and does not intend to tell him? Should a Case Manager warn the authorities when she becomes aware her client intends to commit a homicide? Should a Case Manager inform the insurer when she becomes aware that the medical condition currently being paid for was a "pre-existing condition" and therefore not eligible for coverage under the policy? Some of these examples may appear to be easy decisions, others less so. Each decision involves not only a potential "beneficence" to a third party, but also involves a potential harm to the client. Who does the Case Manager have a duty to? What are the limits of that duty?

REFERENCES

1. Cesta T, Tahan, H, Fink I. *The Case Manager's Survival Guide: Winning Strategies for Clinical Practice.* St. Louis, MO: Mosby Year-Book; 1998.
2. Localio AR, Lawthers AG, Brennan TA, et al. Relation between malpractice claims and adverse events due to negligence. Results of the Harvard Medical Practice Study III. *N Engl J Med.* 1991;325(4):245–251.
3. Brennan TA, Leape LL, Laird NM, et al. Incidence of adverse events and negligence in hospitalized patients. Results of the Harvard Medical Practice Study I. *N Engl J Med.* 1991;324(6):370–376.
4. Huycke LI, Huycke MM. Characteristics of potential plaintiffs in malpractice litigation. *Ann Intern Med.* 1994;120(9):792–798.
5. *Fox v. Healthnet,* No 21692 (Cal Super Ct. Riverside County, filed June 19, 1992: settled April 6, 1994).
6. Quinn C. Avoiding bad faith denials of medical claims. *Managed Care.* April 1997; 79–85.
7. *Schloendorff v. The Society of the New York Hospital,* 211 N.Y. 125, 105 N.E. 92 (1914) [April 14, 1914]. 1914 N.Y. LEXIS 1028.
8. Hogue E. Tips make CMSA standards work for you. *Case Manage Advisor.* 1998;6(5):75–76.
9. Americans with Disabilities Act of 1990. 42 U.S.C. §§ 12101, et seq.
10. EEOC American Medical Association. *Code of medical ethics: current opinions with annotations.* Chicago: American Medical Association, 1997, 1.

1) **Of the following, which are common causes of malpractice litigation?**
   1. Discourteous behavior by the professional
   2. Provider/patient miscommunication
   3. Lack of patient understanding
   4. Failure to inform a patient's family of pertinent issues
      A. 1, 3
      B. 2, 4
      C. 1, 2, 3
      D. All of the above
      E. None of the above

2) **Of the following, which are *not* common causes of malpractice litigation?**
   1. Discourteous behavior by the professional
   2. Poor clinical outcomes
   3. Lack of patient understanding
   4. Substandard medical care
      A. 1, 3
      B. 2, 4
      C. 1, 2, 3
      D. All of the above
      E. None of the above

3) **Common causes of malpractice litigation include which of the following?**
   1. Discourteous behavior by the professional
   2. Poor clinical outcomes
   3. Lack of patient understanding
   4. Substandard medical care
      A. 1, 3
      B. 2, 4
      C. 1, 2, 3
      D. All of the above
      E. None of the above

4) **Case management activities that have the highest risk of malpractice associated with them include which of the following?**
   1. Patient discharge
   2. Claims denials
   3. Patient assessment
   4. Referral to providers
      A. 1, 3
      B. 2, 4
      C. 1, 2, 3
      D. All of the above
      E. None of the above

5) **Of the following Case Management activities, which do *not* have the highest risk of malpractice associated with them?**

1. Patient admissions
2. Patient assessment
3. Claims approvals
4. Referral to providers
   A. 1, 3
   B. 2, 4
   C. 1, 2, 3
   D. All of the above
   E. None of the above

6) **Case Managers may decrease the legal liability associated with patient discharges through which of the following activities?**

1. Decreasing the average length of stay of their clients
2. Confirming the integrity of the patient's support network
3. Reducing the per member per month medical costs of her clients
4. Confirming the adequacy of follow-up outpatient care
   A. 1, 3
   B. 2, 4
   C. 1, 2, 3
   D. All of the above
   E. None of the above

7) **Which of the following activities are *not* associated with a decrease in the legal liability associated with patient discharges?**

1. Decreasing the average length of stay of their clients
2. Confirming the integrity of the patient's support network
3. Reducing the per member per month medical costs of her clients
4. Confirming the adequacy of follow-up outpatient care
   A. 1, 3
   B. 2, 4
   C. 1, 2, 3
   D. All of the above
   E. None of the above

8) **Which of the following activities are associated with a *decrease* in the legal liability associated with bad faith allegations?**

1. Decreasing the average length of stay of their clients
2. Expediting claims adjudication
3. Reducing the per member per month medical costs of her clients
4. Securing an independent medical examination of the patient
   A. 1, 3
   B. 2, 4
   C. 1, 2, 3
   D. All of the above
   E. None of the above

9) **Which of the following activities are associated with an *increase* in the legal liability associated with bad faith allegations?**

1. Decreasing the average length of stay of their clients
2. Unnecessarily delaying claims adjudication
3. Reducing the per member per month medical costs of her clients
4. Refusing an independent medical examination of the patient
   A. 1, 3
   B. 2, 4
   C. 1, 2, 3
   D. All of the above
   E. None of the above

10) Disclosure of confidential information is mandatory when:

A. It is pursuant to judicial proceedings.
B. It is government mandated.
C. A professional has a duty to warn a third party about the illness of a patient.
D. All of the above
E. None of the above

11) Case Managers are committed to obtaining informed consent, providing options for the patient to choose from and educating the patient to make independent decisions. This principle is known as:

A. Veracity
B. Beneficence
C. Autonomy
D. Nonmaleficence

12) Malpractice is _____ that results in harm to another person.

A. A professional's wrongful conduct
B. A professional's failure to meet acceptable standards of care
C. The improper discharge of a professional's duties
D. All of the above
E. None of the above

13) Negligence is:

A. An act of omission
B. An act of commission
C. Failing to use the degree of care a reasonably prudent and careful person would under similar circumstances
D. None of the above
E. All of the above

14) _____ is an unlawful, wrongful act.

A. Negligence
B. Liability
C. Malpractice
D. Malfeasance

15) A tort is:

A. A damage, injury, or wrongful act independent of a contractual relationship
B. An agreement by the parties involved to a resolution of a particular issue
C. A voluntary assignation of a known right to someone else
D. None of the above

16) The court case of *Wickline v. State of California* found that:

1. Medical doctors have a duty to protest adverse determinations by payers.
2. Medical doctors can shift their liability to payers if they do protest adverse determinations.
3. Case Managers are not liable for their roles in adverse determinations.
4. Payers of heath care can be held accountable if their adverse decisions are arbitrary, made for cost containment and are not based on acceptable medical standards of practice in the community.
    A. 1, 2, 3
    B. 2, 3, 4
    C. 1, 2, 4
    D. None of the above

17) **In a malpractice suit the plaintiff must prove two points.**

    1. His compliance with the prescribed treatment plan
    2. Negligence on the part of the Case Manager
    3. Injury from the Case Manager's negligence
    4. Intent on the part of the Case Manager
       A. 1, 4
       B. 2, 3
       C. None of the above
       D. All of the above

18) **Which of the following are subject to state and federal mandates regarding medical record retention?**

    A. Financial files
    B. HMO insurance information
    C. Case Management files
    D. Insurance claims files

19) **Communication failures, lack of information given to the family, lack of patient understanding, and discourteous behavior are all causes of _____.**

    A. Lack of patient compliance
    B. Patient injuries
    C. Patient complaints
    D. Malpractice litigation

20) **Which of the following statements best defines ethics, as they relate to Case Management?**

    1. The rules of conduct that govern a person or members of a profession
    2. The thoughts that govern a person's conduct
    3. A society's ideal for a person's conduct
    4. The minimal acceptable standards for a person's conduct
       A. 1, 3
       B. 2, 4
       C. 1, 2, 3
       D. All of the above
       E. None of the above

21) **Which of the following statements are *not* true regarding ethics as they relate to Case Management?**

    1. They are rules of conduct that govern a person or members of a profession.
    2. They are thoughts that govern a person's conduct.
    3. They are a society's ideal for a person's conduct.
    4. They are the minimal acceptable standards for a person's conduct.
       A. 1, 3
       B. 2, 4
       C. 1, 2, 3
       D. All of the above
       E. None of the above

22) **Which of the following statements can be said to be true, when distinguishing ethical from legal principles?**

    1. Civil punishments usually exist for lapses in legal duties.
    2. Ethical duties usually exceed legal requirements.
    3. Legal duties describe society's minimum acceptable behaviors.
    4. Ethical obligations describe society's ideals for personal and professional behavior.
       A. 1, 3
       B. 2, 4
       C. 1, 2, 3
       D. All of the above
       E. None of the above

23) **When distinguishing ethical from legal principles, which of the following statements are *not* considered to be true?**
   1. Civil punishments usually exist for lapses in legal duties.
   2. Ethical duties usually exceed legal requirements.
   3. Legal duties describe society's minimum acceptable behaviors.
   4. Ethical obligations describe society's ideals for personal and professional behavior.
      A. 1, 3
      B. 2, 4
      C. 1, 2, 3
      D. All of the above
      E. None of the above

24) **Which of the following statements are true regarding ethical dilemmas?**
   1. It involves a decision between two or more possible outcomes.
   2. It involves the breaking of an ethical principle.
   3. The possible outcomes are in conflict.
   4. Solving an ethical dilemma is usually illegal.
      A. 1, 3
      B. 2, 4
      C. 1, 2, 3
      D. All of the above
      E. None of the above

25) **In regard to ethical dilemmas, which of the following statements are <u>not</u> true?**
   1. It involves a decision between two or more possible outcomes.
   2. It involves the breaking of an ethical principle.
   3. The possible outcomes are in conflict.
   4. Solving an ethical dilemma is usually illegal.
      A. 1, 3
      B. 2, 4
      C. 1, 2, 3
      D. All of the above
      E. None of the above

26) **Which of the following are ethical principles promulgated by the Case Management Society of America?**
   1. Autonomy
   2. Beneficence
   3. Nonmalfeasance
   4. Justice
      A. 1, 3
      B. 2, 4
      C. 1, 2, 3
      D. All of the above
      E. None of the above

27) **Which of the following attributes are *not* ethical principles promulgated by the Case Management Society of America?**
   1. Autonomy
   2. Insouciance
   3. Nonmalfeasance
   4. Diversity
      A. 1, 3
      B. 2, 4
      C. 1, 2, 3
      D. All of the above
      E. None of the above

28) **The ethical principle of Justice implies all except which of the following qualities or attributes?**
   1. Upholding what is just or fair
   2. Kindness
   3. Equity of treatment
   4. Charity
      A. 1, 3
      B. 2, 4
      C. 1, 2, 3
      D. All of the above
      E. None of the above

29) **The ethical principle of Beneficence implies all except which of the following qualities or attributes?**
   1. Upholding what is just or fair
   2. Kindness
   3. Equity of treatment
   4. Charity
      A. 1, 3
      B. 2, 4
      C. 1, 2, 3
      D. All of the above
      E. None of the above

30) **The ethical principle of Autonomy is associated with all except which of the following attributes?**
   1. Promoting a patient's freedom to choose
   2. Preventing harm to the patient
   3. Encouraging patient self-advocacy
   4. Encouraging the patient to do what is right for the Case Manager
      A. 1, 3
      B. 2, 4
      C. 1, 2, 3
      D. All of the above
      E. None of the above

31) **The ethical principle of Nonmalfeasance is associated with all except which of the following attributes?**
   1. Promoting a patient's freedom to choose
   2. Preventing harm to the patient
   3. Encouraging patient self-advocacy
   4. Encouraging the patient to do what is right for the Case Manager
      A. 1, 3, 4
      B. 2, 4
      C. 1, 2, 3
      D. All of the above
      E. None of the above

32) **The ethical principle of Veracity implies all except which of the following qualities or attributes?**
   1. Upholding what is just or fair
   2. Adherence to the truth
   3. Equity of treatment
   4. Conforming in one's dealings with others to accuracy or precision
      A. 1, 3
      B. 2, 4
      C. 1, 2, 3
      D. All of the above
      E. None of the above

33) **Which of the following qualities or attributes are associated with the ethical principle of Veracity?**
1. Upholding what is just or fair
2. Adherence to the truth
3. Equity of treatment
4. Conforming in one's dealings with others to accuracy or precision
    A. 1, 3
    B. 2, 4
    C. 1, 2, 3
    D. All of the above
    E. None of the above

34) **The term *ethics* is best defined as:**
    A. Rules or standards that govern a person's behavior
    B. A set of religious laws that govern a person's behavior
    C. A set of juridical laws that govern a person's behavior
    D. Instinctual or inborn standards of behavior

35) **Ethical rules are derived from:**
    A. A set of personal or professional behaviors that embodies the highest ideals of society
    B. A set of personal or professional behaviors that embodies the minimal standards set by society
    C. A set of personal or professional behaviors found in one religious group
    D. A set of personal or professional behaviors that result in personal success or positive clinical outcomes

36) **The differences between ethics and law are:**
1. Ethics represent the highest standards for personal behavior, and law represents the minimal acceptable standards.
2. The law represents the highest standards for personal behavior, and ethics represents the minimal acceptable standards.
3. Lapses in strictly ethical behavior rarely result in punishment outside professional circles, while strictly legal infractions will.
4. Lapses in strictly legal behavior rarely result in punishment outside professional circles, while strictly ethical infractions will.
    A. 1, 2
    B. 1, 3
    C. 1, 4
    D. All of the above

37) **The term *ethical dilemma* is best defined as:**
    A. A conflict between two or more equally desirable outcomes, where only one outcome is possible
    B. A conflict between two or more possible outcomes, where a lack of knowledge as to which outcome will be best prevents adequate decisionmaking
    C. A conflict between two or more possible outcomes that occurs because of the indecisiveness of the Case Manager
    D. A conflict between two or more possible outcomes that occurs because of financial constraints

38) **The solutions to ethical dilemmas usually can be found in:**
    A. Textbooks on ethics
    B. Textbooks on medical care
    C. A more appropriately designed health care system
    D. An examination of the best interests of all parties involved in the dilemma
    E. There are no solutions to ethical dilemmas

39) **According to the code of ethics promulgated by the Case Management Society of America, the five ethical principles of Case Management are:**

   A. Autonomy, veracity, beneficence, nonmalfeasance, and justice
   B. Autonomy, veracity, beneficence, charity, and justice
   C. Autonomy, veracity, malfeasance, charity, and justice
   D. Autonomy, veracity, empathy, virtue, and justice
   E. Autonomy, veracity, forbearance, virtue, and justice

40) **Which of the following activities are associated with an increase in the legal liability associated with negligent patient assessment allegations?**

   1. Failing to inquire about a patient's educational background
   2. Failing to inquire about a patient's cultural background
   3. Failing to inquire about a patient's religious background
   4. Failing to inquire about a patient's social support system
       A. 1, 3
       B. 2, 4
       C. 1, 2, 3
       D. All of the above
       E. None of the above

41) **Which of the following activities are associated with a decrease in legal liability associated with allegations of negligent patient assessment?**

   1. Understanding a patient's family and social support system
   2. Understanding a patient's highest educational achievements
   3. Understanding a patient's religious affiliations
   4. Understanding a patient's cultural background
       A. 1, 3
       B. 2, 4
       C. 1, 2, 3
       D. All the of above
       E. None of the above

42) **Which of the following activities are associated with decreased risk of allegations of negligent referral?**

   1. Understanding the credentialing criteria of the provider network
   2. Making a personal recommendation for a single provider
   3. Providing patients with a list of providers, rather than the name of a single provider
   4. Protecting a provider who provides irregular or suspicious medical treatments
       A. 1, 3
       B. 2, 4
       C. 1, 2, 3
       D. All of the above
       E. None of the above

43) **Which of the following activities are associated with increased risk of allegations of negligent referral?**

   1. Understanding the credentialing criteria of the provider network
   2. Making a personal recommendation for a single provider
   3. Providing patients with a list of providers, rather than the name of a single provider
   4. Protecting a provider who provides irregular or suspicious medical treatments
       A. 1, 3
       B. 2, 4
       C. 1, 2, 3
       D. All of the above
       E. None of the above

44) **Of the following, which activity(s) may increase the risk of allegations of breach of patient confidentiality?**

1. Understanding applicable federal and state regulations on the disclosure of medical information
2. Quickly transferring information to any and all parties who request it, without bothering with notifying patient, attorneys, etc.
3. Informing the patient of his or her right to refuse the disclosure of medical information to any or all parties .
4. Transferring patient information concerning abortions, venereal and psychiatric diseases to third parties, without discussing first with patient and/or attorneys
   A. 1, 3
   B. 2, 4
   C. 1, 2, 3
   D. All of the above
   E. None of the above

45) **Of the following, which activity(s) may decrease the risk of allegations of breach of patient confidentiality?**

1. Understanding applicable federal and state regulations on the disclosure of medical information
2. Quickly transferring information to any and all parties that request it, without bothering with notifying patient, attorneys, etc.
3. Informing the patient of his or her right to refuse the disclosure of medical information to any or all parties
4. Transferring patient information concerning abortions, venereal and psychiatric diseases to third parties, without discussing first with patient and/or attorneys
   A. 1, 3
   B. 2, 4
   C. 1, 2, 3
   D. All of the above
   E. None of the above

46) **Which of the following should be disclosed to the patient when a provider is obtaining consent for a medical, surgical or psychological intervention?**

1. The projected or desired outcomes of the proposed treatment, and the likelihood of success
2. Reasonably foreseeable risks or hazards inherent in the proposed treatment or care (This must be done in a manner that the patient can understand.)
3. Alternatives to proposed care or treatment plan
4. Consequences of foregoing the treatment
   A. 1, 3
   B. 2, 4
   C. 1, 2, 3
   D. All of the above
   E. None of the above

47) **Which of the following need *not* be disclosed to the patient when a provider is obtaining consent for a medical, surgical or psychological intervention?**

1. The projected or desired outcomes of the proposed treatment, and the likelihood of success
2. The mood of the provider and his staff
3. Alternatives to proposed care or treatment plan
4. The names of all the patients the provider has treated with this intervention in the past
   A. 1, 3
   B. 2, 4
   C. 1, 2, 3
   D. All of the above
   E. None of the above

48) Which of the following are requirements for obtaining informed consent?

1. The patient must consent voluntarily.
2. The patient must have the capacity to give consent.
3. The patient must be an adult (under existing state law).
4. In the event that the patient is a minor, or adult without capacity to consent, parents, attorneys or legal guardians may give consent.
   A. 1, 3
   B. 2, 4
   C. 1, 2, 3
   D. All of the above
   E. None of the above

49) In order to decrease patient allegations of lack of informed consent, a Case Manager should assure which of the following?

1. The patient must have a full understanding of the scope of activities of the Case Manager, with all its attendant risks, benefits, and alternatives.
2. The Case Manager must document the consent. (A signed consent agreement is adequate.)
3. The Case Manager must obtain informed consent prior to the beginning of the professional relationship.
4. The Case Manager must consult with an attorney before every consent for treatment is signed.
   A. 1, 3
   B. 2, 4
   C. 1, 2, 3
   D. All of the above
   E. None of the above

50) Which of the following are <u>not</u> requirements for obtaining informed consent?

1. A signed affirmation from an attorney stating that the patient is competent must be obtained.
2. The patient must have the capacity to give consent.
3. The patient must be at least 10 years of age.
4. In the event that the patient is a minor, or adult without capacity to consent, parents, attorneys or legal guardians may give consent.
   A. 1, 3
   B. 2, 4
   C. 1, 2, 3
   D. All of the above
   E. None of the above

51) The legal definition of *Agency* includes which of the following?

1. It is a relationship between two or more parties.
2. One party consents to act on the behalf of the other party.
3. The relationship carries the obligation that the principal is responsible for the actions of the agent.
4. The relationship carries no obligations for the agent to the principal.
   A. 1, 3
   B. 2, 4
   C. 1, 2, 3
   D. All of the above
   E. None of the above

52) **Which of the following are requirements for obtaining informed consent?**
1. The patient may consent voluntarily or may be coerced if uncooperative.
2. The patient must have the capacity to give consent.
3. The patient must be an adult; however, emancipated minors must have parents' consent.
4. In the event that the patient is a minor, or adult without capacity to consent, parents, attorneys or legal guardians may give consent.
    A. 1, 3
    B. 2, 4
    C. 1, 2, 3
    D. All of the above
    E. None of the above

53) **Agents have which of the following legal obligations to their principals?**
1. Using care and skill in the performance of their duties.
2. Acting in good faith in the performance of their duties.
3. Remaining within the limits of their authority.
4. Advancing the interests of the agent.
    A. 1, 3
    B. 2, 4
    C. 1, 2, 3
    D. All of the above
    E. None of the above

54) **Under the rules of *Agency*, agents have which of the following legal obligations to their principals?**
1. Using care and skill in the performance of their duties
2. Assuming new authority and exercising it in the interests of the principal
3. Acting in good faith in the performance of duties
4. Advancing the interests of the agent
    A. 1, 3
    B. 2, 4
    C. 1, 2, 3
    D. All of the above
    E. None of the above

55) **Apparent authority (or ostensible agency) occurs with which of the following?**
1. A principal has taken such actions that would indicate to third parties that someone is his agent.
2. A principal assigns duties and authorities to an agent via a written contract.
3. A principal, aware that a third party is acting as his agent, does nothing to stop it.
4. A principal assigns duties and authorities to an agent via an oral contract.
    A. 1, 3
    B. 2, 4
    C. 1, 2, 3
    D. All of the above
    E. None of the above

56) **Which of the following pairs are examples of principals and their agents?**
1. Hospitals and community physicians (not employed by the hospital)
2. Hospitals and the nurses who work on the wards
3. Case Managers and patients
4. Insurers and Case Managers (employed by the insurer)
    A. 1, 3
    B. 2, 4
    C. 1, 2, 3
    D. All of the above
    E. None of the above

57) **Which of the following pairs are *not* examples of principals and their agents?**

    1.   Hospitals and community physicians (not employed by the hospital)
    2.   Hospitals and phlebotomists (employed by the hospital)
    3.   Case Managers and network physicians
    4.   Insurers and their utilization review departments (employed by the insurer)

    A. 1, 3
    B. 2, 4
    C. 1, 2, 3
    D. All of the above
    E. None of the above

58) **Which of the following statements describes the legal term *abandonment*?**

    1.   Termination of a professional relationship without reasonable notice to the patient
    2.   Termination of a professional relationship without payment of debts
    3.   Termination of a professional relationship without giving the patient an opportunity to acquire alternative care or services
    4.   Termination of a professional relationship because of a disagreement

    A. 1, 3
    B. 2, 4
    C. 1, 2, 3
    D. All of the above
    E. None of the above

59) **Which of the following statements does *not* describe the legal term *abandonment*?**

    1.   Termination of a professional relationship without reasonable notice to the patient
    2.   Termination of a professional relationship without payment of debts
    3.   Termination of a professional relationship without giving the patient an opportunity to acquire alternative care or services
    4.   Termination of a professional relationship because of a disagreement

    A. 1, 3
    B. 2, 4
    C. 1, 2, 3
    D. All of the above
    E. None of the above

60) **The legal term *claim* is best described by which of the following?**

    A. The state or quality of being confidential; treated as private and not for publication
    B. The document by which the plaintiff gives the court and the defendant notice of the transactions, occurrences or series of transactions or occurrences intended to be proved and the material elements of each cause of action or defense
    C. A method of measuring negligence among the participants in a suit, both defense and plaintiff, in terms of percentages of culpability. Damages are then diminished in proportion to the amount of negligence attributable to the complaining party.
    D. A report by the insured to the insurance company based on notification by a patient or the patient's attorney of an event out of which malpractice has been alleged
    E. A failure of a fiduciary duty, refusing to hold secret a privileged communication entrusted by one party to another

61) **The legal term *breach of confidentiality* is best described by which of the following?**

    A. The state or quality of being confidential; treated as private, and not for publication
    B. The document by which the plaintiff gives the court and the defendant notice of the transactions, occurrences or series of transactions or occurrences intended to be proved and the material elements of each cause of action or defense
    C. A method of measuring negligence among the participants in a suit, both defense and plaintiff, in terms of percentages of culpability. Damages are then diminished in proportion to the amount of negligence attributable to the complaining party

    D. A report by the insured to the insurance company based on notification by a patient or the patient's attorney of an event out of which malpractice has been alleged

    E. A failure of a fiduciary duty, refusing to hold secret a privileged communication entrusted by one party to another

62)   The legal term *comparative negligence* is best described by which of the following?

    A. The state or quality of being confidential; treated as private and not for publication

    B. The document by which the plaintiff gives the court and the defendant notice of the transactions, occurrences or series of transactions or occurrences intended to be proved and the material elements of each cause of action or defense

    C. A method of measuring negligence among the participants in a suit, both defense and plaintiff, in terms of percentages of culpability. Damages are then diminished in proportion to the amount of negligence attributable to the complaining party.

    D. A report by the insured to the insurance company based on notification by a patient or the patient's attorney of an event out of which malpractice has been alleged

    E. A failure of a fiduciary duty, refusing to hold secret a privileged communication entrusted by one party to another

63)   The legal term *complaint* is best described by which of the following?

    A. The state or quality of being confidential; treated as private, and not for publication

    B. The document by which the plaintiff gives the court and the defendant notice of the transactions, occurrences or series of transactions or occurrences intended to be proved and the material elements of each cause of action or defense

    C. A method of measuring negligence among the participants in a suit, both defense and plaintiff, in terms of percentages of culpability. Damages are then diminished in proportion to the amount of negligence attributable to the complaining party.

    D. A report by the insured to the insurance company based on notification by a patient or the patient's attorney of an event out of which malpractice has been alleged

    E. A failure of a fiduciary duty, refusing to hold secret a privileged communication entrusted by one party to another

64)   The legal term *confidentiality* is best described by which of the following?

    A. The state or quality of being confidential; treated as private and not for publication

    B. The document by which the plaintiff gives the court and the defendant notice of the transactions, occurrences or series of transactions or occurrences intended to be proved and the material elements of each cause of action or defense

    C. A method of measuring negligence among the participants in a suit, both defense and plaintiff, in terms of percentages of culpability. Damages are then diminished in proportion to the amount of negligence attributable to the complaining party.

    D. A report by the insured to the insurance company based on notification by a patient or the patient's attorney of an event out of which malpractice has been alleged

    E. A failure of a fiduciary duty, refusing to hold secret a privileged communication entrusted by one party to another

65)   Which of the following statements best defines the legal term *corporate negligence*?

    A. A method of obtaining disclosure of information that is material and necessary to the underlying lawsuit by way of sworn oral testimony

    B. The ascertainment of what is not previously known; generally, the pretrial stage of a lawsuit beginning with the service of summons and complaint and concluding with the filing of a "note of issue"

    C. A pecuniary compensation recovered by the courts for acts of tort. These recoveries, or compensations are for both tangible (medical expenses, lost earnings) and intangible (pain and suffering) injuries (torts).

D. A legal doctrine that prohibits corporations from engaging in the practice of medicine. That is the treatment of injuries as well as the discovery of the cause and nature of disease, and the administration of remedies, or the prescribing of treatment.

E. A term that encompasses the legal grounds for managed care organizations liability based on the corporate activities of the managed care organization itself, rather than on the care-related activities of participating health care professionals

66) **Which of the following statements best defines the legal term *corporate practice of medicine*?**

A. A method of obtaining disclosure of information that is material and necessary to the underlying lawsuit by way of sworn oral testimony

B. The ascertainment of what is not previously known; generally, the pretrial stage of a lawsuit beginning with the service of summons and complaint and concluding with the filing of a "note of issue"

C. A pecuniary compensation recovered by the courts for acts of tort. These recoveries, or compensations are for both tangible (medical expenses, lost earnings) and intangible (pain and suffering) injuries (torts).

D. A legal doctrine that prohibits corporations from engaging in the practice of medicine; that is, the treatment of injuries as well as the discovery of the cause and nature of disease, and the administration of remedies, or the prescribing of treatment

E. A term that encompasses the legal grounds for managed care organizations liability based on the corporate activities of the managed care organization itself, rather than on the care-related activities of participating health care professionals

67) **Which of the following statements best defines the legal term *damages*?**

A. A method of obtaining disclosure of information that is material and necessary to the underlying lawsuit by way of sworn oral testimony

B. The ascertainment of what is not previously known; generally, the pretrial stage of a lawsuit beginning with the service of summons and complaint and concluding with the filing of a "note of issue"

C. A pecuniary compensation recovered by the courts for acts of tort. These recoveries, or compensations are for both tangible (medical expenses, lost earnings) and intangible (pain and suffering) injuries (torts).

D. A legal doctrine that prohibits corporations from engaging in the practice of medicine; that is, the treatment of injuries as well as the discovery of the cause and nature of disease, and the administration of remedies, or the prescribing of treatment

E. A term that encompasses the legal grounds for managed care organizations liability based on the corporate activities of the managed care organization itself, rather than on the care-related activities of participating health care professionals

68) **Which of the following statements best defines the legal term *discovery*?**

A. A method of obtaining disclosure of information that is material and necessary to the underlying lawsuit by way of sworn oral testimony

B. The ascertainment of what is not previously known; generally, the pretrial stage of a lawsuit beginning with the service of summons and complaint and concluding with the filing of a "note of issue"

C. A pecuniary compensation recovered by the courts for acts of tort. These recoveries or compensations are for both tangible (medical expenses, lost earnings) and intangible (pain and suffering) injuries (torts).

D. A legal doctrine that prohibits corporations from engaging in the practice of medicine; that is, the treatment of injuries as well as the discovery of the cause and nature of disease, and the administration of remedies, or the prescribing of treatment

E. A term that encompasses the legal grounds for managed care organizations liability based on the corporate activities of the managed care organization itself, rather than on the care-related activities of participating health care professionals

69)   **Which of the following statements best defines the legal term *examination before trial*?**

A.   A method of obtaining disclosure of information that is material and necessary to the underlying lawsuit by way of sworn oral testimony.

B.   The ascertainment of what is not previously known; generally, the pretrial stage of a lawsuit beginning with the service of summons and complaint and concluding with the filing of a "note of issue"

C.   A pecuniary compensation recovered by the courts for acts of tort. These recoveries or compensations are for both tangible (medical expenses, lost earnings) and intangible (pain and suffering) injuries (torts).

D.   A legal doctrine that prohibits corporations from engaging in the practice of medicine; that is, the treatment of injuries as well as the discovery of the cause and nature of disease, and the administration of remedies, or the prescribing of treatment

E.   A term that encompasses the legal grounds for managed care organizations liability based on the corporate activities of the managed care organization itself, rather than on the care-related activities of participating health care professionals

70)   **Which of the following statements best defines the legal term *joint and several liability*?**

A.   A debt, responsibility or obligation

B.   An unwarranted appropriation or exploitation of another's private affairs with which the public has no legitimate concern. A wrongful intrusion into one's private activities in such a manner as to cause mental suffering, shame or humiliation to a person of ordinary sensibilities

C.   A complication that is commonly associated with a procedure, but is not the result of the negligence of the operator (physician, nurse, or other provider performing the procedure or treatment)

D.   A contractual arrangement between the insurer and the provider of service, typically contained in a managed care contract. This provision specifies that the provider assumes the liability for covered services, and cannot sue or assert any claims against enrollees for those covered services, even if the managed care organization becomes insolvent.

E.   An obligation of a group and its individual members. The party that has been harmed is able to sue all of the liable parties as a group, or any one of them individually. He may not, however, recover more compensation by suing each of them individually, than by suing them as a group.

71)   **Which of the following statements best defines the legal term *hold harmless provision*?**

A.   A debt, responsibility or obligation

B.   An unwarranted appropriation or exploitation of another's private affairs with which the public has no legitimate concern. A wrongful intrusion into one's private activities in such a manner as to cause mental suffering, shame or humiliation to a person of ordinary sensibilities.

C.   A complication that is commonly associated with a procedure, but is not the result of the negligence of the operator (physician, nurse, or other provider performing the procedure or treatment)

D.   A contractual arrangement between the insurer and the provider of service, typically contained in a managed care contract. This provision specifies that the provider assumes the liability for covered services, and cannot sue or assert any claims against enrollees for those covered services, even if the managed care organization becomes insolvent.

E.   An obligation of a group and its individual members. The party that has been harmed is able to sue all of the liable parties as a group, or any one of them individually. He may not, however, recover more compensation by suing each of them individually, than by suing them as a group.

72) **Which of the following statements best defines the legal term *inherent risk*?**

A. A debt, responsibility or obligation

B. An unwarranted appropriation or exploitation of another's private affairs with which the public has no legitimate concern. A wrongful intrusion into one's private activities in such a manner as to cause mental suffering, shame or humiliation to a person of ordinary sensibilities

C. A complication that is commonly associated with a procedure, but is not the result of the negligence of the operator (physician, nurse, or other provider performing the procedure or treatment)

D. A contractual arrangement between the insurer and the provider of service, typically contained in a managed care contract. This provision specifies that the provider assumes the liability for covered services, and cannot sue or assert any claims against enrollees for those covered services, even if the managed care organization becomes insolvent.

E. An obligation of a group and its individual members. The party that has been harmed is able to sue all of the liable parties as a group, or any one of them individually. He may not, however, recover more compensation by suing each of them individually, than by suing them as a group.

73) **Which of the following statements best defines the legal term *invasion of privacy*?"**

A. A debt, responsibility or obligation

B. An unwarranted appropriation or exploitation of another's private affairs with which the public has no legitimate concern. A wrongful intrusion into one's private activities in such a manner as to cause mental suffering, shame or humiliation to a person of ordinary sensibilities.

C. A complication that is commonly associated with a procedure, but is not the result of the negligence of the operator (physician, nurse, or other provider performing the procedure or treatment)

D. A contractual arrangement between the insurer and the provider of service, typically contained in a managed care contract. This provision specifies that the provider assumes the liability for covered services, and cannot sue or assert any claims against enrollees for those covered services, even if the managed care organization becomes insolvent.

E. An obligation of a group and its individual members. The party that has been harmed is able to sue all of the liable parties as a group, or any one of them individually. He may not, however, recover more compensation by suing each of them individually, than by suing them as a group.

74) **Which of the following statements best defines the legal term *liability*?**

A. A debt, responsibility or obligation

B. An unwarranted appropriation or exploitation of another's private affairs with which the public has no legitimate concern. A wrongful intrusion into one's private activities in such a manner as to cause mental suffering, shame or humiliation to a person of ordinary sensibilities.

C. A complication that is commonly associated with a procedure, but is not the result of the negligence of the operator (physician, nurse, or other provider performing the procedure or treatment)

D. A contractual arrangement between the insurer and the provider of service, typically contained in a managed care contract. This provision specifies that the provider assumes the liability for covered services, and cannot sue or assert any claims against enrollees for those covered services, even if the managed care organization becomes insolvent.

E. An obligation of a group and its individual members. The party that has been harmed is able to sue all of the liable parties as a group, or any one of them individually. He may not, however, recover more compensation by suing each of them individually, than by suing them as a group.

75) **Which of the following statements is (are) true, regarding the False Claims Act?**

1. It has both civil and criminal penalties.
2. It prohibits the presentation of false claims to the U.S. Government.
3. Penalties for violation include substantial fines and imprisonment.
4. The Act is targeted only at physicians.
   A. 1, 3
   B. 2, 4
   C. 1, 2, 3
   D. All of the above
   E. None of the above

76) **Which of the following statements is (are) *not* true, regarding the False Claims Act?**

1. It prohibits the presentation of false claims to the U.S. Government.
2. Physical therapists are exempt from this act.
3. Penalties for violation include substantial fines and imprisonment.
4. The Act is targeted only at physicians.
   A. 1, 3
   B. 2, 4
   C. 1, 2, 3
   D. All of the above
   E. None of the above

77) **Which of the following statements best defines the legal term *liable*?**

A. A failure on the part of the managed care organization to exercise reasonable care in screening and selection of providers

B. A failure to use such care in making a referral, as a reasonable professional would use under similar circumstances; referring a patient to a provider who does not possess the skills, experience, licensure or certifications to care for that patient

C. A failure to use the degree of care a reasonably prudent and careful person would use under similar circumstances

D. A contractual arrangement between a purchaser and provider—in this arrangement the provider is obligated to render products or services to the purchaser at the same rate as his most favored customer.

E. Bound by law or fairness; responsible, accountable.

78) **Which of the following statements best defines the legal term *most favored nation clause*?**

A. A failure on the part of the managed care organization to exercise reasonable care in screening and selection of providers

B. A failure to use such care in making a referral, as a reasonable professional would use under similar circumstances; referring a patient to a provider who does not possess the skills, experience, licensure or certifications to care for that patient

C. A failure to use the degree of care a reasonably prudent and careful person would use under similar circumstances

D. A contractual arrangement between a purchaser and provider—in this arrangement the provider is obligated to render products or services to the purchaser at the same rate as his most favored customer.

E. Bound by law or fairness; responsible; accountable

79) **Which of the following statements best defines the legal term *negligence*?**

A. A failure on the part of the managed care organization to exercise reasonable care in screening and selection of providers

B. A failure to use such care in making a referral, as a reasonable professional would use under similar circumstances; referring a patient to a provider who does not possess the skills, experience, licensure or certifications to care for that patient

C. A failure to use the degree of care a reasonably prudent and careful person would use under similar circumstances

D. A contractual arrangement between a purchaser and provider—in this arrangement the provider is obligated to render products or services to the purchaser at the same rate as his most favored customer.

E. Bound by law or fairness; responsible; accountable

80) Which of the following statements best defines the legal term *negligent referral*?

A. A failure on the part of the managed care organization to exercise reasonable care in screening and selection of providers

B. A failure to use such care in making a referral, as a reasonable professional would use under similar circumstances; referring a patient to a provider who does not possess the skills, experience, licensure or certifications to care for that patient

C. A failure to use the degree of care a reasonably prudent and careful person would use under similar circumstances

D. A contractual arrangement between a purchaser and provider—in this arrangement the provider is obligated to render products or services to the purchaser at the same rate as his most favored customer.

E. Bound by law or fairness; responsible; accountable

81) Which of the following statements best defines the legal term *negligent credentialing*?

A. A failure on the part of the managed care organization to exercise reasonable care in screening and selection of providers

B. A failure to use such care in making a referral, as a reasonable professional would use under similar circumstances; referring a patient to a provider who does not possess the skills, experience, licensure or certifications to care for that patient

C. A failure to use the degree of care a reasonably prudent and careful person would use under similar circumstances

D. A contractual arrangement between a purchaser and provider—in this arrangement the provider is obligated to render products or services to the purchaser at the same rate as his most favored customer.

E. Bound by law or fairness; responsible; accountable

82) Which of the following components are necessary to constitute a malpractice incident?

1. A deviation from the approved and accepted standards of care
2. A violation of federal law
3. An injury to the patient that resulted from negligence
4. A violation of criminal law
    A. 1, 3
    B. 2, 4
    C. 1, 2, 3
    D. All of the above
    E. None of the above

83) Which of the following components are *not* necessary to constitute a malpractice incident?

1. A deviation from the approved and accepted standards of care
2. A violation of federal law
3. An injury to the patient that resulted from negligence
4. A violation of criminal law
    A. 1, 3
    B. 2, 4
    C. 1, 2, 3
    D. All of the above
    E. None of the above

84) **Which of the following statements best describes the legal term *ombudsman*?**

   A. A person whose occupation consists of investigating customer complaints against his or her employer
   B. An agreement between two litigants to settle the contested matter privately, without being referred to the judge for authorization or approval, before the Court has rendered its decision
   C. The quality or condition of being secluded from the presence or view of others; the state of being free from unsanctioned intrusion
   D. Information that a person authorized to practice medicine, nursing, counseling, etc., acquires in attending to a patient in a professional capacity, and that is necessary to enable him or her to act in that capacity
   E. A doctrine of law where mere proof that an occurrence took place is sufficient under the circumstances to shift the burden of proof upon the defendant to prove that it was not due to his or her negligence

85) **Which of the following statements best describes the legal expression *out of court settlement*?**

   A. A person whose occupation consists of investigating customer complaints against his or her employer
   B. An agreement between two litigants to settle the contested matter privately, without being referred to the judge for authorization or approval, before the Court has rendered its decision
   C. The quality or condition of being secluded from the presence or view of others; the state of being free from unsanctioned intrusion
   D. Information that a person authorized to practice medicine, nursing, counseling, etc., acquires in attending to a patient in a professional capacity, and that is necessary to enable him or her to act in that capacity
   E. A doctrine of law where mere proof that an occurrence took place is sufficient under the circumstances to shift the burden of proof upon the defendant to prove that it was not due to his or her negligence

86) **Which of the following statements best describes the legal term *privacy*?**

   A. A person whose occupation consists of investigating customer complaints against his or her employer
   B. An agreement between two litigants to settle the contested matter privately, without being referred to the judge for authorization or approval, before the Court has rendered its decision
   C. The quality or condition of being secluded from the presence or view of others; the state of being free from unsanctioned intrusion
   D. Information that a person authorized to practice medicine, nursing, counseling, etc., acquires in attending to a patient in a professional capacity, and that is necessary to enable him or her to act in that capacity
   E. A doctrine of law where mere proof that an occurrence took place is sufficient under the circumstances to shift the burden of proof upon the defendant to prove that it was not due to his or her negligence

87) **Which of the following statements best describes the legal term *privileged communication*?**

   A. A person whose occupation consists of investigating customer complaints against his or her employer
   B. An agreement between two litigants to settle the contested matter privately, without being referred to the judge for authorization or approval, before the Court has rendered its decision
   C. The quality or condition of being secluded from the presence or view of others; the state of being free from unsanctioned intrusion

D. Information that a person authorized to practice medicine, nursing, counseling, etc., acquires in attending to a patient in a professional capacity, and that is necessary to enable him or her to act in that capacity

E. A doctrine of law where mere proof that an occurrence took place is sufficient under the circumstances to shift the burden of proof upon the defendant to prove that it was not due to his or her negligence

88) **Which of the following statements best describes the legal expression *res ipsa loquitor*?**

A. A person whose occupation consists of investigating customer complaints against his or her employer

B. An agreement between two litigants to settle the contested matter privately, without being referred to the judge for authorization or approval, before the Court has rendered its decision

C. The quality or condition of being secluded from the presence or view of others; the state of being free from unsanctioned intrusion

D. Information that a person authorized to practice medicine, nursing, counseling, etc., acquires in attending to a patient in a professional capacity, and that is necessary to enable him or her to act in that capacity

E. A doctrine of law where mere proof that an occurrence took place is sufficient under the circumstances to shift the burden of proof upon the defendant to prove that it was not due to his or her negligence

89) **Which of the following statements are true concerning the legal term *res ipsa loquitor*?**

1. It translates from the Latin as "the thing speaks for itself."
2. It proves that the defendant was negligent.
3. It implies that the defendant was negligent.
4. It translates from the Latin "Let the master answer."
   A. 1, 3
   B. 2, 4
   C. 1, 2, 3
   D. All of the above
   E. None of the above

90) **Which of the following statements are *not* true concerning the legal term *res ipsa loquitor*?**

1. It translates from the Latin as "the thing speaks for itself."
2. It proves that the defendant was negligent.
3. It implies that the defendant was negligent.
4. It translates from the Latin "Let the master answer."
   A. 1, 3
   B. 2, 4
   C. 1, 2, 3
   D. All of the above
   E. None of the above

91) **Which of the following statements best describes the legal expression *statute of limitations*?**

A. This maxim means that a master is liable, in certain cases, for the wrongful acts of his servant (and a principal for those of his agent). A master/servant or principal/agent relationship exists where one person, for pay or other valuable consideration, enters into the service of another and devotes his or her personal labor for an agreed period.

B. The period of time in which a plaintiff may bring lawsuit after an incident has occurred

C. A judicial process requiring a witness to give relevant information or testimony "under penalty" of contempt for disobedience

D. A document issued by the plaintiff's attorney that when properly delivered, commences a legal action

E. Legal liability that a person may have for the actions of someone else

92) **Which of the following statements best describes the legal expression** *respondeat superior*?

   A. This maxim means that a master is liable, in certain cases, for the wrongful acts of his servant (and a principal for those of his agent). A master/servant or principal/agent relationship exists where one person, for pay or other valuable consideration, enters into the service of another and devotes his or her personal labor for an agreed period.
   B. The period of time in which a plaintiff may bring lawsuit after an incident has occurred
   C. A judicial process requiring a witness to give relevant information or testimony "under penalty" of contempt for disobedience
   D. A document issued by the plaintiff's attorney that when properly delivered, commences a legal action
   E. Legal liability that a person may have for the actions of someone else

93) **Which of the following statements best describes the legal expression** *summons*?

   A. This maxim means that a master is liable, in certain cases, for the wrongful acts of his servant (and a principal for those of his agent). A master/servant or principal/agent relationship exists where one person, for pay or other valuable consideration, enters into the service of another and devotes his or her personal labor for an agreed period.
   B. The period of time in which a plaintiff may bring lawsuit after an incident has occurred
   C. A judicial process requiring a witness to give relevant information or testimony "under penalty" of contempt for disobedience
   D. A document issued by the plaintiff's attorney that when properly delivered, commences a legal action
   E. Legal liability that a person may have for the actions of someone else

94) **Which of the following statements best describes the legal expression** *vicarious liability*?

   A. This maxim means that a master is liable, in certain cases, for the wrongful acts of his servant (and a principal for those of his agent). A master/servant or principal/agent relationship exists where one person, for pay or other valuable consideration, enters into the service of another and devotes his or her personal labor for an agreed period.
   B. The period of time in which a plaintiff may bring lawsuit after an incident has occurred
   C. A judicial process requiring a witness to give relevant information or testimony "under penalty" of contempt for disobedience
   D. A document issued by the plaintiff's attorney that when properly delivered, commences a legal action
   E. Legal liability that a person may have for the actions of someone else

95) **Which of the following statements are true regarding the legal term** *respondeat superior*?

   1. It translates as "let the master answer."
   2. It proves negligence on the part of the defendant.
   3. It holds that in certain circumstances the employer is responsible for wrongful acts committed by the employee.
   4. It translates as "the thing speaks for itself."
      A. 1, 3
      B. 2, 4
      C. 1, 2, 3
      D. All of the above
      E. None of the above

96) **Which of the following statements are *not* true regarding the legal term *respondeat superior*?**

   1. It translates as "let the master answer."
   2. It proves negligence on the part of the defendant.
   3. It holds that in certain circumstances the employer is responsible for wrongful acts committed by the employee.
   4. It translates as "the thing speaks for itself."
       A. 1, 3
       B. 2, 4
       C. 1, 2, 3
       D. All of the above
       E. None of the above

97) **Which of the following statements are true regarding the legal term *tort*?**

   1. It comes from a Latin word that means "twist."
   2. It implies that testimony has been given falsely.
   3. It refers to damage or injury that is done willfully or negligently.
   4. It refers only to medical malpractice cases.
       A. 1, 3
       B. 2, 4
       C. 1, 2, 3
       D. All of the above
       E. None of the above

98) **Which of the following statements are *not* true regarding the legal term *tort*?**

   1. It comes from a Latin word that means "twist."
   2. It implies that testimony has been given falsely.
   3. It refers to damage or injury that is done willfully or negligently.
   4. It refers only to medical malpractice cases.
       A. 1, 3
       B. 2, 4
       C. 1, 2, 3
       D. All of the above
       E. None of the above

99) **A request by an insured or a provider to re-review a denial of a utilization review organization's decision is also known as:**

   1. An appeal
   2. A reconsideration
   3. An expedited appeal
   4. An IME
       A. 1, 2
       B. 1, 3
       C. 1, 4
       D. All of the above
       E. None of the above

100) **As a result of the case of *Wickline v. State of California*, which of the following is true?**

1. Providers can be held accountable for negative outcomes when they discharge patients solely at the request of the insurer or payer.
2. Case Managers can be held liable for negative outcomes as a consequence of their denials.
3. Insurers or utilization review firms can be held liable for negative outcomes as a consequence of their denials.
4. If a provider appeals an adverse determination and a negative outcome occurs, the liability may be passed to the insurer.
    A. 1, 2, 3
    B. 2, 3. 4
    C. All of the above
    D. None of the above

101) **During a Case Management interview, in a Workers' Compensation case, the patient confides to the Case Manager that he is a recovering alcoholic and has been alcohol free for 5 years. The Case Manager should:**

A. Include the information in the psychosocial section of her insurance company report.
B. Immediately notify the patient's attending physician.
C. Make no comment verbally or in writing as it has no current bearing on a work-related injury.
D. Close the case.

1) **Answer: D**

Discourteous behaviors, communications failures, lack of patient understanding and lack of family understanding are the most common causes of malpractice litigation. Malpractice litigation stems more commonly from poor relationships with patients than from negligent medical care.

2) **Answer: B**

For some, it is surprising that bad clinical outcomes and negligent medical care are not common causes of malpractice litigation. In fact, studies have demonstrated that patients rarely identify most substandard medical care, and most bad clinical outcomes are not litigated. Discourteous behaviors, communications failures, lack of patient understanding and lack of family understanding are the most common causes of malpractice litigation. Malpractice litigation stems more commonly from poor relationships with patients than from negligent medical care.

3) **Answer: A**

For some it is surprising that bad clinical outcomes and negligent medical care are not common causes of malpractice litigation. In fact, studies have demonstrated that patients rarely identify most substandard medical care, and most bad clinical outcomes are not litigated. Discourteous behaviors, communications failures, lack of patient understanding and lack of family understanding are the most common causes of malpractice litigation. Malpractice litigation stems more commonly from poor relationships with patients than from negligent medical care.

4) **Answer: D**

When malpractice is alleged, the Case Manager is commonly accused of negligence in the following areas: premature discharge, bad faith claims denials, negligent patient assessment, negligent referral, invasion of privacy, breach of confidentiality and treating without informed consent.

5) **Answer: A**

When malpractice is alleged, the Case Manager is commonly accused of negligence in the following areas: premature discharge, bad faith claims denials, negligent patient assessment, negligent referral, invasion of privacy, breach of confidentiality and treating without informed consent. Approval of claims, and admissions to hospitals do not carry a high malpractice risk.

6) **Answer: B**

The Case Manager has an obligation of "reasonable care" to the patient. Failing to assure that the discharge is "safe" would be negligent on the part of the Case Manager.

7) **Answer: A**

The Case Manager has an obligation of "reasonable care" to the patient. Failing to assure that the discharge is "safe" would be negligent on the part of the Case Manager. Reducing medical costs or utilization of services is not associated with decreased risk of litigation.

8) **Answer: B**

Bad faith claims occur when there is no reasonable basis for denial of benefits, or when long, purposeful delays in benefit adjudication result in *de facto* denials. Activities that decrease delays and increase communication with the client will decrease allegations of dealing in bad faith.

9)   **Answer: D**

Bad faith claims occur when there is no reasonable basis for denial of benefits, or when long, purposeful delays in benefit adjudication result in *de facto* denials. Activities that decrease delays and increase communication with the client will decrease allegations of dealing in bad faith.

10) **Answer: D**

11) **Answer: C**

12) **Answer: D**

13) **Answer: E**

14) **Answer: D**

15) **Answer: A**

16) **Answer: C**

Case Managers are liable for damages if their referral of patients to providers is negligently performed and harm comes to the patient as a direct result of that referral.

17) **Answer: B**

18) **Answer: C**

Case Management files are the only files in the preceding list that are considered medical records.

19) **Answer: D**

These items are the common causes for malpractice litigation. Although all of them can contribute to A–C, D is the best answer.

20) **Answer: A**

Ethics are the rules or standards that govern the conduct of a person or members of a profession. Ethical rules describe a society's ideal of how a person or professional should conduct him- or herself.

21) **Answer: B**

Ethics are the rules or standards that govern the conduct of a person or members of a profession. Ethical rules describe a society's ideal of how a person or a professional should conduct him- or herself. Thoughts that govern a person's conduct are not necessarily ethical or virtuous.

22) **Answer: D**

Ethical and legal principles are closely related, as both are based on what a given society values as an appropriate standard of conduct. Legal duties are what a society describes as the minimum acceptable standards of conduct. A legal duty usually carries a punishment for those whose conduct falls below its standards. Ethical duties, on the other hand, represent a society's conception of the ideal conduct for an individual or a profession. Lapses in ethical behavior, to the extent that the behavior is also not illegal, are usually not punishable outside of a professional society. In general, the demands of ethical duties usually exceed those of legal duties. For example, the AMA holds that in the rare instances when legal duties and ethical duties are in conflict, a professional's ethical duties should supersede his legal duties.

23) **Answer: E**

Ethical and legal principles are closely related, as both are based on what a given society values as an appropriate standard of conduct. Legal duties are what a society describes as the minimum acceptable standards of conduct. A legal duty usually carries a punishment for those whose conduct falls below its standards. Ethical duties, on the other hand, represent a society's conception of the ideal conduct for an individual or a profession. Lapses in ethical behavior, to the extent that the behavior is also not illegal, are usually not punishable outside of a professional society. In general, the demands of ethical duties usually exceed those of legal duties. For example, the AMA holds that in the rare instances when legal duties and ethical duties are in conflict, a professional's ethical duties should supersede his legal duties.

24) **Answer: A**

An ethical dilemma exists where two or more equally desirable outcomes are in conflict.

25) **Answer: B**

An ethical dilemma exists where two or more equally desirable outcomes are in conflict.

26) **Answer: D**

27) **Answer: B**

28) **Answer: B**

The ethical principle of Justice implies the upholding of what is just, in accordance with honor, standards or law, and is derived from the Case Manager's sense of moral rightness. The qualities of kindness and charity are associated with the ethical principle of beneficence.

29) **Answer: A**

The ethical principle of Justice implies the upholding of what is just or fair, in accordance with honor, standards or law, and is derived from the Case Manager's sense of moral rightness. The qualities of kindness and charity are associated with the ethical principle of Beneficence.

30) **Answer: B**

The ethical principle of autonomy asks the Case Manager to encourage the client to make his own well-informed decisions. Nonmalfeasance is an amplification of beneficence, and this principle requires that the Case Manager not only do good by doing a good job, but actively seek to prevent harm from coming to the patient. It requires the Case Manager to show the patient the course of action that will result in the best outcome.

31) **Answer: A**

The ethical principle of autonomy asks the Case Manager to encourage the client to make his own well-informed decisions. Nonmalfeasance is an amplification of beneficence, and this principle requires that the Case Manager not only do good by doing a good job, but actively seek to prevent harm from coming to the patient. It requires the Case Manager to show the patient the course of action that will result in the best outcome.

32) **Answer: A**

The ethical principle of Justice implies the upholding of what is just or fair, in accordance with honor, standards or law, and is derived from the Case Manager's sense of moral rightness. The qualities of accuracy, precision, and truth are associated with the ethical principle of Veracity.

33) **Answer: B**

The ethical principle of Justice implies the upholding of what is just or fair, in accordance with honor, standards or law, and is derived from the Case Manager's sense of moral rightness. The qualities of accuracy, precision, and truth are associated with the ethical principle of Veracity.

34) **Answer: A**

35) **Answer: A**

Ethical rules are meant to be a challenge to the individual or professional, and represent the ideal behaviors that one should strive for.

36) **Answer: B**

Ethics represent the highest standards of personal or professional behavior. Lapses in ethical behavior are usually not punishable outside of the professional society. Legal infractions, which represent lapses in the minimum standards for behavior, are punishable by society.

37) **Answer: A**

In a situation where two or more equally desirable outcomes are in conflict an ethical dilemma exists. By definition, ethical dilemmas do not depend on the lack of knowledge, money, or skills of the decisionmaker.

38)   Answer: E

While being knowledgeable about ethics, medical care, and health care systems is helpful in avoiding violation of ethical principles, and achieving the best results for one's clients, true ethical dilemmas, by definition, have no solution. (A solution being defined here as a single answer that accommodates all equally deserving and conflicting outcomes.) One may make a decision that accommodates one party, and results in one desirable outcome. However, the other equally desirable outcomes do not occur, and the other deserving parties are disenfranchised. This is the inescapable result of decisions in ethical dilemmas.

39)   Answer: A

40)   Answer: D

The prudent Case Manager should be aware of a patient's intellectual, educational, psychological, social, religious, cultural and financial status. Any of these may present a barrier to a patient's medical care, compliance, and ability to follow up with providers as an outpatient.

41)   Answer: D

The prudent Case Manager should understand a patient's intellectual, educational, psychological, social, religious, cultural and financial status. Any of these may present a barrier to a patient's medical care, compliance, and ability to follow up with providers as an outpatient. While a patient's hobbies may give some insight into intelligence and psychological status, it is generally not thought to be helpful in Case Management patient assessment.

42)   Answer: A

A Case Manager can decrease the risk of allegations of negligent assessment by understanding the network's credentialing criteria, refusing to make personal recommendations for providers, providing the names of several providers, rather than a single provider when asked for a recommendation, and finally, reporting all suspicious, illegal, unethical provider behavior to the proper authorities.

43)   Answer: B

A Case Manager can decrease the risk of allegations of negligent assessment by understanding the network's credentialing criteria, refusing to make personal recommendations for providers, providing the names of several providers, rather than a single provider when asked for a recommendation, and finally, reporting all suspicious, illegal, unethical provider behavior to the proper authorities.

44)   Answer: B

A Case Manager can decrease the risk of allegations of breach of confidentiality by fully understanding the following: the implications of federal and state regulations on the disclosure of medical information, that venereal diseases, abortion, mental illness, and substance abuse are very sensitive topics, and transferring such information should only be done after discussing it with patients and attorneys, that a patient has the right to refuse all information release.

45)   Answer: A

A Case Manager can decrease the risk of allegations of breach of confidentiality by fully understanding the following: the implications of federal and state regulations on the disclosure of medical information, that venereal diseases, abortion, mental illness, and substance abuse are very sensitive topics, and transferring such information should only be done after discussing it with patients and attorneys, that a patient has the right to refuse all information release.

46)   Answer: D

47)   Answer: B

When obtaining consent, the provider is obligated to disclose the following: the desired outcome, all the reasonably foreseeable risks and hazards of treatment, all the reasonable options for care, including the option not to treat, with its foreseeable consequences.

48)   Answer: D

49)   Answer: C

While consulting with an attorney may be necessary in rare cases, it is unnecessary in every case.

50)   Answer: A

Competence is assumed in most patients. In rare cases when the patient's competence is questioned, an affidavit from a physician attesting to competence will do. A patient must be an adult (under applicable state law) in order to give consent.

51)   Answer: C

Agency is defined as the relationship between two or more persons by which one (the principal) consents that the other (the agent) shall act on his behalf. There are legal obligations for both the agent and the principal.

52)   Answer: B

Emancipated minors are considered adults under most states' law. Consent must be given freely, without coercion.

53)   Answer: C

The agent has the following legal obligations to the principal: using care and skill, acting in good faith, staying within the limits of the agent's authority, obeying the principal and carrying out all reasonable instructions, advancing the interests of the principal, and acting solely for the principal's benefit.

54)   Answer: A

The agent has the following legal obligations to the principal: using care and skill, acting in good faith, staying within the limits of the agent's authority, obeying the principal and carrying out all reasonable instructions, advancing the interests of the principal, and acting solely for the principal's benefit. The agent should not act solely for his own benefit, nor should he assume authority not assigned him under the contract.

55)   Answer: A

Apparent authority implies that a person or corporation has no direct assignment of authority or agency, such as occurs in a written or verbal contract. However, when the principal is held to have given "apparent authority" to the agent, he will be held responsible for his actions.

56)   Answer: B

Both the Case Manager and the ward nurse are employed by an entity that grants them authority to act in a certain capacity. They are both agents of the hospital and insurance company, respectively. The physician who works in the community and the Case Manager of the patient are independent agents who work for their own best interests.

57)   Answer: A

Both the UR departments and the phlebotomists are employed by an entity that grants them authority to act in a certain capacity. They are both, by definition, agents. The physician who works in the community and the network physician are independent agents, who work for their own best interests. A Case Manager must be wary of recommending specific network physicians to patients, as this may then be construed as a principal–agent relationship.

58)   Answer: A

The termination of a professional relationship (physician–patient, Case Manager–patient) without reasonable notice to the patient, and without an opportunity for the patient to acquire alternative care or services, thereby resulting in injury to the patient constitutes the legal definition of abandonment.

59)   Answer: B

The termination of a professional relationship (physician–patient, Case Manager–patient) without reasonable notice to the patient, and without an opportunity for the patient to acquire alternative care or services, thereby resulting in injury to the patient constitutes the legal definition of abandonment.

60) **Answer: D**

61) **Answer: E**

62) **Answer: C**

63) **Answer: B**

64) **Answer: A**

65) **Answer: E**

66) **Answer: D**

67) **Answer: C**

68) **Answer: B**

69) **Answer: A**

70) **Answer: E**

71) **Answer: D**

72) **Answer: C**

73) **Answer: B**

74) **Answer: A**

75) **Answer: C**

The False Claims Act is a Federal Act providing for civil and criminal penalties against individuals who knowingly present false claims to the government. The criminal False Claims Act makes it illegal to present a claim upon or against the United States which the claimant knows to be false, fictitious, or fraudulent. The civil False Claims Act says that any person who knowingly presents or causes to be presented, to the United States Government a false or fraudulent claim for payment approval; or knowingly makes, uses, or causes to be made or used a false record or statement to get a false or fraudulent claim paid or approved by the government by getting a false or fraudulent claim allowed or paid violates the Act. The penalties for violation include substantial fines and imprisonment. The Act does not exclude or exempt any party from prosecution or penalties.

76) **Answer: B**

The False Claims Act is a Federal Act providing for civil and criminal penalties against individuals who knowingly present false claims to the government. The criminal False Claims Act makes it illegal to present a claim upon or against the United States which the claimant knows to be false, fictitious, or fraudulent. The civil False Claims Act says that any person who knowingly presents or causes to be presented, to the United States Government a false or fraudulent claim for payment approval; or knowingly makes, uses, or causes to be made or used a false record or statement to get a false or fraudulent claim paid or approved by the government by getting a false or fraudulent claim allowed or paid violates the Act. The penalties for violation include substantial fines and imprisonment. The Act does not exclude or exempt any party from prosecution or penalties.

77) **Answer: E**

78) **Answer: D**

79) **Answer: C**

80) **Answer: B**

81) **Answer: A**

82) **Answer: A**

Malpractice is professional negligence that has two components. The first is negligence or a deviation from the approved and accepted standards of care, as defined within a given specialty. The second is injury or damage to the patient as a result of the stated negligence or deviation from the standard of care.

83) Answer: B

Malpractice is professional negligence that has two components. The first is negligence or a deviation from the approved and accepted standards of care, as defined within a given specialty. The second is injury or damage to the patient as a result of the stated negligence or deviation from the standard of care. It does not require a violation of civil or criminal law.

84) Answer: A

85) Answer: B

86) Answer: C

87) Answer: D

88) Answer: E

89) Answer: A

A doctrine of law with reference to cases where mere proof that an occurrence took place is sufficient under the circumstances to shift the burden of proof upon the defendant to prove that it was not due to his or her negligence. Implied in this doctrine is that the instrumentality causing injury was in the defendant's exclusive control, and that the accident was one that ordinarily does not happen in the absence of negligence. An example of *res ipsa loquitor* would be when a patient is found to have a surgical instrument left in his abdomen after an appendectomy (assuming there was only one surgeon involved, of course).

90) Answer: B

A doctrine of law with reference to cases where mere proof that an occurrence took place is sufficient under the circumstances to shift the burden of proof upon the defendant to prove that it was not due to his or her negligence. Implied in this doctrine is that the instrumentality causing injury was in the defendant's exclusive control, and that the accident was one that ordinarily does not happen in the absence of negligence. An example of *res ipsa loquitor* would be when a patient is found to have a surgical instrument left in his abdomen after an appendectomy (assuming there was only one surgeon involved, of course). *Respondeat superior* translates as "Let the master answer."

91) Answer: B

92) Answer: A

93) Answer: D

94) Answer: E

95) Answer: A

This maxim holds that a master is liable, in certain cases, for the wrongful acts of his servant (and a principal for those of his agent). A master/servant or principal/agent relationship exists where one person, for pay or other valuable consideration, enters into the service of another and devotes his or her personal labor for an agreed period (for example, employee–employer).

96) Answer: B

This maxim holds that a master is liable, in certain cases, for the wrongful acts of his servant (and a principal for those of his agent). A master/servant or principal/agent relationship exists where one person, for pay or other valuable consideration, enters into the service of another and devotes his or her personal labor for an agreed period (for example, employee–employer).

97) Answer: A

The word tort comes from the Latin *torquêre*, to twist, and implies injury. In law, a tort is a damage, injury, or a wrongful act done willfully, negligently, or in circumstances involving strict liability, a legal wrong committed upon the person or property independent of contract. It may be either a direct invasion of some legal right of the individual; or an infraction of some public duty by which special damage accrues to the individual; or the violation of some private obligation by which like damage accrues to the individual. Torts are not specific to medical malpractice cases.

98) Answer: B

The word tort comes from the Latin *torquêre*, to twist, and implies injury. In law, a tort is a damage, injury, or a wrongful act done willfully, negligently, or in circumstances involving strict liability; a legal wrong committed upon the person or property independent of contract. It may be either a direct invasion of some legal right of the individual; or an infraction of some public duty by which special damage accrues to the individual; or the violation of some private obligation by which like damage accrues to the individual. Torts are not specific to medical malpractice cases.

99) Answer: A

An expedited appeal may be requested if an urgent need exists for a particular service or treatment. An IME is an Independent Medical Exam and is most often used in Workers' Compensation or Disability cases.

100) Answer: C

Therefore, Case Managers should aggressively seek all data necessary to make an informed decision that is in the best interests of their patient.

101) Answer: C

According to the Code of Professional Ethics, it is the responsibility of the Case Manager to safeguard the patient's confidentiality unless there is a legal requirement to disclose the information.

Chapter 3

Physical and Psychological Aspects of Case Management

IDENTIFYING PATIENTS FOR CASE MANAGEMENT

Patients that will benefit the most from case management are identified through a series of proactive and often overlapping processes, including catastrophic diagnosis selection, high-risk diagnosis selection, sentinel procedures, high-cost case selection, passive case acquisition, and direct case referral.

Catastrophic Diagnosis Selection

A payer's software system can be pre-programmed to "flag" those diagnoses and procedures that historically result in high utilization of medical resources. These cases are often complex, require multiple care providers, and are very costly for the payer and patient alike. Individual insurers, managed care corporations, and Case Managers have unique lists of diagnosis and procedures. These lists are often based on community or corporate experience; however, all the lists will have diagnoses in common. Below is a short list of diagnoses and procedures that fit this category.

- AIDS
- adult respiratory distress syndrome
- renal failure
- hepatic failure
- head injuries
- spinal cord injuries
- cancer/leukemia
- multi-trauma cases
- neurological surgery
- back surgery
- solid organ transplants
- bone marrow transplants
- premature delivery
- respiratory distress syndrome of infancy

High-Risk Diagnosis Selection

While some diagnoses do not necessarily result in high medical utilization rates, they are placed on these lists because they are often the harbinger of high-cost cases. For example, while diagnoses such as pregnancy-induced diabetes or uncontrolled hypertension will not, in themselves, result in high utilization rates, that small minority of patients that have complications will be exorbitantly expensive. Some examples of high-risk diagnosis and procedures are:

- seizure disorder, new onset
- transient ischemic attack
- syncope
- malignant cardiac arrhythmia
- diabetes gravidarum
- pregnancy-induced hypertension
- premature labor

Sentinel Procedures

The term "sentinel procedures" refers to those procedures that are associated with catastrophic diseases. The procedures themselves do not imply grave diagnosis but are associated with them often enough that they merit investigation by the Case Manager for potential case management services. Some examples of these procedures are:

- exploratory laparotomy
- mediastinoscopy
- lung biopsy
- kidney biopsy
- bone marrow biopsy
- brain biopsy
- liver biopsy
- electrophysiologic testing
- thalidiotomy
- arteriovenous shunt placement
- lymph node biopsy

High-Cost Case Selection

Experienced Case Managers realize that admitting diagnoses can be misleading. An admitting diagnosis of diabetic ketoacidosis may be masking other, more complex diagnoses such as acute myocardial infarction, sepsis, and occult wound infection. Therefore, Case Managers benefit from reviewing those cases that rise above a predetermined dollar limit. The cost limit acts as a proxy for case complexity that would otherwise not be searchable by computer software. For example, a weekly report can be generated that lists all patients whose claims have exceeded $10,000 in the previous 6 months or year. Reviewing this list will reveal cases that had escaped the notice of Case Managers because of irregularities in diagnosis reporting or bill submission.

Passive Case Acquisition and Direct Case Referral

Established Case Managers can have cases directly referred to them. Knowledgeable physicians and other health care providers will refer patients that they believe will benefit from case management. These patients can have a newly identified catastrophic diagnosis or a more common diagnosis with unusual clinical or social complexity. This method of passive case acquisition has historically been responsible for only a minority of the Case Manager's caseload. The increased prevalence of managed care and the growth in case management has resulted in an increased appreciation for the Case Manager as a valuable member of the care team, and so has resulted in an increased number of referrals.

THE CASE MANAGER AS A PATIENT ADVOCATE

The Case Manager's foremost role is that of patient advocate. The selection and identification process results in the presentation of a group of critically or chronically ill patients. Frequently, because of their disease process or as a result of being overwhelmed by the magnitude of their situation, these patients and their families have no idea what their needs are. This is when a Case Manager is most needed. The Case Manager can assist the patient and family to attain autonomy and self-determination by empowering them. This can easily be done through education on the disease process (or injury), offering and explaining the available options to the patient, clarifying the available insurance benefits and community resources, and by listening to the patient verbalize views and perceived needs. The Case Manager can intercede on behalf of the patient with the physician and providers of services, can negotiate rates to minimize the patient's expenses, can assist the patient in finding specialists or special services required, and can help identify resources for those needs not covered by insurance.

The Case Manager also has a legal and ethical responsibility to protect patients from misinformation, omissions, and errors in comprehension. The Case Manager can fill in gaps in knowledge, clarify misunderstandings, and communicate with providers when the patient requires more information or further clarification regarding treatment plans and options. The Case Manager is in the unique position of being able to obtain information regarding the patient's end-of-life treatment decisions. The Case Manager can play a central role in helping patients and their families elucidate their views and feelings on these difficult subjects. Generally it is the Case Manager who assists the patient in documenting his or her wishes regarding withdrawal of care or end-of-life decisions. The Case Manager then has a major advocacy role in ensuring that the patient's wishes are documented and observed.

In order for the Case Manager to effectively advocate for patients, he or she must have adequate contact with the patient. She must spend the time required to understand the patient's concerns and to educate the patient and the patient's family regarding options. She must be able to convey the patient's and family's concerns to the appropriate providers, obtain answers or possible solutions and report back to the patient or family. The Case Manager must be fully aware of the patient's bill of rights and state laws and mandates pertaining to health care. The Case Manager is charged with the responsibility of explaining all of this to the patient and family, with advocating for the patient, with alleviating their worries, with providing emotional support, and with obtaining information or a source for the patient when she doesn't have the answer.

ASSESSING THE PATIENT'S LEVEL OF PHYSICAL / MENTAL IMPAIRMENT

The rehabilitation Case Manager seeks to promote optimal outcomes for his or her patients. He or she is responsible for implementing a quality care plan that is cost effective, realistic, and optimal for the patient. Although rehabilitation Case Managers are often found in institutions, such as acute care facilities, rehabilitation facilities, skilled nursing facilities, etc., they also may be agency based, insurance based, or independent Case Managers. In order to collaborate with the patient and family, the Case Manager must do an assessment, which identifies any temporary or permanent functional changes; physiological, psychological, or social problems; possible difficulties reintegrating back into the community; and the educational deficits of the patient and family.

There are several tools the Case Manager can utilize to assess patients with central nervous system injuries. One of these tools is the Ranchos Los Amigos Levels of Cognitive Functioning (Exhibit 3–1). In general, patients in levels I to III will require skilled nursing placement and are not appropriate for rehabilitation. If the patient progresses he or she can be reassessed for rehabilitation. Levels IV and up are recognized as usually appropriate for rehabilitation.

Another tool frequently utilized to assess comatose/recovering patients is the Glasgow Coma Scale (Exhibit 3–2). Most acute care facilities utilize this objective neurological measurement/assessment system. The assessments with this tool are done frequently. Repetitive scores of 3 indicate a poor prognosis. A score of 3 to 7 indicates coma and above 8 indicates rehabilitation potential.

Exhibit 3–1
RANCHOS LOS AMIGOS LEVELS OF COGNITIVE FUNCTIONING

I	NO RESPONSE	The patient is totally unresponsive to all stimuli.
II	GENERALIZED RESPONSE	The patient reacts inconsistently and nonpurposefully to environmental stimuli in a nonspecific manner. Responses are generally to deep pain and are likely to be delayed.
III	LOCALIZED RESPONSE	The patient reacts specifically but inconsistently to stimuli. He may respond to discomfort by pulling at tubes or responding to a familiar person by turning his head toward the person.
IV	CONFUSED/AGITATED	The patient is confused and excited. He can't process all that is said or done; his attention span is short. His speech may not make sense, he usually cannot cooperate in his treatment plan, and he tires easily.
V	CONFUSED/INAPPROPRIATE	The patient is alert and able to respond to simple commands. He responds best to familiar people. He requires structure, may wander, and his memory may be impaired.
VI	CONFUSED/APPROPRIATE	The patient demonstrates goal-directed behavior but still requires structure. He has an increased awareness of the environment and his own needs, has the ability to learn but requires frequent repetition.
VII	AUTOMATIC/APPROPRIATE	The patient can follow a daily routine automatically but can't deal with unexpected situations. He has a vague understanding of his condition but no real insight and is likely to be unrealistic about his future.
VIII	PURPOSEFUL/APPROPRIATE	The patient is alert and oriented but may not function as well as before the injury. Once a skill is learned he requires no supervision. He is able to function in society but may have occasional problems with unexpected or stressful situations.

Courtesy of Ranchos Los Amigos Medical Center, Downey, California.

Exhibit 3–2
GLASGOW COMA SCALE

Examiner's Test		Patient's Response	Assigned Score
Eye opening	Spontaneous	Opens eyes on own	4
	Speech	Opens eyes in response to a loud voice	3
	Pain	Opens eyes when pinched	2
	Pain	Does not open eyes	1
Best motor response	Commands	Follows simple commands	6
	Pain	Pulls examiner's hand away when pinched	5
	Pain	Pulls a part of body away when examiner pinches patient	4
	Pain	Flexes body inappropriately to pain (decorticate posturing)	3
	Pain	Body becomes rigid in an extended position when examiner pinches patient (decerebrate posturing)	2
	Pain	No motor response to pain	1
Verbal Response	Speech	Carries on a conversation correctly, is oriented to time, place, person	5
	Speech	Seems confused and disoriented	4
	Speech	Speech is clear but makes no sense	3
	Speech	Makes sounds the examiner can't understand	2
	Speech	No speech or noise	1

Source: Reprinted from M. St. Couer, *Case Management Practice Guidelines,* pp. 2–14, © 1996, Mosby.

Case Managers can plan more effectively when they know what deficits to expect. Stroke or brain trauma patients may have the following functional disabilities based on where the injury is located. See Exhibit 3–3.

Patients with spinal cord injuries/lesions will require vastly different treatment plans and equipment depending on the level of the injury. Exhibit 3–4 is a brief guide used to gauge functional ability in patients with spinal cord injuries.

PSYCHOLOGICAL ASPECTS OF CATASTROPHIC ILLNESS AND CHRONIC DISEASE

Case Managers know from firsthand experience what a "change agent" illness can be, not just in the physical sense but psychologically also. The illness need not be as "catastrophic" as a closed head injury, a cervical spine injury or cancer to cause serious changes in a person's life. A carpenter who loses the use of his hand, a dancer who suffers from vertigo, or a professional athlete who injures his knee are examples of patients whose injuries, while not considered catastrophic by most, have serious effects beyond the physical realm and into the social and psychological spheres. These patients have not just suffered a serious and painful injury, but have lost careers, hopes, dreams, social status, and income. As a further example, the father of three, who because of illness is no longer the breadwinner for the family, experiences more than the pain and disability of his illness; he also suffers the loss of self-respect, social status, and independence.

Case Managers who hope to intervene successfully in these situations must assess the effects of the illness or injury beyond the patient's physical self. The assessment must explore what limitations, disabilities, and effects on sense of self, relationships, employment, inter-

Exhibit 3–3
IMPAIRED FUNCTIONAL ABILITIES OF STROKE OR BRAIN TRAUMA PATIENTS

Left hemisphere	Right hemisphere
Speech	Spatial orientation
Language	Picture/pattern sense
Complex motor functions	Performance-like functions
Vigilance	Spatial integration
Paired associate learning	Creative associative thinking
Verbal abilities	Calculation
Linguistic description	Simple language comprehension
Verbal ideation	Nonverbal identification
Conceptual similarities	Facial identification
Time analysis	Recognition of environmental sounds
Detail analysis	Nonverbal paired associate learning
Arithmetic	Tactile perception
Writing	
Calculation	
Finger naming	
Right-left orientation	

Exhibit 3–4
GUIDE TO FUNCTIONAL ABILITIES IN PATIENTS WITH SPINAL CORD INJURIES

Vertebral Level	Functional Ability
C 1–3	Ventilator dependent
	No neck control, no movement in upper or lower extremities
	Cardiac pacer
C 4	May need ventilator support (C4 –phrenic nerve)
	Shoulder shrug/neck control
C 5	Involvement of both hands
	Weakness of triceps
	Severe weakness in trunk and lower extremities
C 6	Involvement of upper extremities and hands
	Normal or good triceps
	Generalized weakness of the trunk and lower extremities impairing balance and ambulation
C 7	Involvement of upper extremities
	Normal or good finger flexion and extension
	Grasp and release
	No intrinsic hand function
	Generalized weakness of trunk and lower extremities
	Poor balance
T 1–5	Total abdominal paralysis or poor muscle strength
	No useful trunk sitting
T 6–10	Upper abdominal and spinal extension musculature sufficient to provide some element of trunk sitting
T 11–L 2	No quadriceps or very weak
L 2 –S 5	Moderate to good quadriceps; ambulation with some support. (S 2 – S 5 loss of bowel & bladder control.)

ests, hopes, and aspirations this illness brings. As a result of these life changes precipitated by major illness and injury, patients commonly experience the following:

- Loss
- Anger
- Fear/anxiety
- Depression
- Dependency

If anticipated by the Case Manager, and noted early, these reactions can be treated with education, support, counseling, and, in some cases, medication. During the intake interview, the Case Manager can ask some questions that may help determine the patient's response to his current situation. Some examples are:

- Have you ever (personally) suffered with a serious injury or illness in the past?
- Have you ever had a serious illness in your family?
- How did you deal with these situations?
- Do you know anyone with this type of illness?
- How did they deal with it?
- What do you know about your current disease?
- What do you know about its treatments?
- What do you know about its prognosis?
- What do you know about possible limitations, disabilities, or handicaps that are sometimes associated with it?
- How do you feel about these?
- What do you think will happen to you? Will you be limited, handicapped, or disabled?
- What are your plans for dealing with them?

Effects of Patient's Illness and Injury on Family and Caregivers

A holistic approach to the care of a patient dictates that the Case Manager examine the environment that the patient is in and how this environment can be used to support and heal the patient during his or her illness. Catastrophic illness and injuries have "ripple effects" that extend outward from the patient and exert their profound effects on the environment. The environment in turn has effects on the patient. Those closest and more dependent on the patient are likely to suffer the greatest amount of turmoil. For example, let us examine the hypothetical case of Mr. Green.

Hypothetical Case

Mr. Green is a 32-year-old owner of his own business. He is a husband and father of four children. While vacationing with his family at a ski resort, he collides with a tree and sustains a fracture of his cervical spine. After several days, his spinal cord injury stabilizes, and he is diagnosed with quadriplegia. The neurosurgeons and rehabilitation specialists report that after a long period of rehabilitation, he may be able to return home, and perhaps even work. During his inpatient stay at the rehabilitation hospital the following questions may be asked.

Questions asked by his wife
- What will we do for income?
- Who will pay the bills?

- Will I have to go to work?
- What can I do that will earn an income?
- Will I ever be able to match my husband's income?
- Do we have enough insurance?
- What does his disability policy allow?
- If I go to work, who will watch the children?
- Will the children have to come out of private schools?
- What about contributions to their college fund?
- If I go to work, who will do the shopping, cleaning, and household chores?
- Can we still afford the house mortgage and taxes?
- Will we have to move?
- Can we afford the payments on the cars?
- Will we have to sell the cars?
- What will I do for transportation?
- Will we have to purchase a specialized van?
- With all the attention on my husband, will the children feel neglected?

Questions asked by his children
- Will Daddy die?
- Will Mommy remarry?
- Will he ever come home?
- Will he have to stay in the wheelchair?
- If I hug him, will it hurt him?
- Will he ever be happy again?
- Will he ever be able to play with me?
- Will we have to move from our home?
- Will we have to leave school?
- Who will rake the leaves and take out the garbage?
- Who will play with the little kids in the family?
- What if something happens to Mommy?
- Could Mommy get sick and die?
- What will happen to us?

Questions asked by business partners
- Will he ever return to work?
- What will we do without his expertise?
- Can the business survive?
- What happens if we replace him, and he wants to come back to work?
- What if he wants to sell his share of the business? Can we afford to buy him out?
- Can we afford to pay him while he rehabilitates? Do we have to?
- What will happen to our clients who depend on Mr. Green's critical skills for their business to go forward?
- What will happen to our suppliers who depend on Mr. Green for their businesses to go forward?

Questions asked by Mr. Green's parents
- What can we do to help our son and his family?
- Can we afford to pay their expenses?
- Do we have enough room for them to live with us?
- Can we live comfortably with his wife and children?

- What if our son dies?
- What about our retirement and our "golden years"?
- Is there any end in sight to these responsibilities?
- Will our helping out our son's family jeopardize or deplete our retirement savings?
- What happens to us when our money's gone? What will happen to our son's family?
- Who will help us? (We were hoping that our son could help us out in our retirement.)
- Who will help out our daughter? (We were hoping that our son could care for his handicapped, dependent sister who lives with us, when we were gone.)

These types of questions can go on and on. The number of people affected by a catastrophic illness is surprisingly large. The family (or caretakers) may also suffer from the symptoms of loss, anger, anxiety, fear, depression, and dependency. The well-tempered Case Manager should be aware of the impact of catastrophic illness on the family and friends of the patient. These are the same people that may be asked to lend the patient financial, social, and psychological support in the future.

Adaptable and Maladaptive Families

Some families are remarkably adaptable to these crisis situations. In a crisis situation such as during a catastrophic illness in a family member, successful families are flexible in their roles within the family, they maintain the ability to solve problems, they communicate with each other and outsiders effectively, they accept help, and they maintain their relationship with the community. This type of family is able to meet the new needs of a sick member without a loss of balance and functioning.

Maladaptive families, on the other hand, are unable to achieve a balance between meeting a patient's needs and maintaining their own functioning. These families may overindulge the patient and foster his dependency. Other family members may be ignored or mistreated in an effort to meet the needs of the sick member. Conversely, maladaptive families may abandon or ignore the patient. They may deny the existence of illness or disability to the detriment of the patient. These maladaptive patterns stem from a family's inability to communicate effectively with each other, with care providers, or with support networks; to seek and accept help; to maintain flexibility in role relationships; and to retain relationships with community.

The following are some questions that can help the Case Manager determine how the family will deal with the catastrophically ill patient.

- Are there other sick family members at home?
- Have there been any in the past?
- How does the family treat these sick family members?
- How did the family function during this illness?
- How have other family crises (financial, social, political) been dealt with in the past?
- Who is available for care giving?
- What are that person's responsibilities now?
- What social or community resources can be brought to bear?
- What financial resources can be brought to bear?
- Is there a leader in the family? (Matriarch, patriarch?)
- Are there any health care professionals in the family?
- What is the level of understanding about the disease or injury?
- What is the level of understanding about the course of treatment?
- What is the level of understanding about the prognosis?
- What is the level of understanding about possible limitations, disabilities, or handicaps that the patient may be left with?

1) _____ refers to the Case Manager having a duty to promote good and to be the patient's advocate.

   A. Nonmaleficence
   B. Beneficence
   C. Advocacy
   D. None of the above

2) A Case Manager is frustrated by her inability to get her patient to agree to occupational therapy. The patient was involved in a high speed motor vehicle accident and suffered severe head injuries. When encouraged to attend therapy sessions the patient refuses, becomes verbally abusive and hangs up. Likely reason(s) for this patient's reaction is (are):

   A. Head injuries can result in emotional lability.
   B. Head injuries can result in cognitive impairments.
   C. Head injuries can result in prolonged head pain and mood depression.
   D. All of the above
   E. None of the above

3) Diagnosis, high costs, multiple admissions or treatments are red flags for:

   A. Pre-existing HMO exclusions
   B. Utilization management review
   C. Case management evaluation
   D. Disability hearings

4) Which of the following diagnoses should trigger an inquiry for potential Case Management services?

   1. Blepharitis
   2. Spinal cord injury
   3. Coryza
   4. Non–Hodgkin's lymphoma
      A. 1, 3
      B. 2, 4
      C. 1, 2, 3
      D. All of the above
      E. None of the above

5) **Of the following diagnoses, which should trigger an inquiry for potential Case Management services?**

1. Blepharitis
2. Varucus vulgaris
3. Coryza
4. Pedis planus
   A. 1, 3
   B. 2, 4
   C. 1, 2, 3
   D. All of the above
   E. None of the above

6) **Of the following, which are "sentinel procedures" that should prompt inquiries for Case Management services?**

1. Brain biopsy
2. Bone marrow biopsy
3. Endocardiac biopsy
4. Skin biopsy
   A. 1, 3
   B. 2, 4
   C. 1, 2, 3
   D. All of the above
   E. None of the above

7) **Of the following, which utilization figure for an individual's medical claims would make an appropriate financial threshold for Case Management evaluation?**

A. Claims exceeding $500 per year
B. Claims exceeding $1,000 per year
C. Claims exceeding $10,000 per year
D. Claims exceeding $100,000 per year
E. Claims exceeding $1,000,000 per year

8) **_____ is the body's response to physical and psychological stress.**

1. Mutate
2. Disease
3. Eliminate toxins
4. Adapt/cope
   A. 1, 3
   B. 2, 4
   C. All of the above
   D. None of the above

9) **The definition of disease can include:**

1. A disturbance of the homeostatic balance
2. Imbalance in the internal environment of the body
3. An attempt to restore balance in the body
4. Mental illness
   A. 1, 2, 3
   B. 2, 3, 4
   C. All of the above
   D. None of the above

10) **A Case Manager is told by a paraplegic "I feel like half a person." The Case Manager's response should be to:**

   A. Distract the patient from self-pity.
   B. Help the patient explore personal feelings.
   C. Ignore the comment.
   D. Actively discourage negative comments.

11) **After a patient sustains a mild head injury, he or she continues to experience dizziness, headache and inability to concentrate. These symptoms most likely are due to:**

   A. An aneurysm
   B. A subdural hematoma
   C. An arachnoid hemorrhage
   D. Post concussion syndrome

12) **Which of the following is needed in order for the Case Manager to ensure an accurate assessment of the impact an injury will have on a patient and his ability to return to work?**

   A. The physical requirements of the patient's position
   B. The coworkers' or employer's opinion of the patient's ability
   C. A history of childhood diseases
   D. All of the above
   E. None of the above

13) **When interviewing a patient, the Case Manager is aware that the patient is being overtly and verbally hostile. The most appropriate response by the Case Manager is:**

   A. Verbal defense by the Case Manager
   B. Complete withdrawal from the patient
   C. Acceptance of the patient's behavior in silence
   D. A, B
   E. All of the above

14) **A Case Manager expects a vocational evaluation to be warranted for:**

   1. A brain injured worker unable to perform his own ADL
   2. A paraplegic with only manual labor work experience
   3. A back strain patient who is expected to return to work in 1 month
   4. An amputee who is expected to return to his regular job in 3 months
       A. 1, 2
       B. 2, 3, 4
       C. 2
       D. All of the above
       E. None of the above

15) **The Case Manager has a patient who continues to focus on his functional loss. Which of the following would be the best response by the Case Manager?**

   1. "You should be making faster progress than this in PT."
   2. "Your last physical therapy report states you have increased your strength and flexibility."
   3. "Other patients with this injury returned to work 2 weeks ago."
       A. 1, 2
       B. 2, 3
       C. 2
       D. All of the above
       E. None of the above

16) **The Case Manager knows that adaptive equipment along with instruction and training in its use results in:**

A. Enhanced self-esteem
B. Independence
C. Decreased reliance on home health aides and others to perform ADLs
D. All of the above
E. None of the above

17) **Which of the following statements are true regarding the clinical consequences of head injuries?**

1. Patients may become depressed.
2. A patient's cognitive ability may be impaired.
3. Emotional lability is common.
4. Chronic headaches may be result.
    A. 1, 3
    B. 1, 2, 4
    C. 1, 2, 3
    D. All of the above
    E. None of the above

18) **Which of the following statements are true regarding the clinical consequences of head injuries?**

1. Patients may become depressed.
2. A patient's cognitive ability may improve as a result.
3. Chronic headaches may be result.
4. Emotional lability is common.
    A. 1, 3
    B. 2, 4
    C. 1, 2, 3
    D. All of the above
    E. None of the above

19) **Which of the following statements are *not* true regarding the clinical consequences of head injuries?**

1. Patients may become depressed.
2. A patient's cognitive ability may improve as a result.
3. Chronic headaches may be result.
4. Emotional lability is common.
    A. 1, 3
    B. 2, 4
    C. 1, 2, 3
    D. All of the above
    E. None of the above

20) **When the Case Manager is planning for timely rehabilitation, she must do which of the following in order to provide for the coordination of the medical care the patient requires?**

A. Arrange for an objective second opinion.
B. Request the diagnostic films for the Medical Director to read.
C. Do an onsite evaluation.
D. Develop and clarify the medical care plan of the attending physician.

21) **A patient has just had a full diagnostic workup of his condition. The need for surgery has been ruled out and the condition has been diagnosed as chronic. Which of the following is true of the patient's follow-up needs?**

   A. The patient should be followed every 2 months by the surgeon, in case his condition changes and he requires surgery.
   B. Several other opinions should be sought to confirm the first diagnosis.
   C. Follow up with the patient's primary care physician is indicated to obtain any needed treatment, monitoring or medications required for the chronic condition.
   D. All of the above
   E. None of the above

22) **Patients with chronic back pain require:**

   A. Supportive conservative treatment
   B. Whatever the patient and his various treating physicians determine is helpful
   C. Chiropractic care three times per week for life
   D. Continual testing to monitor the condition

23) **Of the following methodologies, which are common means that insurers and Case Managers use for identifying potential patients for Case Management services?**

   1. Selecting cases with catastrophic diagnoses, such as head or spine injury
   2. Selecting cases with "sentinel procedures," such as bone marrow biopsy or brain biopsy
   3. Selecting cases with claims costs over $10,000 a year
   4. Selecting cases at random, and investigating for potential problems
       A. 1, 3
       B. 2, 4
       C. 1, 2, 3
       D. All of the above
       E. None of the above

24) **A patient with chronic back pain needs hospital admission:**

   A. For immediate surgery
   B. For IV pain administration
   C. Only in an emergency situation
   D. Every 6 weeks for evaluation

25) **Patients with musculoskeletal disorders frequently require physical therapy as part of the Case Management care plan. The goals of physical therapy are:**

   1. To develop strength and endurance above and beyond the patient's condition prior to getting ill or injured.
   2. To learn massage techniques and other passive modalities
   3. To progress to work hardening
   4. To improve range of motion and strength, to reduce pain, and to teach a home exercise program to the patient
       A. 1, 2, 3
       B. 4
       C. All of the above
       D. None of the above

26) **Which treatment would be the most appropriate for reflex sympathetic dystrophy?**

    A. Physical therapy and anti-inflammatory medications

    B. Anti-inflammatory medications only

    C. Physical therapy and anesthetic or nerve blocks of sympathetic nerve function

    D. Physical therapy: heat or cold therapy

    E. All of the above

27) **The following are all part of treatment for a rotator cuff tendinitis:**

    1. Exercises that bring objects toward the body

    2. Exercises that push objects away from the body

    3. Surgical correction for severe injuries

    4. Rest of the injured tendons

        A. All except 1

        B. All except 2

        C. All of the above

        D. None of the above

28) **The Case Manager has a patient with a recent amputation. The patient expresses concern that his wife will no longer find him attractive. The Case Manager should realize that:**

    A. The patient is in a grieving stage.

    B. The patient is experiencing self-pity, which will pass.

    C. Many patients have a distorted body image when they have an amputation.

    D. All of the above

    E. None of the above

29) **The Case Manager is following a CVA patient at home. In speaking with his family they inform the Case Manager he can no longer feed himself and is having difficulty swallowing. What should the Case Manager do?**

    A. Call the physical therapist on the case.

    B. Call the physician on the case.

    C. Arrange for a swallowing consult by a speech therapist.

    D. Arrange for an assistive device.

30) **The Case Manager is following a patient with a complaint and diagnosis of back pain. The patient has not been at work for more than 2 weeks, has no documented pathology and has no specific treatment plan other than "rest." What should the Case Manager recommend at this point?**

    1. A functional capacity study

    2. A nerve conduction test

    3. An MRI of the area

    4. A second opinion

    5. An independent medical exam

        A. 1, 2

        B. 2, 3

        C. 3, 4

        D. 4, 5

        E. All of the above

31) **A Case Manager can expect an amputee with a new prosthesis to experience which of the following?**

    A. Balance and gait difficulties

    B. Functional issues

    C. Body image acceptance

    D. All of the above

    E. None of the above

32) **The Case Manager receives a referral for a patient with a spinal cord injury at C1–C4. When would the Case Manager expect the patient to be ready for discharge home?**

   A.   When the patient can direct her own care
   B.   When the patient is independent in self-care
   C.   When the patient reaches functional independence at the wheelchair level
   D.   All of the above
   E.   None of the above

33) **A patient has an arthrogram scheduled. The Case Manager knows the following is true of this procedure:**

   A.   An arthrogram aids in the diagnosis of spinal stenosis.
   B.   Crepitus is a potential complication of this procedure.
   C.   An arthrogram aids in diagnosis of injured bursa or cartilage.
   D.   Radiopaque solutions are injected with this procedure.

34) **The Case Manager is working on discharging a brain-injured patient to the home setting with family care. When reviewing his readiness for discharge, in relation to his adaptive equipment, which of the following is/are the most important issue(s)?**

   A.   The length of time the patient requires the equipment
   B.   Whether or not the family has been trained in its use
   C.   Whether or not there are structural barriers to utilizing the equipment in the home
   D.   All of the above
   E.   None of the above

35) **Which of the following statements are *not* true about home infusion therapy?**

   A.   Infusion therapy can be safely administered in the home setting most of the time.
   B.   It is always more cost effective to arrange for infusion therapy to be given at home rather than the hospital.
   C.   Home care patients must be stable to be set up for home infusion therapy.
   D.   The primary caregiver must be capable of managing the infusion therapy at home.

36) **A patient has had successful surgery for his condition, yet he remains anxious and uncertain. The Case Manager should:**

   A.   Explore the patient's concerns and feelings with him.
   B.   Reassure the patient that everything will be fine.
   C.   Provide recommendations regarding rest and relaxation.
   D.   A, B
   E.   None of the above

37) **The Case Manager has been following an amputee in an inpatient rehabilitation program. He has been instructed in using his prosthesis, caring for it and his limb. He is now ready for discharge. What need is most often overlooked when discharging this type of patient?**

   A.   A follow-up appointment with the prosthetist
   B.   A follow-up appointment with his surgeon
   C.   His ability to drive a car
   D.   His ability to problem solve for himself

38) **The Case Manager with a patient who is paraplegic because of a spinal cord injury recognizes that a major early problem will be:**

   A.   Use of ambulation aids
   B.   Patient education
   C.   Bladder control
   D.   All of the above
   E.   None of the above

39) _____ are a variety of implements or equipment utilized to aid individuals in performing tasks or movements.

    A. Prosthetics
    B. Orthotics
    C. Durable medical equipment
    D. Assistive devices

40) A variety of cognitive techniques may be utilized for pain control. The following are examples of some of these techniques.

    1. Distraction
    2. Pain medication
    3. Relaxation training
    4. Biofeedback
        A. 3, 4
        B. 1, 2, 3
        C. 1, 3, 4
        D. All of the above
        E. None of the above

41) _____ is the loss of the ability to express oneself and understand language.

    A. Dysphasia
    B. Aphasia
    C. Apraxia
    D. Amnesia

42) _____ is the impairment of speech resulting from a brain lesion.

    A. Dysphasia
    B. Aphasia
    C. Apraxia
    D. Amnesia

43) _____ is the inability to understand the meaning of things.

    A. Dysphasia
    B. Aphasia
    C. Apraxia
    D. Amnesia

44) _____ is the inability or difficulty in swallowing.

    A. Dysphasia
    B. Aphasia
    C. Apraxia
    D. Dysphagia

45) _____ is the paralysis of the lower half of the body and both legs.

    A. Hemiplegia
    B. Paraplegia
    C. Quadriplegia
    D. Hemiparesis

46) _____ is the paralysis of all four limbs.

    A. Hemiplegia
    B. Paraplegia
    C. Quadriplegia
    D. Quadraparesis

47) _____ is the paralysis of one side of the body.

    A. Hemiplegia
    B. Paraplegia
    C. Quadriplegia
    D. Quadrapara

48) **The Case Manager can expect which of the following after ACL reconstruction surgery?**

    A. Jogging by the twelfth postoperative week
    B. Full weight bearing and range of motion by the fourth postoperative week
    C. Bent knee raises and isometric exercises on the affected leg for the first postoperative week while immobilized in a hinged-type brace
    D. All of the above

49) **Case Managers know that motivating a patient with a knowledge deficit can be problematic. As the Case Manager evaluating the duration and progress of occupational services, what questions would you ask if informed that the patient was making little progress and was noncompliant with his instruction?**

    1. Has anyone explored the reasons for his resistance?
    2. Has anyone discussed his lack of progress and cooperation with his family?
    3. What time of day is he receiving teaching?
    4. Is there a time of day when he is more cooperative and compliant?
        A. 1, 2, 3
        B. 2, 3, 4
        C. All of the above
        D. None of the above

50) **A Case Manager is frustrated by her inability to get her patient to agree to occupational therapy. The patient was involved in a high-speed motor vehicle accident and suffered severe head injuries. When encouraged to attend therapy sessions, the patient refuses, becomes verbally abusive and hangs up. Likely reason(s) for this patient's reaction is (are):**

    A. Head injuries can result in emotional lability.
    B. Head injuries can result in cognitive impairments.
    C. Head injuries can result in prolonged head pain and a depressed mood.
    D. All of the above
    E. None of the above

51) **Which of the following statements are true regarding the psychological aspects of chronic disease and disability?**

    1. Only catastrophic illnesses like cancer and spinal cord injuries have psychological ramifications
    2. Even injuries that are usually considered minor can have severe social and psychological ramifications
    3. Psychological reactions such as euphoria and mania are common in catastrophic illnesses
    4. Psychological reactions such as depression and dependency are common in catastrophic illnesses
        A. 1, 3
        B. 2, 4
        C. 1, 2, 3
        D. All of the above
        E. None of the above

52) **Which of the following statements are *not* true regarding the psychological aspects of chronic disease and disability?**

1. Only catastrophic illnesses like closed head injuries or lymphoma have psychological ramifications
2. Even injuries that are usually considered minor can have severe social and psychological ramifications
3. Psychological reactions such as euphoria and complacency are common in catastrophic illnesses
4. Psychological reactions such as depression and dependency are common in catastrophic illnesses
    A. 1, 3
    B. 2, 4
    C. 1, 2, 3
    D. All of the above
    E. None of the above

53) **Which of the following statements are true regarding the psychological aspects of catastrophic illness or injury?**

1. Certain illnesses have the same or similar effects on all patients.
2. Minor illnesses may cause catastrophic physiological reactions in some patients.
3. Major illnesses and grave prognoses will cause depression in all patients.
4. A patient's reactions to illness may extend beyond the illnesses' pain and disability, and can affect the patient's self-respect and social status.
    A. 1, 3
    B. 2, 4
    C. 1, 2, 3
    D. All of the above
    E. None of the above

54) **Which of the following statements are *not* true regarding the psychological aspects of catastrophic illness or injury?**

1. Certain illnesses have the same or similar effects on all patients.
2. Minor illnesses may cause catastrophic physiological reactions in some patients.
3. Major illnesses and grave prognoses will cause depression in all patients.
4. A patient's reactions to illness may extend beyond the illnesses' pain and disability, and can affect the patient's self-respect and social status.
    A. 1, 3
    B. 2, 4
    C. 1, 2, 3
    D. All of the above
    E. None of the above

55) **Which of the following reactions do patients with major illness or injury commonly experience?**

1. Loss
2. Anger
3. Fear and anxiety
4. Depression
    A. 1, 3
    B. 2, 4
    C. 1, 2, 3
    D. All of the above
    E. None of the above

56) **Which of the following reactions do patients with major illness or injury commonly experience?**

1. Loss
2. Euphoria
3. Fear and anxiety
4. Contentment
    A. 1, 3
    B. 2, 4
    C. 1, 2, 3
    D. All of the above
    E. None of the above

57) **Which of the following reactions do patients with major illness or injury *not* experience?**

1. Loss
2. Happiness
3. Fear and anxiety
4. Peace
    A. 1, 3
    B. 2, 4
    C. 1, 2, 3
    D. All of the above
    E. None of the above

58) **Which of the following statements are true regarding Case Managers dealing with patients with catastrophic illnesses and injury?**

1. Anxiety may be treated with education and counseling.
2. Severe depression may respond to appropriate antidepressant medication and should be recommended.
3. Diagnosing depression may require skillful interviewing.
4. Case Managers should avoid dealing with the psychological aspects of major illnesses.
    A. 1, 3
    B. 2, 4
    C. 1, 2, 3
    D. All of the above
    E. None of the above

59) **Which of the following statements are true regarding Case Managers dealing with patients with catastrophic illnesses and injury?**

1. Anxiety may be treated with education and counseling.
2. Severe depression will never respond to antidepressant medication.
3. Diagnosing depression may require skillful interviewing.
4. Case Managers should avoid dealing with the psychological aspects of major illnesses.
    A. 1, 3
    B. 2, 4
    C. 1, 2, 3
    D. All of the above
    E. None of the above

60) **Which of the following statements are *not* true regarding Case Managers dealing with patients with catastrophic illnesses and injury?**

1. Anxiety may be treated with education and counseling.
2. Severe depression responds only to electroconvulsive therapy and it should be recommended.
3. Diagnosing depression may require skillful interviewing.
4. Case Managers should avoid dealing with the psychological aspects of major illnesses.

A. 1, 3
B. 2, 4
C. 1, 2, 3
D. All of the above
E. None of the above

61) **Which of the following statements are true regarding patients with catastrophic injuries and illnesses?**

1. The negative effects are felt only by the patient.
2. The spouse is never affected by the other spouse's injury.
3. The Case Manager should restrict her inquiries to the patient's reactions, mood and coping abilities.
4. A history of adequately coping with major illness is a negative predictor for a patient's future coping ability.
    A. 1, 3
    B. 2, 4
    C. 1, 2, 3
    D. All of the above
    E. None of the above

62) **Which of the following statements are true regarding patients with catastrophic injuries and illnesses?**

1. The negative effects are felt by the patient, his family, friends, and coworkers among others.
2. The spouse is never affected by the other spouse's injury.
3. The Case Manager should expand her inquiries beyond the patient's reactions, mood and coping abilities to those of the family, friends and caretakers.
4. A history of adequately coping with major illness is a negative predictor for a patient's future coping ability.
    A. 1, 3
    B. 2, 4
    C. 1, 2, 3
    D. All of the above
    E. None of the above

63) **Which of the following statements are *not* true regarding patients with catastrophic injuries and illnesses?**

1. The negative effects are felt by the patient, his family, friends, and coworkers among others.
2. The spouse is never affected by the other spouse's injury.
3. The Case Manager should expand her inquiries beyond the patient's reactions, mood and coping abilities to those of the family, friends and caretakers.
4. A history of adequately coping with major illness is a negative predictor for a patient's future coping ability.
    A. 1, 3
    B. 2, 4
    C. 1, 2, 3
    D. All of the above
    E. None of the above

64) **Which of the following characteristics are commonly associated with "maladaptive families"?**

1. An inability to communicate with each other, health care providers and support networks
2. An inability to seek and accept help
3. An inability to maintain flexibility in role relationships
4. An inability to retain relationships with the community

A. 1, 3
B. 2, 4
C. 1, 2, 3
D. All of the above
F. None of the above

65) Which of the following characteristics are commonly associated with "maladaptive families"?

1. An inability to communicate with each other, health care providers and support networks
2. Fostering dependency in the patient through overindulgence
3. An inability to maintain flexibility in role relationships
4. Ignoring or mistreating other family members to accommodate the sick family member
    A. 1, 3
    B. 2, 4
    C. 1, 2, 3
    D. All of the above
    E. None of the above

66) Which of the following characteristics are commonly associated with "maladaptive families"?

1. An inability to communicate with each other, health care providers and support networks
2. Abandoning the patient
3. An inability to maintain flexibility in role relationships
4. Denying the existence of the family member's illness or disability
    A. 1, 3
    B. 2, 4
    C. 1, 2, 3
    D. All of the above
    E. None of the above

67) Which of the following characteristics are common to the "adaptable" family?

1. Flexibility in their roles within the family
2. Maintains its ability to solve problems within the family
3. The family communicates with each other and outsiders
4. The family seeks and accepts help willingly
    A. 1, 3
    B. 2, 4
    C. 1, 2, 3
    D. All of the above
    E. None of the above

68) Which of the following characteristics are common to the "adaptable" family?

1. Inflexibility in their roles within the family
2. Maintains its ability to solve problems within the family
3. The family communicates poorly with each other and outsiders
4. The family seeks and accepts help willingly
    A. 1, 3
    B. 2, 4
    C. 1, 2, 3
    D. All of the above
    E. None of the above

69) **Which of the following are *not* characteristics common to the "adaptable" family?**

1. Inflexibility in their roles within the family
2. Maintains its ability to solve problems within the family
3. The family communicates poorly with each other and outsiders effectively
4. The family seeks and accepts help willingly
   A. 1, 3
   B. 2, 4
   C. 1, 2, 3
   D. All of the above
   E. None of the above

70) **A patient with damage to the spinal cord at C6–C7 is referred for Case Management. Prior to contacting the patient the Case Manager can expect that the patient will experience which of the following symptoms?**

1. Respiratory paralysis
2. Quadriplegia
3. Paralysis of the legs, wrists, and hands, but retaining motion in the elbows and shoulders
4. Aphasia
   A. 1, 4
   B. 2, 3
   C. 3
   D. All of the above
   E. None of the above

1) **Answer: B**

2) **Answer: D**

3) **Answer: C**

   These are the three criteria for Case Management referrals.

4) **Answer: B**

   Both spinal cord injuries and lymphomas are complex, high-cost and life-threatening illnesses that may potentially benefit from Case Management. Coryza is a common cold, and blepharitis is a minor infection of the eyelid.

5) **Answer: E**

   Coryza is a common cold, and blepharitis is a minor infection of the eyelid. Pedis planus are flat feet, and varrucus vulgaris are common warts. None of these conditions requires the services of a Case Manager.

6) **Answer: C**

   While biopsies of the endocardium, the brain and bone marrow involve high risk and are done infrequently, biopsies of the skin are low risk, are commonly performed and require Case Management services in a small minority of cases.

7) **Answer: C**

   Screening all patients with claims over $500 and $1,000 per year would yield too many claims and too few catastrophic illnesses. Those patients with claims of $100,000 and over would no doubt be well known to the insurers and Case Managers long before the patients hit those thresholds. Thresholds of $5,000 to $10,000 are most commonly seen in the industry.

8) **Answer: B**

   The body's attempt to adapt or cope with physical or psychological stress can result in disease if the adaptation is unsuccessful.

9) **Answer: C**

10) **Answer: B**

   The Case Manager should permit and encourage the patient to explore his or her feelings without judgment, punishment or rejection.

11) **Answer: D**

12) **Answer: A**

   In order to make an accurate determination regarding a patient's ability to return to work, the Case Manager and the team involved in the care of the patient must know the physical requirements of the patient's job.

13) **Answer: C**

Acceptance of the behavior in silence is an effective interpersonal skill demonstrating a nonjudgmental attitude. As the patient may be exhibiting a defensive behavior this is the most appropriate way to begin a nonthreatening relationship with the patient.

14) **Answer: C**

15) **Answer: C**

The Case Manager should be motivating the patient by focusing on his progress, not lack of progress.

16) **Answer: D**

17) **Answer: B**

18) **Answer: A**

19) **Answer: B**

20) **Answer: D**

Second opinions and onsite evaluations are not required in every case. They may be necessary occasionally on a difficult case or a case in dispute. There is no medical necessity for the Medical Director to read the diagnostic films upon setting up a rehabilitation plan.

21) **Answer: C**

Chronic conditions not requiring surgery can be handled by the primary care physician (PCP). The PCP can then make referrals when the patient's condition changes or he deems referrals medically necessary.

22) **Answer: A**

Supportive conservative care is the standard of care for chronic back pain.

23) **Answer: C**

Common methodologies include screening claims with catastrophic diagnoses, sentinel procedures, high claims cost, and through direct case referral from community physicians.

24) **Answer: C**

A patient with chronic back pain generally only requires hospitalization during an emergency situation or when incapacitating, intractable pain occurs. Chronic conditions are best handled on an outpatient basis.

25) **Answer: B**

Work hardening is not always appropriate or necessary. It is not medically necessary to set goals beyond the starting point of the patient. The goals of therapy are not to learn passive modalities, but to increase range of motion and strength while decreasing pain and learning self-management.

26) **Answer: C**

27) **Answer: B**

Exercises that push objects away from the body should be avoided.

28) **Answer: C**

Many patients are embarrassed or ashamed when their body image changes due to illness or injury.

29) **Answer: B**

Although a swallowing consult may be appropriate, it is more appropriate to inform the physician so that he can evaluate the patient and order whatever services or diagnostic tests he feels are appropriate.

30) Answer: D

A second opinion or an independent medical exam is warranted to determine if further diagnostic testing or treatment is medically necessary. The maximum amount of time away from work expected with a nonspecific complaint of back pain, no objective findings and a patient at rest is 2 weeks.

31) Answer: D

32) Answer: A

The patient with an injury at C1–C4 is dependent for care, and must be instructed in their care needs so he or she may direct her own care.

33) Answer: C

Arthrograms are not performed on the spine, but are utilized in injuries to bursa or cartilage.

34) Answer: D

The family must know how to use the equipment safely, there should be no barriers to its safe use and the length of time the equipment is needed is a factor in arranging for and selecting the equipment.

35) Answer: B

If there are multiple infusions and frequent infusion administrations, it may be more cost effective to administer the therapy in the hospital.

36) Answer: A

Communicating openly is always important in relieving anxiety and stress. If this is not done the patient's anxiety could interfere with his recovery.

37) Answer: D

Rehabilitation programs often overlook the fact that this patient will have many problems occur due to such things as falls, weight gain or loss, and weather conditions. All of these things and others can effect the way the prosthesis fits and the patient's ability to function. The Case Manager should explore the patient's ability to cope with his disability and potential problems. She should review typical scenarios and have the physical therapy department have the patient practice getting up off the floor and other difficult situations. The nursing department should review possible scenarios with the fit of the prosthesis, any causes of irritation to the limb and discuss when to seek out the physician or prosthesis.

38) Answer: C

The micturation reflex center is located in the sacral region of the spinal cord. As a result bladder function may be impaired with a lower spinal cord injury.

39) Answer: D

40) Answer: C

Pain medication is not a cognitive technique.

41) Answer: B

42) Answer: A

43) Answer: B

44) Answer: D

45) Answer: B

46) Answer: C

47) Answer: A

48) Answer: C

Postoperatively, the knee is immobilized in a hinged brace in a flexed position.

49) **Answer: C**

All of the above questions can help shed light on the reason for the patient's resistance and assist the team in formulating a more effective care plan.

50) **Answer: D**

51) **Answer: B**

The illness need not be as "catastrophic" as a closed head injury, a cervical spine injury or cancer to cause serious changes in a person's life. A carpenter who loses the use of his hand, a dancer who suffers from vertigo, or a professional athlete who injures his knee are examples of patients whose injuries, while not considered catastrophic by most, have serious effects beyond the physical realm, and into the social and psychological spheres. These patients have not just suffered a serious and painful injury, but have lost careers, hopes, dreams, social status, and income. As a result of the life changes precipitated by major illness and injury patients commonly experience loss, anger, fear and anxiety, depression, and dependency.

52) **Answer: A**

The illness need not be as "catastrophic" as a closed head injury, a cervical spine injury or cancer to cause serious changes in a person's life. A carpenter who loses the use of his hand, a dancer who suffers from vertigo, or a professional athlete who injures his knee are examples of patients whose injuries, while not considered catastrophic by most, have serious effects beyond the physical realm, and into the social and psychological spheres. These patients have not just suffered a serious and painful injury, but have lost careers, hopes, dreams, social status, and income. As a result of the life changes precipitated by major illness and injury patients commonly experience loss, anger, fear and anxiety, depression, and dependency.

53) **Answer: B**

The illness need not be as "catastrophic" as a closed head injury, a cervical spine injury or cancer to cause serious changes in a person's life. A carpenter who loses the use of his hand, a dancer who suffers from vertigo, or a professional athlete who injures his knee are examples of patients whose injuries, while not considered catastrophic by most, have serious effects beyond the physical realm, and into the social and psychological spheres. These patients have not just suffered a serious and painful injury, but have lost careers, hopes, dreams, social status, and income. Others with the same injury would not necessarily be so profoundly affected. For example, a 90-year-old man who is told that he has prostate carcinoma that may kill him in 10 years may not have the same reaction as a 30-year-old man with the same diagnosis. Not every patient has the same reaction to illness or injuries, whether they are minor or catastrophic.

54) **Answer: A**

The illness need not be as "catastrophic" as a closed head injury, a cervical spine injury or cancer to cause serious changes in a person's life. A carpenter who loses the use of his hand, a dancer who suffers from vertigo, or a professional athlete who injures his knee are examples of patients whose injuries, while not considered catastrophic by most, have serious effects beyond the physical realm, and into the social and psychological spheres. These patients have not just suffered a serious and painful injury, but have lost careers, hopes, dreams, social status, and income. Others with the same injury would not necessarily be so profoundly affected. For example, a 90-year-old man who is told that he has prostate carcinoma that may kill him in ten years may not have the same reaction as a 30-year-old man with the same diagnosis. Not every patient has the same reaction to illness or injuries, whether they are minor or catastrophic.

55) **Answer: D**

56) **Answer: A**

As a result of changes precipitated by major illness and injury patients commonly experience loss, fear and anxiety, as well as depression, dependency, and anger.

57) **Answer: B**

58) Answer: C

As a result of changes precipitated by major illness and injury patients commonly experience loss, anger, fear and anxiety, depression, and dependency. If anticipated by the Case Manager, and noted early, these reactions can be treated with education, support, counseling, and in some cases, medication. During the intake interview, the Case Manager can ask some questions that may help determine the patient's response to his current situation.

59) Answer: A

As a result of changes precipitated by major illness and injury patients commonly experience loss, anger, fear and anxiety, depression, and dependency. If anticipated by the Case Manager, and noted early, these reactions can be treated with education, support, counseling, and in some cases, medication. During the intake interview, the Case Manager can ask some questions that may help determine the patient's response to his current situation.

60) Answer: B

As a result of changes precipitated by major illness and injury patients commonly experience loss, anger, fear and anxiety, depression and dependency. If anticipated by the Case Manager, and noted early, these reactions can be treated with education, support, counseling, and in some cases, medication. During the intake interview, the Case Manager can ask some questions that may help determine the patient's response to his current situation.

61) Answer: E

A patient's injury has "ripple effects" that impact the family, friends, and coworkers. Because of these ripple effects, the Case Manager must be aware of what is going on in the patient's environment, make what interventions she can, and recommend more extensive counseling and education when appropriate. A personal history of effectively coping with a major illness in the past is a positive predictor for a patient's future coping abilities.

62) Answer: A

A patient's injury has "ripple effects" that impact the family, friends, and coworkers. Because of these ripple effects, the Case Manager must be aware of what is going on in the patient's environment, make what interventions she can, and recommend more extensive counseling and education when appropriate. A personal history of effectively coping with a major illness in the past is a positive predictor for a patient's future coping abilities.

63) Answer: B

A patient's injury has "ripple effects" that impact the family, friends, and coworkers. Because of these ripple effects, the Case Manager must be aware of what is going on in the patient's environment, make what interventions she can, and recommend more extensive counseling and education when appropriate. A personal history of effectively coping with a major illness in the past is a positive predictor for a patient's future coping abilities.

64) Answer: D

Maladaptive families are unable to achieve a balance between meeting a patient's needs and maintaining their own functioning. These families may overindulge the patient and foster dependency. Other family members may be ignored or mistreated in an effort to meet the needs of the sick member. Conversely, maladaptive families may abandon or ignore the patient. They may deny the existence of illness or disability to the detriment of the patient. These patterns stem from a family's inability to communicate effectively with each other, with care providers or with support networks; seek and accept help; maintain flexibility in role relationships; retain relationships with community.

65)   Answer: D

Maladaptive families are unable to achieve a balance between meeting a patient's needs and maintaining their own functioning. These families may overindulge the patient and foster dependency. Other family members may be ignored or mistreated in an effort to meet the needs of the sick member. Conversely, maladaptive families may abandon or ignore the patient. They may deny the existence of illness or disability to the detriment of the patient. These patterns stem from a family's inability to communicate effectively with each other, with care providers or with support networks; seek and accept help; maintain flexibility in role relationships; retain relationships with community.

66)   Answer: D

Maladaptive families are unable to achieve a balance between meeting a patient's needs and maintaining their own functioning. These families may overindulge the patient and foster dependency. Other family members may be ignored or mistreated in an effort to meet the needs of the sick member. Conversely, maladaptive families may abandon or ignore the patient. They may deny the existence of illness or disability to the detriment of the patient. These patterns stem from a family's inability to communicate effectively with each other, with care providers or with support networks; seek and accept help; maintain flexibility in role relationships; retain relationships with community.

67)   Answer: D

Some families are remarkably adaptable to these crisis situations. In a crisis situation, such as during a catastrophic illness in a family member, successful families are flexible in their roles within the family, they maintain the ability to solve problems, they communicate with each other and outsiders effectively, they accept help, and they maintain their relationship with the community. This type of family is able to meet the new needs of a sick member without a loss of balance and functioning.

68)   Answer: B

Some families are remarkably adaptable to these crisis situations. In a crisis situation, such as during a catastrophic illness in a family member, successful families are flexible in their roles within the family, they maintain the ability to solve problems, they communicate with each other and outsiders effectively, they accept help, and they maintain their relationship with the community. This type of family is able to meet the new needs of a sick member without a loss of balance and functioning.

69)   Answer: A

Some families are remarkably adaptable to these crisis situations. In a crisis situation such as during a catastrophic illness in a family member, successful families are flexible in their roles within the family, they maintain the ability to solve problems, they communicate with each other and outsiders effectively, they accept help, and they maintain their relationship with the community. This type of family is able to meet the new needs of a sick member without a loss of balance and functioning.

70)   Answer: C

The other answers require a higher spinal cord injury or brain trauma.

Chapter 4

Case Management Concepts

DEFINITION OF CASE MANAGEMENT

The Case Management Society of America (CMSA) defines case management[1] as a collaborative process that assesses, plans, implements, coordinates, monitors, and evaluates the options and services required to meet an individual's health needs, using communication and available resources to promote quality, cost-effective outcomes.

The Six Essential Activities of Case Management

As noted above, case management has six essential activities:*

- Assessment
- Planning
- Implementation
- Coordination
- Monitoring
- Evaluation

The Five Core Components of Case Management

These six essential activities of case management are practiced by licensed health professionals in each of the following five core components:*

1. coordination and service delivery
2. physical and psychological factors
3. benefit systems and cost benefit analysis
4. case management concepts
5. community resources

The Commission for Case Manager Certification, from its CM Job Description/Role and Function Study, lists acceptable work activities for each of the five core components.*

---

*Courtesy of Commission for Case Manager Certification, Rolling Meadows, Illinois.

Coordination and Service Delivery

- Understands legal and ethical issues pertaining to confidentiality.
- Understands medical terminology.
- Understands restrictions on the release of confidential information.
- Knows how to obtain an accurate history.
- Establishes treatment goals that meet the client's health care needs and the referral source's requirements.
- Assesses clinical information to develop treatment plans.
- Communicates case objectives to those who need to know them.

Physical and Psychological Factors

- Identifies cases with potential for high-risk complications.
- Acts as an advocate for an individual's health care needs.
- Understands methods for assessing an individual's present level of health care needs.
- Understands the physical characteristics of illness.
- Understands the psychological characteristics of disabling conditions.
- Understands the psychological characteristics of illness.
- Assists individuals with the development of short- and long-term health goals.
- Understands the psychological characteristics of wellness.

Benefit Systems and Cost Benefit Analysis

- Evaluates the quality of necessary medical services.
- Understands requirements for prior approval by payer.
- Identifies cases that would benefit from alternative care.
- Evaluates necessary medical services for cost containment.
- Analyzes data necessary to determine cost of care.
- Understands home health resources.
- Understands health care delivery systems.

Case Management Concepts

- Understands the role of the Case Manager.
- Documents case management services.
- Applies problem-solving techniques to the case management process.
- Understands case management philosophy and principles.
- Knows how to evaluate the effectiveness of case management.
- Understands planning and goal development techniques.
- Understands liability issues for case management activities.
- Develops case management plans that address the individual's needs.

Community Resources

- Understands interviewing techniques.
- Knows how to explain services and available resources (including limitations) to individuals with disabilities.
- Knows how to establish a client's support system.
- Understands assistive devices needed by individuals with disabilities.

- Understands the Americans with Disabilities Act.
- Understands federal legislation affecting individuals with disabilities.
- Understands the client's need for vocational services.

PHILOSOPHY OF CASE MANAGEMENT

Case management is not a profession in itself, but an area of practice within one's profession. Its underlying premise is, when an individual reaches the optimum level of wellness and functional capability, everyone benefits: the individual being served, his or her support systems, the health care delivery systems, and the various reimbursement sources. Case Management Certification[2] documents a level of education, experience, and skill within one's chosen profession and the surrounding health care delivery systems, insurance plans, and social systems. (See Appendix A for case management certification criteria.) This assures the Case Manager's patients and clients that the plans proposed are appropriate and based on sound principles.

ROLE OF THE CASE MANAGER

The Case Manager's role is the same in every setting, whether working in an acute care hospital, sub-acute care setting, rehabilitation facility, psychiatric milieu, home care agency, hospice, insurance industry, or as an independent case manager. The role of the Case Manager is that of an assessor, planner, facilitator, and patient advocate. The Case Manager performs these functions during the case management process.

The method of managing a patient's care progresses through the following eight stages:[3]

1. case finding
2. gathering and assessing information to identify problems
3. planning
4. reporting
5. obtaining approval
6. coordination
7. follow-up/monitoring
8. evaluation

While all Case Managers will perform the above processes, not all Case Managers will function in all settings. Case management is as specialized as the various professions that comprise it. While some Case Managers will deal with discharge planning but never follow a patient after discharge, others may follow a patient from pre-admission through various admissions and treatments until case management services are no longer required. The common denominator for Case Managers is their commitment to *patient advocacy, educating* patients and others involved in their care, *facilitating* a patient's optimal outcome, and *empowering* patients to be active decision makers in their health care.

Case Managers work in the four major areas: medical, financial, behavioral/motivational, and vocational. Medical activity refers to all those activities generally performed by a nurse Case Manager: following a patient throughout his hospital stay or treatment course, contacting and coordinating his care with a team of medical professionals, arranging for discharge needs, etc. Financial activity deals with assisting the patient to cope with the insurance company or claims payers, negotiating with vendors, assisting with applications for Medicare/Medicaid/skilled nursing facilities, etc. Behavioral/motivational activity includes assisting the patient and his family to manage the stress brought about by the disease process/injury, offering counseling (if qualified) or arranging for social work or other intervention as needed. Vocational activity is more often done in a rehabilitation setting or Workers' Compensation case management. However, it may be required in the group health catastrophic Case Manager's position. It can involve testing for function, aptitude, and interests, developing return to work strategies based on testing and working with an employer to get an employee back to work.

The case management process begins with case identification. This can occur in the following ways: self-referral, referral by an employer, referral by a provider, referral by an insurer/third party administrator via a claims person or computer system, referral by a discharge planner, or referral by a utilization reviewer. There are three basic criteria for referring patients for case management evaluation: diagnosis-driven referrals, high dollar referrals, or multiple or repeated service requests.

Assessment

Once a patient has been identified as a potential case management case, the assessment phase begins. The Case Manager should evaluate the information that triggered the referral. It may be clinical treatment or hospitalization history, a diagnosis, or high dollar claim. If the information warrants further action, the Case Manager should contact the patient next. This call is for the purpose of identifying the case management function to the patient, gathering more information, and assessing the needs of the patient. All information gathered at the point of the referral until discharge from case management needs to be systematically documented. The patient should be sent a consent agreement (see Appendix B) so that the Case Manager may contact the physician and other providers on behalf of the patient. The consent form should be clear and state that the information gathered will be shared only with those professionals involved in the care of the patient or in payment of services. The consent form also serves to involve the patient in the case management process. It empowers the patient to participate in decision making and the planning of his health care. All contacts with the patient and family should be utilized to develop a rapport with the patient. The patient should be asked at the beginning of all contacts if it is a good time to talk. If not, a better time can be scheduled, so that the patient may speak freely with the Case Manager. The success of the case management plan and ultimate outcome depends on the cooperation and involvement of the patient and significant others. Therefore, taking the time to understand the patient's grasp of the disease process, value system and beliefs, and ultimate goals will pave the way toward cooperation and positive outcomes.

Planning

Once the patient has been contacted and agrees to accept the Case Manager's services, it is appropriate for the Case Manager to contact the patient's physicians and other health care providers. The signed consent agreement will make this process easier. In order to create a plan with the patient, it is necessary to review the evaluation, treatment plans, and goals from each provider. Being acquainted with the patient's previous health status, physical and mental abilities, and goals is also very important. The Case Manager works as the liaison between all groups interested in the patient's care. These groups include the patient, the patient's family and friends, physicians, and allied health professionals, the employer, and the insurer. The Case Manager coordinates the care being rendered. Good case management plans are objective and have goals that are both attainable and tailored to the individual patient's needs. Plans of care should always have a definable beginning and end. The end of some cases will coincide with the death of the patient, such as in terminal cancer patients or patients with progressive neurologic diseases, such as amyotrophic lateral sclerosis (Lou Gehrig's disease). Other cases have a less grave endpoint, such as where a patient undergoes a hip replacement. In these cases case management intervention should end with the end of the rehabilitation period. All goals require written time frames for achievement or reevaluation of the goal, if it is unmet.

Goal setting is a priority in effective case management. The characteristics of an effective goal can be recalled using the mnemonic device[4] SMART. All case management goals should be:

Specific: Goals should be specific; for example, a physical therapy goal may be to ambulate 100 feet without assistance.

Measurable: The above goal can be measured. After having physical therapy three times a week for 1 week, the patient can ambulate 50 feet with a walker and supervision.

Achievable: If the patient was unable to ambulate prior to hospitalization and only had been able to transfer with assistance, the above goal would not be achievable.

Realistic: Likewise, the above goal of ambulating 100 feet would not be realistic.

Timely: Goals will be set at the appropriate time. The above physical therapy goal would not be timely if set within 24 hours of a cardiovascular accident (CVA) before the patient is stabilized nor would it be appropriately timed 10 years after a CVA.

Implementation

The Case Manager implements a care plan once the assessment and goals have been met. The plan should be agreeable to all concerned parties, particularly the patient.

Coordination

Case Managers do not act in a void. They are the focal point for a team of professionals involved in a patient's health care. As a result, the Case Manager has the role of liaison, coordinator, and communicator to all parties interested in the care of the patient. This is true whether he or she works for an insurance company (payer sector), private sector, provider sector, or as an independent Case Manager.

Monitoring and Evaluation

The processes of monitoring and evaluating a patient's care plan are dynamic and continuous. With every patient contact and every progress report received from the care givers, the plan needs to be reevaluated. Are the strategies working? Is the patient progressing as expected? If not, the Case Manager needs to reassess the goals and set new ones.

Reports that are commonly made available to the Case Manager should include those on the patient's case, cost benefit analysis, summary, and vendor progress. Case Managers should receive regular reports of the patient's progress or status from the vendors and providers in place. Likewise, regular patient case reports should be provided to the payer (see Appendix C). In some case this will be to the insurer, in others to the employer.

Patient case reports should clearly state the following:

- desired outcomes
- progress toward the outcomes
- cost of care without case management intervention
- cost of care with case management intervention
- savings due to case management intervention

Specific patient reports should be produced monthly and upon case closure. Additionally, a cost benefit analysis report should be produced upon closure of a case. Cost benefit analysis reports should contain:

- diagnosis
- summary of intervention
- total time in case management
- total cost without case management intervention
- total cost with case management intervention
- total savings

A Case Manager should produce a cost benefit analysis report for her client on a regular basis. This report should include all the activity on the client's employees in the past reporting period. Quarterly reporting is usually sufficient, unless there is unusually heavy activity with a client. This cost benefit report gives the client an understanding of what the Case Manager is doing for the employees and just how valuable the Case Manager's services are. The Case Management Society of America (CMSA) reports that, on a national basis, from five to 11 dollars are saved for every dollar spent on case management activities.

Summary reports should contain:

- a summary of the activity of a particular client
- the number of cases in case management
- the number of cases referred
- the number of cases closed
- the fees for case management services
- the savings generated by case management intervention
- the ratio of savings per dollar billed

Progress reports should be submitted regularly to the Case Manager (see Appendix D). These reports should be timely and communicate the results of the provider's most recent evaluation, goals, and progress toward the patient's goals. Like the case management plan, they should be specific, measurable, achievable, realistic, and timely. They should include time frames for goal reevaluation if the goals are unmet.

Alternate Benefit Plans

At times, benefit plan limitations and exclusions can hinder the most efficient and cost-effective medical care. In these cases, offering extracontractual benefits is helpful, for instance, a patient's benefit plan may only pay for nursing visits after a hospitalization. A newly diagnosed diabetic with this limited benefit plan may require nursing visits for diabetic education, for initial insulin injections, and for glucometer instruction. While this patient clearly can be managed at home without a costly hospitalization, his only recourse under the limitations of his health plan is to enter the hospital for care or pay significant out-of-pocket expenses for home nursing care. The Case Manager needs to present to the payer the argument for extending the extracontractual benefit of home nursing care before a hospitalization. The request should indicate the desired outcomes and the cost effectiveness of managing the patient at home while avoiding a costly hospitalization. Extracontractual benefits (also called alternate benefit plans) should be approved by the payer prior to their implementation. These extracontractual benefits and confirmation of the payer's approval need to be communicated to the insurance plan's claims adjuster to ensure a smooth payment process and to avoid unintended claims denials. See Appendix E for a sample alternate benefit plan.

Extracontractual benefits are a powerful tool in the Case Manager's armamentarium, but are insufficient to meet all the challenges presented by a catastrophic injury or chronic debilitating illness. A Case Manager must be able to maximize the resources that the patient has at his disposal. These resources include family, friends, and neighbors, community-based philanthropies, religious and other charitable organizations, and federal entitlements, as well as any private insurance coverage. Maximizing resources requires prudent planning, such as instructing the patient and significant others on certain aspects of his care, utilizing lending closets, and free drug programs for indigent patients. It is the Case Manager's responsibility to keep apprised of available family, community, and governmental resources. An excellent reference is the *Case Management Resource Guide*.[5] Additionally, the Case Manager should compile and keep a file of facilities and specialists to whom he or she can refer. This file should include specialized programs and providers with accredited expertise.

Patient Advocate

Case Managers are patient advocates and must always act in the patient's best interest. It is important to document from the initial contact until discharge from case management. Some critical information to document includes discharge planning goals, the medical stability of the patient within 24 hours of discharge, the plan of care agreed on with the patient and his family, falls, injuries, restraints, medication reactions/problems, justification of the need for referrals to specific providers, ongoing evaluation of the patient's condition and progress in light of the treatment, evidence of properly credentialled and competent health care providers, evidence of continuity of care upon discharge from the inpatient setting, summary of nursing and medical history, patient and family education, informed consent, all patient communications including acceptance or refusal of case management services, consultation with the treating physician, precertification and the time it took to obtain it, advanced directives, living wills, health care proxies, do not resuscitate orders, and medical durable power of attorney. Case Managers can be held liable when inappropriate decisions are made regarding medical services. Case Managers are held to a "reasonable standard" and are expected to be the patient's advocate especially if they work for the payer. Case Managers must be aware of national standards and of new treatments and their appropriateness. If an incident should occur with a vendor they put in place, there must be documentation of the investigation, findings, and subsequent actions.

CREDENTIALS

Case Managers have a responsibility to their patients to recommend quality, credentialled providers. When looking to refer patients to providers, it is helpful to refer to nationally recognized providers. Three things to look for when referring patients are:

1. Is the vendor accredited by the Joint Commission on Accreditation of Healthcare Organizations (Joint Commission or JCAHO)?
2. Is the facility accredited by the Rehabilitation Accreditation Commission (CARF)?
3. Is the physician board certified?

Joint Commission on Accreditation of Healthcare Organizations

The Joint Commission is an independent, nonprofit organization, established in 1951, with the sole purpose of improving the quality of care provided to the public through the provision of health care accreditation and related services that support performance improvement in health care organizations. Case Managers should look for accreditation of a health care provider by the Joint Commission when arranging for the following services:

- General, psychiatric, children's, and rehabilitation hospitals;
- Health care networks, including health plans, integrated delivery networks, and preferred provider organizations;
- Home care organizations, including those that provide home health services, personal care and support services, home infusion, and other pharmacy services;
- Nursing homes and other long-term care facilities, including subacute care programs, dementia programs, and long-term care pharmacies;
- Behavioral health care organizations, including those that provide mental health chemical dependency and mental retardation/developmental disabilities services for patients of various ages in various organized service settings; managed behavioral health care organizations;
- Ambulatory care providers, including outpatient surgical facilities, rehabilitation centers, infusion centers, group practices, and others; and
- Clinical laboratories.

Accreditation by the Joint Commission is recognized nationally as a quality symbol. It indicates the organization meets certain quality performance standards. Health care organizations strive to meet Joint Commission standards, since accreditation will accomplish several goals. Accreditation

- Assists the organizations in improving their quality of care;
- May be used to meet certain Medicare certification requirements;
- Enhances community confidence in the organization;
- Enhances staff recruitment;
- Provides an educational tool for the staff;
- Expedites third party reimbursement;
- Often fulfills state licensure requirements;
- May favorably influence liability insurance premiums;
- Enhances access to managed care contracts; and
- May favorably influence bond ratings and access to financial markets.

The Rehabilitation Accreditation Commission

CARF is a private, not-for-profit organization that promotes quality rehabilitation services. Established in 1966, CARF's mission is to promote the quality, value, and optimal outcomes of services through a consultative accreditation process that centers on enhancing the lives of the persons served. CARF establishes standards of quality for organizations to use as guidelines in developing and offering their programs or services to consumers. CARF standards are developed with input from consumers, rehabilitation professionals, state and national organizations, and funders. Every year the standards are reviewed and new ones are developed to keep current with the needs and environment.

CARF believes in three core values:

1. All people have the right to be treated with respect and dignity.
2. All people should have access to needed services that achieve optimal outcomes.
3. All people should be empowered to make informed choices.

When the Case Manager selects an accredited CARF facility, she can be assured that:

- The programs or services actively involve consumers in selecting, planning, and using services.
- The organization's programs and services have met consumer-focused, state-of-the-art national standards of performance.
- These standards were developed with the involvement and input of consumers.
- The organization is focused on assisting each consumer in achieving his or her chosen goals and outcomes.

Board Certification

The American Board of Medical Specialties and the American Medical Association recognize 24 specialty boards that certify that physicians have met certain published standards. The intent of the certification process is to provide assurance to the public that a certified medical specialist has successfully completed an approved educational program and an evaluation, including as examination process designed to assess the knowledge, experience, and skills needed to provide high quality patient care in that specialty. In order to be certified as a medical specialist by one of these boards, a medical doctor must fulfill the following requirements:

- Completion of a course of study leading to the MD or DO degree from a recognized school of medicine.
- Completion of 3 to 7 years of full-time training in an accredited residency program designed to train specialists in the field.
- Some specialty boards require assessments of individual performance and competence from the residency training director or from the chief of service in the hospital where the specialty is practiced.
- Most specialty boards require that the person who seeks certification has an unrestricted license to practice medicine in order to sit for the certification exam.
- Some boards require that the doctor have a period of experience in full-time practice in the specialty prior to taking the certification exam, usually for 2 years after their training period. For specialties that require surgery, there are also minimum requirements regarding the hours spent in surgery.
- Finally, each candidate must pass a written examination given by the specialty board. Fifteen of the specialty boards also require an oral exam conducted by senior specialists in the same field.

Most boards issue certificates for a limited period of time (7 to 10 years) with requirements of continuing education and review of credentials to be recertified.

The Case Manager should use these credentials as a baseline. He or she must also obtain feedback from patients regarding their experiences with these providers and observe for outcomes. Whenever an irregularity is detected or suspected, there is a duty to investigate and to report to the appropriate credentialing body or National Physician's Database when appropriate.

LIFE CARE PLANS

A life care plan is a systematic analysis of clinical and financial information, which results in an estimation of the lifetime utilization of medical resources and other resources for the patient. Those who will be responsible for the lifetime care of a patient use these plans. It allows them to anticipate utilization, seek out community resources, and plan for the care of the patient when the parents (or legal guardians) no longer can.

A life care plan is reflected in a comprehensive document that contains an analysis and narrative report of a patient's needs. These needs projections include original acquisition costs of services and medical items as well as their replacement costs, replacement frequency, repair, maintenance, and upgrading costs. These costs are reported in the cost of the present year. A medical economist is usually enlisted to evaluate cost projections and adjust them for inflation and other financial trends.

Attorneys, insurers, providers, and families use the life care plan to help determine current and future needs of a patient over his or her life span. A patient's caretaker, be it providers, family members, or legal guardians, must plan for the care of the patient, both medically and financially. To be able to review projections of costs against current and future resources is a great help. In the court system, the life care plan becomes the groundwork for settlements in tort claims for personal injury or medical liability cases. Further, the insurer needs this information to allocate sufficient money reserves for the care of this patient.

The categories in which needs are usually assessed include the following:

- current and projected financial status
- current and projected medical utilization
- current and projected psychological services utilization
- current and projected physical rehabilitation utilization
- current and projected vocational needs
- current and projected pharmaceutical and medical supply needs
- current and projected social support resources
- current and projected housing needs or architectural modifications
- current and projected transportation needs
- current and projected prosthesis and assistive devices needs

MALPRACTICE RISK MANAGEMENT

Case Managers are at risk for malpractice litigation. These litigations can arise from acts of omission as well as commission. Failure to do something that should be done (omission) is a "breach of obligation" for the Case Manager, just as doing something that should not be done (an act of commission) is a "breach of obligation.[6] Both of these events can result in malpractice actions.

To perfect a malpractice suit, a plaintiff (the person who sues) must prove two points: (1) negligence on the part of the Case Manager, and (2) injury resulting from the Case Manager's negligence. Negligence (by omission or commission) that occurs without injury does not constitute grounds for a malpractice incidence. For example, failure to recommend cardiac rehabilitation after a myocardial infarction is not a litigatable offense if the patient does not have another heart attack. (i.e., suffers no injury as a result of the negligence). Similarly, a suit based on an injury that does not arise from negligence cannot be litigated successfully. For example, if a patient developed aplastic anemia after an appropriately prescribed and delivered course of chemotherapy, he is not entitled to sue, because no negligence was involved.

In sum then, patients must suffer an injury as a result of the Case Manager's breach of duty for the legal system to find that the Case Manager "caused" the injury. In order to reduce the risk of liability, a Case Manager should practice the following precautions:

- Utilize credentialled reputable providers.
- Offer the patient several choices of providers, whenever possible.
- Develop written guidelines.
- Be consistent in decision making.
- Document justification when varying from established criteria.
- Document all contacts with patient, and those associated with the care, especially the patient's participation in the decision making process.
- Document compliance or lack of compliance with treatment plan.
- Establish quality assurance programs to monitor for consistency in decision making and payment guidelines.
- Implement grievance procedures, following state guidelines for timeliness and specialty peer review.
- Always address the patient's concerns.
- Always contact the patient's physician.

Negligent Referral

This is a relatively new term applied to case management. Case Managers need to be aware of court cases that address the liability of Case Managers performing utilization review. Case Managers are at risk for damages if their referral of patients to providers is negligently performed and harm comes to the patient as a result.[7] An example of this is *Wickline v. State of California*. Mrs. Wickline had surgery for a vascular disease followed by a number of complications. The Medicaid (MediCal) program stopped payment for inpatient hospital care. Mrs. Wickline's physician asked for payment for 8 additional days of acute care. Medicaid agreed to pay for an additional 4 days. After 4 days the physician took no further action and the patient went home. She developed additional complications and lost her leg. She sued the Medicaid program, claiming she would not have lost her leg if she hadn't been discharged early due to termination of payment. The courts stated that a physician cannot shift their legal responsibility for the welfare of their patient to a third party by complying with a cost containment program.[8] However, the courts also stated that providers can shift their liability to payers for adverse determination as long as they satisfy their "duty to protest" such decisions.[9] The California Court of Appeals further stated that third party payers of health care services can be held legally accountable when medically inappropriate decisions result from defects in the design or implementation of cost containment mechanisms, as, for example, when appeals made on a patient's behalf for medical or hospital care are arbitrarily ignored or unreasonably disregarded or overridden.[7]

ETHICAL CONSIDERATIONS

There are many ethical challenges that face Case Managers daily. Generally, when one thinks of ethical challenges, one's thoughts revolve around how to attain the best outcome for your patient given the constraints of a limited benefit plan or resources. However, the challenges can be subtler and more complex than that. As long as the Case Manager is truly the patient's advocate, these dilemmas can be worked out with some assertiveness and creativity. For example, awareness of insurance limits, specialty programs such as charitable specific disease organizations, and other community resources allows case management plans to be put into place to meet a patient's needs without causing an ethical dilemma. Similarly, "flexing" benefits (asking payers to put alternative benefit plans into place) where they make financial and clinical sense, are ethically appropriate, and should be done.

"Dual relationships"[10] are one of the least understood and one of the most serious ethical issues that face Case Managers today. A dual relationship is defined as a relationship where a Case Manager has assumed more than one role with respect to a client, a subordinate, or a student. This concept may also extend to "multiple relationships." A Case Manager may have to balance obligations to the patient, the patient's family, the patient's employer, her own employer, and the payer. This can occur when the employer expects the Case Manager to save benefit dollars, the patient and family want the best for the patient regardless of cost, and the payer wants to pay at the normal benefit level (not at 100% of a negotiated fee); in some cases putting in services prior to a severe need will save benefit dollars later on, but the employer or payer cannot see the potential savings. This is an ethical dilemma the Case Manager has to face each and every day. It is only natural when managing a particular case to become close to the patient and his family. However, a Case Manager must remember that the patient, the employer, the vendor, the subordinate, etc., do not exist to meet the Case Manager's needs. Avoiding dual relationships may not always be entirely possible; however, the Case Manager has an obligation to set appropriate boundaries and constantly reevaluate those relationships in an ethical context. If the Case Manager feels his or her objectivity is threatened, he or she should set up a mechanism to consult with an impartial third party at regular intervals. Whether dealing with a patient or subordinate, expectations should be clearly defined and ongoing feedback should occur regularly. If objectivity and professionalism become an impossibility, such as in the situation of being asked to manage a family member or close friend, the patient should be reassigned to another Case Manager.

CMSA 1996 Statement Regarding Ethical Case Management Practices

The CMSA developed a written ethical position in 1996; the CMSA 1996 Statement regarding Ethical Case Management Practices* (see Appendix I). There are five principles cited in the ethical statement:

1. Autonomy
2. Beneficence
3. Nonmaleficence
4. Justice
5. Veracity

Autonomy refers to the patient's freedom to choose his own treatment course. Case management is committed to patient autonomy. This includes informed consent, providing options for the patient to choose from, educating the patient and empowering the patient, to be independent and self-directed.

Beneficence refers to the Case Manager as having a duty to promote good and to be the patient's advocate. Nonmaleficence refers to doing no harm. Justice refers to the allocation of

---

*Courtesy of Case Management Society of America, Little Rock, Arkansas.

health care resources based on individual need in a fair manner. Decisions are not made based on whims, and the same criteria are utilized for all patients. Veracity or telling the truth is essential to developing a rapport with the patient and significant others. The ethical Case Manager is accountable to everyone she deals with for her decisions and actions.

In the managed care environment the role of the case manager is to balance the best possible ethical outcome with the responsibility to the employer to be judicious with finances and to be certain that distribution is fair and equitable to all patients.[11]

INFORMED CONSENT

In order for consent to be considered informed,[3] it must have the following elements:

- Information is given verbally and in writing.
- An opportunity is given for questions and answers to clarify the patient's understanding.
- Disclosure of information is provided that a reasonable medical practitioner would disclose under the same or similar circumstances.
- Disclosure of background information needed to make the decision-making process meaningful is given.
- The patient signs a written consent form with specific permission spelled out in the agreement.
- The consent form is signed by a witness, preferably other than the Case Manager.

UTILIZATION MANAGEMENT/UTILIZATION REVIEW

Utilization review can be prospective, as in precertification of an elective hospital admission; concurrent, as in an unexpected or emergent admission; or retrospective, as occurs when claims are received and reviewed after services have been rendered. Utilization review is concerned with ensuring that the appropriate service is being performed at the appropriate level of care, by the appropriate provider, at an appropriate cost. Utilization review is especially effective in identifying potential case management cases. Furthermore, due to the nature of utilization review, it is possible to impact the length of stay and patient outcome from the time the procedure or hospitalization is called into the precertification unit. An example of this is having a patient, who is scheduled for a hip replacement, being taught postoperative physical therapy exercises and obtaining a raised toilet seat and walker prior to the surgery. This reduces discharge planning delays to get equipment and teaches the patient ambulation with a walker. The patient can also get more out of the teaching before the surgery, when he or she is not uncomfortable. One of the most noted consequences of utilization review is the sentinel effect. This hypothesis was extrapolated from research in industrial psychology that also yielded the Hawthorne effect. This sentinel effect states that a case would be better managed, and therefore less costly, simply because a neutral, third party was *observing*.[12] In other words, for the purposes of utilization review, the knowledge that someone is doing utilization review impacts the process. Those being "observed" are aware and want to do well, and thus more timely interventions and discharges occur.

REFERENCES

1. *Standards of Practice for Case Management.* Case Management Society of America; 1995.
2. CCM Certification Guide. Commission for Case Manager Certification; 1995.
3. Mullahy, C. *The Case Manager's Handbook.* Gaithersburg, MD: Aspen Publishers; 1995.
4. St. Coeur, M. *Case Management Practice Guidelines.* St. Louis: Mosby; 1996.
5. *Case Management Resource Guide.* Center for Consumer Health Care Information. 1-800-627-2244.

6. Hogue, EE. *J of Care Manage.* August 1995; 36.
7. Powers, Pyles & Verville. Legal hazards on the case management highway. *The Case Manager.* July/August/September 1994; 102.
8. Powell. *Nursing Case Management. A Practical Guide to Success in Managed Care.* New York: Lippincott 1996.
9. Hogue, EE. Hitting the mark—ethics in case management. *Continuing Care.* 1997; vol. 45.
10. Commission for Case Manager Certification. *J of Care Manage.* December 1997 and February 1998.
11. Keffer MJ. Ethical decisions with limited resources. How is that possible? *Nurs Case Manage.* 1997; 2(5):196–200.
12. Thorn K. *The Birth of Third Generation Case Management.* Canoga Park, CA: Thorn Associates; 1990.

1) **Case Management is defined by the Case Management Society of America (CMSA) as a process that includes which of the following?**

1. Managed care
2. Assessing, planning, and monitoring
3. Collaboration, coordination, and communication
4. Implementation and evaluation
   A. 1, 2, 3
   B. 2, 3, 4
   C. All of the above
   D. None of the above

2) **Arranging for continuity of care upon discharge from the hospital is also known as:**

A. Discharge status
B. Effective utilization review
C. Discharge planning
D. Timeliness

3) **Which of the following answers are not included in the five core areas of Case Management?**

A. The return to work process
B. Benefit systems and cost benefit analysis
C. Case Management concepts
D. Community resources

4) **Case Management documentation should:**

1. Be done upon closure of the case.
2. Be done as close to the time of all contacts as possible.
3. Be thorough.
4. Reflect the patient's level of involvement in care planning.
   A. 1, 2, 3
   B. 1, 3, 4
   C. 2, 3, 4
   D. All of the above

5) **Assessment, planning, implementation, coordination, monitoring and evaluation are referred to as:**

A. The nursing process
B. The scientific method
C. The six components of Case Management
D. None of the above

6)   **Accurate, thorough Case Management Documentation:**

    A.   Limits or reduces liability
    B.   Is a legal medical record subject to state record retention laws
    C.   Is confidential
    D.   None of the above
    E.   All of the above

7)   **The role of the Case Manager is that of:**

    A.   Educator, facilitator, insurance advocate
    B.   Assessor, planner, educator, facilitator and patient advocate
    C.   Claims adjuster, planner, educator, facilitator
    D.   Assessor, medical planner, facilitator

8)   **Case finding, gathering and assessing information and problem identification are all part of:**

    A.   Patient advocacy
    B.   The return to work assessment
    C.   The case management process
    D.   The precertification process

9)   **Diagnosis, high costs, multiple admissions or treatments are red flags for:**

    A.   Pre-existing HMO exclusions
    B.   Utilization management review
    C.   Case Management evaluation
    D.   Disability hearings

10) **The Case Manager never contacts:**

    A.   The patient
    B.   The caregivers
    C.   The employer
    D.   The patient's coworkers

11) **A Case Management consent agreement provides for which of the following?**

    1.   Release of clinical information to the Case Manager
    2.   Claims payment
    3.   Permission to review the case information with the parties involved in the care of the patient or the payment of services
    4.   Provision of durable medical equipment
        A. 1, 2
        B. 2, 3
        C. 1, 3
        D. 3, 4

12) **Which of the following is *not* true about Case Management?**

    A.   It is a new profession.
    B.   It is an area of practice within one's profession.
    C.   It is performed by a variety of health care providers.
    D.   It is performed in a variety of settings.

13) **In the Case Management Process the stage of "obtaining approval" refers to:**

    A.   Permission from the patient to implement Case Management
    B.   Permission from the payer to implement a care plan
    C.   Permission from claims to negotiate fees
    D.   None of the above

14) **Case Managers work in a variety of settings. The following are examples of the provider sector.**
   1.   Third party administrators
   2.   Infusion company
   3.   Rehabilitation center
   4.   Hospital
      A.   1, 2, 3
      B.   2, 3, 4
      C.   None of the above
      D.   All of the above

15) **Case Managers perform their function in the following four areas: Medical, Financial, Vocational and _____:**
   A.   Workers' Compensation
   B.   Social
   C.   Legal
   D.   Behavioral/motivational

16) **Although Case Managers work in a variety of settings, they all have a common denominator of patient advocacy, educating patients and facilitating patient's optimal outcomes. But the focal point of their work is:**
   A.   Empowering physicians to be gatekeepers
   B.   Empowering patients to be active decision makers in their health care
   C.   Mandating care plans to patients and their families
   D.   Mandating services to be provided by their physicians

17) **Case Managers deal with vocational activity most often in a:**
   A.   Subacute setting
   B.   Acute care facility
   C.   Rehabilitation center
   D.   None of the above

18) **Continual assessment of the care plan is part of which process(es):**
   A.   Initial evaluation
   B.   Goal setting
   C.   Implementation
   D.   Monitoring and evaluation

19) **The following information should be included in which report:**
   - Desired outcomes
   - Progress toward outcomes
   - Cost without Case Management intervention
   - Cost with Case Management intervention
   - Savings due to Case Management intervention
      A.   Cost benefit analysis reports
      B.   Patient case reports
      C.   Summary reports
      D.   Vendor progress reports

20) **The CMSA states that nationally the typical savings for every dollar spent on Case Management services are:**
   A. $1–$5
   B. $5–$7
   C. $5–$11
   D. $11–$15

21) **Which of the following are true regarding client cost benefit analysis reporting?**

1. Reports should be generated only when requested.
2. Regular reports should be generated.
3. Reports should include specific cases.
4. Reports should include the ratio of savings per dollar billed.
5. Reports should never include billed amounts for Case Management services.
   - A. 1, 2, 3
   - B. 3, 4, 5
   - C. 2, 4
   - D. None of the above
   - E. All of the above

22) **Which of the following are important areas for Case Managers to document?**

1. Medical stability of patient upon discharge
2. Refusal of Case Management services
3. Social history
4. Living wills
   - A. 1, 2, 3
   - B. 2, 3 , 4
   - C. None of the above
   - D. All of the above

23) **Alternate benefit plans are also known as:**

- A. A secondary insurance plan
- B. A plan option when electing coverage
- C. Extra-contractual benefits
- D. None of the above

24) **The following are all true of alternate benefit plans:**

1. They require preapproval by the patient.
2. They require preapproval by the payer.
3. They require cost effectiveness justification.
4. They require prior hospitalization.
5. They require claims notification.
   - A. 1, 2, 3
   - B. 2, 3, 5
   - C. 2, 3, 4
   - D. All of the above

25) **Which of the following is *not* true regarding the planning process?**

1. The coordinator is the primary care physician.
2. Care plans should be objective.
3. Care plans should be individualized by disease process.
4. Case Managers act as coordinator and liaison.
5. Care plans should have time frames for reaching and reevaluating goals.
   - A. 2, 4
   - B. 1, 2, 3
   - C. None of the above
   - D. All of the above

26) **In goal setting the mnemonic SMART should be utilized. This refers to goals being:**

- A. Specific, Measurable, Achievable, Realistic and Timely
- B. Standardized, Medical, Action Oriented, Reasonable and Timely
- C. None of the above
- D. A, B

27) **Which of the following are true regarding the practice of Case Management?**
   1. It is a relatively new profession.
   2. Certification assures appropriate care plans.
   3. All Case Managers are nurses.
   4. Case Management is based on the premise that when an individual reaches his or her optimal level of wellness and functional capability everyone benefits.
      A. 1
      B. 2
      C. 1, 3
      D. 2, 4
      E. All of the above

28) **Informed consent must contain which of the following elements?**
   1. Disclosure of all possible side effects
   2. Disclosure of meaningful background information
   3. A chance for the patient to ask questions
   4. It must be done by an RN
      A. 1, 2, 3
      B. 2, 3, 4
      C. 2, 3
      D. All of the above

29) **The hypothesis that states that a case would be better managed, and therefore less costly, simply because a neutral party is observing is known as:**
   A. The Sentinel Effect
   B. Utilization Review
   C. The Hawthorne Effect
   D. None of the above

30) **Utilization Review can be done in the following manner:**
   1. Retrospectively
   2. Prospectively
   3. Concurrently
   4. Ambulatory
      A. 1, 2, 3
      B. 2, 3, 4
      C. None of the above
      D. All of the above

31) **Dual relationships refers to:**
   A. The relationship between the Case Manager and the physician
   B. The relationship where the Case Manager has more than one role in respect to a patient, subordinate or a student
   C. The relationship between the Case Manager and the patient and his family
   D. None of the above

32) **The court case of *Wickline v. State of California* found:**
   1. Medical doctors have a duty to protest adverse determinations by payers.
   2. Medical doctors can shift their liability to payers if they do protest adverse determinations.
   3. Case Managers are not liable for their roles in adverse determinations.
   4. Payers of heath care can be held accountable if their adverse decisions are arbitrary, for cost containment and are not based on acceptable medical standards of practice in the community.
      A. 1, 2, 3
      B. 2, 3, 4
      C. 1, 2, 4
      D. None of the above

33)   **In a malpractice suit the plaintiff must prove two points:**

    1.   His compliance with the prescribed treatment plan
    2.   Negligence on the part of the Case Manager
    3.   Injury from the Case Manager's negligence
    4.   Intent on the part of the Case Manager

        A.   1, 4
        B.   2, 3
        C.   None of the above
        D.   All of the above

34)   **A systemic analysis of an individual's clinical and financial information which results in a lifetime estimate of utilization of medical and other resources is known as a _____.**

    A.   Discharge plan
    B.   Critical pathway
    C.   Life care plan
    D.   Rehabilitation plan

35)   **The purpose of a life care plan is:**

    A.   To provide the insurer with a reasonable expectation of future costs
    B.   To provide the groundwork for settlements in lawsuits
    C.   To provide for the lifetime needs of the patient
    D.   All of the above

36)   **Assessment, problem definition, selection/planning the solution, implementation, and evaluation/monitoring are all part of which process?**

    A.   Coordination and service delivery
    B.   Problem solving
    C.   Life care planning
    D.   None of the above

37)   **Negotiated services and verbal agreements with vendors of medical equipment or services should be confirmed in writing and include the following information:**

    A.   Time frame of the negotiation
    B.   Service approved, number of units approved, frequency approved
    C.   Fees negotiated (itemized)
    D.   B, C
    E.   All of the above

38)   **Case Managers should do a provider and service comparison to:**

    A.   Obtain cost information for the insurer and her own files.
    B.   Ensure the quality of the services arranged.
    C.   Choose the most cost-effective provider available.
    D.   B, C
    E.   All of the above

39)   **The Case Manager needs to be knowledgeable regarding charitable and not-for-profit programs and services available in the community because:**

    A.   They are qualitatively superior to those that can be purchased privately.
    B.   PIP policy limits may restrict the range of options available to the client.
    C.   A higher quality of life index is associated with these programs.
    D.   All of the above
    E.   None of the above

40) **Accurate, thorough Case Management documentation:**

    A. Limits or reduces liability
    B. Is a legal medical record subject to state record retention laws
    C. Is confidential
    D. None of the above
    E. All of the above

41) **Health care needs provided over a period of time to patients who do not require acute hospital care but still require nursing, medical and other health care services is covered under:**

    A. Group health
    B. Disability
    C. Workers' Compensation
    D. Long-term care

42) **Reports that demonstrate Case Management savings to the payer of services in terms of dollars spent as compared to dollars saved are:**

    A. Outcome reports
    B. Cost benefit analysis reports
    C. Case closure reports
    D. Claims reports

43) **The following are all types of utilization review:**

    A. Preadmission/precertification
    B. Concurrent
    C. Retrospective
    D. All of the above

44) **Identification of potential high risk or high cost patients is known as:**

    A. Case finding and targeting
    B. Planning
    C. Gathering and assessing information
    D. None of the above

45) **Utilization review evaluates the following in regards to medical services:**

    1. The medical appropriateness
    2. The medical necessity
    3. The efficiency
    4. The level of care
    5. The provider of care
        A. 1, 2,.3, 4
        B. 2, 3, 4, 5
        C. All of the above
        D. None of the above

46) **The Case Manager can reduce her potential for liability by:**

    1. Purchasing Case Management liability insurance
    2. Keeping the lines of communication open between the patient, family, provider and herself
    3. Educating the patient and family, and testing for understanding
    4. Empowering the patient to participate in planning his care
    5. Documenting all discussions with the patient, family and his caregivers
        A. 1, 2, 3, 4
        B. 2, 3, 4, 5
        C. All of the above
        D. None of the above

47) **During the _____ the Case Manager determines how the family members see their role.**

  A. Implementation phase
  B. Initial assessment
  C. Referral process
  D. All of the above

48) **In evaluating a medical plan, what are the main considerations?**

  1. Quality of life
  2. Number of treating providers
  3. Quantity of money spent on health care
  4. Progress of patient
      A. 1, 2, 3
      B. 1, 3, 4
      C. All of the above
      D. None of the above

49) **The process of Case Management includes which of the following categories?**

  1. Case finding and targeting
  2. Planning, reporting and obtaining approval
  3. Gathering and assessing information
  4. Coordination, follow up and evaluation
      A. 1, 2, 3
      B. 2, 3, 4
      C. All of the above
      D. None of the above

50) **Items that a Case Manager should review in her initial assessment are:**

  A. Vocational status
  B. Leisure activities
  C. Socioeconomic and psychological factors
  D. All of the above

51) **Case Management is:**

  A. A way of reducing costs
  B. A method of following the referral source instructions
  C. A profitable business
  D. A collaborative process which assesses, plans, implements, coordinates, monitors and evaluates options and services to meet an individual's health service needs through communication and available resources to promote quality and cost-effective outcomes.

52) **The focus of Case Management is to :**

  A. Save money
  B. Report to the referral source
  C. Empower patients
  D. All of the above

53) **The Case Manager needs to keep the referral source informed regarding:**

  A. Total Case Management charges
  B. Case Management interventions and outcomes
  C. Large cases in terms of money and time
  D. All of the above

54) **A Case Manager's records should be scrupulously accurate, unbiased, and completed in a timely fashion because:**

A. Orderliness of records is scored by state inspectors during reviews, and therefore can affect state reimbursement rates.
B. A client may become involved in litigation that may require the testimony or written records of the Case Manager.
C. A Case Manager's records have an impact on the policy limits of PIP coverage.
D. All of the above
E. None of the above

55) **After a Case Management plan is implemented, the Case Manager should:**

1. Monitor compliance and communicate noncompliance to the treating physician.
2. Always arrange for a second opinion to determine if the treatment plan is medically necessary.
3. Monitor the patient's progress and change the patient's goals as necessary.
4. Cancel the physician's orders if the insurer disagrees with the care plan.
    A. 1, 2
    B. 1, 3
    C. 1, 2, 3
    D. All of the above
    E. None of the above

56) **When the Case Manager is arranging for durable medical equipment, ordered by the physician, she should:**

1. Order the equipment as quickly as possible without contacting the payer for approval to avoid delays in delivery.
2. Determine if renting or purchasing is more cost effective.
3. Monitor progress, patient recovery and use of equipment to avoid charges for unused equipment.
4. Contact the insurer to request information on benefits, preferred providers and any other pertinent information required.
    A. 1, 3
    B. 2, 3
    C. 2, 3, 4
    D. All of the above
    E. None of the above

57) **The Case Manager can facilitate the treatment plan ordered by the physician and the patient's recovery by:**

1. Facilitating approval for all authorizations required
2. Arranging for all medically necessary services in a timely fashion
3. Evaluating effectiveness of the services or care plan on a regular basis
4. Communicating with the providers of services and physician regularly and as needed
5. Providing hands-on care when needed
    A. 1, 2, 3
    B. 2, 3, 4
    C. 1, 2, 3, 4
    D. All of the above
    E. None of the above

58) **Following a back injury, it is important for the Case Manager to communicate to the providers of care and those involved in the care plan the physical requirements of the job the patient has, that way:**

1. The treatment team can meet the patient's needs.
2. Appropriate treatment goals can be identified.
3. Vocational rehabilitation can begin immediately.
4. Disability papers can be filed.
    A. 1, 2
    B. 1, 2, 3
    C. 1, 3
    D. All of the above
    E. None of the above

59) **The primary goals of medical Case Management include all of the following except:**

A. To assure the effectiveness of medical treatment and that rehabilitative services are arranged for in a timely and progressive manner
B. To assist in cost containment
C. To minimize the recovery period without jeopardizing medical stability or quality of care
D. To provide hands-on nursing care

60) **The effectiveness of the entire Case Management process depends on which of the following?**

1. Physician cooperation
2. Patient cooperation
3. Obtaining an accurate history
4. Family cooperation
    A. 1, 2
    B. 1, 2, 3
    C. 1, 3
    D. All of the above
    E. None of the above

61) **Obtaining an accurate medical history is important to the Case Management process. Toward that end the Case Manager should:**

1. Obtain a signed consent agreement or release of medical information from the patient.
2. Obtain the history directly from the patient.
3. Interview the employer.
4. Request medical records for review.
5. Interview the physician.
    A. 1, 2, 3
    B. 1, 2, 3, 4
    C. 1, 2, 4, 5
    D. All of the above
    E. None of the above

62) **When conducting an interview to obtain an accurate history, after a work-related accident, which of the following are essential?**

1. Investigating the legal issues of the accident
2. Current treatment and medications
3. Employment history and job requirements
4. Description of the incident
5. Previous medical history
    A. 1, 2, 3, 4
    B. 2, 3, 4, 5
    C. 3 only
    D. All of the above
    E. None of the above

63) **To assess the appropriateness of the treatment plan the Case Manager should:**

1. Discuss job requirements and whether the possibility for light duty or modified duty exists.
2. Interview the injured worker to obtain information regarding the injury and response to treatment to date.
3. Obtain medical information from the attending physician.
4. Complete an in-person assessment.
   A. 1, 2, 3
   B. 2, 3, 4
   C. All of the above
   D. None of the above

64) **Case Managers spend most of their time managing high-cost cases. In this role, the focus of the Case Manager is:**

1. To arrange services and supplies with vendors the physician has a relationship with
2. To obtain supplies from the closest and most convenient vendor
3. To contact several vendors and select the lowest cost vendor
4. To obtain specifics regarding credentials, accreditation status, scope of services, dependability and costs in order to select the best vendor for cost, availability and dependability
   A. 1, 2, 3
   B. 2, 3, 4
   C. 4
   D. 3
   E. All of the above

65) **When the Case Manager arranges for medical supplies to be delivered to the patient's home, she should keep the following in mind:**

A. The best selection is the vendor recommended by the attending physician, regardless of price and other factors.
B. The goal is to meet the patient's needs in a safe, quality and cost-effective manner.
C. The goal is to pick the most expensive vendor, as this will assure a quality service.
D. The goal is to maximize the patient's benefit dollars; therefore, the least expensive vendor should always be chosen.

66) **Case Management care plans should be continually reevaluated to ensure:**

1. The treatment is cost effective.
2. The treatment meets the patient's needs.
3. The treatment is effective.
4. The patient is progressing.
   A. 1, 2
   B. 1, 3
   C. 3, 4
   D. All of the above
   E. None of the above

67) **Case Managers must balance their obligations; which of the following should be their priority?**

A. Interacting with the patient's attorney
B. Interests of the insurance carrier
C. Their employer
D. The patient

68) When establishing working relationships with referral sources it is important to describe:

1. Reporting expectations
2. Role expectations of the referral source
3. Business lines involved
4. Work flow processes
   A. 1, 2, 3
   B. 2, 3, 4
   C. All of the above
   D. None of the above

69) When the Case Manager is arranging for supplies and services, it is important for her to know the following:

1. The patient's diagnosis and support system
2. The physician's orders and treatment plan
3. The benefit coverage and any guidelines to be utilized in obtaining supplies and services
4. Any barriers to delivery or use of the supplies or services in the home
   A. 1, 2, 3
   B. 2, 3, 4
   C. All of the above
   D. None of the above

70) Case Management care plans should

1. Be included in case reports.
2. Include specific goals and timeframes for achieving them.
3. Include short and long term goals and objectives.
4. Be followed without deviation once implemented.
   A. 1, 2, 3
   B. 2, 3, 4
   C. All of the above
   D. None of the above

71) Case Management care plans are constantly reevaluated and revised. Which of the following statements is the most precise?

A. Care plans remain constant once implemented and do not change because patient status has changed.
B. Care plans are revised whenever patient status changes.
C. Short-term Case Management problems are always short-lived.
D. Short-term Case Management problems always turn into long-term problems.

72) When a patient has a spinal cord injury the Case Manager should:

A. Leave the rehabilitation plans up to the patient and his family to plan.
B. Begin planning for the rehabilitation stay early in the hospitalization.
C. Not worry about rehabilitation, as the patient will probably not be able to work again, and therefore will not need resources that can be utilized for someone else.
D. Not worry about rehabilitation, as the patient will probably return to his former activity level upon discharge.

73) Which of the following is a common side effect of nonsteroidal anti-inflammatory (NSAID) medication?

A. Impaired kidney function
B. Impaired coordination
C. Gastrointestinal irritation
D. All of the above
E. None of the above

74) **When the Case Manager reports to the referral source regarding alternate treatment options, she should include:**

A. Availability of options
B. Expected costs of options
C. Approval of the attending physician
D. All of the above
E. None of the above

75) **Which of the following statements is (are) *not* true?**

A. The insurances governed by state regulations include: disability, auto and Workers' Compensation.
B. The Case Manager must know the medical policy framework of the injured individual before beginning the Case Management process.
C. A Case Manager working on an auto policy case needs to know the dollars available, medical coverage, lost wages and the covered years.
D. Plan flexibility is not an influencing factor in the Case Manager's ability to impact the case.

76) **Case Managers can receive cases from the following referral sources:**

1. Insurers
2. Employers
3. TPAs
4. Attorneys
5. Providers
   A. 1, 2, 3, 5
   B. 1, 2, 4, 5
   C. 1, 2, 3, 4
   D. All of the above
   E. None of the above

77) **A Case Management report should contain which of the following?**

1. The physician's recommendations for optimal recovery
2. The diagnosis
3. The prognosis
4. The employer's assessment of the patient
5. The expected length of the disability
   A. 1, 2, 3, 4
   B. 1, 2, 3, 5
   C. 1, 2, 4, 5
   D. All of the above
   E. None of the above

78) **_____ is a systematic process of data collection and analysis involving multiple components and sources:**

A. Assessment
B. Evaluation
C. Implementation
D. Planning

79) **Excellent Case Management services delivered in an appropriate and timely fashion promote which of the following?**

A. RTW outcomes
B. Quality health care services
C. Cost-effective health care services
D. All of the above
E. None of the above

80) _____ is tuberculosis of the vertebra.

    A. Spondylocace
    B. Spondylolisthesis
    C. Spondylolysis
    D. Spondylexarthrosis

81) _____ is the breaking down of the a vertebral structure.

    A. Spondylocace
    B. Spondylolisthesis
    C. Spondylolysis
    D. Spondylexarthrosis

82) _____ is a dislocation of a vertebra.

    A. Spondylocace
    B. Spondylolisthesis
    C. Spondylolysis
    D. Spondylexarthrosis

83) _____ is a forward subluxation of the lower lumbar vertebrae on the sacrum.

    A. Spondylocace
    B. Spondylolisthesis
    C. Spondylolysis
    D. Spondylexarthrosis

1) **Answer: B**

2) **Answer: C**

3) **Answer: A**

The return to work (RTW) process is part of Worker's Compensation Case Management, not a core component of Case Management. The five core areas consist of B, C, D, physical and psychological factors and coordination and service delivery.

4) **Answer: D**

Proper documentation will minimize a Case Manager's liability risk.

5) **Answer: C**

6) **Answer: E**

7) **Answer: B**

Case Managers are patient advocates, not insurance advocates. They do not adjust claims, nor are they medical planners—that is the physician's role.

8) **Answer: C**

The Case Management process, which also includes planning, reporting, obtaining approval, coordination, follow-up, monitoring and evaluation.

9) **Answer: C**

These are the three criteria for Case Management referrals.

10) **Answer: D**

The first three choices are involved in the patient's care or benefit payment. The caregivers are contacted for the assessment of the patient and his progress. The employer is contacted for approval of benefit plans or return to work information. The patient is contacted to collaborate with the Case Manager on his care plan.

11) **Answer: C**

12) **Answer: A**

Case Management by itself is not a profession, but an area of practice within one's profession.

13) **Answer: B**

14) **Answer: B**

HMOs, insurance companies and third party administrators are examples of the payer sector.

15) **Answer: D**

16) **Answer: B**

17) **Answer: C**

Vocational activity is most often necessary in rehabilitation centers and on Workers' Compensation cases.

18) **Answer: D**

19) **Answer: B**

20)) **Answer: C**

21) **Answer: C**

22) **Answer: D**

The medical stability of a patient upon discharge is important in assuring a safe discharge. Refusal of Case Management services with an explanation and an offer for the patient to call should he change his mind protects the Case Manager from claims of negligence. Information regarding significant others is important in setting up the care plan. Knowledge of living wills also helps the Case Manager and patient develop a plan of care consistent with his wishes.

23) **Answer: C**

24) **Answer: B**

Alternate benefit plans include services that are not normally part of the benefit package. They therefore need preapproval by the payer, cost justification and claims notification to prevent denial of benefits.

25) **Answer: B**

26) **Answer: A**

27) **Answer: D**

28) **Answer: C**

29) **Answer: A**

The Sentinel Effect is a hypothesis that was extrapolated from the research principle called the Hawthorne Effect. The hypothesis is the basis for the impact of Utilization Review on hospital admissions.

30) **Answer: D**

Utilization Review can be performed in all of the categories mentioned plus in-patient or on selected procedures.

31) **Answer: B**

Dual relationship is a term that reflects the conflict between the Case Manager and another individual due to the nature of having more than one role with the individual. An example of this is being the Case Manager and the mother of the patient.

32) **Answer: C**

Case Managers are liable for damages if their referral of patients to providers is negligently performed and harm comes to the patient as a direct result of that referral.

33) **Answer: B**

34) **Answer: C**

35) **Answer: D**

The insurer needs to allocate sufficient money reserves, the lawsuit will be settled with consideration of the medical and financial needs, the caretakers need to plan for supplementing health care needs with community resources, maintenance or replacements of equipment, etc.

36) **Answer: B**

37) **Answer: E**

The date of the negotiation and the signature of the agreeing party with title should also be included.

38) **Answer: E**

This is part of assessing the resources available to meet the patient's needs. The Case Manager needs to utilize her professional and clinical judgment to choose cost-effective and quality providers.

39) **Answer: B**

PIP policy minimums are set by the state insurance department. These minimums may not be sufficient to cover the medical costs of more severe injuries.

40) **Answer: E**

41) **Answer: D**

Group health, disability and Workers' Compensation do not specifically provide for health care services that are required outside of an acute care facility for an extended period of time.

42) **Answer: B**

43) **Answer: D**

Preadmission/precertification is commonly known as prospective review. Concurrent review occurs during the event as in concurrent hospital review. Retrospective review is after the event as in chart review or claims review.

44) **Answer: A**

45) **Answer: C**

46) **Answer: B**

All of these strategies will assist the Case Manager in building a positive relationship with the patient. Poor relationships are one of the foremost reasons for litigation. The first answer, purchasing Case Management liability insurance, is effective after you have a malpractice case but will not reduce your potential for liability.

47) **Answer: B**

48) **Answer: B**

Case Management is concerned with quality and cost. Additionally all medical plans should evaluate the progress of the patient.

49) **Answer: C**

50) **Answer: D**

51) **Answer: D**

This is the official definition of the CMSA.

52) **Answer: C**

While A and B can be outcomes of Case Management, choice C, empowering the patient, is the focus of Case Management.

53) **Answer: D**

54) **Answer: B**

During litigation, all medical records are subpoenaed for review by the courts. The quality or orderliness of a Case Manager's record has no impact on the policy limits of PIP coverage, nor does the state change reimbursement rates based on this.

55)   Answer: B

The role of the Case Manager, after implementing a care plan includes monitoring for compliance, re-evaluation of goals and communicating with the treating physician. Second opinions are not necessary on every case and the Case Manager has no authority to "cancel" physicians' orders.

56)   Answer: C

The Case Manager should always seek approval, benefit information, and preferred provider information prior to putting equipment into place.

57)   Answer: C

Case Managers do not provide hands-on care.

58)   Answer: A

Vocational training may not be necessary and it certainly does not begin immediately after the back injury. Likewise, disability papers may need to be filed but that is not the reason for communicating with the providers of care. The primary reason for communicating the physical job requirements to the providers of care is to choose appropriate treatment goals, therein meeting the patient's specific individual needs.

59)   Answer: D

Case Managers do not provide hands-on care.

60)   Answer: D

61)   Answer: C

Interviewing the employer for medical information is inappropriate.

62)   Answer: B

The Case Manager should not get into any discussions regarding legal issues. They are not pertinent to her Case Management role.

63)   Answer: A

An on-site review of a case should be saved for the very complex cases. The Case Manager will be able to assess the treatment plan, in most cases, by discussing and obtaining information from the employer, patient and provider.

64)   Answer C

Arranging services based on prior physician relationships, convenience and lowest cost is not in the best interests of the patient. While cost and convenience are factors, it is more important to deal with a reputable, dependable credentialed vendor.

65)   Answer: B

Price alone should never be the determining factor. The goal of Case Management is to meet the patient's needs in a safe, quality and cost-effective manner.

66)   Answer: D

67)   Answer: D

Case Managers should not be dealing with patients' attorneys, but refer them to their legal representative. While the interests of the employer and insurance carrier are important, the first priority is the patient, the Case Manager is their advocate.

68)   Answer: C

69)   Answer: C

70)   Answer: A

Case Management plans need to be evaluated frequently and changed as the patient's needs change. It is in the patient's best interest to change the care plan whenever re-evaluation demonstrates a need to do so. Care plans should be specific and have target dates for achieving goals and they should be part of the standard reports.

71) **Answer: B**

72) **Answer: B**

Discharge planning begins upon admission, especially in a spinal injury case.

73) **Answer: C**

74) **Answer: D**

75) **Answer: D**

76) **Answer: D**

77) **Answer: B**

The medical and clinical issues are relevant in evaluating the appropriateness of the treatment plan, anticipated length of disability and costs involved. The employer is not equipped to assess the patient's medical condition.

78) **Answer: A**

79) **Answer: D**

80) **Answer: A**

81) **Answer: C**

82) **Answer: D**

83) **Answer: B**

Chapter 5

Benefits and Cost Analysis

Case Managers need to have an understanding of the various health care delivery systems in order to effectively balance the patient's needs with plan benefits and the available resources. The following is information regarding the various insurance benefits and legislation impacting the delivery of services.

FEDERAL INSURANCE INFORMATION

What Is the Health Care Financing Administration?

The Health Care Financing Administration (HCFA) is a federal agency within the U.S. Department of Health and Human Services. HCFA runs the Medicare and Medicaid programs, two national health care programs that benefit about 75 million Americans. Along with the Health Resources and Services Administration, HCFA runs the Children's Health Insurance Program (CHIP), a program that is expected to cover many of the approximately 10 million uninsured children in the United States. (A detailed description of this program is found later in this chapter.)

HCFA also regulates all laboratory testing (except research) performed on humans in the United States. Approximately 158,000 laboratory entities fall within HCFA's regulatory responsibility. HCFA, with the departments of Labor and Treasury, helps millions of Americans and small companies get and keep health insurance coverage and helps eliminate discrimination based on health status for people buying health insurance.

HCFA spends over $360 billion a year buying health care services for beneficiaries of Medicare, Medicaid, and the Children's Health Insurance Program. In this context, HCFA:

- ensures that the Medicaid, Medicare, and Children's Health Insurance Programs are properly run by its contractors and state agencies;
- establishes policies for paying health care providers;
- conducts research on the effectiveness of various methods of health care management, treatment, and financing;
- assesses the quality of health care facilities and services; and
- takes enforcement actions as appropriate.

HCFA protects the fiscal integrity of its Medicare, Medicaid, and child health programs. Working with other federal departments and state and local governments, HCFA has a comprehensive program to combat fraud and abuse. Strong enforcement action against those who commit fraud and abuse protects taxpayer dollars and guarantees security for these programs.

HCFA also is improving the quality of health care provided to Medicare, Medicaid, and the Children's Health Insurance Program beneficiaries. Quality improvement is based on:

- developing and enforcing standards through surveillance;
- measuring and improving outcomes of care;
- educating health care providers about quality improvement opportunities; and
- educating beneficiaries to make good health care choices.

The Medicare Program

The Medicare program was created by Title XVIII of the Social Security Act. The program, which went into effect in 1966, was first administered by the Social Security Administration; in 1977 the Medicare program was transferred to the newly created HCFA.

Medicare is divided into two parts, Part A and Part B. Part A is the Hospital Insurance Program, which is funded by Social Security taxes and is provided to eligible individuals at no personal expense. As one might suspect, Part A is a basic hospital-insurance plan covering hospital care, extended care, home health services, and hospice care for terminally ill patients. Part B helps pay for various services. Both parts are described in more detail later in this chapter.

Who Is Eligible for Medicare Benefits?

As previously stated, HCFA administers Medicare, the nation's largest health insurance program, which covers 37 million Americans. Medicare provides insurance to people who are:

- *65 years old.* Generally, people age 65 and older are eligible for Medicare benefits on their own or through their spouse's employment. Any one of the following must be true.
  - The patient receives benefits under the Social Security or Railroad Retirement Systems.
  - The patient is eligible for benefits under the Social Security or Railroad Retirement System, but has not filed for them.
  - The patient's spouse has Medicare-covered government employment.
- *Disabled.* A person becomes entitled to Medicare on the basis of disability after he or she have been entitled to Social Security disability benefits for 24 months. An individual has a 5-month waiting period before receiving Social Security disability payments, which means that, in most instances, there will be a 29-month period before the individual becomes entitled to Medicare.
- *Diagnosed with permanent kidney failure.* A person is considered to have end-stage renal disease (ESRD) if they have irreparable kidney damage that requires a transplant or dialysis to maintain life. A person becomes eligible for Medicare if he requires dialysis, or has a kidney transplant, and meets the following requirements:
  - The patient has worked the required amount of time under Social Security, the Railroad Retirement Board, or is a government employee.
  - The patient is receiving or is eligible for Social Security or Railroad Retirement benefits.

– The patient is a spouse or dependent child of a person who has worked the required amount of time, or who is receiving Social Security or Railroad Retirement benefits.

How long is the waiting period for people with ESRD? If a person becomes entitled to Medicare solely because of ESRD, he or she has a 3-month wait until coverage begins (or the third month after the month in which a regular course of dialysis starts).

When does eligibility for Medicare end for people with ESRD? For those beneficiaries entitled to Medicare solely because of ESRD, Medicare protection ends 12 months after the month the patient no longer requires maintenance dialysis treatments, or 36 months after a successful kidney transplant.

What is the limitation of benefits under the renal failure eligibility rule? It should also be noted that if a person less than 65 years old becomes eligible for Medicare due to ESRD, the benefits extended to the patient by Medicare will only cover those medical expenses that are attendant to the treatment of the disease. For example, if a person under 65, who was eligible for Medicare because of ESRD were to also suffer from rheumatoid arthritis, the cost of the medical care for the treatment of arthritis would not be covered by Medicare, but that for renal dialysis would be.

If a patient has permanent kidney failure, he cannot join a Medicare Managed Care Plan/health maintenance organization (HMO). However, if the patient is already enrolled in the Medicare HMO, the plan will provide, pay for, or arrange for the patient's care.

What Are the Benefits from Medicare?

Medicare benefits come in two parts: Hospital Insurance (Part A) and Medical Insurance (Part B). Medicare Part A benefits provide coverage for inpatient hospital services, skilled nursing facilities, home health services and hospice care.

Medicare Part A helps pay for up to 90 days of medically necessary inpatient hospital care in each benefit period. From the first through the 60th day of in-hospital treatment, Medicare pays for all covered services (except the Part A deductible) during each benefit period. During the 61st to the 90th day of in-hospital treatment, Medicare will pay for all medically necessary services, except for an amount called Part A Coinsurance (Table 5–1). Medicare Part A helps pay for up to 100 days in a skilled nursing facility after a hospital stay (under certain conditions) (Table 5–2). Medicare Part A helps pay for up to 210 days of hospice care. When necessary, an extended period of coverage may be allowed. Patients pay no deductible, but may pay a coinsurance amount for outpatient drugs and respite care (Table 5–3).

Medicare Part B helps pay for the cost of physician services, outpatient hospital services, medical equipment and supplies, and other health services and supplies.

What is a "benefit period?" Medicare defines a benefit period as that period of time that begins the first day of a patient's admission to a hospital, skilled nursing facility or hospice, and ends after he or she has been discharged for sixty contiguous days. There *is no limit to the number of benefit periods* a beneficiary may have for hospital and skilled nursing care. But there is a limit to the number of days of care a beneficiary may claim payment for.

What is a "reserve day?" A reserve day is one of 60 "extra days" of hospital care that Medicare will pay for during the lifetime of a beneficiary. Medicare Part A includes an extra 60 hospital days that can be used if the patient has a prolonged illness necessitating a hospital stay of longer than 90 days. A Medicare beneficiary has only 60, non-renewable reserve days in a lifetime. The beneficiary has the right to choose when to use these "reserve days."

Table 5–1 Medicare Payments for Hospital Treatment

In-Hospital Day	Medicare Pays	Patient Pays
1st–60th	100% of allowable charges less deductible	Part A Deductible = $764.00
61st–90th	100% of allowable charges less Part A coinsurance	Part A coinsurance = $191.00*
91st–151st	100% of allowable charges less Part A coinsurance	Part A coinsurance = $382.00*

*Amount charged per day

Table 5–2 Medicare Payments for Skilled Nursing Facility

Skilled Nursing Facility Days	Medicare Pays	Patient Pays
1st–20th	100% of allowable charges	0
21st–100th	100% of allowable charges	Part A coinsurance = $95.00*

*Amount charged per day

Table 5–3 Medicare Payments for Hospice Care

Hospice Care	Medicare Pays	Patient Pays
1st – 210th	100% of allowable charges	0
Outpatient drugs	100% of allowable charges less coinsurance	Coinsurance
Respite care	100% of allowable charges less coinsurance	Coinsurance

Medigap Insurance

Though Medicare covers many health care costs, patients will still have to pay Medicare's coinsurance and deductibles. There are also many medical services that Medicare does not cover; because of this, Medicare recipients sometimes buy a Medicare supplemental insurance (Medigap) policy. Medigap is private insurance that is designed to help pay the patient's Medicare cost-sharing amounts. There are 10 standard Medigap policies, and each offers a different combination of benefits. The best time to buy a policy is during the Medigap open enrollment period. For a period of 6 months from the date a patient is first enrolled in Medicare Part B and is age 65 or older, he has a right to buy the Medigap policy of his choice. That is his open enrollment period. Patients cannot be turned down or charged higher premiums because of poor health if they buy a policy during this period. Once the Medigap open enrollment period ends, the patient may not be able to buy the policy of his or her choice. The patient may have to accept whatever Medigap policy an insurance company is willing to sell.

If the patient has Medicare Part B but is not yet 65, the 6-month Medigap open enrollment period begins when he or she turns 65. However, several states (Connecticut, Maine, Massachusetts, Minnesota, New Jersey, New York, Oklahoma, Oregon, Pennsylvania, Virginia, Washington, and Wisconsin) require at least a limited Medigap open enrollment period for Medicare beneficiaries under 65. The state health insurance assistance program can answer questions about Medicare and other health insurance for patients. The services are free.

Medicare SELECT

Medicare SELECT is another type of Medicare supplemental health insurance sold by insurance companies and HMOs throughout most of the country. Medicare SELECT is the same as standard Medigap insurance in nearly all respects. The only difference between Medicare SELECT and standard Medigap insurance is that each insurer has specific hospitals, and in some cases specific doctors, that the patient must use, except in an emergency, in order to be eligible for full benefits. Medicare SELECT policies generally have lower premiums than other Medigap policies because of this requirement.

When Do Other Insurance Policies Pay before Medicare?

Other health insurance policies may have to pay, before Medicare pays its share of an individual's bill. For those individuals who have other health insurance policies and are eligible for Medicare (not including Medigap policies), the other insurance will pay first if:

- The individual is 65 or older.
- The individual or his or her spouse is currently working at an employer with 20 or more employees, with group health insurance based on that employment.
- The individual is under age 65 and is disabled.
- The individual or any member of his family is currently working at an employer with 100 or more employees, with group health insurance based on that employment.
- The individual has Medicare because of permanent kidney failure. (See further explanation below.)
- The individual has an illness or injury that is covered under Workers' Compensation, the federal black lung program, no-fault insurance, or any liability insurance.

Prior to enactment of the Balanced Budget Act of 1997, Medicare benefits were secondary to benefits payable under a group health plan in the case of individuals entitled to benefits on the basis of end-stage renal disease during a 30-month coordination period. This coordination period begins with the first month the individual is eligible for Medicare, whether or not the individual is actually entitled or enrolled. Medicare is secondary during this period even though the employer policy or plan contains a provision stating that its benefits are secondary to Medicare, or otherwise excludes or limits payments to Medicare beneficiaries. Under this provision, the group health plan must be billed first for services provided to the Medicare end-stage renal disease beneficiary. If the group health plan does not pay for covered services in full, Medicare may pay secondary benefits in accordance with current billing instructions. This provision applies to all Medicare covered items and services (not just those pertaining to end-stage renal disease) furnished to beneficiaries who are in the coordination period.

Assistance for Low Income Beneficiaries

For individuals that have a low income and limited resources, the state may pay for their Medicare costs, including premiums, deductibles, and coinsurance. To qualify, the individual must be entitled to Medicare hospital insurance (Part A), his annual income level must be at or below the national poverty guidelines, and he cannot have resources such as bank accounts or stocks and bonds worth more than $4,000 for one person or $6,000 for a couple (home and first car don't count).

Balanced Budget Act of 1997

An awareness of the cost-efficiency of preventative care over restorative treatments has prompted the federal government to add to the Medicare benefits package. The following changes in Medicare coverage have been made by the Balance Budget Act of 1997.

Effective October 1, 1997, regarding vaccines outreach: Currently Medicare pays for one influenza vaccination per year, and one pneumococcal vaccine per lifetime. This program will be extended into the year 2002.

Effective January 1, 1998, regarding breast cancer screening: Medicare will pay for yearly screening mammograms for women over age 40. The Part B deductible will be waived for this procedure. With regard to cervical cancer screening, Medicare will pay for screening PAP smears every three years, and will cover screening pelvic exams every three years or yearly for women at high risk. The Part B deductible will be waived. For colorectal cancer screening, Medicare will pay for yearly colorectal screening for people over age 50.

Effective July 1, 1998, for diabetic education: Medicare will cover educational programs aimed at outpatient self-management. For glucose test strips, Medicare will pay for glucose test strips for diabetics who are not insulin dependent. For osteoporosis screening, Medicare will cover the costs of bone mass tests for beneficiaries who are at clinical risk for osteoporosis.

Effective January 1, 2000, Medicare will pay for yearly prostate cancer screening for men over the age of 50.

Medicaid

Medicaid is a national insurance program aimed at serving the poor and the "needy." All 50 states, the District of Columbia, Guam, Puerto Rico, and the Virgin Islands operate Medicaid plans. It was created by Title XIX of the Social Security Act, and is part of the federal and state welfare system. State welfare or health departments usually operate the Medicaid program, within the guidelines issued by the HCFA, and they are funded by the general tax revenues of the federal and state governments. Persons covered by the Medicaid program have no "out of pocket" expense for coverage.

Though Medicaid benefits can vary from state to state, the program must furnish the federally mandated services that include the following:

- inpatient hospital care and outpatient services
- physicians' services
- skilled nursing home services for adults
- laboratory and X-ray services
- family planning services
- early and periodic screening, diagnosis, and treatment for children under age 21 (EPSDT)

Eligibility requirements for Medicaid benefits are set by each state, although the HCFA has set some minimum standards. The people who are eligible under these standards include the categorically needy and the medically needy. The categorically needy includes families and certain children who qualify for public assistance, that is, they are eligible for Aid to Families with Dependent Children (AFDC) or Supplemental Security Income (SSI). Examples are the aged, blind, and physically disabled adults and children. The medically needy are those people that earn enough to meet their basic needs but have inadequate resources to pay health care bills, for example, persons infected with tuberculosis (TB) who would be financially eligible for Medicaid at the SSI level (but only for TB-related ambulatory services and TB drugs).

Mandatory Coverage for the Categorically Needy

States have some discretion in determining which groups their Medicaid programs will cover and the financial criteria for Medicaid eligibility. To be eligible for federal funds, states are required to provide Medicaid coverage for most individuals who receive federally assisted income maintenance payments, as well as for related groups not receiving cash payments. Some examples of the mandatory Medicaid eligibility groups are:

- AFDC recipients
- SSI recipients (or, in states using more restrictive criteria, aged, blind, and disabled individuals who meet criteria that are more restrictive than those of the SSI program and that were in place in the state's approved Medicaid plan as of January 1, 1972)
- infants born to Medicaid-eligible pregnant women. (Medicaid eligibility must continue throughout the first year of life so long as the infant remains in the mother's household and she remains eligible or would be eligible if she were still pregnant)
- children under age 6 and pregnant women who meet the state's AFDC financial requirements or whose family income is at or below 133% of the federal poverty level (FPL). (The minimum mandatory income level for pregnant women and infants in certain states may be higher than 133%, if, as of certain dates, the state had established a higher percentage for covering those groups. States are required to extend Medicaid eligibility until age 19 to all children born after September 30, 1983 in families with incomes at or below the federal poverty level. This phases in coverage, so that by the year 2002, all poor children under age 19 will be covered. Once eligibility is established, pregnant women remain eligible for Medicaid through the end of the calendar month ending 60 days after the end of the pregnancy regardless of any change in family income. States are not required to have a resource test for these poverty-level related groups. However, any resource test imposed can be no more restrictive than that of the AFDC program for infants and children and the SSI program for pregnant women.)
- recipients of adoption assistance and foster care under Title IV - E of the Social Security Act, certain Medicare beneficiaries (described later), and special protected groups who lose cash assistance because of the cash programs' rules, but who may keep Medicaid for a period of time. (Examples are persons who lose AFDC or SSI payments due to earnings from work or increased Social Security benefits and two-parent, unemployed families whose AFDC cash assistance time is limited by the state and who are provided a full 12 months of Medicaid coverage following termination of cash assistance.)

Optional Coverage for the Categorically Needy

States also have the option to provide Medicaid coverage for other categorically needy groups. These optional groups share characteristics of the mandatory groups, but the eligibility criteria are somewhat more liberally defined. Examples of the optional groups that states may cover as categorically needy (and for which they will receive federal matching funds) under the Medicaid program are:

- infants up to age 1 and pregnant women not covered under the mandatory rules whose family income is below 185% of the federal poverty level (the percentage to be set by each state)
- certain aged, blind, or disabled adults who have incomes above those requiring mandatory coverage, but below the federal poverty level
- children under age 21 who meet income and resources requirements for AFDC, but who otherwise are not eligible for AFDC
- institutionalized individuals with income and resources below specified limits
- persons who would be eligible if institutionalized but are receiving care under home and community-based services waivers
- recipients of state supplementary payments
- TB-infected persons who would be financially eligible for Medicaid at the SSI level (only for TB-related ambulatory services and TB drugs)

Medically Needy Eligibility Groups

The option to have a medically needy program allows states to extend Medicaid eligibility to additional qualified persons who may have too much income to qualify under the mandatory or optional categorically needy groups. This option allows them to "spend down" to Medicaid eligibility by incurring medical or remedial care expenses to offset their excess income, thereby reducing it to a level below the maximum allowed by that state's Medicaid plan. States may also allow families to establish eligibility as medically needy by paying monthly premiums to the state in an amount equal to the difference between family income (reduced by unpaid expenses, if any, incurred for medical care in previous months) and the income eligibility standard.

Eligibility for the medically needy program does not have to be as extensive as the categorically needy program. However, states that elect to include the medically needy under their plans are required to include certain children under age 18 and pregnant women who, except for income and resources, would be eligible as categorically needy. These states may choose to provide coverage to other medically needy persons: aged, blind, or disabled persons; certain relatives of children deprived of parental support and care; and certain other financially eligible children up to age 21. In 1995 there were 40 medically needy programs that provided at least some services to recipients.

Amplification on Medicaid Eligibility

Medicaid coverage may be applied retroactively for up to 3 months prior to application, if the individual would have been eligible during that period. Coverage generally stops at the end of the month in which a person's circumstances change. Most states have additional "state-only" programs to provide medical assistance for specified poor persons who do not qualify for the Medicaid program. No federal funds are provided for state-only programs.

Medicaid does not provide medical assistance for all poor persons. Even under the broadest provisions of the federal statute (except for emergency services for certain persons), the Medicaid program does not provide health care services, even for very poor persons, unless they are in one of the groups designated above. Low income is only one test for Medicaid eligibility; assets and resources are also tested against established thresholds. As noted earlier, categorically needy persons who are eligible for Medicaid may or may not also receive cash assistance from the AFDC program or from the SSI program. Medically needy persons who would be categorically eligible except for income or assets may become eligible for Medicaid solely because of excessive medical expenses.

States may use more liberal income and resource methodologies to determine Medicaid eligibility for certain AFDC-related and aged, blind, and disabled individuals under section 1902(r)(2) of the Social Security Act. The more liberal income methodologies cannot result in the individual's income exceeding the limits prescribed for federal matching (for those groups that are subject to these limits).

Significant changes were made in the Medicare Catastrophic Coverage Act (MCCA) of 1988 that affected Medicaid. Although much of the MCCA was repealed, the portions affecting Medicaid remain in effect. The law also accelerated Medicaid eligibility for some nursing home patients by protecting assets for the institutionalized person's spouse at home at the time of the initial eligibility determination after institutionalization. Before an institutionalized person's monthly income is used to pay for the cost of institutional care, a minimum monthly maintenance needs allowance is deducted from the institutionalized spouse's income to bring the income of the community spouse up to a moderate level.

Medicaid–Medicare Relationship

The Medicare program (Title XVIII of the Social Security Act) provides hospital insurance (HI), also known as Part A coverage, and supplementary medical insurance (SMI), which is known as Part B coverage as previously noted. For people aged 65 and older (and for certain disabled persons) who have insured status under Social Security or Railroad Retirement, coverage for HI is automatic. Coverage for SMI, however, requires payment of a monthly premium. Some aged or disabled persons are covered under both the Medicaid and Medicare programs.

For Medicare beneficiaries who are also fully eligible for Medicaid, Medicare coverage is supplemented by health care services that are available under the state's Medicaid program. If a person is a Medicare beneficiary, payments for any services covered by Medicare are made by the Medicare program before the Medicaid program makes any payments. *Medicaid is always the "payer of last resort."* As each state elects, the Medicaid program may provide services such as eyeglasses, hearing aids, and nursing facility care not covered by Medicare.

Limited Medicaid benefits are available for certain qualified disabled working individuals (QDWIs), who have earnings sufficiently high to preclude entitlement to Medicare coverage except if the individual purchases coverage, and whose earnings are less than 200% of the federal poverty level (FPL). State Medicaid programs must pay the HI premium for QDWIs with income less than 150% of the FPL, and may pay some or all of the HI premium for QDWIs with earnings between 150 and 200% of the FPL. Medicaid does not pay SMI premiums for these individuals.

For certain poor Medicare recipients known as "Qualified Medicare Beneficiaries" (QMBs) (those beneficiaries with incomes below the federal poverty level and with resources at or below twice the standard allowed under the SSI program), the Medicaid program pays the Medicare premiums and cost-sharing expenses for Medicare HI and SMI. For "Specified Low-Income Medicare Beneficiaries" (SLMBs) (those like QMBs, but with slightly higher incomes), the Medicaid program pays only the SMI premiums.

Spousal Impoverishment

Placing a spouse in a nursing home can be a very expensive proposition. With monthly expenses running $2,000 to $3,000, it does not take very long for these bills to wipe out a lifetime of savings, leaving the community-based spouse destitute. This situation has come to be called "spousal impoverishment."

In an attempt to prevent this spousal impoverishment, Congress enacted provisions in 1988[1] that allow a couple to have Medicaid benefits without "spending down" their resources. These provisions help ensure that this spousal impoverishment will not occur and that community spouses are able to live out their lives with independence and dignity.

In order to be eligible for Medicaid under this provision, the member of the couple who is in a nursing facility or medical institution must be expected to remain there for at least 30 days. The state then evaluates the couple's resources. After the state's evaluation, it determines the spousal resource amount (SRA). The SRA is the number the state measures against its minimum resource standard for an institutionalized patient to receive Medicaid. An institutionalized spouse who has less than this amount is eligible for Medicaid. The SRA is equal to the following: the combined spousal assets, minus the house, car, household goods, and burial costs, divided by two. It is described in the following formula:

$$SRA = \frac{1}{2} \times (\text{couple's combined assets}) - (\text{house, car, etc.})$$

In order to determine whether the spouse residing in a medical facility is eligible for Medicaid, the SRA must be less than the state's minimum resource standard. This number was $76,740 in 1996. If the SRA is greater than the state's minimum resource standard, the remainder becomes attributable to the spouse that is residing in a medical institution as countable or depletable resources.

What the Community-Based Spouse Is Entitled To. The community spouse is entitled to protection of a certain amount of the couple's combined assets under this provision. These assets are known as the spouse's protected resource amount (PRA). Said another way, the PRA is that amount of the couple's combined assets that the community spouse keeps for her own benefit and that is not available to the institutionalized spouse. This PRA is the greatest of:

- the spousal resource amount,
- the state spousal resource standard, which is the amount that the state has determined will be protected for the community spouse,
- an amount transferred to the community spouse for her/his support as directed by a court order, or
- an amount designated by a state hearing officer to raise the community spouse's protected resources up to the minimum monthly maintenance needs standard.

If the amount of resources for the institutionalized spouse is below the state's resource standard, the individual is eligible for Medicaid. Once resource eligibility is determined, resources of the community spouse are not attributed to the spouse in the medical facility.

Income Eligibility. The community spouse's income is not considered available to the spouse who is in the medical facility, and the two individuals are not considered a couple for these purposes. The state is to use the income eligibility standards for one person rather than two. Therefore, the standard income eligibility process for Medicaid is used.

Posteligibility Treatment of Income. This process is followed after an individual in a nursing facility/medical institution is determined to be eligible for Medicaid. After this determination, the post-eligibility process is used to determine how much the spouse in the medical facility must contribute toward his/her cost of nursing facility/institutional care. This process also determines how much of the income of the spouse who is in the medical facility is actually protected for use by the community spouse. Deductions are made from the total income of the spouse who is residing in the medical facility in the following order:

- a personal needs allowance of at least $30;
- the community spouse's monthly income allowance (between $1,295 and $1,918.50 for 1996), as long as the income is actually made available to her/him;
- a family monthly income allowance; and
- an amount for medical expenses incurred by the spouse who is in the medical facility.

The sum of these deductions subtracted from the income of the individual who is in the medical facility will result in the amount the individual must contribute to his/her cost of care.

Transfers of Assets Prior to Institutionalization or Medicaid Application

When a patient is transferred to any of the following facilities (long-term care facility, receiving home, or community-based waiver services) and state/federal funding is requested, the state will examine the financial records of the individual for assets transferred for less than their fair market value.[2] In common parlance, this financial examination undertaken by the state is called a "look back." (For the state's purposes, assets are defined both as real financial assets and income.)

States "look back" into an individual's financial records during the evaluation of eligibility for Medicaid. The state looks to find transfers of assets for 36 months prior to the date the individual is institutionalized or, if later, the date he or she applies for Medicaid. For certain trusts, this look-back period extends to 60 months. If a transfer of assets for less than fair market value is found, the state will impose a penalty period. A penalty period is that amount of time that a state will withhold payment for a nursing facility and certain other long-term care services. There is no limit to the length of the penalty period.

The penalty period is calculated by determining the fair market value of the transferred asset, and dividing the value of the asset by the average monthly private pay rate of a nursing facility in that state. For example, if an asset worth $120,000 has been transferred, and the average cost of a nursing facility in that state is $2,000 per month, then the penalty period would be calculated as: $120,000/$2,000 per month = 60 months penalty period.

For certain types of transfers, these penalties are not applied. The principal transfer exceptions are:

- to a spouse or to a third party for the sole benefit of the spouse
- by a spouse to a third party for the sole benefit of the spouse
- to certain disabled individuals or to trusts established for those individuals
- for a purpose other than to qualify for Medicaid
- where imposing a penalty would cause undue hardship

Treatment of Trusts

A trust is a legal title to property, held by one party, for the benefit of another. There are usually three parties involved in a trust. The first is the grantor. The grantor is the person or entity that establishes the trust and donates the assets. A trustee is a person or qualified trust company, who holds and manages the assets for the benefit of another. The beneficiary is the recipient of some or all of the trust's assets. The assets held by a trust can exist in many forms, for example, money, real estate, art, businesses, stocks, bonds, or other tangible assets. Trusts usually come in two varieties. Revocable trusts (those trusts whose terms or beneficiaries can be changed) and irrevocable trusts (those trusts whose terms and beneficiaries are unchangeable).

Putting an asset in a trust transfers that asset from the individual's ownership to that of the trustee, who holds the property for the beneficiary(s). For most purposes, the law looks at these assets as if the trustee now owned them. But not HCFA. HCFA would like to prevent asset transfers made only to ensure that the individual appears eligible for Medicaid benefits. It therefore has a process to evaluate the financial history of individuals applying for benefits and for imposing penalties for what it terms inappropriate transfers of assets.

Trusts and Medicaid Eligibility. How a trust is treated by HCFA depends to some extent on the type of trust it is, for example, whether it is revocable or irrevocable, and what specific requirements and conditions the trust contains. In general, however, payments actually made to or for the benefit of the individual are treated as income to the individual. HCFA considers amounts that could be paid to or for the benefit of the individual, but are not, are treated as available resources. Further, amounts that could be paid to or for the benefit of the individual, but are paid to someone else, are treated as transfers of assets for less than fair market value. Amounts that cannot, in any way, be paid to or for the benefit of the individual are also treated as transfers of assets for less than fair market value.

Certain trusts are not counted as being available to the individual. They are those:

- established by a parent, grandparent, guardian, or court for the benefit of an individual who is disabled and under the age of 65, using the individual's own funds
- established by a disabled individual, parent, grandparent, guardian, or court for the disabled individual, using the individual's own funds, where the trust is made up of pooled funds and managed by a nonprofit organization for the sole benefit of each individual included in the trust
- composed only of pension, Social Security, and other income of the individual, in states that make individuals eligible for institutional care under a special income level, but do not cover institutional care for the medically needy
- where the state determines that counting the trust would cause an undue hardship

In all of the above instances, the trust must provide that the state receives any funds, up to the amount of Medicaid benefits paid on behalf of the individual, remaining in the trust when the individual dies. Where an individual, his or her spouse, or anyone acting on the individual's behalf establishes a trust using at least some of the individual's funds, that trust can be considered available to the individual for purposes of determining eligibility for Medicaid.

Social Security

Social Security is a group of federally funded public programs designed to provide income and services to individuals in the event of retirement, sickness, disability, death, or unemployment. The Social Security Act that established these programs was enacted in 1935. The six original program titles of the Social Security Act were Old-Age Assistance, Old-Age (retirement) Benefits, Unemployment Compensation, Aid to Dependent Children (ADC), Maternal and Child Welfare, and Aid to the Blind. Title II, Old-Age Benefits for retired adults, was the keystone measure of the act and is the portion most often referred to as Social Security. Monthly cash benefit payments are made to the following:

- retired workers who have reached at least the age of 62
- spouses and dependents of retired workers
- divorced spouses of retired or disabled workers
- workers who become disabled

- spouses and dependents of disabled workers
- survivors of deceased workers
- divorced spouses of deceased workers

To be eligible to collect Social Security benefits, an individual must meet two criteria. First, the individual must have worked 40 quarters (or 10 years) in a job that paid social security premiums to be fully insured. (Individuals who have less than 10 years may not be excluded as there are many exceptions to this rule.) Second, the individual must meet the requirements to collect the benefits (i.e., be the right age, be able to prove disability or dependence on an insured worker, or be the survivor of an insured deceased worker).

Since its inception in 1935, the Social Security Act has been modified more than 20 times by major amendments. A 1950 amendment added Cost of Living Adjustments (COLAs) to increase benefit payments in keeping with inflation. Another major amendment to the Act in 1956 added benefits for disabled workers. All of the amendments up to this time created what is now known as the centerpiece of social security, Old-Age, Survivors' and Disability Insurance (OASDI). A 1965 amendment created a program that provides hospital insurance to the elderly, along with supplementary medical insurance for other medical costs. In 1972, the original Old-Age Assistance and Aid to the Blind titles were combined with new provisions for assistance to disabled people to create the SSI program.

In 1983, concern for the financial integrity of Social Security prompted the passage of major legislative changes, including the ending and, in some cases, taxation of certain benefits. At this time, the Congress of the United States also legislated a gradual increase in the standard retirement age, raising it from 65 to 67 for individuals born in 1960 or later. In 1996 welfare reform bills were submitted by the U.S. Congress that created Temporary Aid for Needy Families (TANF) as a replacement for AFDC, which was a revision of the original ADC title. These bills also made changes to the provision of SSI, in particular denying benefits for most non-citizens.

TANF is administered by state governments and is supported by the Administration for Children and Families within the U.S. Department of Health and Human Services, which took over the health and social welfare components of the Department of Health, Education and Welfare in 1979. The Social Security Administration (SSA) and the HCFA of HHS jointly administer Medicare, as mentioned previously, while the U.S. Employment and Training Administration of the Department of Labor administers unemployment compensation.

Programs

OASDI, Medicare hospital insurance, and Medicare SMI are separately financed segments of the social security program. The OASDI program provides benefits for the aged, for the disabled, and for survivors of deceased workers. In 1995, OASDI benefits, the largest of all social insurance payments, amounted to 4.5% of the gross domestic product (GDP). The cash benefits for OASDI are financed by earmarked payroll taxes levied on employees, their employers, and the self-employed. The rate of these contributions is based on the employee's taxable earnings, up to a maximum taxable amount, with the employer contributing an equal amount. Self-employed people contribute twice the amount levied on payrolled employees.

The hospital insurance portion of Medicare is, for the most part, similarly financed through payroll taxes. In 1996, some 124 million people contributed to social security funds; during an average month, 43 million people drew social security cash benefits. The amount of a person's cash benefit is determined by the combined wages, salaries, and self-employment income of the primary earner or earners in a family; dependent children and a noncontributing spouse receive additional amounts. The law specifies certain minimum and maximum monthly benefits. To keep the cash benefits in line with inflation, they are annually indexed to the increase in the cost of living as it is gauged in the consumer price index.

The 1986 amendments to the Age Discrimination in Employment Act state that, with some exceptions (such as firefighters, police officers, and tenured university faculty), an individual cannot be compelled to retire because of age. Since 1983 individuals aged 70 and older are entitled to receive full social security benefits even if they continue working. For other eligible workers, the amount of benefits is based on age and earnings. In 1995, for example, working persons aged 65 to 69 with earnings of $11,280 or less would not lose any social security benefits; for those under age 65, the limit would be $8,160. In accord with the automatic adjustment provisions of the law, these limits are raised yearly in proportion to the increase in average annual wages. Above the limit, for each $2 in earnings, $1 of social security benefits is deducted.

Social security benefits replace a stated portion of a person's former earned income, expressed as a percentage of earnings in the year before retirement. Low earners receive a larger percentage of their former income as benefits than recipients from higher income brackets. An earner's noncontributing spouse, first claiming benefits at age 65 or older, receives 50% of the amount paid to the earner. Similar percentages are payable to disabled individuals and their spouses. Surviving spouses and children receive a percentage of the retirement benefit computed from the earnings of the deceased earner.

Under the SSI, the federal government provides payments to needy, aged, blind, and disabled individuals. While the SSI program is run by the Social Security Administration, one does not have to be eligible for Social Security to receive benefits (i.e., a work history is not needed). Eligibility criteria for SSI includes an individual with very limited and personal property and at least one of the following characteristics: 65 years or older, blind, or disabled.

HCFA defines income as money the individual has coming in, such as earnings, Social Security checks, and pensions. Non-cash items received such as food, clothing, or shelter also count as income. Federal eligibility rules define limited income and personal property as less than $2,000 in assets for an individual, or $3,000 for a couple. However, the amount an individual can have each month and still receive SSI depends on where he or she lives. In some states one can have more income than in other states. If the individual doesn't work, he or she may be able to get SSI if his or her monthly income is less than $490 for one person or $725 for a couple. If the individual works, he or she can have more income each month. If all the income is from working, he or she may be able to get SSI if he or she makes less than $1,250 a month for one person or $1,495 a month for a couple.

As with so many of these laws, there are assets that are protected or exempt from this calculation. These assets include the following items:

- an individual's home
- household goods valued up to $2,000
- wedding rings
- car (especially if it is needed for employment or getting to medical appointments)
- trade or business property needed for self-support
- value of burial plot
- up to $1,500 burial expense
- cash value of life insurance, if the face value is less than $1,500 (if the face value is higher, it is considered an asset)

Blind means you are either totally blind or have very poor eyesight. Children as well as adults can get benefits because of blindness.

Criteria for disability include the following three items:

1. An individual's inability to engage in substantial gainful employment;
2. An individual cannot engage in work due to a medically determinable physical or mental impairment; and
3. The medically determinable impairment can be expected to result in death, or in a disability lasting at least 12 months.

Children as well as adults can get benefits because of a disability.

In determining the amount of aid given, programs take into consideration the income and resources of individuals and families. However, once you qualify for disability benefits, payments continue for as long as you remain medically disabled and unable to work. There are periodic medical reviews made to determine your health status. Those who receive SSI can receive Social Security benefits at the same time. Individuals that receive SSI are eligible in most states to receive medical care through the Medicaid program and food stamps. The basic monthly SSI check is the same in all states. It is $470 for one person or $705 for a couple.

Not all who are eligible get this exact amount. Individuals may get more if they live in a state that supplements the SSI check. Less may be given if the individual or his family has another source of monthly income.

Unemployment Compensation

The U.S. Unemployment Compensation program, established by the Social Security Act of 1935, and employment service programs, established in 1933, form a federal-state cooperative system. The federal Unemployment Tax Act levied taxes on employers' payrolls to finance unemployment payments. Most of this federal tax can be offset by employer contributions to state funds under an approved state unemployment compensation law. The federal government, in order to pay for the administrative costs of the unemployment compensation and employment service programs, and for loans to states whose funds run low, retains a small portion of the tax.

State financing and benefit laws vary widely. In general, unemployment compensation benefits under state laws are intended to replace about 50% of an average worker's previous wages. Maximum weekly benefits provisions, however, result in benefits of less than 50% for most higher-earning workers. All states pay benefits to some unemployed persons for 26 weeks. In some states, the duration of benefits depends on the amount earned and the number of weeks worked in a previous year. In others, all recipients are entitled to benefits for the same length of time. During periods of heavy unemployment, federal law authorizes extended benefits, in some cases up to 39 weeks; in 1975, extended benefits were payable for up to 65 weeks. Extended benefits are financed in part by federal employer taxes.

Workers' Compensation Insurance

Workers' Compensation is payments made to employees by employers, in accordance with statutory provisions, for injuries and disabilities incurred in the course of employment. Prior to the enactment of legislation compelling employers to insure their employees for any injuries sustained in the course of their employment, the employee had the right to sue his employer to obtain damages for such injuries. The employee had an uphill battle in proving that he or she was not responsible for the accident, that no fellow worker was responsible, and that the accident was not a normal risk of the industry. The worker also had to prove the nature and extent of the injury. The employers aggressively defended themselves against these suits and countersuits were advanced claiming employee negligence. The workers' legal forays were expensive, time consuming, and resulted in a very small number of successful suits. This resulted in serious financial, social, and psychological consequences for injured workers and their families.

Nevertheless, the number of injuries and subsequent lawsuits increased to a point where governmental intervention encouraged the employers to adopt some form of compulsory Workers' Compensation insurance. Workers' Compensation insurance was designed as a contract between the employer and employee to provide a no-fault source of insurance for work-related injuries.

Workers' Compensation legislation was enacted in 1911 and was adopted by all states by 1948. Under Workers' Compensation legislation, scales of compensation are established for accidental injuries arising out of, and in the course of, employment; that is, the injury or illness occurred while they were at work and was caused by a work-related task. Workers' Compensation benefits are awarded to the worker regardless of who was responsible for the accident.

The scope of coverage varies by state with respect to benefits payable in case of death, of total disability, and of partial disability due to specific injuries or continuing during specified periods. Though they vary between states, these benefits generally include the cost of medical bills attendant to treating the illness or injury, as well as some percentage of lost wages. The compensation benefits, set forth by the state, take precedence over the funding source. Employees are entitled to the level of benefits mandated by the state without regard to the financial status or desires of the employers. Therefore, even if the employer is self-funded or self-administered, he is bound to offer the full level of benefits required by the state's Workers' Compensation commission. Self-funded group health insurance plans may be exempt from state mandated benefits under ERISA (Employee Retirement Income Security Act) guidelines, but are not exempt under Workers' Compensation regulations. Administrative requirements compel the reporting of all accidents to a public board that is charged with the responsibility for making compensation awards to workers injured or, in case of death, to their families. In recent years, coverage for occupational diseases has been added to state Workers' Compensation statutes.

Workers' Compensation is the exclusive remedy to a worker's entitlements. If the worker is covered by Workers' Compensation insurance, he or she is excluded from claiming benefits for a covered injury under a group insurance policy and, further, is excluded from bringing suit against the employer for work-related injuries.

In many states the compensation laws are not compulsory but elective, such as in the state of Texas. Here, the employer may elect to be governed by the provisions of the act or not. An employer electing not to be so governed is liable to suit by injured workers. This employer cannot assert as a defense to an action for damages that the employee's negligence was a contributory factor, that the accident was due to the actions of a fellow employee, or that the accident was a normal risk of the business.

The cost of the Workers' Compensation insurance premiums are borne by the employer, with no contribution by the employee. The authors of the Workers' Compensation legislation intended that the significant cost of this compulsory insurance would provide an incentive to employers to increase workers' safety programs and result in decreased work-related injuries. Stringent safety programs instituted by the major corporations have nevertheless failed to stop the rise in industrial accident rates. It is estimated that industrial accidents have cost U.S. manufacturers more than $11 billion per year.

Children's Health Insurance Program

There are at least 5 million children in the United States who have no health insurance coverage. Responsive to this need, the federal government designed the Children's Health Insurance Program (CHIP) to increase coverage for uninsured children. It is run by HCFA, along with the Health Resources and Services Administration, and it provides $24 billion in federal matching funds to the states over 5 years, beginning in 1997.

Like Medicaid, states set eligibility and coverage but must follow federal guidelines. Basic eligibility requirements mandate that recipients must have low incomes, be otherwise ineligible for Medicaid, and be uninsured.

State programs differ, but all states must cover at least these services:

- inpatient and outpatient hospital services
- doctors' surgical and medical services
- laboratory and X-ray services
- well-baby/child care, including immunizations

Some states may provide additional benefits.

FEDERAL LEGISLATION

Among various federal legislation that is pertinent to the Case Manager is the Tax Equity and Fiscal Responsibility Act of 1982 (TEFRA). This legislation was designed to provide incentives for cost containment. Under TEFRA the following were established:

- A case-based reimbursement system, the Diagnosis Related Groups or DRGs. This prospective payment system determined the cost of care for selected diagnosis, while also placing limits on rate increases in hospital revenues.
- Exempted medical rehabilitation from DRGs. Rehabilitation would continue as a cost-based reimbursement system, subject to certain limits.
- Amended the Social Security Act and made Medicare secondary to employer group health plans for active employees 65 to 69 years old and their spouses in the same age group.
- It revised the Age Discrimination in Employment Act (ADEA) of 1967 by requiring employers to offer active employees age 65 to 69 and their spouses the same health benefits as those made available to younger employees.
- Established Peer Review Organizations (PROs). A PRO is an entity that is selected by HCFA to reduce costs associated with the hospital stays of Medicare and Medicaid patients. Further, they are charged with conducting reviews of hospital-based care on these patients to assure quality of care and appropriateness of admissions, readmissions and discharges. Through this review procedure, PROs can maintain or lower admission rates and reduce lengths of stay while insuring against inadequate treatment.

The Mental Health Parity Act of 1996

The Mental Health Parity Act (MHPA) of 1996 is a federal law that protects individuals with mental health problems against discrimination by prohibiting lifetime or annual dollar limits on mental health care, unless comparable limits apply to medical or surgical treatment. Enforcement began during plan years beginning on or after January 1, 1998, and will sunset on September 30, 2001.

The scope of the MHPA is limited, as is its likely impact on mental health services. Some important issues in this law are:

- The MHPA's definition of mental health excludes chemical dependency. Therefore, plans will be able to have separate limits for the treatment of substance abuse.
- Under the MHPA, plans are *not* required to cover mental health treatment. However, if a plan does have mental health coverage, it cannot set a separate dollar limit on medical care.
- While annual or lifetime dollar limits cannot be set under the provisions of the MHPA, other limits are allowed. Examples of these limits are:
  – Limited number of annual outpatient visits
  – Limited number of annual inpatient days
  – A per-visit fee limit
  – Higher deductibles and copayments are allowed in mental health benefits under MHPA, without parity in medical and surgical benefits

Some employers are exempt from this law. These include employers with 50 or fewer employees and any group plan that can demonstrate that the MHPA's requirements will result in a significant hardship. Specifically, if parity would require an increase of 1% or more in its health care costs, the plan would be exempt.

The Pregnancy Discrimination Act

The Pregnancy Discrimination Act is a federal law that extends to disabilities associated with pregnancies and childbirth the same rights and benefits offered to employees with other medical disabilities. This federal law was created as an amendment to Title VII of the Civil Rights Act of 1964.

The Pregnancy Discrimination Act expects employers to treat equally individuals with disabilities attendant to medical and surgical conditions as they do disabilities associated with pregnancy and childbirth. This *"same treatment"* includes:

- Health insurance benefits
- Short-term sick leave
- Disability benefits
- Employment policies (such as seniority, leave extensions, and reinstatement)

The "same treatment" means that in regard to choice, access, cost, and quality, maternity benefits will be the equal of medical benefits. An individual cannot be discriminated against in any of the following fashions:

- Limiting the number of physicians or hospitals who provide maternity care, when medical and surgical care providers are not limited.
- Limiting the number of plans that offer maternity care, without corresponding limits on medical and surgical care.
- Limiting the reimbursement for maternity care, when there are no corresponding limits on medical and surgical care.
- Exacting higher deductibles, copayments or out of pocket maximums for maternity care, than would be on medical and surgical care.

Who is covered by the Pregnancy Discrimination Act

Coverage standards for employees have been interpreted broadly by the courts, and all of the following are considered eligible under the Pregnancy Discrimination Act:

- Full-time employees
- Part-time employee
- Independent contractors
- Employees of successor corporations
- Employees of parent-subsidiary groups

The Pregnancy Discrimination Act is enforced, independent of the marital status of the employee. Benefits *not* covered under the Pregnancy Discrimination Act include abortions and mandatory maternity leave.

As with most laws, there are employers that are exempt from the Pregnancy Discrimination Act's restrictions. These include private employers with less than fifteen employees.

Newborns' and Mothers' Health Protection Act of 1996

Among the phrases brought into common parlance by the managed care industry, the term "drive through delivery" engendered more controversy than most. This term refers to insurers who would only cover 24 hours of hospitalization for mother and child after a normal vaginal delivery or 3 days for a cesarean section. Though little clinical evidence existed linking this policy with increased risk to mother or child, a few tragic cases of out-of-hospital morbidity and mortality began a hue and cry for reform. Reform came in the guise of the Newborns' and Mothers' Health Protection Act of 1996 (NMHPA). This law was enacted on September 26, 1996 to provide protection for mother and newborns with regard to hospital lengths of stay following childbirth.

Compliance with the Act

This law applies to private and public employer plans and health insurance issuers.

Non-Federal Governmental self-insured plans may elect to "opt out" of this Act's requirements, in the same manner as they may opt out of the requirements of the Health Insurance Portability and Accountability Act of 1996 (HIPAA), the Mental Health Parity Act, and the Women's Health and Cancer Rights Act.

Under this law (NMHPA), group health plans and health insurance issuers may *not*:

- Restrict benefits for any hospital length of stay in connection with childbirth for mother or newborn child to less than 48 hours following a normal vaginal delivery, or less than 96 hours following a delivery by cesarean section.
- Require that a provider obtain authorization for prescribing a length of stay up to 48 hours for a normal vaginal delivery or 96 hours for a delivery by cesarean section.
- Increase an individual's coinsurance for any later portion of a 48-hour (or, if applicable, 96-hour) hospital stay.
- Deny a mother or her newborn child eligibility or continued eligibility to enroll, or to renew coverage, under the terms of the plan solely to avoid the NMHPA requirements.
- Provide monetary payments, payments in kind, or rebates to a mother to encourage her to accept less than the minimum protections available under the NMHPA.

- Penalize, or otherwise reduce or limit, the reimbursement of an attending provider because the provider furnished care to a mother or newborn in accordance with the NMHPA.
- Provide monetary or other incentives to an attending provider to induce the provider to furnish care to a mother or newborn in a manner inconsistent with the NMHPA.

An attending physician may discharge the mother and/or child before the 48 and 96 hours limits, when both the mother and the physician agree that it is safe and appropriate to do so.

How does the law define the "hospital length of stay"?

The hospital stay begins at the time of the newborn's delivery, when that delivery occurs in the hospital. In cases of multiple births, the time and date of the last delivery begins the hospital stay. When the delivery occurs outside the hospital, the hospital length of stay begins at the time the mother or newborn is admitted to the hospital in connection with the childbirth. The physician alone will determine if the hospital admission is "in connection with childbirth."

Women's Health and Cancer Rights Act of 1998

This new law was enacted as part of an Omnibus Appropriations Bill and becomes effective for plan years beginning on or after October 21, 1998. This Act amended ERISA to require group health plans, including self-insured plans, which provide coverage for mastectomies, to provide certain reconstructive and related services following mastectomies.

What is Covered?

These services mandated by the Act include:

- Reconstruction of the breast upon which the mastectomy has been performed;
- Surgery and reconstruction of the other breast to produce a symmetrical appearance; and
- Breast prosthesis
- Treatment for physical complications attendant to the mastectomy, for example, lymphedema.

It should be noted that the law specifically states that these services may be subject to annual deductibles and coinsurance under the plan's normal terms.

Prohibitions

This Act imposes prohibitions on the insurers that include:

- A group health plan is prohibited from denying a patient eligibility to enroll or renew coverage solely for the purpose of avoiding the requirements of the Act; and
- A group health plan is prohibited from inducing an attending physician to limit the care which is required under the Act, whether that takes the form of penalty, or reducing or limiting the reimbursement to such physician. This prohibition should not be thought of as an impediment to effective price negotiation. The Act specifically states that its provisions shall not be construed to prevent a group health plan from negotiating the level and type of reimbursement with a provider for care provided in accordance with the Act.

Compliance with the Act

This law applies to private and public employer plans, and health insurance issuers. Non-Federal Governmental self-insured plans may elect to "opt out" of this Act's requirements, in the same manner as they may opt out of the requirements of HIPAA, the Mental Health Parity Act, and the Newborns' and Mothers' Health Protection Act.

Americans with Disabilities Act of 1990 (ADA)

The Americans with Disabilities Act (ADA) is a federal law that prohibits discrimination against individuals with disabilities. The scope of the ADA is broad, and its goals include the elimination of the discrimination against persons with disabilities in the following areas:

- Employment
- Education
- Recreation
- Transportation
- Telecommunication
- Access to public facilities (such as theatres, stores, banks, restaurants, places of employment, and senior centers)
- Access to public services (especially state and local government services and programs)

Organizations Exempt from ADA

While this law is broad and its goals far reaching, the ADA does have some exceptions. The exceptions to the ADA are:

- Religious organizations or private membership clubs (except when these organizations sponsor a public event).
- The federal government or corporations owned by the federal government.
- Native American Tribes.
- Small Employers. Compliance with this Act can prove a hardship for small employers. Therefore, employers with less than 15 employees are exempt. Because an accommodation is expensive for an employer does not automatically make it a "hardship."
- Housing. This aspect of discrimination is covered by the Fair Housing Amendments Act.

Defining Disability

The federal legislators defined disability as:

1. Any physiological disorder or condition, cosmetic disfigurement, or anatomical loss affecting one or more systems of the body including the following: the neurological system; the musculoskeletal system; the special sense organs and respiratory organs, including speech organs; the cardiovascular system; the reproductive system; the digestive system; the genitourinary systems; the skin; and the endocrine system.
2. Any mental or psychological disorder, such as mental retardation, organic brain syndrome, emotional or mental illness, and specific learning disabilities.

Excluded Populations

While the federal government hopes to end all discrimination against U.S. citizens, there are certain conditions that do not qualify as disabilities under the ADA, and individuals with these conditions are *not* entitled to protection under the ADA. These conditions include:

- Transvestitism
- Transsexualism
- Homosexuality and bisexuality
- Pedophilia, exhibitionism and voyeurism
- Gender identity disorders (unless there is a physical cause)
- Compulsive gambling
- Pyromania
- Kleptomania
- Current alcohol or drug abuse (illegal or prescription)
- A person with a communicable disease, which can be transmitted through food handling, may be denied employment in a job involving food handling if there is no reasonable accommodation, which would eliminate that risk.

One should note an apparent disparity in the law as it relates to drugs and alcohol. The current use of drugs illegally is never protected under the ADA. A history of drug abuse is a protected disability. In contradistinction, the current use of alcohol is protected, as long as the alcohol does not impair the employee's job performance. Employees with alcohol dependence can be held to the same performance and conduct standards as their nondisabled co-workers. Prescription drug use is protected under the ADA, but the illegal use of prescription drugs is not.

Qualified Employee Criteria Under ADA

The employment provisions of the ADA do not pertain to all individuals of working age who meet the legal definition of disability. The ADA's provisions only apply to "qualified individuals." A person is considered qualified for a job if he or she has the requisite skill, experience, and education, as well as being able to, with or without reasonable accommodation, perform the *essential functions of the job* as determined by the employer. The ADA does not require that the essential functions of the job be changed in order to make a "reasonable accommodation."

Essential Functions of a Job

One can see that the definition of essential functions of the job is critical to any ADA discrimination action. An employer can claim that while he is willing to make accommodations, the disabled candidate is unable to perform the essential functions of the job, and therefore is not qualified. The candidate can claim that what the employer is demanding are not essential functions of the job. While job analysis of essential functions can be a very complex determination, there are a few rules of thumb to guide you.

- Essential job functions recorded in the written descriptions of a job, prepared prior to advertising for the job or interviewing candidates, are considered evidential when determining the essential functions of the job.
- If the job function in question takes up the majority of the job's time.

- If the job function in question is considered "essential" to the jobs of others in the same or similar job.
- If the job function is described in a collective bargaining agreement.

Reasonable Accommodation

The employer is obligated to make "reasonable accommodations" to an individual's disability that allows the employee to perform his job. Reasonable accommodations in employment may include:

- Making existing facilities readily accessible to, and useable by, an individual with disabilities.
- Offering job restructuring, part-time or modified work schedules, reassignment to a vacant position, acquisition or modification of equipment or devices, appropriate adjustment or modification of examinations, training materials or policies, the provision of qualified readers or interpreters, and other similar accommodations for individuals with disabilities.

PRIVATE INSURANCE TOPICS FOR THE CASE MANAGER

Indemnity Health Insurance Plans

An indemnity health insurance plan is a legal entity, licensed by the state insurance department. It exists to provide health insurance to its enrollees. An indemnity health insurer "indemnifies" or reimburses the enrollee for the costs of health care claims. Indemnity insurers historically had not spent money or time on utilization or quality management. Now, because of savings demonstrated by the managed care companies, some indemnity companies have adopted these cost saving approaches. These companies are now referred to as "managed indemnity" companies.

Self-insured Products

The high cost of health insurance premiums has encouraged employers to seek alternative ways to insure their employees. One option is to "self-insure." Self-insurance is a method where the employer assumes the risk, in whole or in part, of insuring his employees. In doing so, the employer decreases significantly his cost of insurance.

The employer makes himself responsible for the cost of medical claims up to a "threshold" amount for the individual employee and the employed group. For costs incurred above this "threshold amount" the employer purchases a reinsurance policy to limit the extraordinary liability. Reinsurance policies are also called "stop-loss" or "threshold" policies.

Benefits of a Self-insured Program

A well-run self-insurance program can achieve the following benefits for an employer:

- Reduce the service costs that are usually incurred by conventional insurers
- Exemption from providing benefits mandated by ERISA
- Eliminate the costs of premium taxes
- Improve cash flow

Large employers (greater than 500 employees) tend to self-insure. Conversely, employers with less than 500 employees find it difficult to self-insure, because they lack the cash reserves necessary to handle large claims losses. An employer's decision to self-insure should be based on the size of the employee base, employer cash reserves, group claims experience, employee health status, and the ability to find reinsurance for catastrophic losses.

Third Party Administrators

Third Party Administrators (or TPAs) usually operate in the environment of the self-insured employer. While they may act as an agent of the "insurer," the TPA is not party to the insurance contract between the employer and the employee. The TPA does not incur any risk for employer or employee losses. A TPA's sole function is to perform "insurance type" administrative services for self-insured employers. These services include, but are not limited to, performing claims adjudication and payment, maintaining all records, and providing utilization management, case management and provider network management.

Benefits of Using a TPA

When employers self-insure, they often utilize a TPA for the following reasons:

- *Decrease start-up time:* The use of a TPA decreases the conversion time from external insurance coverage to self-insured coverage. It would be very time consuming for the employer to develop the systems for claims adjudication and payment alone.
- *Increase expertise:* The TPA "rents" the administrative talent it would take years for the employer to develop "in-house."
- *Decrease employee expense:* The employer does not incur the expense of hiring and finding space for full-time insurance administration personnel.
- *Decreased systems expense:* The TPA utilizes state-of-the-art hardware and software for claims administration. It would be prohibitively expensive for the employer to purchase the same equipment.
- *Privacy and Objectivity:* The TPA insures discretion and objectivity in claims adjudication.

Automobile Insurance

Car owners are financially responsible for any accidents or damage to property that they cause. Most states, therefore, require automobile insurance for those that own autos. Each state mandates the minimum allowable limits of policy coverage for medical expenses and lost wages. These policy limits vary from state to state. In some states, the policy limit is as low as $10,000. Some states have enacted "no fault" or "PIP" (personal injury protection) statutes to deter the incidence of tort claims. Under "no fault" coverage, the injured are paid, regardless of who is to blame for the accident. Under the PIP system, the individual can choose as payer either the auto insurance company or the health insurance company who currently insures the person. (Unless Medicare or Medicaid is the health insurer. These federal programs do not allow PIP coverage of their insured.) When a presentation for benefits is made by a patient injured in an automobile collision, a determination must be made as to whether the car in which he or she was riding had PIP coverage.

Patients injured in automobile accidents are characterized by their youth, the severity of their injuries, the high incidence of head and spine injuries, and the high rate of litigation. Many are left permanently disabled as a result of their accidents. These patients can require long periods of rehabilitation, with extensive physical therapy, as well as speech, occupational, cognitive, and psychological therapy. Unlike Workers' Compensation, where there may be no limit to medically necessary care, automobile insurance has policy limits. Therefore, patients may not be able to afford all the care they require. Case Managers must be knowledgeable of community programs and resources that can supplement or replace purchased services.

Many of these automobile accident cases will go to trial, and Case Managers' records will be subpoenaed. Case Managers must therefore keep clear, concise documentation of all patient and family interactions and recommendations.

Patients asserting related tort claims irrespective of the source of funding of medical bills have a tendency to be treated paternalistically by physicians. In other words, there is a tendency toward "over treatment." The Case Manager must assess this type of presentation against the standard of what is reasonable and necessary.

Managed Care

Managed care is, at its base, a payer driven system of cost containment. It is traditionally defined as any health care delivery system in which a third party (i.e., a party other than the physician or the patient) actively manages both a defined, comprehensive set of health care benefits and the financial aspects of a patient's care. The enrolled population is voluntary, and pays premiums in advance to the managed care organization for medical care.

Managed care began in the 1930s when the first prepaid group practices were established as a way to improve access to quality health care and as a vehicle to provide preventative health care services. Included under the rubric of managed care organizations are HMOs (health maintenance organizations), PPOs (preferred provider organizations), EPOs (exclusive provider organizations), and POS (point of service) plans.

Health Maintenance Organization (HMO)

The HMO is the most common form of managed care. It is a legal entity, licensed by the state or federal government as a health care insurer, and is regulated by state and federal HMO laws. It accepts premium payments in advance of disbursements, and manages both the medical and financial aspects of care. HMOs often use primary care physicians to act as coordinators (or gatekeepers) of the enrollee's health care. The coordinator or gatekeeper's role in the HMO is to maximize the effectiveness of the care delivered, and to do so at the least possible cost and consistent with good medical care.

There are four basic types of HMO:

- *Staff Model:* In this model the physicians are employed solely by the HMO. They see only the HMO's enrollees and are usually paid a salary. This is the oldest form of HMO, and is rarely practiced today.
- *Group Model:* The group model varies from the staff model in that the physicians are not employed by the HMO, but are employed by the physician group. The physician group contracts with the HMO to provide a defined set of services for a fixed monthly rate per enrollee (capitated rate). The physician group then distributes the proceeds of the capitated reimbursement to its physicians according to its own schedule.
- *Independent Practice Association (IPA):* In this model, an IPA contracts with the HMO to provide medical services to its enrollees. An IPA is a legal entity sponsored by physicians that exists to contract with HMOs. An IPA is composed of independent physicians, or physician groups, who agree to be bound by the terms of a contract with an HMO. These physicians have their own practices, see their own patients (i.e., non-HMO patients), and care for the HMO's enrollees at the rate contracted by the IPA. The IPA

negotiates payment for the physicians in the IPA as either a capitated fee or a discounted fee-for-service rate.

- *Network Model:* The HMO contracts individually with IPAs, medical groups, and independent physicians to form its provider network. Fees are negotiated as either a capitated rate or a discounted fee-for-service rate.

The Gatekeeper

The use of a gatekeeper is a method of physician case management practiced widely in HMOs, EPOs and PPOs. The gatekeeper is a primary care physician who has a group of patients assigned to him or her. The gatekeeper responsibility to these patients is to direct, authorize, and coordinate medical care, as well as provide basic care that is in the scope of his or her practice. Before one of these assigned patients can receive health care that is reimbursable by the HMO, the gatekeeper must approve it.

Exclusions of the gatekeeper model include true medical or surgical emergencies and routine gynecological care. Benefits of the gatekeeper model are that it controls costs, controls utilization, and channels utilization of services to "in-network" providers.

This method of physician case management has proven effective in reducing unnecessary health care expenditures, especially when the gatekeeper is at financial risk for the cost of care. While managed care companies have encouraged the gatekeeper concept, patients used to referring themselves to specialists have chafed under this system.

Accusations that gatekeepers and HMOs deny medically appropriate care in order to save money have been leveled. The idea, however erroneous, that the gatekeeper model restricts patients' freedom and may not be in their best interest has gained currency among some consumers and the lay press.

Preferred Provider Organizations (PPOs)

As managed care became more popular, the perception grew that HMOs limited a patient's choice of provider. Consumers demanded more flexibility in choosing providers than that made available in the standard HMO. PPOs were formed to accommodate this desire for more freedom in provider selection. Typically, a PPO is formed when an insurer contracts with a large group of providers (i.e., a provider network) to provide medical services for its enrollees at a negotiated fee schedule. PPOs do not depend on gatekeepers to control specialty referrals, nor do they rely upon capitation to control costs. Providers are usually paid on a discounted fee-for-service schedule and enrollees can seek specialty care as they see fit. While enrollees are encouraged to seek care from the provider network, they can also receive care from non-affiliated providers by paying a higher coinsurance fee. Aggressive utilization management and fee negotiations are used to control costs.

Exclusive Provider Organizations (EPOs)

An EPO uses the same model of organization as the PPO. It uses a network of contracted physicians who agree to care for the EPO's enrollees at a discounted rate. Gatekeepers and capitation are not employed. However, the enrollee is not free to choose a provider outside the network. Care from non-affiliated providers is not reimbursed by the EPO.

Point of Service Plans (POS)

The POS is a hybrid between the PPO and the HMO. The POS plan uses a contracted network of providers. The primary care physician acts as a gatekeeper to control specialty referrals. Enrollees who seek care from network physicians pay little or no out-of-pocket expenses. Those that seek care from non-network physicians are reimbursed, but are responsible for paying a higher deductible and coinsurance payment. Through this methodology, insurers have managed to keep up to 85% of care provided through the HMO product line.

Specialty Managed Care Arrangements (Carve Outs)

As managed care became more prevalent, difficulties in managing specialty care arose. Escalating specialty costs and a lack of understanding of the intricacies of specialty care prompted managed care organizations to look for new options. New organizations with experience in handling specialty care began to negotiate with the managed care plans to provide services. These specialty organizations have their own contracted specialty provider panels and possess sophisticated management services that allowed them to offer the specialty care more efficiently and effectively. Typically, mental health and substance abuse, prescription drug services, dental care, and vision (prescription eyeglasses) are "carved out" services. However, cancer care, HIV/AIDS care, cardiology, audiology, and radiology are also becoming common carve outs.

Capitation

Capitation is a payer driven, prepayment methodology aimed at reducing costs. It accomplishes cost reduction by removing the provider's incentive to provide more services than are needed. This "perverse incentive" to over-prescribe and over-treat is seen commonly under the fee-for-service system. Capitation permits the provider and the managed care organization to predict the expenses and revenues that will be generated by a defined population. The capitated amount is set by the number of lives covered, rather than the number of services provided, and is usually expressed in units of dollars per member per month, abbreviated as PMPM.

This means that the primary care physician is paid the same amount of money each month regardless of how many patients he or she sees (in the capitated population), or what services he or she provides to those patients. This results in fixed payment amount, providing no economic advantage for increasing utilization.

When catastrophic cases occur, requiring increased amounts of care, the primary care physician limits his or her degree of financial risk by purchasing reinsurance or stop-loss insurance. One of the advantages under capitation is the incentive for physicians to appreciate the need to manage the health of the entire population as a way of keeping costs under control. It brings into better focus the need to increase preventative services, and identify diseases early. For example, mammography screening becomes not just a public health issue, but may save the physician the expense of caring for an end-stage breast cancer patient.

As a means of limiting utilization, capitation has proven very effective. When capitation is introduced into a fee-for-service market, a 25% reduction in outpatient utilization results. The minority of the reductions represent a decrease in utilization in specialty consultations and specialty procedures.

Critics of capitation have alleged that it encourages physicians to make choices that will maximize practice revenue and minimize expense, rather than ensuring the best care for their enrolled patients. While most physicians and their staffs are conscientious and ethical, a bias to minimize the utilization of capitated patients, and increase the utilization of fee-for-service patients, does exist. This bias has done much to promote the impression that physicians are not working in the best interest of their patients when their patients are capitated.

Advantages of Capitation:

- Decrease utilization and costs (especially costs associated with specialty services)
- Decrease primary care physician's tendency to "over treat"
- Improve cash flow
- Increase tendency to offer preventative services
- Increase tendency to focus on the early detection of disease

Disadvantages of Capitation include:

- Increase tendency to under treat capitated patients
- Increase tendency of physicians to focus on fee-for-service patients
- Increase suspicion of patients about motivations of physicians

Coordination of Benefits (COB)

Coordination of benefits is a process utilized by insurers to coordinate claims payments. The COB process is structured so that the payments made to the insured do not exceed the expenses incurred. Without COB, an individual might be reimbursed more than 100% of the cost for medical care.

Coordination of benefits provisions were developed during the 1950s when it became common for people to have more than one source of insurance. Almost all group health insurers have COB provisions in their contracts with enrollees. COB rules are not federally mandated, but are adopted by states and individual insurance companies. Despite the voluntary nature of these rules, the compliance rate is very high. COB saves between 4 and 9% in claims costs.

A set of rules has been agreed to by the National Association of Insurance Commissioners (NIAC). The rules specify who pays for an individual's health care claims when the individual has more than one insurance coverage. Most states and insurance companies have adopted these rules. In fact, insurance plans without COB provisions always pay first.

The following are the rules of COB adopted by the National Association of Insurance Commissioners:

1. The insurance plan covering the individual as an employee pays first.
2. The plan covering the individual as a dependent pays second.
3. If both plans cover the individual as a dependent, the plan of the employee, whose birthday occurs earliest in the year pays first. This rule ("the birthday rule") applies only if both plans have adopted the birthday rule and the parents are married.
4. If either plan has not adopted the birthday rule and the parents are married, the plan of the male parent will pay first.
5. If the parents are divorced, the plan awarded primary responsibility by the court will pay first.
6. If the parents are divorced and there is no court-determined primary, then the following order will be used:
   - The plan of the parent with custody of the child will pay first.
   - The plan of the spouse of the parent with custody will be second.
   - The plan of the parent without custody will be next.
   - The plan of the spouse of the non-custodial parent will be last.

7.   The plan covering an individual as an active employee will pay first; the plan covering that individual as an inactive employee (such as a retiree, or laid-off employee) will pay second.
8.   The plan covering an individual as a COBRA (Consolidated Omnibus Budget Reconciliation Act) will be secondary to a plan covering that individual as an employee, a member, or a dependent.
9.   If none of the above rules results in a determination, then the plan covering the individual for the longest period of time will pay first.

Medical Necessity

Defining medical necessity is a problem that gets to the heart of health insurance. All health insurance policies state in some fashion that only "medically necessary" care will be reimbursed. However, the definition of the term "medical necessity" is ambiguous at best and leads to a lack of consistency among insurance plans in the way that they interpret medical necessity. In fact, a 1994 survey by the U.S. General Accounting Office revealed "substantial variation" in the denial rates for lack of medical necessity.

Problems with the Definition

Current corporate definitions of medical necessity are crafted in weak terms or in circular language. For example, a typical corporate definition describes medical necessity as: "Those procedures, treatments or supplies that are recommended by a licensed physician are appropriate, reasonable and accepted in the medical community for treating the disease in question and are not experimental or investigational, and are not custodial."

What is "appropriate, reasonable and acceptable?" What is experimental? What is custodial? It is not made clear to either the insured or the insurer's administrators.

Further complicating this issue is the fact that the insurer or the insurer's review organization typically reserves the right to determine what procedures are medically necessary. With the spectrum of meanings available in this definition, discrepancies over coverage issues naturally arise. When litigated, the courts have consistently construed the meaning in favor of the insured.

Reasonable Expectations

When cases of medical necessity are litigated, the courts place significant weight on the *reasonable expectations* of a layperson in the position of a patient. The court implies that if "reasonable laypersons" could expect a certain medical benefit under their contract, then they may be entitled to it. This expectation principle is used by the courts to justify granting a wide range of benefits to the subscriber that the insurer's policy language appears to exclude. In the *Ponder* case, the insurer denied treatment for temporomandibular joint syndrome, because it was excluded by the contract. The fairness of the contract was questioned because the purchaser of the insurance did not understand the meaning of the exclusionary criteria in the contract. As the court stated, subscribers "could only discover what they had bought with their premiums as their diseases were diagnosed, and they found out to their sorrow, the true meaning of those mysterious words in their insurance contracts."

Solutions

A procedural approach to defining medical necessity effectively bolsters an insurance company's contractual definition, especially when the definition is contested in court. The solution lies in the hands of the medical director. His or her responsibility is to manage the process of claims adjudication for medical necessity. The medical director must ensure, on the one hand, that subscribers receive everything they paid for and are not subjected to ineffective or harmful treatment and, on the other hand, that the process for making these decisions is fair, reproducible, and based on the best medical information available. This is called a *procedural definition* of medical necessity.

The best solution, therefore, lies not only in improving a contractual definition that contains exhaustive exclusionary criteria, but also in defining a process for determining medical necessity. The goal of this process is to improve the health of subscribers and protect them from harm through rigorous, scientifically sound, and manifestly fair methods. This process entails the following procedures:

- *Firmly establish the intent of the medical necessity clause in all documentation.* The intent of medical necessity determinations is to protect the subscribers from irregular, dangerous, or unnecessary procedures. The intent of medical necessity should be clearly stated in the contract, the subscribers' handbook, and any other communications between the subscriber and the insurer.
- *Implement medical oversight.* The medical director, a licensed physician, should review and approve all benefit denials.
- *Eliminate perverse incentives.* The compensation of the medical director and the utilization staff should not depend on the number of dollars saved through claims denials, but on their adherence to the tenets and goals of the review process.
- *Be aware of high-profile cases.* The medical director, risk manager, and corporate counsel should be aware of all high-profile cases (i.e., those most likely to be legally contested or result in unfavorable media coverage, such as expensive, high-risk procedures; bone marrow transplants, neurosurgeries, and treatment of infants in pediatric intensive care units or oncology wards). These cases, which have a high potential for grievances and appeals, are more intensely scrutinized by subscribers, regulators, and the courts. They should therefore generate a commensurate amount of investigation and consideration by the medical director and the case management staff.
- *Consult objective specialists.* Cases that fall outside the medical director's area of expertise should be reviewed by independent, external, unbiased medical consultants.
- *Request and review the medical records.* The medical director must be alert to extenuating circumstances or clinical issues that may mitigate the claims denial. Medical directors should record the time, date, and finding from the chart review and any subsequent interviews or examination in their case notes.
- *Speak with the patient's attending physician.* To obtain the complete clinical picture, the medical director should speak with all physicians involved in the patient's care.
- *Document all decisions.* Documentation of decisions surrounding denials is essential. These documents should include both the cause of denial (e.g., not medically necessary) and the reasons for it (e.g., does not meet inclusion criteria). Any literature or expert testimony relied on in making the decision should be included in the file.
- *Maintain denial database.* When denying claims, the medical director should review past decisions regarding the type of treatment under consideration. Lack of consistency in decision making opens the insurer to criticisms of arbitrary and capricious conduct. Insurers should maintain a database of prior decisions on medical necessity, so that

these decisions can be reviewed and used to guide research and investigations into future claims issues.

- *Address subscribers' expectations.* Insurers must address the reasonable expectations of their subscribers. Although a full explanation in the subscribers' manual is a good start, most subscribers do not read this document. Timely information about benefits and education about disease states is useful to subscribers and can be carried out by the case management staff.
- *Regularly review utilization review procedures, including software edits in the claims system that defines covered benefits.* Inaccuracies in the claims system may lead to unwarranted denials.

A comprehensive definition of medical necessity, while highly desirable, no longer satisfies subscribers or protects insurers against litigation. In determining medical necessity, insurers should strive to provide subscribers with the safest, most efficacious care needed. Insurer's attention to this process, rather than a slavish dependence on the definition alone, will improve subscriber satisfaction and decrease liability. Educating subscribers about the contract's benefits will temper their expectations when benefits are required. The medical director should control the process of determining what is medically necessary, consult experts liberally, and document extensively. An effective Case Manager should understand the definition of medical necessity as stated in the insured's contract, as well as the limitations of that definition. Counseling the insureds on what medical necessity means, how it is defined, and how discrepancies are adjudicated will help to manage their expectations and needless anxieties.

Reinsurance or Stop-Loss Insurance

To reinsure is defined as the act of insuring again, especially by transferring in whole or in part a risk already covered under an existing contract. Reinsurance then is an insurance policy purchased by an insurer in order to reduce financial risk. Reinsurance policies insure against the occurrence of losses greater than some predefined limit.

Health care plans, insurance companies, and individual physicians (operating under risk contracts) purchase reinsurance policies to reduce their financial risk when paying the health care claims of an individual or a group. This reinsurance is sometimes called stop-loss or threshold insurance and may apply to the aggregate expense of multiple individuals (i.e., total claims for an insured population for 1 year) or to the expenses of a single enrollee. For example, Health Plan A receives a million dollars of premium for insuring the health care of 1,000 enrollees. A single catastrophic case, such as a premature infant in the neonatal intensive care unit for 6 months could eliminate all profits, and perhaps bring the company to insolvency. Even a small group of severely ill patients could wipe out the health plan's earnings. For these two types of occurrence, the health care plan purchases stop-loss insurance or reinsurance. The first type of reinsurance sets a predefined dollar limit on any *individual's loss*, for example, $2,500 per enrollee. In this example, the health care plan is at risk up to $2,500 on any one enrollee; after that, the reinsurance company pays the bills for that enrollee's care. The second type of reinsurance sets a predefined dollar limit on the *aggregate loss* of the health care plan. To use Health Plan A as an example, it might buy a reinsurance policy that would set a limit of $500,000 in losses. After that limit is reached, the reinsurer would cover losses above one-half million dollars.

Reinsurers of health care companies base their premiums (or cost of their insurance) on several variables. They are:

Threshold: At what dollar level does the reinsurer start paying. An insurer makes plans to cover health care claims up to a certain limit. This limit may be $5,000, $10,000, or $50,000. When claims are received for amounts above this limit, the reinsurer pays. The higher the threshold the insurer sets, the lower the reinsurance rate.

Health Risk of Population: Insurers and reinsurers base their premiums on the likelihood of the patients requiring medical services. The higher the risk of illness or injury, the higher the insurance premium will be. The risk of getting ill or injured is related to the age, occupation and health experience of an individual or group. For example, those that work in heavy construction are more likely to get injured than those that do office work, therefore, their health insurance premiums will be higher. Similarly, those groups or individuals that have a history of high medical resource utilization are expected to have a similar pattern of utilization in the future. They will therefore pay higher premiums for health insurance.

Benefits: The liability or risk of exceeding the claims threshold is related to the benefits an insurer extends to a group. The more generous the benefit package, the easier it will be for an individual or group to exceed its threshold. An insurer can reduce his risk of exceeding his reinsurance threshold by eliminating high cost or highly utilized procedures or treatments from the benefits package. For example, cosmetic surgery or treatments for infertility are commonly excluded in health insurance policies.

When a Case Manager Extends "Extracontractual" Benefits

It should be noted, that when a Case Manager extends (working for the insurer) "extracontractual" benefits to an individual, this unfairly changes the assumptions upon which a reinsurer has based his premiums. In order to avoid a breech of the reinsurance contract, the insurer does not charge the costs of extracontractual benefits against his reinsurance threshold.

Alternate Benefit Plans/Extracontractual Benefits

Alternate benefit plans and extracontractual benefits are health insurance benefits given to a beneficiary that are not contained in the beneficiary's insurance policy. The insurer extends these benefits to the insured when two conditions can be met. These are:

- The benefit will aid the patient (i.e., it is medically necessary for the patient)
- The utilization of the extracontractual benefit will decrease the overall cost of care for the insurer (i.e., financially advantageous to the insurer)

For example, an insured is a patient in the hospital receiving only wound care that could be offered at home. The patient's insurance policy does not have a home care benefit, therefore wound care must be offered at the hospital at considerable expense. It makes economic sense for the insurer to offer the patient a home care benefit, because doing so saves the insurer the cost of hospitalization.

The provision of extracontractual benefits is not a discretionary right of the Case Manager. Case Managers, acting as agents for the insurer, are empowered through their job description or by provisions in their contract to offer extracontractual benefits. This is an instance when the Case Manager's obligation to act as an advocate for the patient and the insurer has a harmonious resolution.

Case Managers Responsibilities When Offering Alternate Benefit Plans/Extracontractual Benefits

In order to prevent confusion on the part of the patient and other insureds, the Case Manager should abide by the following rules when offering extracontractual benefits:

- *Obtain Approval from the Referral Source.* The referral source must approve alternate benefit plans prior to the patient and provider being alerted. The request to the referral source is best done interactively, as over the telephone. This way the Case Manager can present the entire case, the rationale for "flexing" the benefit, the cost savings projected for the alternate benefit plan, and answer any questions that may arise. It is prudent to then obtain the approval in writing.
- *Inform the insured of the nature of the benefit.* The insured should be made aware that the benefit being offered is outside his benefit package and is being offered because it is financially advantageous for the insurer. It is helpful to memorialize this information in a letter to the insured. This will help to manage the patient's expectations when he or she requests other "non-covered" benefits.
- *Set time limits.* Extracontractual benefits are only financially advantageous to the insurer when the extent of the benefit is known. For example, when offering home physical rehabilitation care to a patient recovering from an injury, a Case Manager assumes that the cost of home rehabilitation is less expensive than hospital-based rehabilitation. In order to correctly determine the cost of home rehabilitation versus the hospital-based rehabilitation, a Case Manager must know not just the per-diem cost, but the total number of days of rehabilitation as well. Once begun, some benefits are difficult to stop, especially when the patient and family become used to or dependent upon the benefit. The costs of these "prolonged" benefits can far outstrip the costs of the "expensive" care they were meant to replace. It is imperative, therefore, for the Case Manager to describe to the insured the reason for the benefit and clearly articulate the length of time it will be offered.
- *Document, Document, Document.* As stated above, confusion can occur when extracontractual benefits are offered and not only with the insured receiving the benefit. Other persons insured by the same company might request benefits that they have seen others receive. These others may be family members, neighbors, coworkers and health care providers. It becomes difficult to deny these requests when the insurer has no record of why he disregarded the benefits contract in the past. Accusations of arbitrary and capricious conduct or discrimination may be leveled at the insurer who appears to offer different levels of benefits to different enrollees. The need for adequate documentation is clear. The documentation should include, but not be limited to:
  - Letter to the insurer notifying them what benefits are being offered, what they are replacing or trying to avoid, and what the cost, and savings will be.
  - Letter to the employer (in the case of third party administration) notifying them what benefits are being offered, what they are replacing or trying to avoid, and what the cost, and the savings will be.
  - Letter to the insured notifying him or her of the new benefit, the reason for the benefit and the limits of the benefit.
  - Letters to the providers of care in the case notifying them of the new benefit, the reason for the benefit, and the limits of the benefit.
  - Letters to the claims administrator notifying them of the alternate benefit so that claims are adjudicated per the alternate benefit agreement.

- Case Manager's report: the narrative summary of individual case activity and cost savings.
- An extracontractual benefits log: the database for all extracontractual benefits offered by the Case Manager or all Case Managers in a single office. It contains the names of the insured, the benefit extended, benefit replaced, and saving accrued.

Extracontractual Benefits and Reinsurance

Reinsurance companies are institutions that indemnify insurance companies. The cost of extracontractual benefits is the sole responsibility of the insurer. Therefore, the careful documentation of all costs associated with extracontractual benefits must be reported to the insurer, so that the reinsurer will not be billed.

Prior Approval

It is important for Case Managers to understand the insurance policy and benefits the patient has in planning his care. One of the most important aspects of the policy is whether or not there is a precertification requirement and, if so, what requires prior approval. The Case Manager will need to coordinate the needed referrals for precertification with the primary physician. The limitations of certain benefits come into play when a patient requires extensive rehabilitation. Does the patient have a maximum of 40 visits per calendar year for physical therapy? Is the patient's inpatient rehabilitation benefit unlimited? Does the patient only have access to a durable medical equipment benefit if arranged through a specific network vendor? Does the case management benefit allow for free rein in choosing providers and arranging alternate benefit plans? Most payers want to be involved in approving alternate benefit plans or extracontractual benefits. It is important to document the payer source's approval and to communicate that approval to the actual claims processor. It is recommended that the Case Manager speak to the person delegated to approve or deny such benefit plan recommendations rather than initially putting the request in writing. That way any questions can be answered immediately, and the entire situation can be spelled out, including the cost effectiveness of the outlined plan. It is important to communicate estimated timeframes, negotiated rates, and any comparison to whatever other treatment is contemplated. For instance, if there is no home care benefit without a hospitalization and a patient requires a course of intravenous (IV) antibiotics for 6 weeks, it is effective to compare the cost of the hospitalization versus the cost of home IV therapy. That difference is often called *hard savings*. The total daily rate for the hospitalization that was avoided is referred to as *soft savings or potential savings*. Another way of looking at the hard savings is that it is the difference between the costs that would have been incurred had there been no case management intervention and the actual cost due to case management intervention. Soft savings are usually "in lieu" of some other therapy or treatment plan. The savings realized from subtracting the cost of a subacute facility from an acute care facility is considered soft savings, while the savings from negotiating off the usual fee at the subacute facility is considered hard savings. Once the payer or referral source has agreed to the alternate benefit plan or extracontractual benefit, it is recommended that a specific letter detailing the agreement be faxed or mailed to the payer or referral source for signature and the returned for the Case Manager's records. If the bills are sent to the Case Manager for approval prior to sending them for claims adjudication, it is advantageous to attach a copy of the extracontractual agreement to assure proper payment.

Negotiating

Case Managers need to maintain a file of basic costs for the items they negotiate routinely. Most insurance companies have predetermined fee schedules. They are usually based on *reasonable and customary* or *usual, customary and reasonable (R&C/UCR)*. Although there are many methods to determining these fees, they are generally based on submitted bills in a geographic region (zip code), and the charges are either averaged or the bottom and top 10% are thrown out and the median charge is deemed reasonable and customary. Another method is to utilize some statistical database such as HIAA (Health Insurance Association of America) data to set usual, customary, and reasonable. A third method is to base R&C/UCR on the Medicare fee schedule. It is common to negotiate durable medical equipment, IVs, nursing visits, etc., at a percentage off the Medicare fee schedule. The *Red Book*[3] is an invaluable tool when negotiating prescription medications. This lists the AWP (average wholesale price) for all medications. The Case Manager can be more effective when utilizing national resources such as the *Red Book* as a basis for negotiating discounts.

Quality Medical Services

The Case Manager has a dual responsibility in arranging for medically necessary services, providing cost effective care *and* quality services. The Case Manager has several options to assure quality providers. He or she can use an established network of providers that have been credentialled by the insurer, he or she can look for board certified providers, for institutions accredited by the Joint Commission for Accreditation of Health Organizations (JCAHO or Joint Commission), Centers of Excellence, facilities accredited by the Commission on Accreditation of Rehabilitation Facilities (CARF), or specialty centers. By utilizing well-established or credentialled providers, the risk is minimized for a poor outcome and the opportunity maximized for the best outcome for the patient and all concerned in his or her care.

REFERENCES

1.   Section 1924 of the Social Security Act; 42 U.S.C. 1396r-5.
2.   Section 1917(c) of the Social Security Act; 42 U.S.C. 1396p(c).
3.   *The Red Book*. Montvale, NJ: Medical Economics; 1998.

1) **Which of the following organizations are exempt from the mandates of the Americans with Disabilities Act?**

    1. Small businesses with fewer than 15 employees
    2. The federal government
    3. Native American tribes
    4. Software manufacturers
        A. 1, 3
        B. 2, 4
        C. 1, 2, 3
        D. All of the above
        E. None of the above

2) **Which of the following organizations must comply with the mandates of the Americans with Disabilities Act?**

    1. Small businesses with less than 100 employees
    2. The federal government
    3. Multinational corporations with headquarters in the USA
    4. Native American tribes
        A. 1, 3
        B. 2, 4
        C. 1, 2, 3
        D. All of the above
        E. None of the above

3) **Under the proscriptions of the Americans with Disabilities Act, which of the following are considered "reasonable accommodations" by the employer?**

    1. Providing automatic doors and wheelchair ramps in the employer's facilities
    2. Modifying equipment to accommodate disabled employees
    3. Providing qualified readers for the visually handicapped
    4. Providing qualified interpreters for the hearing impaired
        A. 1, 3
        B. 2, 4
        C. 1, 2, 3
        D. All of the above
        E. None of the above

4)   Under the proscriptions of the Americans with Disabilities Act, which of the following are considered "reasonable accommodations" by the employer?

1. Making the disabled "typist" a receptionist who answers phones only
2. Modifying equipment to accommodate disabled employees
3. Making the paralyzed "ballet dancer" a "theatrical director" of the ballet company
4. Providing qualified interpreters for the hearing impaired
   A. 1, 3
   B. 2, 4
   C. 1, 2, 3
   D. All of the above
   E. None of the above

5)   Under the proscriptions of the Americans with Disabilities Act, which of the following are *not* considered "reasonable accommodations" by the employer?

1. Making the disabled "typist" a receptionist who answers phones only
2. Modifying equipment to accommodate disabled employees
3. Making the paralyzed "ballet dancer" a "theatrical director" of the ballet company
4. Providing qualified interpreters for the hearing impaired
   A. 1, 3
   B. 2, 4
   C. 1, 2, 3
   D. All of the above
   E. None of the above

6)   Which of the following would help to define the "essential functions of the job" under the mandates of the Americans with Disabilities Act?

1. The job function takes up the majority of the employee's time.
2. The job function is described in the collective bargaining agreement.
3. The job function is recorded in the written job description.
4. The job function in question is considered "essential" to the jobs of others in the same or similar job.
   A. 1, 3
   B. 2, 4
   C. 1, 2, 3
   D. All of the above
   E. None of the above

7)   Which of the following would *not* help to define the "essential functions of the job" under the mandates of the Americans with Disabilities Act?

1. The job function takes up the minority of the employee's time.
2. The job function is described in the collective bargaining agreement.
3. The job function is recorded in the written job description; the job description was developed after the employee was hired.
4. The job function in question is considered "essential" to the jobs of others in the same or similar job.
   A. 1, 3
   B. 2, 4
   C. 1, 2, 3
   D. All of the above
   E. None of the above

8) **Which of the following would be helpful in defining the "essential functions of the job" under the mandates of the Americans with Disabilities Act?**

   1. The job function takes up the minority of the employee's time.
   2. The job function is described in the collective bargaining agreement.
   3. The job function is recorded in the written job description; the job description was developed after the employee was hired.
   4. The job function in question is considered "essential" to the jobs of others in the same or similar job.
      A. 1, 3
      B. 2, 4
      C. 1, 2, 3
      D. All of the above
      E. None of the above

9) **Under the tenets of the Americans with Disabilities Act, which of the following is (are) true regarding the definition of "qualified individuals"?**

   1. Not all disabled individuals of working age are "qualified individuals" under the ADA.
   2. Requisite job skills are essential to be a "qualified individual" under the ADA.
   3. Requisite job experience is essential to be a "qualified individual" under the ADA.
   4. Requisite educational background for the job is essential to be a "qualified individual" under the ADA.
      A. 1, 3
      B. 2, 4
      C. 1, 2, 3
      D. All of the above
      E. None of the above

10) **Under the tenets of the Americans with Disabilities Act, which of the following is (are) true regarding the definition of "qualified individuals"?**

   1. The individual must meet the legal definition of "disability" under the ADA.
   2. Requisite job skills are essential to be a "qualified individual" under the ADA.
   3. Requisite job experience is essential to be a "qualified individual" under the ADA.
   4. Requisite educational background for the job is not essential to be a "qualified individual" under the ADA.
      A. 1, 3
      B. 2, 4
      C. 1, 2, 3
      D. All of the above
      E. None of the above

11) **Under the tenets of the Americans with Disabilities Act, which of the following is (are) *not* true regarding the definition of "qualified individuals"?**

   1. All disabled individuals of working age are "qualified individuals" under the ADA.
   2. Requisite job skills are essential to be a "qualified individual" under the ADA.
   3. Requisite job experience is *not* essential to be a "qualified individual" under the ADA, since disabled workers often cannot get job experience.
   4. Requisite educational background for the job is essential to be a "qualified individual" under the ADA.
      A. 1, 3
      B. 2, 4
      C. 1, 2, 3
      D. All of the above
      E. None of the above

12)   **Which of the following statements concerning alcoholism is (are) true, under the tenets of the Americans with Disabilities Act?**

1.   An employer may not discriminate because of a history of alcohol abuse.
2.   An employer may not discriminate because of current alcohol abuse.
3.   An employer may not monitor alcohol intake when the employee is on his own time.
4.   An employer may not fire an alcoholic due to poor job performance, if the poor performance is due to alcohol abuse.
   A.   1, 3
   B.   2, 4
   C.   1, 2, 3
   D.   All of the above
   E.   None of the above

13)   **Which of the following statements concerning alcoholism is (are) true, under the tenets of the Americans with Disabilities Act?**

1.   An employer may not discriminate against an employee because of a history of alcohol abuse.
2.   An employer may not discriminate against an employee because of behavior problems due to alcohol abuse.
3.   An employer may not discriminate against an employee because of current alcohol abuse.
4.   An employer may not fire an alcoholic due to poor job performance, if the poor performance is due to alcohol abuse.
   A.   1, 3
   B.   2, 4
   C.   1, 2, 3
   D.   All of the above
   E.   None of the above

14)   **Which of the following statements concerning drug abuse is (are) true, under the tenets of the Americans with Disabilities Act?**

1.   An employer may not discriminate against an employee because of a history of drug abuse.
2.   An employer may not discriminate against an employee because of behavior problems due to illicit drug abuse.
3.   An employer may discriminate against an employee because of current drug abuse.
4.   An employer may not fire an employee with a drug addiction due to poor job performance, if the poor performance is due to drug abuse.
   A.   1, 3
   B.   2, 4
   C.   1, 2, 3
   D.   All of the above
   E.   None of the above

15)   **Which of the following statements concerning drug abuse is (are) *not* true, under the tenets of the Americans with Disabilities Act?**

1.   An employer may not discriminate against an employee because of a history of drug abuse.
2.   An employer may not discriminate against an employee because of behavior problems due to illicit drug abuse.
3.   An employer may discriminate against an employee because of current drug abuse.
4.   An employer may not fire an employee with a drug addiction due to poor job performance, if the poor performance is due to drug abuse.
   A.   1, 3
   B.   2, 4
   C.   1, 2, 3
   D.   All of the above
   E.   None of the above

16) **Which of the following statements are true, regarding the Women's Health and Cancer Rights Act?**

1. It is a new law, enacted as part of the Omnibus Appropriations Bill.
2. It assures coverage for surgery of the contralateral breast to provide a symmetrical appearance after mastectomy.
3. It amended ERISA to require both health plans and self-insured plans to provide coverage for mastectomies and certain reconstructive surgeries.
4. It assures coverage for breast prostheses after mastectomy.
   - A. 1, 3
   - B. 2, 4
   - C. 1, 2, 3
   - D. All of the above
   - E. None of the above

17) **Which of the following statements are true, regarding the Women's Health and Cancer Rights Act?**

1. It assures rehabilitative therapies such as physical therapy to postmastectomy patients.
2. It assures coverage for surgery of the contralateral breast to provide a symmetrical appearance after mastectomy.
3. It assures coverage for postsurgical care such as lymphedema treatment.
4. It assures coverage for breast prostheses after mastectomy.
   - A. 1, 3
   - B. 2, 4
   - C. 1, 2, 3
   - D. All of the above
   - E. None of the above

18) **Which of the following statements are true, regarding the Women's Health and Cancer Rights Act?**

1. It was instituted as part of an Amendment to the Civil Rights Act of 1963.
2. It assures coverage for surgery of the contralateral breast to provide a symmetrical appearance after mastectomy.
3. It amended ERISA to require only health care plans to provide coverage for mastectomies and certain reconstructive surgeries; self-insured plans are excluded from the mandates of this Act.
4. It assures coverage for breast prostheses after mastectomy.
   - A. 1, 3
   - B. 2, 4
   - C. 1, 2, 3
   - D. All of the above
   - E. None of the above

19) **Which of the following statements are *not* true, regarding the Women's Health and Cancer Rights Act?**

1. It assures that coverage for purely cosmetic surgery of the breast after mastectomy is not allowed.
2. It assures coverage for surgery of the contralateral breast to provide a symmetrical appearance after mastectomy.
3. It amended ERISA to require only health care plans to provide coverage for mastectomies and certain reconstructive surgeries; self-insured plans are excluded from the mandates of this Act.
4. It assures coverage for breast prostheses after mastectomy.
   - A. 1, 3
   - B. 2, 4
   - C. 1, 2, 3
   - D. All of the above
   - E. None of the above

20) **Which of the following statements are true, regarding the Women's Health and Cancer Rights Act?**

1. Costs associated with a plan's coinsurance are waived by this Act.
2. It assures coverage for surgery of the contralateral breast to provide a symmetrical appearance after mastectomy.
3. Costs associated with a plan's deductibles are waived by this Act.
4. It assures coverage for breast prostheses after mastectomy.
   - A. 1, 3
   - B. 2, 4
   - C. 1, 2, 3
   - D. All of the above
   - E. None of the above

21) **Which of the following statements are *not* true, regarding the Women's Health and Cancer Rights Act?**

1. Costs associated with a plan's coinsurance are waived by this Act.
2. It assures coverage for surgery of the contralateral breast to provide a symmetrical appearance after mastectomy.
3. Costs associated with a plan's deductibles are waived by this Act.
4. It assures coverage for breast prostheses after mastectomy.
   - A. 1, 3
   - B. 2, 4
   - C. 1, 2, 3
   - D. All of the above
   - E. None of the above

22) **Which of the following statements are true, regarding the Women's Health and Cancer Rights Act?**

1. A group health plan is prohibited from denying a patient eligibility to enroll or renew coverage solely for the purpose of avoiding the requirements of the Act.
2. A group health plan is prohibited from inducing an attending physician to limit the care that is required under the Act.
3. The Act specifically states that its provisions shall not be construed to prevent a group health plan from negotiating the level and type of reimbursement with a provider for care provided in accordance with the Act.
4. A group health plan may penalize, reduce or limit the reimbursement to physicians who provide women's health care in order to reduce the utilization of services associated with this Act.
   - A. 1, 3
   - B. 2, 4
   - C. 1, 2, 3
   - D. All of the above
   - E. None of the above

23) **Which of the following statements are true, regarding the Women's Health and Cancer Rights Act?**

1. A group health plan may deny a patient eligibility to enroll or renew coverage solely for the purpose of avoiding the requirements of the Act.
2. A group health plan may induce an attending physician to limit the care that is required under the Act.
3. A group health plan may penalize, reduce or limit the reimbursement to physicians who provide women's health care in order to reduce the utilization of services associated with this Act.
4. The Act specifically states that its provisions shall be construed to prevent a group health plan from negotiating the level and type of reimbursement with a provider for care provided in accordance with the Act.

    A. 1, 3
    B. 2, 4
    C. 1, 2, 3
    D. All of the above
    E. None of the above

24) **Which of the following statements are *not* true, regarding the Women's Health and Cancer Rights Act?**

  1. A group health plan may not deny a patient eligibility to enroll or renew coverage solely for the purpose of avoiding the requirements of the Act.
  2. A group health plan may induce an attending physician to limit the care that is required under the Act.
  3. A group health plan may not penalize, reduce or limit the reimbursement to physicians who provide women's health care in order to reduce the utilization of services associated with this Act.
  4. The Act specifically states that its provisions shall be construed to prevent a group health plan from negotiating the level and type of reimbursement with a provider for care provided in accordance with the Act.

    A. 1, 3
    B. 2, 4
    C. 1, 2, 3
    D. All of the above
    E. None of the above

25) **Which of the following plan types are bound by the requirements of the Women's Health and Cancer Rights Act?**

  1. Private employer plans
  2. Public employer plans
  3. Health insurance companies
  4. Non–federal government self-insured plans

    A. -1, 3
    B. 2, 4
    C. 1, 2, 3
    D. All of the above
    E. None of the above

26) **Which of the following plan types are *not* bound by the requirements of the Women's Health and Cancer Rights Act?**

  1. Private employer plans
  2. Self-insured automotive manufacturers
  3. Health insurance companies
  4. Self-insured pharmaceutical manufacturers

    A. 1, 3
    B. 2, 4
    C. 1, 2, 3
    D. All of the above
    E. None of the above

27) **Which of the following statements are true regarding unemployment insurance?**

  1. Financing of unemployment benefits are uniform from state to state.
  2. Unemployment compensation benefits guarantee a replacement of 50% of salary.
  3. Benefits are never extended past the usual maximum length of benefit.
  4. All states pay a minimum of 46 weeks of unemployment benefits.

    A. 1, 3
    B. 2, 4
    C. 1, 2, 3
    D. All of the above
    E. None of the above

28) **Which of the following statements are true regarding unemployment insurance?**
1. Financing of unemployment benefits varies from state to state.
2. Unemployment compensation benefits guarantee a replacement of 50% of salary.
3. Benefits may be extended past the usual maximum length of benefit, during periods of heavy unemployment.
4. All states pay a minimum of 46 weeks of unemployment benefits.
   A. 1, 3
   B. 2, 4
   C. 1, 2, 3
   D. All of the above
   E. None of the above

29) **Which of the following statements are true regarding unemployment insurance?**
1. Financing of unemployment benefits are uniform from state to state.
2. Unemployment compensation benefits are intended to replace of 50% of an average worker's salary.
3. Benefits are never extended past the usual maximum length of benefit.
4. All states pay a minimum of 26 weeks of unemployment benefits.
   A. 1, 3
   B. 2, 4
   C. 1, 2, 3
   D. All of the above
   E. None of the above

30) **Which of the following statements are *not* true regarding unemployment insurance?**
1. Financing of unemployment benefits varies from state to state.
2. Unemployment compensation benefits guarantee a replacement of 50% of salary.
3. Benefits may be extended past the usual maximum length of benefit, during periods of heavy unemployment.
4. All states pay a minimum of 46 weeks of unemployment benefits.
   A. 1, 3
   B. 2, 4
   C. 1, 2, 3
   D. All of the above
   E. None of the above

31) **Which of the following statements are *not* true regarding unemployment insurance?**
1. Financing of unemployment benefits are uniform from state to state.
2. Unemployment compensation benefits are guaranteed to replace 50% of an average worker's salary.
3. Benefits are never extended past the usual maximum length of benefit.
4. All states pay a minimum of 26 weeks of unemployment benefits.
   A. 1, 3
   B. 2, 4
   C. 1, 2, 3
   D. All of the above
   E. None of the above

32) **Which of the following is (are) true regarding Workers' Compensation insurance?**
1. The scope of coverage varies from state to state.
2. Benefits generally include the cost of medical benefits and lost wages.
3. Employees are entitled to the level of benefit mandated by the state.
4. Self-funded health insurance programs are exempt from the mandates of Workers' Compensation regulations.

A. 1, 3
B. 2, 4
C. 1, 2, 3
D. All of the above
E. None of the above

33) **Which of the following is (are) true regarding Workers' Compensation insurance?**

1. The scope of coverage varies from state to state.
2. Benefits generally include the cost of legal bills only.
3. Employees are entitled to the level of benefit mandated by the state.
4. Self-funded health insurance programs are exempt from the mandates of Workers' Compensation regulations.
    A. 1, 3
    B. 2, 4
    C. 1, 2, 3
    D. All of the above
    E. None of the above

34) **Which of the following is (are) true regarding Workers' Compensation insurance?**

1. The scope of coverage for compensation benefits is uniform from state to state.
2. Benefits generally include the cost of legal bills only.
3. Employees are entitled to the level of benefit mandated by the employer only.
4. Self-funded health insurance programs are exempt from the mandates of Workers' Compensation regulations.
    A. 1, 3
    B. 2, 4
    C. 1, 2, 3
    D. All of the above
    E. None of the above

35) **Which of the following statements about the Workers' Compensation insurance program is (are) true?**

1. The cost of Workers' Compensation insurance is borne by the employer only.
2. The employee is expected to contribute 3% of his earned income toward Workers' Compensation premiums.
3. The Workers' Compensation program was intended to provide an impetus for an increase in employer safety programs.
4. Employer safety programs have dramatically decreased the industrial accident rate.
    A. 1, 3
    B. 2, 4
    C. 1, 2, 3
    D. All of the above
    E. None of the above

36) **Which of the following statements about the Workers' Compensation insurance program is (are) *not* true?**

1. The cost of Workers' Compensation insurance is borne by the employer only.
2. The employee is expected to contribute 3% of his earned income toward Workers' Compensation premiums.
3. The Workers' Compensation program was intended to provide an impetus for an increase in employer safety programs.
4. Employer safety programs have dramatically decreased the industrial accident rate.
    A. 1, 3
    B. 2, 4
    C. 1, 2, 3
    D. All of the above
    E. None of the above

37) **Which of the following statements about indemnity health insurance plans is (are) true?**
   1. It is a legal entity.
   2. It is licensed by the Federal Department of the Interior.
   3. It exists to provide health insurance to enrollees.
   4. It reimburses enrollees for the cost of any health care they desire.
      A. 1, 3
      B. 2, 4
      C. 1, 2, 3
      D. All of the above
      E. None of the above

38) **Which of the following statements about indemnity health insurance plans is (are) *not* true?**
   1. It is a legal entity.
   2. It is licensed by the Federal Department of the Interior.
   3. It exists to provide health insurance to enrollees.
   4. It reimburses enrollees for the cost of any health care they desire.
      A. 1, 3
      B. 2, 4
      C. 1, 2, 3
      D. All of the above
      E. None of the above

39) **Of the following, which are benefits that accrue to employers who choose to self-insure their employees' health care costs?**
   1. Increased service costs above those that are usually incurred by conventional insurers
   2. Exemption from providing benefits mandated by ERISA
   3. Increases in the costs of premium taxes
   4. Improved cash flow
      A. 1, 3
      B. 2, 4
      C. 1, 2, 3
      D. All of the above
      E. None of the above

40) **Of the following, which are *not* benefits that accrue to employers who choose to self-insure their employees' health care costs?**
   1. Increased service costs above those that are usually incurred by conventional insurers
   2. Exemption from providing benefits mandated by ERISA
   3. Increases in the costs of premium taxes
   4. Improved cash flow
      A. 1, 3
      B. 2, 4
      C. 1, 2, 3
      D. All of the above
      E. None of the above

41) **Which of the following reasons are important when considering if an employer should self-insure for employee health care costs?**
   1. Size of the president's yearly production bonus
   2. Size of employees' cash reserves
   3. Claims processing speed of the production workers
   4. Employer health status
      A. 1, 3
      B. 2, 4
      C. 1, 2, 3
      D. All of the above
      E. None of the above

42) **Which of the following reasons are important when considering if an employer should self-insure for employee health care costs?**
1. Size of the president's yearly production bonus
2. Size of employers' cash reserves
3. Claims processing speed of the production workers
4. Employees' health status
   A. 1, 3
   B. 2, 4
   C. 1, 2, 3
   D. All of the above
   E. None of the above

43) **Which of the following statements is (are) *not* true regarding Third Party Administrators (TPAs)?**
1. The TPA usually operates in the environment of the self-insured employer.
2. The TPA is an agent of the insurer.
3. The TPA is not party to the insurance contract and is not liable for losses incurred by employees.
4. The TPAs sole function is to provide "insurance type" administrative services to the employer.
   A. 1, 3
   B. 2, 4
   C. 1, 2, 3
   D. All of the above
   E. None of the above

44) **Which of the following statements is (are) true regarding Third Party Administrators (TPAs)?**
1. The TPA usually operate in the environment of the self-insured employer.
2. The TPA is an agent of the insurer.
3. The TPA is not party to the insurance contract and is not liable for losses incurred by employees.
4. The TPAs sole function is to provide "insurance type" administrative services to the employer.
   A. 1, 3
   B. 2, 4
   C. 1, 2, 3
   D. All of the above
   E. None of the above

45) **Which of the following statements is (are) *not* true regarding Third Party Administrators (TPAs)?**
1. The TPA is an agent of the employee.
2. The TPA usually operates in the environment of the self-insured employer.
3. The TPA is party to the insurance contract and is liable for losses incurred by employees.
4. The TPAs sole function is to provide "insurance type" administrative services to the employer.
   A. 1, 3
   B. 2, 4
   C. 1, 2, 3
   D. All of the above
   E. None of the above

46) **All of the following are functions normally provided by TPAs for employers:**
1. Medical claims adjudication and payment
2. Maintaining all records
3. Providing Case Management, utilization management, and quality management
4. Collecting and investing premium dollars

A. 1, 3
B. 2, 4
C. 1, 2, 3
D. All of the above
E. None of the above

47) **All of the following are functions normally provided by TPAs for employers, except:**
1. Medical claims adjudication and payment
2. Providing medical care for the employees
3. Providing Case Management, utilization management, and quality management
4. Collecting and investing premium dollars
   A. 1, 3
   B. 2, 4
   C. 1, 2, 3
   D. All of the above
   E. None of the above

48) **Which of the following is (are) benefits associated with employers utilizing a TPA?**
1. Access to state of the art hardware and software claims processing systems
2. Collection of premiums and investment of premium dollars for the employer
3. Objectivity and privacy in claims processing
4. Risk sharing with the TPA
   A. 1, 3
   B. 2, 4
   C. 1, 2, 3
   D. All of the above
   E. None of the above

49) **Which of the following is (are) *not* benefits associated with employers utilizing a TPA?**
1. Access to state of the art hardware and software claims processing systems
2. Collection of premiums, and investment of premium dollars for the employer
3. Objectivity and privacy in claims processing
4. Risk sharing with the TPA
   A. 1, 3
   B. 2, 4
   C. 1, 2, 3
   D. All of the above
   E. None of the above

50) **Of the following, who is *not* financially responsible for any personal injury or damaged property caused by car accidents?**
1. The state insurance fund
2. The car owner
3. The highway department
4. The car owner's insurer
   A. 1, 3
   B. 2, 4
   C. 1, 2, 3
   D. All of the above
   E. None of the above

51) **Which of the following determines minimum policy limits of Personal Injury Protection (PIP) automobile insurance?**
1. State insurance department
2. Accident rate in local community
3. State Insurance Commissioner
4. Driver's record of accidents

A. 1, 3
B. 2, 4
C. 1, 2, 3
D. All of the above
E. None of the above

52) **Which of the following does not determine minimum policy limits of PIP automobile insurance?**

1. State insurance department
2. Accident rate in local community
3. State Insurance Commissioner
4. Driver's record of accidents
    A. 1, 3
    B. 2, 4
    C. 1, 2, 3
    D. All of the above
    E. None of the above

53) **Which of the following characteristics are common to victims of automobile accidents?**

1. Senescence
2. Seriousness of injuries
3. Low incidence of head injuries
4. High incidence of spinal injuries
    A. 1, 3
    B. 2, 4
    C. 1, 2, 3
    D. All of the above
    E. None of the above

54) **Which of the following characteristics are *not* common to victims of automobile accidents?**

1. Senescence
2. Seriousness of injuries
3. Low incidence of head injuries
4. High incidence of spinal injuries
    A. 1, 3
    B. 2, 4
    C. 1, 2, 3
    D. All of the above
    E. None of the above

55) **Victims of automobile accidents may require which of the following services?**

A. Speech therapy
B. Cognitive therapy
C. Occupational therapy
D. All of the above
E. None of the above

56) **Personal Injury Protection (PIP) is designed to provide insurance coverage for which of the following people?**

1. Passengers involved in an auto accident
2. Drivers involved in an auto accident
3. Pedestrians involved in an auto accident
4. A window washer who falls off a ladder while at work
    A. 1, 3
    B. 2, 4
    C. 1, 2, 3
    D. All of the above
    E. None of the above

57) **Personal Injury Protection (PIP) is designed to provide insurance coverage for which of the following people?**

1. Passengers involved in an auto accident
2. Pedestrians involved in a drive by shooting
3. Pedestrians involved in an auto accident
4. A window washer who falls off a ladder while at work
    A. 1, 3
    B. 2, 4
    C. 1, 2, 3
    D. All of the above
    E. None of the above

58) **Which of the following people are protected by a Personal Injury Protection (PIP) policy?**

1. Passengers involved in an auto accident
2. Pedestrians involved in a slip and fall accident
3. Pedestrians involved in an auto accident
4. A driver who is the victim of domestic violence
    A. 1, 3
    B. 2, 4
    C. 1, 2, 3
    D. All of the above
    E. None of the above

59) **Which of the following people are *not* protected by a Personal Injury Protection (PIP) policy?**

1. Passengers involved in an auto accident
2. Pedestrians involved in a slip and fall accident
3. Pedestrians involved in an auto accident
4. A driver who is the victim of domestic violence
    A. 1, 3
    B. 2, 4
    C. 1, 2, 3
    D. All of the above
    E. None of the above

60) **If a worker is injured during his employment through the negligence of another worker he is entitled to:**

A. The full benefits of Workers' Compensation insurance allowable in his state
B. The full benefits allowable by the Workers' Compensation Commission in that state, minus the percentage of "contributory negligence" of the other employee, which is determined by the courts
C. No benefits, because the injury was not caused by the employer
D. Half the allowable state benefits

61) **A worker injured in the state of Florida is entitled to the same benefits as a worker injured in the state of Minnesota, when:**

A. The injury is exactly the same as the former worker.
B. The treating physician in Minnesota is in the same specialty as the treating physician in Florida.
C. The ICD-9 codes and the CPT codes are identical.
D. All of the above are true.
E. All of the above are false.

62) **If a part-time worker is injured while at work, he is entitled to the following WC benefits:**

   A. One-half the WC benefits of a full-time worker
   B. A percentage of benefits commensurate with the percentage of full-time employment that he works
   C. A percentage of WC benefits commensurate with the number of months worked, reaching full-time WC benefits after one year
   D. No WC benefits
   E. Full WC benefits

63) **Workers' Compensation benefits vary by:**

   A. State
   B. Term of employment
   C. Status of worker (full-time, part-time, temporary)
   D. Type of injury
   E. None of the above

64) **WC insurance differs from group health insurance in the following ways:**

   A. WC insurance must cover lost wages as well as the medical costs of injury.
   B. WC insurance benefits cannot be limited by ERISA pre-emptions.
   C. WC Insurance benefits are guaranteed to temporary and part-time workers.
   D. All of the above
   E. None of the above

65) **The length of time a patient is on disability can be prolonged by which of the following elements?**

   1. The availability of modified job functions
   2. Compliance with the medical regime
   3. Timely treatment
   4. Heavy lifting without light duty; alternate work availability
      A. 1, 3
      B. 2, 4
      C. 1, 2, 3
      D. All of the above
      E. None of the above

66) **A worker is injured at his job as a welder in the state of Texas. The employer has opted not to insure his employees by WC insurance. The employer may use which of the following defense strategies to defend himself from the employee's lawsuit?**

   A. Blame a coworker for causing the accident.
   B. Blame the employee for his own negligence.
   C. State that the injury is a risk inherent to the nature of the job.
   D. All of the above
   E. None of the above

67) **At what point in his employment is a worker entitled to WC insurance?**

   A. The first day of his employment
   B. After his probationary period is over
   C. After three months have elapsed
   D. Concurrent with his eligibility for group health insurance coverage
   E. None of the above

68) **In which of the following instances can a medical bill for an injured worker be denied by a WC policy administrator?**

   A. When the treatment is determined to be not medically necessary
   B. When the treatment is for a nonwork-related injury or illness
   C. When the treatment is thought to be excessive or inappropriate
   D. All of the above
   E. None of the above

69) **The Americans with Disabilities Act provides equal opportunity for persons with disabilities in all the following areas except:**

    1. Employment
    2. Government programs and services
    3. Telecommunications
    4. Housing
    5. Transportation
        A. 2
        B. 1, 2
        C. 4
        D. All of the above
        E. None of the above

70) **All of the following groups or institutions are exempt from compliance with the ADA recommendations except:**

    A. Native American tribes
    B. Federal government
    C. Employers with less than 15 employees
    D. Small business employers with 29 or less employees
    E. Private membership clubs

71) **Under the Americans with Disabilities Act, "reasonable accommodations" to a disabled individual include all the following, except:**

    A. Altering the "essential functions" of the job
    B. Making environmental changes
    C. Providing specialized devices or equipment
    D. Altering work schedules
    E. Providing qualified readers or interpreters

72) **Under the ADA, the essential functions of a job can be determined by all of the following except:**

    A. The job description written before the job opening was advertised
    B. The job description written after the job candidate was interviewed
    C. The job description as reported in a collective bargaining agreement
    D. The amount of time spent on the job performing those functions
    E. The current work experience of incumbents in the same or similar jobs

73) **The ADA defines a "qualified person with a disability" as a job candidate with the requisite education and experience who:**

    A. Is able to perform 100% of the essential functions of the job, with or without the employer's reasonable accommodations to his or her disability
    B. Is able to perform at least 75% of the essential functions of the job, with or without the employer's reasonable accommodations to his or her disability
    C. Is able to perform at least 50% of the essential functions of the job, with or without the employer's reasonable accommodations to his or her disability
    D. Is able to perform at least 25% of the essential functions of the job, with or without the employer's reasonable accommodations to his or her disability
    E. Is able to perform at least 15% of the essential functions of the job, with or without the employer's reasonable accommodations to his or her disability

74) An employee is notified of his termination, due to poor job performance noted over the previous six months. He sues his employer for wrongful termination, stating he (the employee) is an alcoholic, and this disability is protected under the Americans with Disabilities Act. The employer must:

   A. Rehire the employee because the employee is protected under the ADA.
   B. Rehire the employee because the employee is protected under the EEOC.
   C. Fire him, because the employee is unable to perform his essential job functions.
   D. Suspend him, and offer the employee a rehabilitation program, as required under the Rehabilitation Act.
   E. None of the above

75) An employer discovers that one of his employees is taking methadone as part of a heroin rehabilitation program. The employee's performance is unchanged, and equal to his fellow workers in the same job. Under the ADA, the employer may legally:

   A. Terminate employment, since a history of drug abuse is not considered a protected disability under the ADA.
   B. Terminate employment because the employee did not notify the employer of his condition as required by the ADA.
   C. Terminate employment, because while history of addiction is protected as a disability under the ADA, current drug abuse is not.
   D. Offer reasonable accommodations to this employee's disabilities
   E. None of the above

76) The length of a patient's disability duration can be shortened by:
   1. Encouraging compliance with treatment
   2. Offering light duty or modified work duties while the patient recuperates
   3. Returning to heavy-duty work as soon as possible
   4. Seeking treatment infrequently to maximize dollar savings
      A. 1, 2
      B. 1, 3
      C. 1, 4
      D. All of the above

77) Many of the victims of automobile accidents have which of the following needs?
   A. Speech therapy
   B. Cognitive therapy
   C. Occupational therapy
   D. All of the above
   E. None of the above

78) PIP insurance is the portion of an automobile policy that covers:
   A. Damage to the owner's automobile
   B. Damage to another's automobile
   C. Bodily injury to the driver, passengers, or pedestrians
   D. Damage to engine, drive train and transmission only
   E. All of the above

79) A Case Manager's records should be scrupulously accurate, unbiased, and completed in a timely fashion because:
   A. Orderliness of records is scored by state inspectors during reviews, and therefore can affect state reimbursement rates.
   B. A client may become involved in litigation that may require the testimony or written records of the Case Manager.
   C. A Case Manager's records have an impact on the policy limits of PIP coverage.
   D. All of the above
   E. None of the above

80) A driver has a no-fault policy. An uninsured driver strikes him while driving his vehicle. The uninsured driver of the second vehicle is noted to have alcohol on his breath, and subsequent testing reveals a blood alcohol level of 203 mg/dl. Both drivers are seriously injured. The first driver's insurance company can successfully deny medical coverage to the uninsured driver because:

A. He was driving while intoxicated.
B. He was driving while uninsured.
C. He has demonstrated negligence, and disregard for safety.
D. All of the above
E. None of the above

81) All except which of the following asset transfers are exempted from state-imposed penalties during a "look back" for inappropriately transferred assets?

A. Transfers to a spouse or to a third party for the sole benefit of the spouse
B. Transfers by a spouse to a third party for the sole benefit of the spouse
C. Transfers to a sibling, for the sole benefit of the sibling
D. Transfers for a purpose other than to qualify for Medicaid
E. Transfers where imposing a penalty would cause undue hardship

82) An individual transfers his house to his sister for consideration of $1, one year prior to his entrance into a nursing home. The house's fair market value is $100,000. During the state's look back they find this asset transfer, and apply a penalty period. If the average cost of the individual's medical care is $500/month, average pharmacy cost is $50/month and the average nursing home cost in that state is $2,000/month, how long is the penalty period?

A. 50 months
B. 100 months
C. 200 months
D. 2000 months
E. None of the above

83) The time limit for a state-imposed "penalty period" for the inappropriate transfer of assets is:

A. 100 months
B. 60 months
C. 36 months
D. No limit
E. None of the above

84) The "look back" period for asset transfer, performed by the state for a Medicaid applicant is:

A. 36 months prior to the date the individual is institutionalized or, if later, the date he or she applies for Medicaid
B. 60 months for certain types of trusts
C. 90 months prior to the date the individual is institutionalized or, if later, the date he or she applies for Medicaid
D. C
E. A, B

85) Which of the following will result in a "penalty period" imposed by the state, when the state reviews financial records during a "look back" for a Medicaid applicant?

A. When an individual's financial asset is transferred at a cost higher than the fair market value
B. When an individual's financial asset is transferred at a cost equal to the fair market value
C. When an individual's financial asset is transferred for a cost less than the fair market value
D. All of the above
E. None of the above

86) **A healthy individual creates an irrevocable trust, and makes his grandson the beneficiary of his trust. He transfers the majority of his real estate holdings into this trust. Six months elapse, and the individual suffers a massive stroke, and requires nursing home care. Which of the following is true regarding how Medicaid will view the assets in trust.**

    A. The assets will be considered not available to the individual because they are placed in an irrevocable trust.

    B. The assets will be considered not available to the individual because the title to the assets are held by the trust.

    C. The assets will be considered available to the individual because the trust was established within the "look back" period.

    D. None of the above

    E. All of the above

87) **A father establishes a trust for his 12-year-old mentally retarded son. The trust is funded by the son's social security benefits. Which of the following statements describes how HCFA will view these assets upon the son's application for Medicaid benefits?**

    A. The assets will be considered not available to the individual because they are placed in an irrevocable trust.

    B. The assets will be considered not available to the individual because the title to the assets is held by the trust.

    C. The assets will be considered available to the individual because the trust was established within the "look back" period.

    D. None of the above

    E. All of the above

88) **All of the following statements are true regarding the Mental Health Parity Act (MHPA), except:**

    A. It is a federal law, enacted to protect the rights of individuals with mental health problems.

    B. It prohibits employers or plans from setting annual dollar limits on mental health treatment benefits, unless similar limits are set on medical and surgical care.

    C. It prohibits employers or plans from setting lifetime dollar limits on mental health treatment benefits, unless similar limits are set on medical and surgical care.

    D. It requires all plans to provide mental health benefits.

    E. None of the above

89) **All employers are bound under the MHPA, except:**

    1. Airlines

    2. Employers with 50 or less employees

    3. Munitions and weapons manufacturers

    4. Employers that can demonstrate that compliance will cause financial hardship

    5. Employers with 100 or less employees

        A. 1, 3

        B. 2, 4

        C. 1, 2, 3

        D. None of the above

90) **The MHPA requires nonexempt employers to offer their employees all of the following benefits, except:**

    1. Mental health benefits equal to medical and surgical benefits

    2. Mental health copayments equal to those of the medical and surgical benefits

    3. Parity in the number of outpatient visits for mental health care, as offered in medical and surgical benefits

    4. Parity in the number of inpatient days for mental health care, as offered in medical or surgical benefits

    5. Parity in the number of inpatient days for chemical dependency as offered in medical or surgical benefits

    A. 1, 3
    B. 2, 4
    C. 1, 2, 3
    D. All of the above
    E. None of the above

91) **Which of the following individuals (is) are protected under the Pregnancy Discrimination Act (PDA)?**

1. An employee's spouse
2. A pregnant but unwed employee
3. A part-time employee
4. An independent contractor
5. Employee of a successor corporation
    A. 1, 2
    B. 3, 4
    C. 1, 2, 3
    D. All of the above
    E. None of the above

92) **Though employers must provide maternity benefits along with health care benefits under the Pregnancy Discrimination Act, they are permitted to recoup some of their cost by which of the following?**

1. Limiting the terms of reimbursement, including maximal reimbursable amount
2. Increasing the deductibles for maternity related benefits
3. Increasing the copayments for maternity related benefits
4. Limiting the choice of physicians and hospitals to those that offer steep discounts for network participation
5. Limiting the number of plans available to employees that offer maternity benefits
    A. 1, 2
    B. 2, 4
    C. 1, 2, 3
    D. All of the above
    E. None of the above

93) **The wife of an eligible part-time employee requests payment for a termination of pregnancy from her husband's employer. This is the wife's second abortion, and the fetus is in its 12th week. Under the Pregnancy Discrimination Act, the employer may legally refuse, because:**

1. Wives of eligible employees are not covered under PDA regulations.
2. Wives of part-time employees are not covered under PDA regulations.
3. First trimester pregnancies are not covered under PDA regulations.
4. Terminations of pregnancies (abortions) are not covered under PDA regulations.
5. The Pregnancy Discrimination Act's lifetime limit on the number of abortions is one.
    A. 1, 3
    B. 2, 4
    C. 1, 2, 3
    D. 4
    E. None of the above

94) **A female employee is out of work for three months secondary to complications of pregnancy and childbirth. Under the policies of the PDA, her employer can legally deny her disability benefits if:**

1. Disability benefits are not available to other employees for disabilities related to medical and surgical treatment.
2. She is not a full-time employee.
3. The employer has less than 50 employees.

4. The employee is not married.
5. The employee has not worked for at least eighteen months for that employer.
   A. 1
   B. 2, 4
   C. 3, 5
   D. All of the above
   E. None of the above

95) **A hybrid insurance plan that provides the employee with provider choice and a contracted network with a gatekeeper is known as:**

A. PPO
B. HMO
C. POS
D. Indemnity

96) **_____ is an organization that collects a predetermined fee per member per month; provides health care for a geographic area; and accepts responsibility to deliver a specified health benefit package to a voluntary enrolled group of employees.**

A. A PPO
B. An HMO
C. A POS plan
D. An indemnity program

97) **Which of the following types of insurance is subject to the guidelines of the state in which the policy is written?**

A. Short-term disability
B. Long-term disability
C. Group medical insurance
D. Workers' Compensation insurance

98) **_____ is a system of cost containment programs.**

A. Case Management
B. Managed Care
C. Workers' Compensation
D. All of the above

99) **_____ made the employer's health plan the primary payer for all active Medicare eligible employees and their spouses, regardless of age; mandated the extension of medical benefits after termination from employment and after a person becomes ineligible under a medical plan; and required that employers with health care plans provide health care coverage to former employees, divorced or widowed spouses of employees and former dependent children of employees at group rates for a specific time frame.**

A. Medicare
B. COBRA
C. SSI
D. FELA

100) **_____ is a system of health care delivery focused on managing the cost and quality of access to health care. It is used by HMOs, PPOs, and certain indemnity plans to improve the delivery of health care services and contain costs.**

A. Capitation
B. Workers' Compensation
C. Managed Care
D. All of the above

101) A _____ is established to share the costs to the insurer of unpredictable catastrophic losses among all policyholders.

    A. Reinsurance reserve
    B. Contingency reserve
    C. Monetary reserve
    D. Legal reserve

102) In complex or disputed cases, _____ may be done to determine an individual's diagnosis, present status, need for continued treatment, type of appropriate treatment, degree of disability or ability to return to work.

    A. A second surgical opinion
    B. An agreed upon medical exam
    C. A qualified medical exam
    D. An independent medical exam

103) A _____ is an employee who has the necessary skills to examine claims and make decisions on whether to approve, investigate or deny the claims.

    A. Medical examiner
    B. Claims examiner
    C. Insurance investigator
    D. Case Manager

104) HMOs designate that all primary care physicians are the _____ in the patient's care regarding specialty referrals and needs.

    A. Internal medicine doctors
    B. Chiropractors
    C. Gatekeepers
    D. Medical directors

105) The amount payable by the insurer to the insured under his group health coverage is called:

    A. Coinsurance
    B. Copayment
    C. Deductible
    D. Benefits

106) Which of the following statements (is) are true regarding current definitions of medical necessity in insurance contracts?

    1. They are clear.
    2. They are concise.
    3. They are unambiguous.
    4. They are uniform throughout the industry.
        A. 1, 3
        B. 2, 4
        C. 1, 2, 3
        D. All of the above
        E. None of the above

107) In standard health insurance contracts, which of the following terms are made clear in the definition of medical necessity?

    1. Appropriate medical care
    2. Reasonable medical care
    3. Custodial medical care
    4. Experimental medical care
        A. 1, 3
        B. 2, 4
        C. 1, 2, 3
        D. All of the above
        E. None of the above

108) **Which of the following statements is (are) true regarding the definition of medical necessity in insurance contracts?**

1. It is largely a "nonissue" discussed only by academics.
2. It is an important issue that affects the adjudication of all health insurance claims.
3. It is a problem solved easily by crafting the "right words" into the definition.
4. The definition of what is medically necessary is best approached through a "procedural methodology."
   - A. 1, 3
   - B. 2, 4
   - C. 1, 2, 3
   - D. All of the above
   - E. None of the above

109) **When determining what is medically necessary in a particular case, which of the following should be evaluated?**

1. The reasonable expectations of the patient
2. The opinion of objective specialists in the field of medicine in question
3. The patient's medical record
4. The opinion of the treating physician
   - A. 1, 3
   - B. 2, 4
   - C. 1, 2, 3
   - D. All of the above
   - E. None of the above

110) **Which of the following is not important in the determination of what is medically necessary in a particular case?**

1. The reasonable expectations of the patient
2. The opinion of objective specialists in the field of medicine in question
3. The patient's medical record
4. The opinion of the treating physician
   - A. 1, 3
   - B. 2, 4
   - C. 1, 2, 3
   - D. All of the above
   - E. None of the above

111) **Which of the following describes the intent of the insurance company when making a determination of what is medically necessary?**

1. Protect the subscriber from irregular medical practices.
2. Protect the subscriber from dangerous medical treatments.
3. Protect the subscriber from ineffective medical treatments.
4. Assure the policy holders that the insurer is paying for only care that is necessary and appropriate.
   - A. 1, 3
   - B. 2, 4
   - C. 1, 2, 3
   - D. All of the above
   - E. None of the above

112) **When making a determination of what care is medically necessary, the Medical Director's intent includes all except which of the following?**

1. Protect the subscriber from dangerous medical treatments.
2. To decrease the utilization of medical resources at all costs.
3. Protect the subscriber from ineffective medical treatments.
4. To decease medical costs, and so raise his year-end bonus.

A. 1, 3
B. 2, 4
C. 1, 2, 3
D. All of the above
E. None of the above

113) **Which of the following statements should characterize the decision-making process that determines what is medically necessary?**

1. The process is fair.
2. The process utilizes the best available information.
3. The process is reproducible.
4. The process is managed by the insurance carrier's medical director.
   A. 1, 3
   B. 2, 4
   C. 1, 2, 3
   D. All of the above
   E. None of the above

114) **The decision to deny a claim payment because it is determined that the proposed treatment was not medically necessary should be made by which of the following persons?**

A. Senior Vice President of Claims Operations
B. Claims Manager
C. Case Manager
D. Medical Director
E. Manager of Network Services

115) **Aside from the Medical Director, who should be authorized to make claim denials for lack of medical necessity?**

1. Claims Supervisor
2. Manager of the Provider Network
3. Chief Operating Officer
4. Vice President of Medical Informatics
   A. 1, 3
   B. 2, 4
   C. 1, 2, 3
   D. All of the above
   E. None of the above

116) **Of the following statements about Unemployment Compensation, which is (are) true?**

1. It is a program established by the Social Security Act of 1935.
2. It is designed to replace 100% of an employee's previous wages.
3. It is financed by unemployment taxes or employer contributions to an approved state unemployment fund.
4. The minimum duration of benefits is 26 months.
   A. 1, 3, 4
   B. 2, 4
   C. 1, 2, 3
   D. All of the above
   E. None of the above

117) **Of the following statements, which is (are) true regarding Children's Health Insurance Program (CHIP)?**

1. It was created by the federal government.
2. It is run by Health Care Financing Administration.
3. It is run by Health Resources and Services Program.
4. It provides federal matching funds to states.

    A. 1, 3
    B. 2, 4
    C. 1, 2, 3
    D. All of the above
    E. None of the above

118) Eligibility criteria for the Children's Health Insurance Program include all except which of the following?

1. Recipients must have been insured in the previous 12 months.
2. Recipients must be from families with low incomes.
3. Recipients must be between the ages of 10 and 19 years.
4. Recipients must be uninsured.
5. Recipients must be otherwise ineligible for Medicaid.
    A. 1, 3
    B. 2, 4
    C. 1, 2, 3
    D. All of the above
    E. None of the above

119) Of the following benefits listed, which are federally mandated benefits for Children's Health Insurance Program?

1. Inpatient and outpatient hospital services
2. Doctor's surgical and medical services
3. Laboratory and x-ray services
4. Well baby/child care, including immunizations
    A. 1, 3
    B. 2, 4
    C. 1, 2, 3
    D. All of the above
    E. None of the above

120) Which of the following is true about an indemnity Health Insurance Plan?

1. It is a legal entity.
2. It is licensed by the State Insurance Department.
3. It exists to provide health insurance to enrollees.
4. It reimburses enrollees for the cost of health care goods and services covered in the insurance contract.
    A. 1, 3
    B. 2, 4
    C. 1, 2, 3
    D. All of the above
    E. None of the above

121) Which of the following is true about indemnity health insurance companies?

1. They historically have had very active utilization review departments.
2. They historically have invested heavily in health care quality managed programs.
3. They exert tight control on network physicians.
4. They negotiate prices with capitated contracts.
    A. 1, 3
    B. 2, 4
    C. 1, 2, 3
    D. All of the above
    E. None of the above

122) **Of the following, which are benefits that accrue to employers who choose to self-insure?**

1. Reduced service costs that are usually incurred by conventional insurers
2. Exemption from providing benefits mandated by ERISA
3. Elimination of the costs of premium taxes
4. Improved cash flow
   - A. 1, 3
   - B. 2, 4
   - C. 1, 2, 3
   - D. All of the above
   - E. None of the above

123) **Which of the following reasons are important when considering if an employer should self-insure for employee health care costs?**

1. Size of the employee base
2. Size of cash reserves
3. Group claims experience
4. Employee health status
   - A. 1, 3
   - B. 2, 4
   - C. 1, 2, 3
   - D. All of the above
   - E. None of the above

124) **Of the following, who is financially responsible for any personal injury or damaged property caused by car accidents?**

1. The state insurance fund
2. The car owner
3. The highway department
4. The car owner's insurer
5. The Department of the Interior
   - A. 1, 3
   - B. 2, 4
   - C. 1, 2, 3
   - D. All of the above
   - E. None of the above

125) **A type of automobile insurance in which each person's own insurance company pays for injury or damage up to a certain limit, regardless of whether its insured was actually at fault, is referred to as:**

- A. Malpractice insurance
- B. Excess and omission insurance
- C. No-fault insurance
- D. Personal injury protection
- E. Reinsurance

126) **Of the following, who determines the minimum allowable limits of car insurance coverage for medical expenses and lost wages?**

- A. Car manufacturers
- B. Federal government
- C. State government
- D. Car owner
- E. Insurance companies

127) Which of the following statements is true concerning Coordination of Benefits (COB) as a process utilized by insurance companies?

1. Coordinates claims payments between two or more insurance companies
2. Helps human resources departments determine which of their employees requires which type of insurance
3. Insures that the claimant does not receive more than 100% of the cost of medical care
4. Helps charitable organizations coordinate the financial gifts of donors
   A. 1, 3
   B. 2, 4
   C. 1, 2, 3
   D. All of the above
   E. None of the above

128) Of the following statements, which is not true concerning Coordination of Benefits (COB) rules?

1. Almost all group health insurers have COB provisions in their contracts.
2. COB provisions are federally mandated.
3. Compliance with COB rules is voluntary.
4. Compliance rates among insurers are low.
   A. 1, 3
   B. 2, 4
   C. 1, 2, 3
   D. All of the above
   E. None of the above

129) A man is hospitalized for treatment of his chronic gallbladder disease. He is covered by his employer-sponsored health plan, as well as being covered as a dependent on his wife's employee-sponsored health plan. According to COB rules, which of the following companies pays first for his health care?

A. His wife's health insurance policy
B. His employee health insurance policy
C. His Workers' Compensation policy
D. His wife's no-fault insurance policy
E. His excess and omissions policy

130) A man is hospitalized for treatment of his chronic gallbladder disease. He is covered by his employer-sponsored health plan, as well as being covered as a dependent on his wife's employee-sponsored health plan. According to COB rules, which of the following companies will pay second for his health care?

A. His wife's health insurance policy
B. His employee health insurance policy
C. His Workers' Compensation policy
D. His wife's no-fault insurance policy
E. His excess and omissions policy

131) A nurse is hospitalized for treatment of a ruptured ovarian cyst. She has health insurance coverage by her employee-sponsored health plan, as well as being covered as a dependent on her husband's health plan. According to COB rules, which of the following companies pays first for her health care?

A. Her husband's health insurance policy
B. Her employee health insurance policy
C. Her Workers' Compensation policy
D. Her husband's no-fault insurance policy
E. His excess and omissions policy

132) **A nurse is hospitalized for treatment of an arthritic ankle. She has health insurance coverage by her employee-sponsored health plan, as well as being covered as a dependent on her husband's health plan. According to COB rules, which of the following companies pays *second* for her health care?**

A. Her husband's health insurance policy
B. Her employee health insurance policy
C. Her Workers' Compensation policy
D. Her husband's no-fault insurance policy
E. His excess and omissions policy

133) **When determining the order of insurance payment for a dependent child, when is the "birthday rule" invoked?**

1. When the parents are divorced
2. When both the insurance companies involved have adopted the "birthday rule" in their contracts
3. When the parents agree to coordinate benefits
4. When each of the married parents has named the child as a dependent in their health insurance policies.
   A. 1, 3
   B. 2, 4
   C. 1, 2, 3
   D. All of the above
   E. None of the above

134) **Of the following statements concerning the "birthday rule" in the coordination of benefits process, which is true?**

1. It is invoked when two or more plans cover an individual as a dependent.
2. It bases the order of payment on the order of birthdays of the parents of the dependent.
3. It can only be used when both insurance companies have adopted the birthday rule.
4. It bases the order of payment on the birthday of the claimant.
   A. 1, 3
   B. 2, 4
   C. 1, 2, 3
   D. All of the above
   E. None of the above

135) **When a child is covered as a dependent on both of his parents' policies, if his mother's insurance company does not ascribe to the "birthday rule," which insurance company pays first?**

A. The father's insurance company will sue the mother's insurer to invoke the birthday rule.
B. The father's insurance company will pay in accord with the male/female rule.
C. The mother's insurance company will pay first in accord with the male/female rule.
D. The mother's insurance company will pay first because they have not adopted the birthday rule.
E. Neither insurance company pays, and the claim is sent to the national insurance fund for payment.

136) **A child of divorced parents becomes ill. Which of the following statements is true regarding the coordination of benefits for his case?**

1. The insurance plan that is awarded primary responsibility by the courts pays first.
2. The insurance plan of the parent with the earliest birthday pays first, if the courts have not determined a primary carrier.
3. The insurance plan of the parent with custody pays first, if the courts have not determined a primary carrier.
4. The insurance plan of the parent without custody pays first, if the courts have not determined a primary carrier.

A. 1, 3
B. 2, 4
C. 1, 2, 3
D. All of the above
E. None of the above

137) **A couple is divorced; they have four children from that union. The father has custody of the children. The mother of the children remarries, the father of the children remains single. When one of the children becomes ill, whose insurance company pays *first*?**

A. The mother's insurance carrier
B. The father's insurance carrier
C. The mother's spouse's insurance carrier
D. The father's girlfriend's insurance carrier
E. The National Allied Insurance Fund (NAIF)

138) **A couple is divorced; they have four children from that union. The father has custody of the children. The mother of the children remarries, the father of the children remains single. When one of the children becomes ill, whose insurance company pays *second*?**

A. The mother's insurance carrier
B. The father's insurance carrier
C. The mother's spouse's insurance carrier
D. The father's girlfriend's insurance carrier
E. The National Allied Insurance Fund (NAIF)

139) **A couple with a single child is divorced; the mother has custody of the child. Each of the parents subsequently remarries. When the child gets ill, which of the following insurance companies pays first?**

A. The mother's insurance carrier
B. The father's insurance carrier
C. The mother's spouse's insurance carrier
D. The father's spouse's insurance carrier
E. The National Allied Insurance Fund

140) **A couple with a single child is divorced; the mother has custody of the child. Each of the parents subsequently remarries. When the child gets ill, which of the following insurance companies pays second?**

A. The mother's insurance carrier
B. The father's insurance carrier
C. The mother's spouse's insurance carrier
D. The father's spouse's insurance carrier
E. The National Allied Insurance Fund

141) **A couple with a single child is divorced; the mother has custody of the child. Each of the parents subsequently remarries. When the child gets ill, which of the following insurance companies pays last?**

A. The mother's insurance carrier
B. The father's insurance carrier
C. The mother's spouse's insurance carrier
D. The father's spouse's insurance carrier
E. The National Allied Insurance Fund

142) **A nurse, after working in a hospital for 25 years, retires with retiree health insurance benefits. She subsequently takes a job as an executive in an insurance company. When she becomes ill, which insurance company pays health insurance costs first?**

   A. Her retiree health insurance benefit from the hospital, since that is where she was insured first
   B. Her current employer's insurance carrier, since that is where she is insured now
   C. Her spouse's insurance company
   D. Her malpractice insurance company
   E. Her Workers' Compensation insurance

143) **A police officer retires after 30 years on the force. His retirement package includes health care benefits. He takes a full-time job as a security guard; this job has health insurance as a benefit to full-time employees. When he gets ill, which insurance company pays first?**

   A. His retiree health insurance benefit from the police force, since that is where he was insured first
   B. The current employer's insurance carrier, since that is where he is insured now as an active employee
   C. His spouse's health insurance company
   D. His professional malpractice insurance company
   E. His wife's Workers' Compensation insurance policy

144) **A man usually employed as a bricklayer is laid off. He is able to maintain his health benefits as a laid-off employee. He also has health care benefits as a dependent on his wife's health insurance policy. When he becomes ill, which carrier pays first?**

   A. His health insurance benefit from his job as a bricklayer
   B. Workers' Compensation insurance
   C. His spouse's health insurance company, where he is covered as dependent
   D. His Unemployment Insurance benefit
   E. His wife's Workers' Compensation insurance policy

145) **A man usually employed as a bricklayer is laid off. He is able to maintain his health benefits as a laid off employee. He also has health care benefits as a dependent on his wife's health insurance policy. When he becomes ill, which carrier pays *second*?**

   A. His health insurance benefit from his job as a bricklayer
   B. Workers' Compensation insurance
   C. His spouse's health insurance company, where he is covered as dependent
   D. His Unemployment Insurance benefit
   E. His wife's Workers' Compensation insurance policy

146) **A nurse, after working in a hospital for 25 years, retires with retiree health insurance benefits. She subsequently takes a job as an executive in an insurance company. When she becomes ill, which insurance company pays health insurance costs second?**

   A. Her retiree health insurance benefit from the hospital, since that is where she was insured first
   B. The current employer's insurance carrier, since that is were she is insured now
   C. Her spouse's insurance company
   D. Her malpractice insurance company
   E. Her Workers' Compensation insurance

147) **A hospital employee is fired from his job. He continues his health insurance benefits under COBRA, though he is also a dependent on his wife's employee-sponsored health insurance policy. He subsequently is employed as a day laborer without benefits. If he becomes ill, who pays his medical bills first?**

   A. His current employer's excess and omissions insurance plan
   B. His health insurance plan maintained by his COBRA coverage
   C. His wife's insurance plan, where he is listed as a dependent
   D. Unemployment benefits insurance plan
   E. National Laborer's Relief Organization (NLRO)

148) **A hospital employee is fired from his job. He continues his health insurance benefits under COBRA, though he is also a dependent on his wife's employee-sponsored health insurance policy. He subsequently is employed as a day laborer without benefits. If he becomes ill, who pays his medical bills second?** `

   A. His current employer's excess and omissions insurance plan
   B. His health insurance plan maintained by his COBRA coverage
   C. His wife's insurance plan, where he is listed as a dependent
   D. Unemployment benefits insurance plan
   E. National Laborer's Relief Organization (NLRO)

149) **Victims of automobile accidents are characterized by which of the following?**

   1. Youth
   2. Seriousness of injuries
   3. High incidence of head injuries
   4. High incidence of spinal injuries
   5. High incidence of permanent disability
      A. 1, 3
      B. 2, 4
      C. 1, 2, 3
      D. All of the above
      E. None of the above

150) **When managing a patient who was injured in a car accident, the Case Manager needs to be knowledgeable regarding charitable and not-for-profit programs and services available in the community because:**

   A. They are qualitatively superior to those that can be purchased privately.
   B. PIP policy limits may restrict the range of options available to the client.
   C. A higher quality of life index is associated with these programs.
   D. All of the above
   E. None of the above

151) **Utilization Review is a process that:**

   1. Reviews medical bills to identify overcharging, billing errors and overutilization
   2. Screens hospital admissions for appropriateness of service and service site
   3. Compares medical services to national standards of care to determine appropriateness of care for specific diagnoses
   4. Reviews ambulatory procedures for reasonable and customary charges
      A. 1, 2
      B. 1, 3
      C. 2, 3
      D. 2, 4

152) **The object of an initial interview in a Workers' Compensation case is to:**

   A. Identify indications of malingering.
   B. Set up an individual medical exam.
   C. Obtain an overview of the patient's relative medical history and job demands.
   D. All of the above
   E. None of the above

153) **The "utilization of services that are in excess of a beneficiary's medical needs or receiving a capitated Medicare payment and failing to provide services to meet a beneficiary's medical needs" defines which of the following terms according to HCFA?**

   A. Inappropriate utilization
   B. Abuse
   C. Fraud
   D. Theft
   E. Collusion

154) **Which of the following terms refers to an intentional deception on the part of a person that could result in some unauthorized benefit to himself or some other person(s)?**

    A. Abuse
    B. Inappropriate utilization
    C. Collusion
    D. Fraud
    E. Fiscal affirmation

155) **Which of the following is true regarding the Medicare Program?**

    1. It was created by Title XVIII of the Social Security Act.
    2. It went into effect in 1966.
    3. It is currently managed by the Health Care Financing Administration (HCFA).
    4. It was started as a "make work" program for underutilized physicians.

        A. 1, 3
        B. 2, 4
        C. 1, 2, 3
        D. All of the above
        E. None of the above

156) **Which of the following statements are true concerning the Medicare Program?**

    1. It is divided into two parts, Part A and Part B
    2. Part A is the Hospital Insurance Program
    3. Part B is the out-of-hospital care and physicians' services insurance program
    4. Part A is funded by Social Security taxes

        A. 1, 3
        B. 2, 4
        C. 1, 2, 3
        D. All of the above
        E. None of the above

157) **Medicare provides health insurance benefits to which of the following?**

    1. Persons 65 years old who receive Social Security benefits
    2. Persons 65 years old who receive Railroad Retirement benefits
    3. Persons 65 years old who have a spouse who has Medicare covered government employment
    4. Persons 65 years old who have never worked or been married to a worker who has paid Social Security taxes

        A. 1, 3
        B. 2, 4
        C. 1, 2, 3
        D. All of the above
        E. None of the above

158) **Which of the following statements are *not* true concerning the Medicare Program?**

    1. Part B is the Hospital Insurance Program.
    2. It was enacted under Title XIV of the Social Security Act.
    3. Part A is the out-of-hospital care and physicians' services insurance program.
    4. Part A is funded by Social Security taxes.

        A. 1, 3
        B. 2, 4
        C. 1, 2, 3
        D. All of the above
        E. None of the above

159) Medicare provides health insurance benefits to which of the following?

1. Persons 55 years old who receive Social Security benefits
2. Persons 55 years old who receive Railroad Retirement benefits
3. Persons 55 years old who have a spouse who has Medicare-covered government employment
4. Persons 55 years old who have never worked or been married to a worker who has paid Social Security taxes
    A. 1, 3
    B. 2, 4
    C. 1, 2, 3
    D. All of the above
    E. None of the above

160) Which of the following is (are) *not* true regarding the Medicare Program?

1. It was created by Title XVIII of the Social Security Act.
2. It went into effect in 1956.
3. It is currently managed by the Health Care Financing Administration (HCFA).
4. It was started as a "make work" program for underutilized physicians.
    A. 1, 3
    B. 2, 4
    C. 1, 2, 3
    D. All of the above
    E. None of the above

161) Medicare provides health insurance benefits to which of the following?

1. Persons who have been entitled to Social Security benefits for 24 months
2. Persons who have been in active duty in the armed forces
3. Persons who are disabled and who are entitled to Social Security benefits
4. Persons who have been treated in a Veteran's Administration hospital
    A. 1, 3
    B. 2, 4
    C. 1, 2, 3
    D. All of the above
    E. None of the above

162) Persons are entitled to Medicare benefits when they have permanent kidney failure and which of the following?

1. He has worked the required amount of time under Social Security, the Railroad Board, or is a government employee.
2. He is receiving or is eligible to receive Social Security or Railroad Retirement Case benefits
3. He is the spouse or a dependent child of a person who has worked the required amount of time, or who is receiving Social Security or Railroad cash benefits.
4. He is a foreign national who has never worked in this country, nor is he a dependent of an eligible worker.
    A. 1, 3
    B. 2, 4
    C. 1, 2, 3
    D. All of the above
    E. None of the above

163) Persons are *not* entitled to Medicare benefits if they have permanent kidney failure and which of the following?

1. He has not worked the required amount of time under Social Security, the Railroad Board or is a government employee.
2. He is receiving or is eligible to receive Social Security or Railroad Retirement case benefits.
3. He is not the spouse or a dependent child of a person who has worked the required amount of time, or who is receiving Social Security or Railroad cash benefits.
4. He is a foreign national who has never worked in this country, or he is a dependent of an eligible worker.
   A. 1, 3, 4
   B. 2, 4
   C. 1, 2, 3
   D. All of the above
   E. None of the above

164) Medicare will *not* provide health insurance benefits to which of the following?

1. Persons who are not entitled to Social Security benefits
2. Persons who have been in active duty in the armed forces, but are not entitled to Social Security benefits
3. Persons who have been treated in a Veteran's Administration hospital
4. Persons who are disabled and who are entitled to Social Security benefits
   A. 1, 3
   B. 2, 4
   C. 1, 2, 3
   D. All of the above
   E. None of the above

165) When a person becomes entitled to Medicare solely because of end-stage renal disease, he must wait how long until he is covered by Medicare?

A. 1 month
B. 2 months
C. 3 months
D. 4 months
E. 5 months

166) Which of the following is true regarding Medicare coverage for persons with end-stage renal disease?

1. He is considered to have end-stage renal disease if he has irreparable damage that requires a transplant or dialysis to maintain life.
2. If he becomes entitled to Medicare benefits solely because of end-stage renal disease, he must wait 3 months before he is covered by Medicare benefits.
3. If he becomes entitled to Medicare benefits solely because of end-stage renal disease, his protection ends 12 months after the month he no longer needs maintenance dialysis treatments.
4. If he becomes entitled to Medicare benefits solely because of end-stage renal disease, his protection ends 36 months after a successful kidney transplant.
   A. 1, 3
   B. 2, 4
   C. 1, 2, 3
   D. All of the above
   E. None of the above

167) If a person is entitled to Medicare benefits solely because of end-stage renal disease, when do his benefits expire?

1. His protection ends 3 years after maintenance dialysis begins.
2. His protection ends 12 months after the month he no longer needs maintenance dialysis treatments.
3. His protection ends 24 months after his diagnosis of end-stage renal disease is made.
4. His protection ends 36 months after a successful kidney transplant.
   A. 1, 3
   B. 2, 4
   C. 1, 2, 3
   D. All of the above
   E. None of the above

168) Which of the following is *not* true regarding Medicare coverage for persons with end-stage renal disease?

1. He is considered to have end-stage renal disease if he has irreparable damage that requires a transplant or dialysis to maintain life.
2. If he becomes entitled to Medicare benefits solely because of end-stage renal disease, he must wait 6 months before he is covered by Medicare benefits.
3. If he becomes entitled to Medicare benefits solely because of end-stage renal disease, his protection ends 12 months after the month he no longer needs maintenance dialysis treatments.
4. If he becomes entitled to Medicare benefits solely because of end-stage renal disease, his protection ends 12 months after a successful kidney transplant.
   A. 1, 3
   B. 2, 4
   C. 1, 2, 3
   D. All of the above
   E. None of the above

169) Medicare benefits under the Part A program include which of the following?

1. Inpatient hospital services
2. Skilled nursing facilities
3. Home health services
4. Hospice care
   A. 1, 3
   B. 2, 4
   C. 1, 2, 3
   D. All of the above
   E. None of the above

170) Medicare benefits under the Part A program include all except which of the following?

1. Physician fees
2. Skilled nursing facilities
3. Outpatient hospital services
4. Hospice care
   A. 1, 3
   B. 2, 4
   C. 1, 2, 3
   D. All of the above
   E. None of the above

171) Medicare benefits under the Part A program include which of the following?

1. Inpatient hospital services
2. Hemodialysis (outpatient)
3. Home health services
4. Ambulatory surgery

    A. 1, 3
    B. 2, 4
    C. 1, 2, 3
    D. All of the above
    E. None of the above

172) Medicare benefits under the Part A program include all except which of the following?

1. Inpatient hospital services
2. Hemodialysis (outpatient)
3. Home health services
4. Ambulatory surgery
    A. 1, 3
    B. 2, 4
    C. 1, 2, 3
    D. All of the above
    E. None of the above

173) Medicare Part A will pay for how many days of inpatient hospital care for each benefit period?

A. Medicare will pay for 90 days of medically necessary inpatient hospital care.
B. Medicare will pay for 60 days of medically necessary inpatient hospital care.
C. Medicare will pay for 50 days of medically necessary inpatient hospital care.
D. Medicare will pay for 120 days of medically necessary inpatient hospital care.
E. Medicare will pay for 90 days of medically unnecessary inpatient hospital care.

174) Medicare Part A will help pay for how many days of care in a skilled nursing facility for each benefit period?

A. Medicare will pay for 160 days of medically necessary care in a skilled nursing facility after a hospital stay.
B. Medicare will pay for 50 days of medically necessary care in a skilled nursing facility after a hospital stay.
C. Medicare will pay for 100 days of medically necessary care in a skilled nursing facility after a hospital stay.
D. Medicare will pay for 90 days of medically necessary care in a skilled nursing facility after a hospital stay.
E. Medicare will pay for 100 days of medically necessary care in a skilled nursing facility without a hospital stay.

175) Medicare Part A will help pay for how many days of hospice care?

A. Medicare will help pay for 220 days of hospice care.
B. Medicare will help pay for 310 days of hospice care.
C. Medicare will help pay for 90 days of hospice care.
D. Medicare will help pay for 210 days of hospice care.
E. Medicare will help pay for 50 days of hospice care.

176) Which of the following statements is (are) true regarding the Medicare Part A program?

1. Medicare Part A will help to pay for 210 days of hospice care.
2. Medicare will pay for 100 days of medically necessary care in a skilled nursing facility after a hospital stay.
3. Medicare will pay for 90 days of medically necessary inpatient hospital care.
4. Medicare will pay for 50 days of medically unnecessary inpatient hospital care.
    A. 1, 3
    B. 2, 4
    C. 1, 2, 3
    D. All of the above
    E. None of the above

177) Which of the following statements is (are) *not* true regarding the Medicare Part A program?

1. Medicare Part A will help to pay for 210 days of hospice care.
2. Medicare will pay for 200 days of medically necessary care in a skilled nursing facility after a hospital stay.
3. Medicare will pay for 90 days of medically necessary inpatient hospital care.
4. Medicare will pay for 50 days of medically unnecessary inpatient hospital care.
   A. 1, 3
   B. 2, 4
   C. 1, 2, 3
   D. All of the above
   E. None of the above

178) Medicare Part B helps pay for the cost of which of the following services?

1. Physician services
2. Outpatient hospital services
3. Medical equipment and supplies
4. Inpatient hospital stays
   A. 1, 3
   B. 2, 4
   C. 1, 2, 3
   D. All of the above
   E. None of the above

179) Medicare Part B helps pay for the cost of all except which of the following services?

1. Physician services
2. Hospice care services
3. Medical equipment and supplies
4. Inpatient hospital stays
   A. 1, 3
   B. 2, 4
   C. 1, 2, 3
   D. All of the above
   E. None of the above

180) A 45-year-old patient becomes eligible for Medicare benefits solely because of end-stage renal disease. Which of the following services are covered by Medicare?

1. Hemodialysis
2. Arthroscopic surgery to treat osteoarthritis of the knee
3. Surgical placement of an arteriovenous fistula for hemodialysis access
4. Retinal surgery
   A. 1, 3
   B. 2, 4
   C. 1, 2, 3
   D. All of the above
   E. None of the above

181) A 33-year-old patient becomes eligible for Medicare benefits solely because of end-stage renal disease. Which of the following services are *not* covered by Medicare?

1. Hemodialysis
2. Speech therapy
3. Surgical placement of an arteriovenous fistula for hemodialysis access
4. Clipping of a cerebral aneurysm surgery
   A. 1, 3
   B. 2, 4
   C. 1, 2, 3
   D. All of the above
   E. None of the above

182) Which of the following statement is (are) true regarding Medicare "reserve days"?

1. The beneficiary has the right to choose when to use a reserve day.
2. It is one of sixty "extra days" of hospital care that Medicare will pay for.
3. There are only sixty reserve days in a beneficiary's lifetime.
4. They can be used if the patient has a prolonged illness necessitating a hospital stay longer than 90 days.
   A. 1, 3
   B. 2, 4
   C. 1, 2, 3
   D. All of the above
   E. None of the above

183) Which of the following statement is (are) *not* true regarding Medicare "reserve days"?

1. Only the provider has the right to choose when to use a reserve day.
2. It is one of sixty "extra days" of hospital care that Medicare will pay for.
3. There are only ninety reserve days in a beneficiary's lifetime.
4. They can be used if the patient has a prolonged illness necessitating a hospital stay longer than 90 days.
   A. 1, 3
   B. 2, 4
   C. 1, 2, 3
   D. All of the above
   E. None of the above

184) Which of the following statements is (are) true regarding a Medicare "benefit period"?

1. A benefit period begins the first day of a patient's admission to a hospital, skilled nursing facility or hospice.
2. A benefit period ends after the patient had been discharged for sixty contiguous days.
3. There is no limit to the number of benefit periods a patient may have for hospital and skilled nursing facilities.
4. There is no limit to the number of days a beneficiary may claim payment for during a benefit period.
   A. 1, 3
   B. 2, 4
   C. 1, 2, 3
   D. All of the above
   E. None of the above

185) Which of the following statements is (are) *not* true regarding a Medicare "benefit period"?

1. A benefit period begins the first day of a patient's admission to a hospital, skilled nursing facility or hospice.
2. A benefit period ends after the patient had been discharged for 90 contiguous days.
3. There is no limit to the number of benefit periods a patient may have for hospital and skilled nursing facilities.
4. There is no limit to the number of days a beneficiary may claim payment for during a benefit period.
   A. 1, 3
   B. 2, 4
   C. 1, 2, 3
   D. All of the above
   E. None of the above

186) **Which of the following statements is (are) true regarding a Medicare "benefit period"?**
   1. A benefit period begins the first day of a patient's admission to a hospital, skilled nursing facility or hospice.
   2. A benefit period ends after the patient had been discharged for 90 contiguous days.
   3. There is no limit to the number of benefit periods a patient may have for hospital and skilled nursing facilities.
   4. There is no limit to the number of days a beneficiary may claim payment for during a benefit period.
      A. 1, 3
      B. 2, 4
      C. 1, 2, 3
      D. All of the above
      E. None of the above

187) **Which of the following is (are) true regarding Medicare benefits?**
   1. Medicare recipients still have to pay Medicare coinsurance.
   2. Medicare recipients have no "out of pocket" financial obligations to providers.
   3. Medicare recipients still have to pay Medicare deductibles.
   4. Medicare recipients pay no Medicare deductibles after their 65th birthday.
      A. 1, 3
      B. 2, 4
      C. 1, 2, 3
      D. All of the above
      E. None of the above

188) **Which of the following is (are) *not* true regarding Medicare benefits?**
   1. Medicare recipients still have to pay Medicare coinsurance.
   2. Medicare recipients have no "out of pocket" financial obligations to providers.
   3. Medicare recipients still have to pay Medicare deductibles.
   4. Medicare recipients pay no Medicare deductibles after their 65th birthday.
      A. 1, 3
      B. 2, 4
      C. 1, 2, 3
      D. All of the above
      E. None of the above

189) **Which of the following is (are) true regarding coverage for Medicare benefits?**
   1. There are many medical services that Medicare does not cover.
   2. Beneficiaries are not responsible for paying for medical services not covered by Medicare.
   3. Medicare Supplemental Insurance policy (Medigap) is sometimes purchased by beneficiaries to pay for services not covered by Medicare.
   4. Medicare pays for all medically necessary care.
      A. 1, 3
      B. 2, 4
      C. 1, 2, 3
      D. All of the above
      E. None of the above

190) **Of the following statements, which is (are) *not* true regarding coverage for Medicare benefits?**
   1. There are many medical services that Medicare does not cover.
   2. Beneficiaries are not responsible for paying for medical services not covered by Medicare.
   3. Medicare Supplemental Insurance policy (Medigap) is sometimes purchased by beneficiaries to pay for services not covered by Medicare.
   4. Medicare pays for all medically necessary care.

    A. 1, 3
    B. 2, 4
    C. 1, 2, 3
    D. All of the above
    E. None of the above

191) Which of the following statements are true regarding Medigap policies?

1. Medigap is private insurance.
2. Medigap is designed to help pay for Medicare cost sharing amounts.
3. Medigap has at least 10 standard policies, each with different combinations of benefits.
4. The best time to purchase a Medigap policy is during the open enrollment period.

    A. 1, 3
    B. 2, 4
    C. 1, 2, 3
    D. All of the above
    E. None of the above

192) Which of the following statements is (are) *not* true regarding Medigap policies?

1. Medigap is federal insurance.
2. Medigap is designed to help pay for Medicare cost sharing amounts.
3. Medigap has a single policy with a single group of benefits.
4. The best time to purchase a Medigap policy is during the open enrollment period.

    A. 1, 3
    B. 2, 4
    C. 1, 2, 3
    D. All of the above
    E. None of the above

193) Which of the following statements are true regarding the purchase of a Medigap policy during the open enrollment period?

1. The best time for a beneficiary to buy a policy is during the open enrollment period.
2. During the open enrollment period the beneficiary has the right to buy the Medigap policy of his choice.
3. During the open enrollment period the beneficiary cannot be turned down for a Medigap policy.
4. During the open enrollment period the beneficiary cannot be charged a higher premium for a Medigap policy because of poor health.

    A. 1, 3
    B. 2, 4
    C. 1, 2, 3
    D. All of the above
    E. None of the above

194) Which of the following statements is (are) *not* true regarding the purchase of a Medigap policy during the open enrollment period?

1. The best time for a beneficiary to buy a policy is after 36 months of Medicare enrollment.
2. During the open enrollment period the beneficiary has the right to buy the Medigap policy of his choice.
3. The beneficiary can be turned down for a Medigap policy if he is a particularly high health risk.
4. During the open enrollment period the beneficiary cannot be charged a higher premium for a Medigap policy because of poor health.

    A. 1, 3
    B. 2, 4
    C. 1, 2, 3
    D. All of the above
    E. None of the above

195) **Which of the following statements is (are) true regarding the purchase of a Medigap policy during the open enrollment period?**

1. The best time for a beneficiary to buy a policy is after 36 months of Medicare enrollment.
2. During the open enrollment period the beneficiary has the right to buy the Medigap policy of his choice.
3. The beneficiary can be turned down for a Medigap policy if he is a particularly high health risk.
4. During the open enrollment period the beneficiary cannot be charged a higher premium for a Medigap policy because of poor health.
    A. 1, 3
    B. 2, 4
    C. 1, 2, 3
    D. All of the above
    E. None of the above

196) **Which of the following statements defines Medicare's open enrollment period?**

A. A period that begins the date the person who is 65 or older first enrolls in Medicare, and ends 6 months later
B. A period that begins the date the person who is 75 or older first enrolls in Medicare, and ends 4 months later
C. A period that begins the date the person who is 65 or older first enrolls in Medicare, and ends 36 months later
D. A period that begins the date the person who is 55 or older first enrolls in Medicare, and ends 6 months later
E. A period that begins the date the person who is 45 or older first enrolls in Medicare, and ends 12 months later

197) **Which of the following statements is (are) true regarding a Medicare beneficiary's open enrollment period?**

1. The beneficiary must be 65 years of age or older.
2. The open enrollment period begins the first day of Medicare enrollment.
3. The open enrollment period lasts for 6 months.
4. Outside the continental United States the period lasts for 12 months.
    A. 1, 3
    B. 2, 4
    C. 1, 2, 3
    D. All of the above
    E. None of the above

198) **Which of the following statements is (are) *not* true regarding a Medicare beneficiary's open enrollment period?**

1. The beneficiary must be 65 years of age or older.
2. The open enrollment period begins after 6 months of Medicare enrollment.
3. The open enrollment period lasts for 6 months.
4. Outside the continental United States the periods last for 12 months.
    A. 1, 3
    B. 2, 4
    C. 1, 2, 3
    D. All of the above
    E. None of the above

199) Which of the following statements are true regarding Medicare Select?

1. It is another type of Medicare supplemental health insurance.
2. Insurance companies and HMOs sell it.
3. It offers benefits similar to Medigap.
4. It limits treatment to specific hospitals and physicians except in emergencies.
   A. 1, 3
   B. 2, 4
   C. 1, 2, 3
   D. All of the above
   E. None of the above

200) Which of the following statements are *not* true regarding Medicare Select?

1. It is more expensive than Medigap insurance.
2. It offers benefits similar to Medigap.
3. It is sold by the federal government.
4. It limits treatment to specific hospitals and physicians except in emergencies.
   A. 1, 3
   B. 2, 4
   C. 1, 2, 3
   D. All of the above
   E. None of the above

201) Which of the following statements are true regarding Medicare Select?

1. It is more expensive than Medigap insurance.
2. It offers benefits similar to Medigap.
3. The federal government sells it.
4. It limits treatment to specific hospitals and physicians except in emergencies.
   A. 1, 3
   B. 2, 4
   C. 1, 2, 3
   D. All of the above
   E. None of the above

202) Other insurance companies will pay before Medicare when which of the following occur?

1. The individual is 65 or over.
2. The individual is under 65 and disabled.
3. The individual has Medicare because of permanent kidney failure.
4. The individual has an illness or injury that is covered under Workers' Compensation, the federal black lung program, no-fault insurance or any liability insurance.
   A. 1, 3
   B. 2, 4
   C. 1, 2, 3
   D. All of the above
   E. None of the above

203) The state may pay for an individual's Medicare costs when which of the following are true?

1. The individual must be entitled to Medicare hospital insurance (Part A Program).
2. The individual's income level must be at or below the national poverty guidelines.
3. The individual cannot have resources worth more than $4,000 (home and first car don't count).
4. The couple cannot have resources worth more than $6,000 (home and first car don't count).
   A. 1, 3
   B. 2, 4
   C. 1, 2, 3
   D. All of the above
   E. None of the above

204) The state may pay for an individual's Medicare costs when which of the following are true?

1. The individual must be entitled to Workers' Compensation insurance.
2. The individual's income level must be at or below the national poverty guidelines.
3. The individual cannot have resources worth more than $8,000 (home and first car don't count).
4. The couple cannot have resources worth more than $6,000 (home and first car don't count).
   A. 1, 3
   B. 2, 4
   C. 1, 2, 3
   D. All of the above
   E. None of the above

205) Which of the following statements is (are) true regarding the Balanced Budget Act of 1997?

1. Medicare will pay for yearly colorectal screening for people over the age of 50.
2. Medicare will pay for screening mammograms for women over the age of 40.
3. Medicare will pay for screening PAP smears every 3 years.
4. Medicare will pay for diabetic educational programs aimed at self-management.
   A. 1, 3
   B. 2, 4
   C. 1, 2, 3
   D. All of the above
   E. None of the above

206) Which of the following statements is (are) true regarding the Balanced Budget Act of 1997?

1. Medicare will pay for one influenza vaccine per year, and one pneumococcal vaccine per lifetime.
2. Medicare will pay for glucose test strips for diabetics who are not insulin dependent.
3. Medicare will pay for bone mass tests for those at risk for osteoporosis.
4. Medicare will pay for diabetic educational programs aimed at self-management.
   A. 1, 3
   B. 2, 4
   C. 1, 2, 3
   D. All of the above
   E. None of the above

207) Which of the following statements is (are) true regarding the Balanced Budget Act of 1997?

1. Medicare will pay for one cosmetic surgical procedure per year.
2. Medicare will pay for glucose test strips for diabetics who are not insulin dependent.
3. Medicare will pay for CT scans to rule out coronary artery disease.
4. Medicare will pay for diabetic educational programs aimed at self-management.
   A. 1, 3
   B. 2, 4
   C. 1, 2, 3
   D. All of the above
   E. None of the above

208) Which of the following statements is (are) *not* true regarding the Balanced Budget Act of 1997?

1. Medicare will pay for one cosmetic surgical procedure per year.
2. Medicare will pay for prostate screening for men over the age of 50.
3. Medicare will pay for CT scans to rule out coronary artery disease.
4. Medicare will pay for diabetic educational programs aimed at self-management.

A. 1, 3
B. 2, 4
C. 1, 2, 3
D. All of the above
E. None of the above

209) Which of the following statements are true regarding the Health Care Financing Administration (HCFA)?

1. It is a federal agency within the U.S. Department of Health and Human Services.
2. It runs the Medicare and Medicaid programs.
3. It helps to run the Children's Health Insurance Program (CHIP).
4. It regulates all laboratory testing performed on humans in the United States.
    A. 1, 3
    B. 2, 4
    C. 1, 2, 3
    D. All of the above
    E. None of the above

210) Which of the following statements are true regarding the Health Care Financing Administration (HCFA)?

1. It helps eliminate discrimination based on health status for people buying health insurance.
2. It runs the Medicare and Medicaid programs.
3. It helps to run the Children's Health Insurance Program (CHIP).
4. It regulates research laboratory testing.
    A. 1, 3
    B. 2, 4
    C. 1, 2, 3
    D. All of the above
    E. None of the above

211) Which of the following statements are true regarding the Health Care Financing Administration (HCFA)?

1. It is a state agency within the U.S. Department of Agriculture.
2. It runs the Medicare and Medicaid programs.
3. It helps to run the Social Security Administration.
4. It regulates all laboratory testing performed on humans in the United States.
    A. 1, 3
    B. 2, 4
    C. 1, 2, 3
    D. All of the above
    E. None of the above

212) Which of the following statements is (are) *not* true regarding the Health Care Financing Administration (HCFA)?

1. It is a state agency within the U.S. Department of Agriculture.
2. It runs the Medicare and Medicaid programs.
3. It helps to run the Social Security Administration.
4. It regulates all laboratory testing performed on humans in the United States.
    A. 1, 3
    B. 2, 4
    C. 1, 2, 3
    D. All of the above
    E. None of the above

213) **Which of the following are true regarding a "claims edit"?**
1. It is software logic within an electronic claims processing system.
2. It selects certain claims for evaluation.
3. It compares certain claims against normative data.
4. It can "decide" to pay the claim in full or in part.
   A. 1, 3
   B. 2, 4
   C. 1, 2, 3
   D. All of the above
   E. None of the above

214) **Which of the following are true regarding a "claims edit"?**
1. It is software logic within an electronic claims processing system.
2. It randomly selects claims for evaluation.
3. It compares certain claims against normative data.
4. It can only "suspend" claims for manual review.
   A. 1, 3
   B. 2, 4
   C. 1, 2, 3
   D. All of the above
   E. None of the above

215) **Which of the following is (are) *not* true regarding a "claims edit"?**
1. It is software logic within an electronic claims processing system.
2. It randomly selects claims for evaluation.
3. It compares certain claims against normative data.
4. It can only "suspend" claims for manual review.
   A. 1, 3
   B. 2, 4
   C. 1, 2, 3
   D. All of the above
   E. None of the above

216) **Which of the following is (are) true regarding "authoritative evidence" in the determination of medical necessity?**
1. It is written medical or scientific conclusions.
2. It demonstrates the effectiveness of a treatment or procedure.
3. It is produced by controlled clinical trials.
4. It is produced by assessments initiated by HCFA.
   A. 1, 3
   B. 2, 4
   C. 1, 2, 3
   D. All of the above
   E. None of the above

217) **A patient that meets the following criteria is entitled to _____.**
- Has a defined disability
- Has a filed application for workers' benefits
- Has achieved a minimum employment period covered by social security
- Is less than 65 years old
- Has been disabled for 5 months
   A. SSI
   B. CHIP
   C. SSDI
   D. Workers' Compensation

218) Which of the following are needed to be eligible for a work conditioning program?

1. The patient must have permanent work restrictions.
2. The patient must have diagnosed neuromusculoskeletal physical and functional deficits that interfere with work.
3. Be physically cleared to participate.
4. Be willing to participate.
   A. 1, 2, 3
   B. 2, 3, 4
   C. All of the above
   D. None of the above

219) In 1965 Medicare legislation provided health benefits to persons over 65 and:

A. Veterans
B. Disabled veterans
C. Welfare recipients
D. Disabled individuals

220) Which of the following statements is correct?

A. COB coordinates Workers' Compensation with group health coverage.
B. With COB patients can obtain benefits exceeding 100% of the fee charged.
C. COB rules vary by state.
D. COB determines the manner in which medical and dental benefits will be paid when a patient has coverage from multiple health care insurers.

221) Which of the following statements are incorrect?

1. COB coordinates Workers' Compensation with group health coverage.
2. Without COB patients can obtain benefits exceeding 100% of the fee charged.
3. COB rules are promulgated by the National Association of Insurance Commissioners.
4. COB determines the manner in which medical and dental benefits will be paid when a patient has coverage from multiple health care insurers.
   A. 1
   B. 2, 3, 4
   C. All of the above
   D. None of the above

222) Which of the following statements is (are) true regarding Medicaid?

1. It is a national health insurance program.
2. It is aimed at serving the poor and needy.
3. It was created by Title XIX of the Social Security Act.
4. State welfare or state health departments operate it.
   A. 1, 3
   B. 2, 4
   C. 1, 2, 3
   D. All of the above
   E. None of the above

223) Which of the following statements is (are) true regarding Medicaid?

1. It is a national health insurance program.
2. It is operated within the guidelines set by HCFA.
3. It was created by Title XIX of the Social Security Act.
4. There are no "out of pocket" expenses for persons covered by this program.
   A. 1, 3
   B. 2, 4
   C. 1, 2, 3
   D. All of the above
   E. None of the above

224) Which of the following statements is (are) true regarding Medicaid?

1. It is a national health insurance program.
2. It is aimed at providing medical insurance for the aged.
3. It was created by Title XIX of the Social Security Act.
4. It is operated by the Health Care Financing Administration (HCFA).
    A. 1, 3
    B. 2, 4
    C. 1, 2, 3
    D. All of the above
    E. None of the above

225) Which of the following statements is (are) *not* true regarding Medicaid?

1. It is a national health insurance program.
2. It is aimed at providing medical insurance for the aged.
3. It was created by Title XIX of the Social Security Act.
4. It is operated by the Health Care Financing Administration (HCFA).
    A. 1, 3
    B. 2, 4
    C. 1, 2, 3
    D. All of the above
    E. None of the above

226) Which of the following statements is (are) true regarding Medicaid?

1. It is a state health insurance program.
2. It is operated within the guidelines set by HCFA.
3. It was created by Title XVI of the Social Security Act.
4. There are no "out of pocket" expenses for persons covered by this program.
    A. 1, 3
    B. 2, 4
    C. 1, 2, 3
    D. All of the above
    E. None of the above

227) Which of the following statements regarding Medicaid is (are) *not* true ?

1. It is a state health insurance program.
2. It is operated within the guidelines set by HCFA.
3. It was created by Title XVI of the Social Security Act.
4. There are no "out of pocket" expenses for persons covered by this program.
    A. 1, 3
    B. 2, 4
    C. 1, 2, 3
    D. All of the above
    E. None of the above

228) Which of the following services are federally mandated by the Medicaid program?

1. Inpatient hospital care and outpatient services
2. Physician services
3. Skilled nursing home services for adults
4. Laboratory and x-ray services
    A. 1, 3
    B. 2, 4
    C. 1, 2, 3
    D. All of the above
    E. None of the above

229) **Which of the following services are federally mandated by the Medicaid program?**

1. Inpatient hospital care and outpatient services
2. Carpentry services
3. Skilled nursing home services for adults
4. Electrician's services
    A. 1, 3
    B. 2, 4
    C. 1, 2, 3
    D. All of the above
    E. None of the above

230) **Which of the following services is (are) *not* federally mandated by the Medicaid program?**

1. Inpatient hospital care and outpatient services
2. Carpentry services
3. Skilled nursing home services for adults
4. Electrician's services
    A. 1, 3
    B. 2, 4
    C. 1, 2, 3
    D. All of the above
    E. None of the above

231) **Groups that are eligible for Medicaid under HCFA standards include which of the following?**

1. Categorically needy
2. Spiritually needy
3. Medically needy
4. Ethnically needy
    A. 1, 3
    B. 2, 4
    C. 1, 2, 3
    D. All of the above
    E. None of the above

232) **Groups that are ineligible for Medicaid under HCFA standards include which of the following?**

1. Categorically needy
2. Spiritually needy
3. Medically needy
4. Ethnically needy
    A. 1, 3
    B. 2, 4
    C. 1, 2, 3
    D. All of the above
    E. None of the above

233) **Which of the following statements regarding Medicaid eligibility are true?**

1. Eligibility standards are set by each state.
2. Minimum eligibility standards are set by HCFA.
3. The categorically needy are usually eligible for Medicaid.
4. The medically needy are usually eligible for Medicaid.
    A. 1, 3
    B. 2, 4
    C. 1, 2, 3
    D. All of the above
    E. None of the above

234) Which of the following statements regarding Medicaid eligibility are true?

1. Eligibility standards are set by each state.
2. Minimum eligibility standards are set by HCFA.
3. The categorically needy are usually eligible for Medicaid.
4. The spiritually impoverished are usually eligible for Medicaid.
   A. 1, 3
   B. 2, 4
   C. 1, 2, 3
   D. All of the above
   E. None of the above

235) Which of the following statements regarding Medicaid eligibility are *not* true?

1. Eligibility standards are set by each state.
2. Minimum eligibility standards for Medicaid are set by the Social Security Administration.
3. The categorically needy are usually eligible for Medicaid.
4. The spiritually impoverished are usually eligible for Medicaid.
   A. 1, 3
   B. 2, 4
   C. 1, 2, 3
   D. All of the above
   E. None of the above

236) Which of the following groups is (are) considered a "mandatory Medicaid eligibility group"?

1. Recipients of Aid to Families with Dependent Children (AFDC)
2. Recipients of Supplemental Security Income (SSI)
3. Infants born to Medicaid-eligible pregnant women
4. Children under age six and pregnant women who meet the state's AFDC financial requirements
   A. 1, 3
   B. 2, 4
   C. 1, 2, 3
   D. All of the above
   E. None of the above

237) Which of the following groups is (are) considered a "mandatory Medicaid eligibility group"?

1. Recipients of Aid to Families with Dependent Children (AFDC)
2. Recipients of Workers' Compensation insurance
3. Infants born to Medicaid-eligible pregnant women
4. Children under age six who are the beneficiaries of a no-fault tort action
   A. 1, 3
   B. 2, 4
   C. 1, 2, 3
   D. All of the above
   E. None of the above

238) Which of the following groups is (are) *not* considered a "mandatory Medicaid eligibility group"?

1. Recipients of Aid to Families with Dependent Children (AFDC)
2. Recipients of Workers' Compensation insurance
3. Infants born to Medicaid-eligible pregnant women
4. Children under age six, who are the beneficiaries of a no-fault tort action
   A. 1, 3
   B. 2, 4
   C. 1, 2, 3
   D. All of the above
   E. None of the above

239) **Which of the following asset transfers are exempted from state imposed penalties during a "look back" for inappropriately transferred assets?**

1. Transfers to a spouse or to a third party for the sole benefit of the spouse
2. Transfers by a spouse to a third party for the sole benefit of the spouse
3. Transfers where imposing a penalty would cause undue hardship
4. Transfers to a sibling for the sole benefit of the sibling
   A. 1, 3
   B. 2, 4
   C. 1, 2, 3
   D. All of the above
   E. None of the above

240) **Which of the following asset transfers are *not* exempted from state imposed penalties during a "look back" for inappropriately transferred assets?**

1. Transfers to a spouse or to a third party for the sole benefit of the spouse
2. Transfers by a spouse to a third party for the sole benefit of the third party
3. Transfers where imposing a penalty would cause undue hardship
4. Transfers to a sibling for the sole benefit of the sibling
   A. 1, 3
   B. 2, 4
   C. 1, 2, 3
   D. All of the above
   E. None of the above

241) **Which of the following asset transfers are exempted from state imposed penalties during a "look back" for inappropriately transferred assets?**

1. Transfers to a spouse or to a third party for the sole benefit of the spouse
2. Transfers by a spouse to a third party for the sole benefit of the third party
3. Transfers where imposing a penalty would cause undue hardship
4. Transfers to a sibling for the sole benefit of the sibling
   A. 1, 3
   B. 2, 4
   C. 1, 2, 3
   D. All of the above
   E. None of the above

242) **Which of the following statements are true regarding a "penalty period" imposed by the state?**

1. It is the amount of time the state will withhold payment from nursing homes and other long-term care facilities.
2. There is no limit to the length of time in a penalty period.
3. Penalty periods are imposed by the state when an "inappropriate transfer of assets" has occurred.
4. The length of the penalty period is based on the fair market value of the transferred asset, and the monthly cost of the long-term care facility.
   A. 1, 3
   B. 2, 4
   C. 1, 2, 3
   D. All of the above
   E. None of the above

243) **Which of the following statements is (are) true regarding a "penalty period" imposed by the state?**

1. It is the amount of time the state will withhold payment from nursing homes and other long-term care facilities.
2. There is a 2-year limit to the length of a penalty period.
3. Penalty periods are imposed by the state when an "inappropriate transfer of assets" has occurred.
4. The length of the penalty period is based on the fair market value of all the marital assets divided by the predicted length of stay in the long-term care facility.
    A. 1, 3
    B. 2, 4
    C. 1, 2, 3
    D. All of the above
    E. None of the above

244) **Which of the following statements are *not* true regarding a "penalty period" imposed by the state?**

1. It is the amount of time the state will withhold payment from nursing homes and other long-term care facilities.
2. There is a 2-year limit to the length of a penalty period.
3. Penalty periods are imposed by the state when an "inappropriate transfer of assets" has occurred.
4. The length of the penalty period is based on the fair market value of all the marital assets divided by the predicted length of stay in the long-term care facility.
    A. 1, 3
    B. 2, 4
    C. 1, 2, 3
    D. All of the above
    E. None of the above

245) **Which of the following statements is (are) true, regarding the "look back" or financial evaluation of an individual's eligibility for Medicaid?**

1. It is a financial evaluation undertaken by the state to establish Medicaid eligibility.
2. Recent transfers of assets are examined.
3. The look back commonly examines financial records for 36 months prior to the date of an individual's institutionalization.
4. Transfers of assets for less than fair market value may invoke penalties from the state.
    A. 1, 3
    B. 2, 4
    C. 1, 2, 3
    D. All of the above
    E. None of the above

246) **Which of the following statements is (are) true, regarding the "look back" or financial evaluation of an individual's eligibility for Medicaid?**

1. It is a financial evaluation undertaken by the federal government to establish Workers' Compensation eligibility.
2. Recent transfers of assets are examined.
3. The look back commonly examines financial records for 6 months prior to the date of an individual's institutionalization.
4. Transfers of assets for less than fair market value may invoke penalties from the state.
    A. 1, 3
    B. 2, 4
    C. 1, 2, 3
    D. All of the above
    E. None of the above

247) **Of the following statements, which is (are) *not* true, regarding the "look back" or financial evaluation of an individual's eligibility for Medicaid?**

1. It is a financial evaluation undertaken by the federal government to establish Workers' Compensation eligibility.
2. Recent transfers of assets are examined.
3. The look back commonly examines financial records for 6 months prior to the date of an individual's institutionalization.
4. Transfers of assets for less than fair market value, may invoke penalties from the state.
    A. 1, 3
    B. 2, 4
    C. 1, 2, 3
    D. All of the above
    E. None of the above

248) **The penalty period imposed by the state for inappropriate transfers of assets prior to Medicaid application is calculated by which of the following formulas?**

A. Fair market value of transferred asset/average monthly cost of nursing facility in the state=months of penalty period
B. Medicaid approved value of transferred asset/Standard Monthly Medicaid Allowance (SMMA) for nursing homes in that state=months of penalty period
C. Average cost of an individuals assets/Standard Monthly Medicaid Allowance (SMMA) for nursing homes in that state=months of penalty period
D. Medicare approved value of transferred asset/Standard Monthly Medicaid Allowance (SMMA) for nursing homes in that state=months of penalty period
E. Medicare approved value of transferred asset/Standard Monthly Medicare Allowance (SMMA) for nursing homes in that state=months of penalty period

249) **Which of the following statements is true regarding the term "spousal impoverishment" before Medicaid eligibility?**

1. It refers to the depletion of a couple's life savings that occurs when one is paying the expenses associated with the institutionalization of the spouse.
2. It refers to the government protection from savings depletion that is granted only to those who are Medicare eligible.
3. Amendments to the Social Security Act in 1988 allow a couple to have Medicaid benefits without spending down their resources.
4. Federal Medicaid guidelines mandate the "community spouse" first reach 161% of the federal poverty level, before the institutionalized spouse is eligible for Medicaid benefits.
    A. 1, 3
    B. 2, 4
    C. 1, 2, 3
    D. All of the above
    E. None of the above

250) **Which of the following statements is (are) *not* true regarding the term "spousal impoverishment" before Medicaid eligibility?**

1. It refers to the depletion of a couple's life savings that occurs when one is paying the expenses associated with the institutionalization of the spouse.
2. It refers to the government protection from savings depletion that is granted only to those who are Medicare eligible
3. It refers to amendments to the Social Security Act in 1988 that allow a couple to have Medicaid benefits without spending down their resources.
4. Federal Medicaid guidelines mandate the "community spouse" first reach 161% of the federal poverty level, before the institutionalized spouse is eligible for Medicaid benefits.
    A. 1, 3
    B. 2, 4
    C. 1, 2, 3
    D. All of the above
    E. None of the above

251) **Which of the following statements is (are) true regarding the eligibility of an institutionalized spouse for Medicaid?**

1. The institutionalized spouse must remain in the medical facility for at least 30 days.
2. The state must evaluate the couple's resources.
3. The spousal resource amount (SRA) must be calculated.
4. Spousal resources amounts (SRAs) that are above the state's minimum resource standard are depletable resources.
   A. 1, 3
   B. 2, 4
   C. 1, 2, 3
   D. All of the above
   E. None of the above

252) **Which of the following statements is (are) true regarding the eligibility of an institutionalized spouse for Medicaid?**

1. The institutionalized spouse must remain in the medical facility for at least 90 days.
2. The state must evaluate the couple's resources.
3. The Spousal Poverty Depletion Rate (SPDR) must be calculated.
4. Spousal resources amounts that are above the State's Minimum Resource Standard are depletable resources.
   A. 1, 3
   B. 2, 4
   C. 1, 2, 3
   D. All of the above
   E. None of the above

253) **Which of the following statements is (are) *not* true regarding the eligibility of an institutionalized spouse for Medicaid?**

1. The institutionalized spouse must remain in the medical facility for at least 90 days.
2. The state must evaluate the couple's resources.
3. The Spousal Poverty Depletion Rate (SPDR) must be calculated.
4. Spousal resources amounts that are above the State's Minimum Resource Standard are depletable resources.
   A. 1, 3
   B. 2, 4
   C. 1, 2, 3
   D. All of the above
   E. None of the above

254) **Which of the following is (are) true, regarding Medicaid eligibility for a couple with a spouse in a medical facility or nursing home?**

1. The community spouse's income is not considered available to the spouse in the medical facility.
2. For the purposes of Medicaid eligibility, the two individuals are not considered a couple.
3. The state will use the income eligibility standards for one person rather than two.
4. For the purposes of Medicaid eligibility, the institutionalized spouse is considered to own all the matrimonial assets.
   A. 1, 3
   B. 2, 4
   C. 1, 2, 3
   D. All of the above
   E. None of the above

255) **Which of the following is (are) true, regarding Medicaid eligibility for a couple with a spouse in a medical facility or nursing home?**

1. The community spouse's income is not considered available to the spouse in the medical facility.
2. For the purposes of Medicaid eligibility, the community spouse is considered to own all the matrimonial assets.
3. The state will use the income eligibility standards for one person rather than two.
4. For the purposes of Medicaid eligibility, the institutionalized spouse is considered to own all the matrimonial assets.

    A. 1, 3
    B. 2, 4
    C. 1, 2, 3
    D. All of the above
    E. None of the above

256) **Which of the following is (are) *not* true, regarding Medicaid eligibility for a couple with a spouse in a medical facility or nursing home?**

1. The community spouse's income is not considered available to the spouse in the medical facility.
2. For the purposes of Medicaid eligibility, the community spouse is considered to own all the matrimonial assets.
3. The state will use the income eligibility standards for one person rather than two.
4. For the purposes of Medicaid eligibility, the institutionalized spouse is considered to own all the matrimonial assets.

    A. 1, 3
    B. 2, 4
    C. 1, 2, 3
    D. All of the above
    E. None of the above

257) **Which of the following statements regarding a trust are true?**

1. It is a legal title to property, held by one party for the benefit of another party.
2. There are usually at least three parties involved in the establishment of a trust.
3. A trust's grantor donates the assets of a trust.
4. A trust's beneficiary is the recipient of some or all of the trust's assets.

    A. 1, 3
    B. 2, 4
    C. 1, 2, 3
    D. All of the above
    E. None of the above

258) **Which of the following statements regarding a trust are true?**

1. It is a legal title to property, held by one party for the benefit of another party.
2. There are usually at least six parties involved in the establishment of a trust.
3. A trust's grantor donates the assets of a trust.
4. A trust's beneficiary is the entity that donates the trust's assets.

    A. 1, 3
    B. 2, 4
    C. 1, 2, 3
    D. All of the above
    E. None of the above

259) **Which of the following statements regarding a trust are true?**

1. It is a legal title to property, held by one party for the benefit of another party.
2. A trust's trustee holds and manages the assets in the trust for the beneficiary.
3. A trust's grantor donates the assets of a trust.
4. A revocable trust is a trust whose terms or beneficiaries can be changed.

A. 1, 3
B. 2, 4
C. 1, 2, 3
D. All of the above
E. None of the above

260) Which of the following statements regarding a trust are true?

1. It is a legal title to property, held by one party for the benefit of that party.
2. A trust's assets can exist in many forms, such as cash, real estate, businesses or stocks.
3. A trust's trustee donates the assets of a trust.
4. An irrevocable trust is a trust whose terms or beneficiaries cannot be changed.
    A. 1, 3
    B. 2, 4
    C. 1, 2, 3
    D. All of the above
    E. None of the above

261) Which of the following statements regarding trusts are true?

1. It is a legal title to property, held by one party, for the benefit of another party
2. A trust's assets can exist in many forms, such as cash, real estate, businesses or stocks
3. A trust's grantor donates the assets of a trust
4. An irrevocable trust is a trust whose terms or beneficiaries cannot be changed
    A. 1, 3
    B. 2, 4
    C. 1, 2, 3
    D. All of the above
    E. None of the above

262) Which of the following statements regarding a trust are true?

1. It is a legal title to property, held by one party, for the benefit of another party.
2. A trust's assets can exist only as cash or stock.
3. A trust's grantor donates the assets of a trust.
4. An irrevocable trust is a trust whose terms or beneficiaries can be changed.
    A. 1, 3
    B. 2, 4
    C. 1, 2, 3
    D. All of the above
    E. None of the above

263) Which of the following is true, regarding the treatment of trusts under HCFA regulations?

1. HCFA would like to prevent the use of trusts created only to transfer assets to assure Medicaid eligibility.
2. How HCFA treats a trust depends upon what type of trust it is.
3. Monies that are paid from a trust to an individual are treated as income to that individual.
4. Monies from a trust that could be paid to an individual, but are not, are treated as available resources.
    A. 1, 3
    B. 2, 4
    C. 1, 2, 3
    D. All of the above
    E. None of the above

264) **Which of the following is true, regarding the treatment of trusts under HCFA regulations?**

1. HCFA would like to encourage the use of trusts created only to transfer assets to assure Medicaid eligibility.
2. How HCFA treats a trust depends upon what type of trust it is (revocable or irrevocable).
3. Monies that are paid from a trust to an individual are treated as protected assets.
4. Monies from a trust that could be paid to an individual, but are not, are treated as available resources.
   - A. 1, 3
   - B. 2, 4
   - C. 1, 2, 3
   - D. All of the above
   - E. None of the above

265) **Which of the following is (are) *not* true, regarding the treatment of trusts under HCFA regulations?**

1. HCFA would like to encourage the use of trusts created only to transfer assets to assure Medicaid eligibility.
2. How HCFA treats a trust depends upon what type of trust it is (revocable or irrevocable).
3. Monies that are paid from a trust to an individual are treated as protected assets.
4. Monies from a trust that could be paid to an individual, but are not, are treated as available resources.
   - A. 1, 3
   - B. 2, 4
   - C. 1, 2, 3
   - D. All of the above
   - E. None of the above

266) **A local court establishes an irrevocable trust for a severely disabled individual. The trust is funded by the individual's Social Security benefits. Which of the following statements describes how HCFA will view these assets upon the individual's application for Medicaid benefits?**

- A. The assets will be considered not available to the individual because they are placed in an irrevocable trust.
- B. The assets will be considered not available to the individual because the title to the assets are held by the Trust.
- C. The assets will be considered available to the individual because the trust was established within the "look back" period.
- D. The assets will not be considered available to the individual because he is disabled.
- E. The assets will be considered available to the individual because the assets are from Social Security.

267) **Which of the following statements (is) are true, regarding current definitions of medical necessity in insurance contracts?**

1. They are inconsistent.
2. They are concise.
3. They are ambiguous.
4. They are uniform throughout the industry.
   - A. 1, 3
   - B. 2, 4
   - C. 1, 2, 3
   - D. All of the above
   - E. None of the above

268) **Which of the following statements (is) are *not* true, regarding current definitions of medical necessity in insurance contracts?**

    1.   They are inconsistent.
    2.   They are concise.
    3.   They are ambiguous.
    4.   They are uniform throughout the industry.
        A.   1, 3
        B.   2, 4
        C.   1, 2, 3
        D.   All of the above
        E.   None of the above

269) **In standard health insurance contracts, which of the following terms (is) are *not* made clear in the definition of medical necessity?**

    1.   Appropriate medical care
    2.   Reasonable medical care
    3.   Custodial medical care
    4.   Experimental medical care
        A.   1, 3
        B.   2, 4
        C.   1, 2, 3
        D.   All of the above
        E.   None of the above

270) **Which of the following statements is (are) *not* true regarding the definition of medical necessity in insurance contracts?**

    1.   It is largely a "nonissue" discussed only by academics.
    2.   It is an important issue that affects the adjudication of all health insurance claims.
    3.   It is a problem solved easily by crafting the "right words" into the definition.
    4.   The definition of what is medically necessary is best approached through a "procedural methodology."
        A.   1, 3
        B.   2, 4
        C.   1, 2, 3
        D.   All of the above
        E.   None of the above

271) **When determining what is medically necessary in a particular case, which of the following should be evaluated?**

    1.   The reasonable expectations of the hospital's nursing staff
    2.   The opinion of objective specialists in the field of medicine in question
    3.   The patient's financial record
    4.   The opinion of the treating physician
        A.   1, 3
        B.   2, 4
        C.   1, 2, 3
        D.   All of the above
        E.   None of the above

272) **When determining what is medically necessary in a particular case, which of the following should *not* be evaluated?**

    1.   The reasonable expectations of the hospital's billing staff
    2.   The opinion of objective specialists in the field of medicine in question
    3.   The patient's financial record
    4.   The opinion of the treating physician

A. 1, 2, 3
B. 2, 4
C. 1, 3
D. All of the above
E. None of the above

273) **When determining the medical necessity of a claim, which of the following is (are) true regarding the "reasonable expectations" of the claimant?**

1. The reasonable expectations of the claimant are unimportant in the adjudication of the claim.
2. If a certain medical benefit can be reasonably expected, then the claimant should be entitled to it.
3. The ability for the insured to understand the complex terminology in the contract is irrelevant.
4. The fairness of any insurance contract is suspect when the claimant does not or cannot understand its benefits or the meaning of its exclusions.
   A. 1, 3
   B. 2, 4
   C. 1, 2, 3
   D. All of the above
   E. None of the above

274) **When determining the medical necessity of a claim, which of the following is (are) *not* true regarding the "reasonable expectations" of the claimant?**

1. The reasonable expectations of the claimant are unimportant in adjudication of the claim.
2. If a certain medical benefit can be reasonably expected, then the claimant should be entitled to it.
3. The ability for the insured to understand the complex terminology in the contract is irrelevant.
4. The fairness of any insurance contract is suspect when the claimant does not or cannot understand its benefits or the meaning of its exclusions.
   A. 1, 3
   B. 2, 4
   C. 1, 2, 3
   D. All of the above
   E. None of the above

275) **When determining the medical necessity of a claim, which of the following is (are) *not* true regarding the "reasonable expectations" of the claimant?**

1. The reasonable expectations of the claimant are unimportant in adjudication of the claim.
2. Just because a certain medical benefit can be reasonably expected by the average layperson, does not mean that the claimant should be entitled to it.
3. The ability for the insured to understand the complex terminology in the contract is irrelevant.
4. The fairness of any insurance contract is suspect when the claimant does not or cannot understand its benefits or the meaning of its exclusions.
   A. 1, 3
   B. 2, 4
   C. 1, 2, 3
   D. All of the above
   E. None of the above

276) **When working with Workers' Compensation patients, a Case Manager should keep in mind that the most effective method to ensure a successful outcome in regards to vocational rehabilitation is to:**

    A. Recommend self-employment to the patient.
    B. Return the injured worker to his former position if at all possible.
    C. Perform a thorough evaluation by doing as many vocational tests as possible.
    D. All of the above
    E. None of the above

277) **Which of the following statements (is) are true regarding the Mental Health Parity Act of 1996?**

    1. It is a federal law.
    2. It is aimed at protecting the rights of individuals with mental health problems.
    3. It forbids lifetime or annual dollar limits on mental health care (unless comparable limits apply to medical and/or surgical treatment).
    4. Its definition of mental illness excludes chemical dependency.
        A. 1, 3
        B. 2, 4
        C. 1, 2, 3
        D. All of the above
        E. None of the above

278) **Which of the following statements (is) are true regarding the Mental Health Parity Act of 1996?**

    1. It is a county law.
    2. It is aimed at protecting the rights of individuals with mental health problems.
    3. It assures lifetime or annual dollar limits on mental health care.
    4. Its definition of mental illness excludes chemical dependency.
        A. 1, 3
        B. 2, 4
        C. 1, 2, 3
        D. All of the above
        E. None of the above

279) **Which of the following statements (is) are *not* true regarding the Mental Health Parity Act of 1996?**

    1. It is a county law.
    2. It mandates that insurance plans cover mental health treatments.
    3. It assures lifetime or annual dollar limits on mental health care.
    4. Its definition of mental illness excludes chemical dependency.
        A. 1, 3
        B. 2, 4
        C. 1, 2, 3
        D. All of the above
        E. None of the above

280) **Which of the following types of employers are bound under the tenets of the Mental Health Parity Act?**

    1. Airlines
    2. Employers with 50 or less employees
    3. Munitions and weapons manufacturers
    4. Employers who can demonstrate that compliance will cause financial hardship
        A. 1, 3
        B. 2, 4
        C. 1, 2, 3
        D. All of the above
        E. None of the above

281) **Which of the following types of employers are *not* bound under the tenets of the Mental Health Parity Act?**

1. Airlines
2. Employers with 50 or less employees
3. Munitions and weapons manufacturers
4. Employers who can demonstrate that compliance will cause financial hardship
   A. 1, 3
   B. 2, 4
   C. 1, 2, 3
   D. All of the above
   E. None of the above

282) **Which of the following mental health benefit limitations are allowable under the tenets of the Mental Health Parity Act?**

1. Limited number of annual outpatient visits
2. Limited number of inpatient days annually
3. Per-visit fee limit
4. Higher deductibles and copayments for mental health treatments than for medical and surgical treatments
   A. 1, 3
   B. 2, 4
   C. 1, 2, 3
   D. All of the above
   E. None of the above

283) **Which of the following mental health benefit limitations are allowable under the tenets of the Mental Health Parity Act?**

1. Per-visit fee limit
2. Limited number of annual outpatient visits
3. Limited number of inpatient days annually
4. No mental health benefits
   A. 1, 3
   B. 2, 4
   C. 1, 2, 3
   D. All of the above
   E. None of the above

284) **Which of the following mental health benefit limitations are allowable under the tenets of the Mental Health Parity Act?**

1. Annual dollar limit for mental health care
2. Limited number of annual outpatient visits
3. Lifetime dollar limit on mental health care
4. Limited number of inpatient days annually
   A. 1, 3
   B. 2, 4
   C. 1, 2, 3
   D. All of the above
   E. None of the above

285) **Which of the following mental health benefit limitations are not allowable under the tenets of the Mental Health Parity Act?**

1. Annual dollar limit for mental health care
2. Limited number of annual outpatient visits
3. Lifetime dollar limit on mental health care
4. Limited number of inpatient days annually

A. 1, 3
B. 2, 4
C. 1, 2, 3
D. All of the above
E. None of the above

286) Which of the following statements are true regarding the Pregnancy Discrimination Act?

1. It is a federal law.
2. It extends to pregnant individuals the same rights and benefits extended to those with medical problems.
3. It is an amendment to the Civil Rights Act of 1964.
4. It extends to pregnant individuals the same rights and benefits extended to those with surgical problems.
   A. 1, 3
   B. 2, 4
   C. 1, 2, 3
   D. All of the above
   E. None of the above

287) Which of the following statements are true regarding the Pregnancy Discrimination Act?

1. It is a state law.
2. It extends to pregnant individuals the same rights and benefits extended to those with medical problems.
3. It is an amendment to the Social Security Act.
4. It extends to pregnant individuals the same rights and benefits extended to those with surgical problems.
   A. 1, 3
   B. 2, 4
   C. 1, 2, 3
   D. All of the above
   E. None of the above

288) Which of the following statements are *not* true regarding the Pregnancy Discrimination Act?

1. It is a state law.
2. It extends to pregnant individuals the same rights and benefits extended to those with medical problems.
3. It is an amendment to the Social Security Act.
4. It extends to pregnant individuals the same rights and benefits extended to those with surgical problems.
   A. 1, 3
   B. 2, 4
   C. 1, 2, 3
   D. All of the above
   E. None of the above

289) Under the terms of the Pregnancy Discrimination Act, in which of the following categories are pregnant individuals to be treated the same as individuals with medical and surgical problems?

1. Health insurance benefits
2. Short-term sick leave
3. Disability benefits
4. Employment policies (such as seniority, leave extensions and reinstatement)
   A. 1, 3
   B. 2, 4
   C. 1, 2, 3
   D. All of the above
   E. None of the above

290) **Under the terms of the Pregnancy Discrimination Act, in which of the following categories are pregnant individuals to be treated the same as individuals with medical and surgical problems?**

1. Health insurance benefits
2. "Lead-off hitter status" in company softball league
3. Disability benefits
4. Car insurance benefits
    A. 1, 3
    B. 2, 4
    C. 1, 2, 3
    D. All of the above
    E. None of the above

291) **Which of the following types of limitations are prohibited under the terms of the Pregnancy Discrimination Act?**

1. Provider choice
2. Provider access
3. Cost of providers or services
4. Quality of providers or services
    A. 1, 3
    B. 2, 4
    C. 1, 2, 3
    D. All of the above
    E. None of the above

292) **Which of the following limitations are prohibited under the terms of the Pregnancy Discrimination Act?**

1. Limiting the number of physicians or hospitals who provide maternity care, when medical and surgical care providers are limited
2. Limiting the number of plans that offer maternity care, without corresponding limits on medical and surgical care
3. Limiting the reimbursement for maternity care, when there are corresponding limits on medical and surgical care
4. Exacting higher deductibles, copayments or out-of-pocket maximums for maternity care, than medical and surgical care
    A. 1, 3
    B. 2, 4
    C. 1, 2, 3
    D. All of the above
    E. None of the above

293) **Which of the following limitations are prohibited under the terms of the Pregnancy Discrimination Act?**

1. Limiting the number of physicians or hospitals who provide maternity care, when medical and surgical care providers are not limited
2. Limiting the number of plans that offer maternity care, without corresponding limits on medical and surgical care
3. Limiting the reimbursement for maternity care, when there are no corresponding limits on medical and surgical care
4. Exacting higher deductibles, copayments or out-of-pocket maximums for maternity care, than medical and surgical care
    A. 1, 3
    B. 2, 4
    C. 1, 2, 3
    D. All of the above
    E. None of the above

294) Which of the following limitations are prohibited under the terms of the Pregnancy Discrimination Act?

1. Limiting the number of physicians or hospitals who provide maternity care, when medical and surgical care providers are not limited
2. Limiting the number of plans that offer maternity care, with corresponding limits on medical and surgical care
3. Limiting the reimbursement for maternity care, when there are no corresponding limits on medical and surgical care
4. Exacting deductibles, copayments or out-of-pocket maximums for maternity care
    A. 1, 3
    B. 2, 4
    C. 1, 2, 3
    D. All of the above
    E. None of the above

295) Which of the following individuals (is) are *not* protected under the Pregnancy Discrimination Act?

1. A pregnant but unwed employee
2. A part-time employee
3. An independent contractor
4. Employee of a successor corporation
    A. 1, 2
    B. 3, 4
    C. 1, 2, 3
    D. All of the above
    E. None of the above

296) Which of the following benefits are *excluded* under the terms of the Pregnancy Discrimination Act?

1. Home health care
2. Abortions
3. Home physical therapy care
4. Mandatory maternity leave
    A. 1, 3
    B. 2, 4
    C. 1, 2, 3
    D. All of the above
    E. None of the above

297) Which of the following benefits are usually *included* under the terms of the Pregnancy Discrimination Act?

1. Home health care
2. Abortions
3. Home physical therapy care
4. Mandatory maternity leave
    A. 1, 3
    B. 2, 4
    C. 1, 2, 3
    D. All of the above
    E. None of the above

298) **Which of the following statements is (are) true, regarding the Tax Equity and Fiscal Responsibility Act (TEFRA)?**

1. It established a case-based reimbursement system called Diagnosis Related Groups, or DRGs.
2. It amended the Social Security Act and made Medicare secondary to employer group health plans for active employees 65 to 69 years old and their spouses in the same age group.
3. It established peer review organizations (PROs).
4. It revised the Age Discrimination in Employment Act.
   A. 1, 3
   B. 2, 4
   C. 1, 2, 3
   D. All of the above
   E. None of the above

299) **Which of the following statements is (are) true, regarding the Tax Equity and Fiscal Responsibility Act (TEFRA)?**

1. It established a case-based reimbursement system called Diagnosis Related Groups, or DRGs.
2. It amended the Social Security Act and made Medicare secondary to employer group health plans for active employees 65 to 69 years old and their spouses in the same age group.
3. It established peer review organizations (PROs).
4. It revised the Mental Health Parity Act.
   A. 1, 3
   B. 2, 4
   C. 1, 2, 3
   D. All of the above
   E. None of the above

300) **Which of the following statements is (are) true, regarding the Tax Equity and Fiscal Responsibility Act (TEFRA)?**

1. It established a reimbursement system called Health Maintenance Organizations, or HMOs.
2. It amended the Social Security Act and made Medicare secondary to employer group health plans for active employees 65 to 69 years old and their spouses in the same age group.
3. It revised the Mental Health Parity Act.
4. It established peer review organizations (PROs).
   A. 1, 3
   B. 2, 4
   C. 1, 2, 3
   D. All of the above
   E. None of the above

301) **Under the Tax Equity and Fiscal Responsibility Act of 1982 (TEFRA), which of the following statements are true regarding Diagnosis Related Groups?**

1. It is a case-based reimbursement system.
2. It is a prospective payment program.
3. It places limits on the rate increases in hospital revenues.
4. It is a cost containment system.
   A. 1, 3
   B. 2, 4
   C. 1, 2, 3
   D. All of the above
   E. None of the above

302) **Under the terms of the Tax Equity and Fiscal Responsibility Act of 1982 (TEFRA), which of the following statements are true regarding Diagnosis Related Groups?**

1. It is a case-based reimbursement system.
2. It is a retrospective payment program.
3. It places limits on the rate increases in hospital revenues.
4. It is a clinical quality improvement system.
   A. 1, 3
   B. 2, 4
   C. 1, 2, 3
   D. All of the above
   E. None of the above

303) **Under the terms of the Tax Equity and Fiscal Responsibility Act of 1982 (TEFRA), which of the following statements are *not* true regarding Diagnosis Related Groups?**

1. It is a case-based reimbursement system.
2. It is a retrospective payment program.
3. It places limits on the rate increases in hospital revenues.
4. It is a clinical quality improvement system.
   A. 1, 3
   B. 2, 4
   C. 1, 2, 3
   D. All of the above
   E. None of the above

304) **Under the terms of the Tax Equity and Fiscal Responsibility Act, which of the following medical specialties were exempted from the Diagnosis Related Groups (DRGs) Program?**

A. Cardiology
B. Endocrinology
C. Rehabilitation medicine
D. Radiation oncology
E. Family medicine

305) **Which of the following was amended or revised under the Tax Equity and Fiscal Responsibility Act?**

1. The Mental Health Parity Act
2. The Social Security Act
3. The Tuberculosis Containment Act
4. The Age Discrimination in Employment Act
   A. 1, 3
   B. 2, 4
   C. 1, 2, 3
   D. All of the above
   E. None of the above

306) **Which of the following was *not* amended or revised under the Tax Equity and Fiscal Responsibility Act?**

1. The Mental Health Parity Act
2. The Social Security Act
3. The Tuberculosis Containment Act
4. The Age Discrimination in Employment Act
   A. 1, 3
   B. 2, 4
   C. 1, 2, 3
   D. All of the above
   E. None of the above

307) **Which of the following was established under the terms of the Tax Equity and Fiscal Responsibility Act?**

1. Peer Review Organizations (PROs)
2. Health Maintenance Organizations (HMOs)
3. Diagnosis Related Groups (DRGs)
4. Independent Practice Organizations (IPAs)
    A. 1, 3
    B. 2, 4
    C. 1, 2, 3
    D. All of the above
    E. None of the above

308) **Which of the following was *not* established under the terms of the Tax Equity and Fiscal Responsibility Act?**

1. Peer Review Organizations (PROs)
2. Health Maintenance Organizations (HMOs)
3. Diagnosis Related Groups (DRGs)
4. Independent Practice Organizations (IPAs)
    A. 1, 3
    B. 2, 4
    C. 1, 2, 3
    D. All of the above
    E. None of the above

309) **Which of the following is (are) true regarding Peer Review Organizations (PROs)?**

1. They were established under the Tax Equity and Fiscal Responsibility Act.
2. They are entities selected by HCFA to reduce medical costs.
3. They are entities selected by HCFA to assure quality of care and appropriateness of admissions, readmissions and discharges.
4. PROs concern themselves with the care of Medicare and Medicaid patients.
    A. 1, 3
    B. 2, 4
    C. 1, 2, 3
    D. All of the above
    E. None of the above

310) **Which of the following is (are) true regarding Peer Review Organizations (PROs)?**

1. They were established under the Social Security Act.
2. They are entities selected by HCFA to reduce medical costs.
3. They are entities selected by the Social Security Administration to assure that cost of care is reduced regardless of consequences to the quality of care.
4. PROs concern themselves with the care of Medicare and Medicaid patients.
    A. 1, 3
    B. 2, 4
    C. 1, 2, 3
    D. All of the above
    E. None of the above

311) **Which of the following is (are) *not* true regarding Peer Review Organizations (PROs)?**

1. They were established under the Social Security Act.
2. They are entities selected by HCFA to reduce medical costs.
3. They are entities selected by the Social Security Administration to assure that cost of care is reduced regardless of consequences to the quality of care.
4. PROs concern themselves with the care of Medicare and Medicaid patients.

    A. 1, 3
    B. 2, 4
    C. 1, 2, 3
    D. All of the above
    E. None of the above

312) Which of the following is true of Utilization Review?

1. Utilization Review reviews services for medical appropriateness.
2. Utilization Review reviews services for medical necessity.
3. Utilization Review is only done retrospectively.
4. Utilization Review compares services rendered to national acceptable standards and protocols.
5. Utilization Review denies care over certain pre-established dollar amount.
    A. 1, 2, 3
    B. 1, 2, 4
    C. 1, 3, 5
    D. All of the above
    E. None of the above

313) A 35-year-old male engineer, who is wheelchair bound secondary to a spinal injury, applies for a job in a large engineering firm. The job advertisement calls for candidates with a PhD in engineering, yet he only has a master's degree. The applicant reasons that under the proscriptions of the ADA, the employer must make "reasonable accommodations" to the disabled, and therefore his degree should be good enough to get the job. The employer is justified (under the ADA) in denying this applicant employment because:

A. The candidate cannot perform the "essential functions" of the job, because he is wheelchair bound and therefore cannot use the existing computer equipment.
B. The candidate is not "qualified" for the job, because he does not have the requirements requested in the written job advertisement.
C. The candidate cannot enter the building because it lacks a ramp.
D. The candidate cannot perform the job adequately, because it requires adherence to a strict time schedule, and his disability requires advance notice for his transportation.
E. The candidate cannot work in the building because it lacks appropriate bathroom facilities.

314) When an injured worker is released to work with permanent restrictions the Case Manager should immediately:

A. Inform the employer that accommodations must be made for the employee.
B. Advise the worker that he must look for work elsewhere.
C. Discuss the restrictions with the employer to explore possible alternative work options.
D. Set up a vocational evaluation.

315) When applying for SSI it is important for the patient to know:

A. The criteria are state specific and have explicit eligibility criteria.
B. That SSI is based on low income and medical criteria.
C. That SSI is for children, the disabled and elderly.
D. All of the above
E. None of the above

316) Which of the following defines "disability"?

A. The inability to perform any activities
B. The inability to perform ADLs
C. The inability to perform age- and gender-specific roles in a particular social and physical environment
D. All of the above
E. None of the above

317) **Which of the following reasons would make it difficult for the Case Manager to affect positively a Workers' Compensation case?**

1. The employer's benefit plan offers financial incentives for an injured worker to remain out of work.
2. The employer won't offer modified duty.
3. The medical improvement of the injured worker must reach the functional level for the individual to be able to safely perform his or her full job duty.
    A. 1, 2
    B. 2, 3
    C. All of the above
    D. None of the above

318) **Why is a job description important to a Case Manager when managing a Workers' Compensation case?**

1. It is necessary to understand the job requirements, tasks and duties of the job the patient will need to return to.
2. It is helpful in determining why the patient was injured.
3. It is helpful in determining how to avoid future injury.
4. It is necessary in order to determine how the patient was injured.
    A. 1
    B. 1, 2, 3
    C. 2, 3, 4
    D. 4
    E. All of the above

319) **When managing a patient who was injured in a car accident, the Case Manager needs to be knowledgeable regarding charitable and not-for-profit programs and services available in the community. Which of the following statements are *not* true in regards to these programs?**

1. They are qualitatively superior to those that can be purchased privately.
2. PIP policy limits may restrict the range of options available to the client.
3. A higher quality of life index is associated with these programs.
4. The costs of health care may exceed the finances of the patient and insurer.
    A. 1, 3
    B. 2, 4
    C. 1, 2, 3
    D. All of the above
    E. None of the above

320) **A driver has a no-fault policy. An uninsured driver strikes him while driving his vehicle. The uninsured driver of the second vehicle is noted to have alcohol on his breath, and subsequent testing reveals a blood alcohol level of 203 mg/dl. Both drivers are seriously injured. The first driver's insurance company can successfully deny medical coverage to the uninsured driver because:**

A. He was driving while intoxicated.
B. He was driving while uninsured.
C. He has demonstrated negligence and disregard for safety.
D. All of the above
E. None of the above

321) **Under the Medicare program, the phrase "assignment of benefits" means:**

1. The patient or beneficiary directs Medicare to pay covered benefits directly to the provider of services.
2. The provider must accept Medicare's allowable charge as payment in full.
3. The patient assigns, or turns over, his benefits to a family member.
4. The Medicare patient has benefit coverage under Medicare.

A. 1, 2
B. 2, 3
C. 3, 4
D. All of the above
E. None of the above

322) What type of insurance generally pays for:
- Medically necessary treatments
- Lost wages
- Rehabilitation services
- Vocational services
  A. Group health insurance
  B. Automobile insurance
  C. Workers' Compensation
  D. Medicare
  E. All of the above

1) **Answer: C**

The exceptions to the ADA are:
- Religious organizations or private membership clubs, except when these organizations sponsor a public event
- The federal government or corporations owned by the federal government
- Native American tribes
- Compliance with this act can prove a hardship for small employers. Therefore, if an employer has less than 15 employees, he is exempt. (Note: Because an accommodation is expensive for an employer, does not automatically make it a "hardship.")

2) **Answer: A**

The exceptions to the ADA are:
- Religious organizations or private membership clubs, except when these organizations sponsor a public event
- The federal government or corporations owned by the federal government
- Native American tribes
- Compliance with this act can prove a hardship for small employers. Therefore, if an employer has less than 15 employees, he is exempt. (Note: Because an accommodation is expensive for an employer, does not automatically make it a "hardship.")

3) **Answer: D**

The employer is obligated to make "reasonable accommodations" to an individual's disability that allows the employee to perform his job. Reasonable accommodations in employment may include:
- Making existing facilities readily accessible to, and usable by an individual with disabilities
- Job restructuring, part-time or modified work schedules, reassignment to a vacant position
- Acquisition or modification of equipment or devices
- Appropriate adjustment or modification of examinations, training materials or policies
- Provision of qualified readers or interpreters, and other similar accommodations for individuals with disabilities

4) **Answer: B**

The employer is obligated to make "reasonable accommodations" to an individual's disability that allows the employee to perform his job. Reasonable accommodations in employment may include:
- Making existing facilities readily accessible to, and usable by an individual with disabilities
- Job restructuring, part-time or modified work schedules, reassignment to a vacant position
- Acquisition or modification of equipment or devices
- Appropriate adjustment or modification of examinations, training materials or policies
- Provision of qualified readers or interpreters, and other similar accommodations for individuals with disabilities

In the examples given, the individual hired as a typist must be able to type; similarly, a ballet dancer must be able to dance. Changing the essential job functions, while laudatory, is not mandated by the ADA.

5)   Answer: A

The employer is obligated to make "reasonable accommodations" to an individual's disability that allows the employee to perform his job. Reasonable accommodations in employment may include:

- Making existing facilities readily accessible to, and usable by an individual with disabilities
- Job restructuring, part-time or modified work schedules, reassignment to a vacant position
- Acquisition or modification of equipment or devices
- Appropriate adjustment or modification of examinations, training materials or policies
- The provision of qualified readers or interpreters, and other similar accommodations for individuals with disabilities

In the examples above, the individual hired as a typist must be able to type; similarly, a ballet dancer must be able to dance. Changing the essential job functions, while laudatory, is not mandated by the ADA.

6)   Answer: D

The following are rules of thumb to help determine if a job function is an "essential function" of the job:

- Essential job functions recorded in the written descriptions of job, prepared prior to advertising for the job or interviewing candidates are considered evidential when determining the essential functions of the job.
- If the job function in question takes up the majority of the job's time
- If the job function in question is considered "essential" to the jobs of others in the same or similar job
- If the job function is described in a collective bargaining agreement

7)   Answer: A

The following are rules of thumb to help determine if a job function is an "essential function" of the job:

- Essential job functions recorded in the written descriptions of job, prepared prior to advertising for the job or interviewing candidates are considered evidential when determining the essential functions of the job.
- If the job function in question takes up the majority of the job's time
- If the job function in question is considered "essential" to the jobs of others in the same or similar job
- If the job function is described in a collective bargaining agreement

8)   Answer: B

The following are rules of thumb to help determine if a job function is an "essential function" of the job:

- Essential job functions recorded in the written descriptions of job, prepared prior to advertising for the job or interviewing candidates are considered evidential when determining the essential functions of the job.
- If the job function in question takes up the majority of the job's time
- If the job function in question is considered "essential" to the jobs of others in the same or similar job
- If the job function is described in a collective bargaining agreement

9)   Answer: D

The employment provisions of the ADA do not pertain to all individuals of working age who meet the legal definition of disability. The ADA's provisions only apply to *qualified individuals*. A person is considered qualified for a job, if he or she has the requisite skill, experience, and education, as well as being able to, with or without reasonable accommodation, perform the *essential functions of the job* as determined by the employer. The ADA does not require that the essential functions of the job be changed in order to make a "reasonable accommodation."

10) Answer: C

The employment provisions of the ADA do not pertain to all individuals of working age who meet the legal definition of disability. The ADA's provisions only apply to *qualified individuals*. A person is considered qualified for a job, if he or she has the requisite skill, experience, and education, as well as being able to, with or without reasonable accommodation, perform the *essential functions of the job* as determined by the employer. The ADA does not require that the essential functions of the job be changed in order to make a "reasonable accommodation."

11) Answer: A

The employment provisions of the ADA do not pertain to all individuals of working age who meet the legal definition of disability. The ADA's provisions only apply to *qualified individuals*. A person is considered qualified for a job, if he or she has the requisite skill, experience, and education, as well as being able to, with or without reasonable accommodation, perform the *essential functions of the job* as determined by the employer. The ADA does not require that the essential functions of the job be changed in order to make a "reasonable accommodation."

12) Answer: C

The current use of drugs illegally is never protected under the ADA. A history of drug abuse is a protected disability. In contradistinction, the current use of alcohol is protected, as long as the alcohol does not impair the employee's job performance. Employees with alcohol dependence can be held to the same performance and conduct standards as their nondisabled coworkers. Prescription drug use is protected under the ADA, but the illegal use of prescription drugs is not.

13) Answer: A

The current use of drugs illegally is never protected under the ADA. A history of drug abuse is a protected disability. In contradistinction, the current use of alcohol is protected, as long as the alcohol does not impair the employee's job performance. Employees with alcohol dependence can be held to the same performance and conduct standards as their nondisabled coworkers. Prescription drug use is protected under the ADA, but the illegal use of prescription drugs is not.

14) Answer: A

The current use of drugs illegally is never protected under the ADA. A history of drug abuse is a protected disability. In contradistinction, the current use of alcohol is protected, as long as the alcohol does not impair the employee's job performance. Employees with alcohol dependence can be held to the same performance and conduct standards as their nondisabled coworkers. Prescription drug use is protected under the ADA, but the illegal use of prescription drugs is not.

15) Answer: B

The current use of drugs illegally is never protected under the ADA. A history of drug abuse is a protected disability. In contradistinction, the current use of alcohol is protected, as long as the alcohol does not impair the employee's job performance. Employees with alcohol dependence can be held to the same performance and conduct standards as their nondisabled coworkers. Prescription drug use is protected under the ADA, but the illegal use of prescription drugs is not.

16) Answer: D

The Women's Health and Cancer Rights Act is a new law that was enacted as part of an Omnibus Appropriation Bill, and becomes effective for plan years beginning on or after October 21, 1998. This Act amended ERISA to require group health plans, including self-insured plans, which provide coverage for mastectomies to provide certain reconstructive and related services following mastectomies. The services mandated by the Act include:
- Reconstruction of the breast upon which the mastectomy has been performed
- Surgery and reconstruction of the other breast to produce a symmetrical appearance
- Prosthesis and treatment for physical complications attendant to the mastectomy, for example, lymphedema

17)   **Answer: D**

The Women's Health and Cancer Rights Act is a new law that was enacted as part of an Omnibus Appropriation Bill, and becomes effective for plan years beginning on or after October 21, 1998. This Act amended ERISA to require group health plans, including self-insured plans, which provide coverage for mastectomies to provide certain reconstructive and related services following mastectomies. The services mandated by the Act include:

- Reconstruction of the breast upon which the mastectomy has been performed
- Surgery and reconstruction of the other breast to produce a symmetrical appearance
- Prosthesis and treatment for physical complications attendant to the mastectomy, for example, lymphedema

18)   **Answer: B**

The Women's Health and Cancer Rights Act is a new law that was enacted as part of an Omnibus Appropriation Bill, and becomes effective for plan years beginning on or after October 21, 1998. This Act amended ERISA to require group health plans, including self-insured plans, which provide coverage for mastectomies to provide certain reconstructive and related services following mastectomies. The services mandated by the Act include:

- Reconstruction of the breast upon which the mastectomy has been performed
- Surgery and reconstruction of the other breast to produce a symmetrical appearance
- Prosthesis and treatment for physical complications attendant to the mastectomy, for example, lymphedema

19)   **Answer: A**

The Women's Health and Cancer Rights Act is a new law that was enacted as part of an Omnibus Appropriation Bill, and becomes effective for plan years beginning on or after October 21, 1998. This Act amended ERISA to require group health plans, including self-insured plans, which provide coverage for mastectomies to provide certain reconstructive and related services following mastectomies. The services mandated by the Act include:

- Reconstruction of the breast upon which the mastectomy has been performed
- Surgery and reconstruction of the other breast to produce a symmetrical appearance
- Prosthesis and treatment for physical complications attendant to the mastectomy, for example, lymphedema

20)   **Answer: B**

21)   **Answer: A**

The Women's Health and Cancer Rights Act is a new law that was enacted as part of an Omnibus Appropriation Bill, and becomes effective for plan years beginning on or after October 21, 1998. This Act amended ERISA to require group health plans, including self-insured plans, which provide coverage for mastectomies to provide certain reconstructive and related services following mastectomies. The services mandated by the Act include:

- Reconstruction of the breast upon which the mastectomy has been performed
- Surgery and reconstruction of the other breast to produce a symmetrical appearance
- Prosthesis and treatment for physical complications attendant to the mastectomy, for example, lymphedema

It should be noted that the law specifically states that these services may be subject to annual deductibles and coinsurance under the plan's normal terms.

22)   **Answer: C**

This Act imposes prohibitions on the insurers that include: A group health plan is prohibited from denying a patient eligibility to enroll or renew coverage solely for the purpose of avoiding the requirements of the Act, and a group health plan is prohibited from inducing an attending physician to limit the care which is required under the Act, whether that takes the form of penalty, reducing or limiting the reimbursement to such physician. This prohibition should not be thought of as an impediment to effective price negotiation. The Act specifically states that its provisions shall *not* be construed to prevent a group health plan from negotiating the level and type of reimbursement with a provider for care provided in accordance with the Act.

23)   Answer: E

This Act imposes prohibitions on the insurers that include: A group health plan is prohibited from denying a patient eligibility to enroll or renew coverage solely for the purpose of avoiding the requirements of the Act; a group health plan is prohibited from inducing an attending physician to limit the care which is required under the Act, whether that takes the form of penalty, reducing or limiting the reimbursement to such physician. This prohibition should not be thought of as an impediment to effective price negotiation. The Act specifically states that its provisions shall *not* be construed to prevent a group health plan from negotiating the level and type of reimbursement with a provider for care provided in accordance with the Act.

24)   Answer: B

This Act imposes prohibitions on the insurers that include: A group health plan is prohibited from denying a patient eligibility to enroll or renew coverage solely for the purpose of avoiding the requirements of the Act, and a group health plan is prohibited from inducing an attending physician to limit the care which is required under the Act, whether that takes the form of penalty, reducing or limiting the reimbursement to such physician. This prohibition should not be thought of as an impediment to effective price negotiation. The Act specifically states that its provisions shall *not* be construed to prevent a group health plan from negotiating the level and type of reimbursement with a provider for care provided in accordance with the Act.

25)   Answer: C

This law applies to private and public employer plans and health insurance issuers. Non–federal government self-insured plans may elect to "opt out" of this Act's requirements, in the same manner as they may opt out of the requirements of HIPAA, the Mental Health Parity Act, and the Newborns' and Mothers' Health Protection Act.

26)   Answer: B

This law applies to private and public employer plans and health insurance issuers. Non–federal government self-insured plans may elect to "opt out" of this Act's requirements, in the same manner as they may opt out of the requirements of HIPAA, the Mental Health Parity Act, and the Newborns' and Mothers' Health Protection Act.

27)   Answer: E

State financing and benefit laws vary widely. In general, unemployment compensation benefits under state laws are intended to replace about 50% of an average worker's previous wages. Maximum weekly benefits provisions, however, result in benefits of less than 50% for most higher-earning workers. All states pay benefits to some unemployed persons for 26 weeks. In some states, the duration of benefits depends on the amount earned and the number of weeks worked in a previous year. In others, all recipients are entitled to benefits for the same length of time. During periods of heavy unemployment, federal law authorizes extended benefits, in some cases up to 39 weeks; in 1975 extended benefits were payable for up to 65 weeks. Extended benefits are financed in part by federal employer taxes.

28)   Answer: A

State financing and benefit laws vary widely. In general, unemployment compensation benefits under state laws are intended to replace about 50% of an average worker's previous wages. Maximum weekly benefits provisions, however, result in benefits of less than 50% for most higher-earning workers. All states pay benefits to some unemployed persons for 26 weeks. In some states, the duration of benefits depends on the amount earned and the number of weeks worked in a previous year. In others, all recipients are entitled to benefits for the same length of time. During periods of heavy unemployment, federal law authorizes extended benefits, in some cases up to 39 weeks; in 1975 extended benefits were payable for up to 65 weeks. Extended benefits are financed in part by federal employer taxes.

29)   Answer: B

State financing and benefit laws vary widely. In general, unemployment compensation benefits under state laws are intended to replace about 50% of an average worker's previous wages. Maximum weekly benefits provisions, however, result in benefits of less than 50% for most higher-earning workers. All states pay benefits to some unemployed persons for 26 weeks. In some states, the duration of benefits depends on the amount earned and the number of weeks worked in a previous year. In others, all recipients are entitled to benefits for the same length of time. During periods of heavy unemployment, federal law authorizes extended benefits, in some cases up to 39 weeks; in 1975 extended benefits were payable for up to 65 weeks. Extended benefits are financed in part by federal employer taxes.

30)   Answer: B

State financing and benefit laws vary widely. In general, unemployment compensation benefits under state laws are intended to replace about 50% of an average worker's previous wages. Maximum weekly benefits provisions, however, result in benefits of less than 50% for most higher-earning workers. All states pay benefits to some unemployed persons for 26 weeks. In some states, the duration of benefits depends on the amount earned and the number of weeks worked in a previous year. In others, all recipients are entitled to benefits for the same length of time. During periods of heavy unemployment, federal law authorizes extended benefits, in some cases up to 39 weeks; in 1975 extended benefits were payable for up to 65 weeks. Extended benefits are financed in part by federal employer taxes.

31)   Answer: C

State financing and benefit laws vary widely. In general, unemployment compensation benefits under state laws are intended to replace about 50% of an average worker's previous wages. Maximum weekly benefits provisions, however, result in benefits of less than 50% for most higher-earning workers. All states pay benefits to some unemployed persons for 26 weeks. In some states, the duration of benefits depends on the amount earned and the number of weeks worked in a previous year. In others, all recipients are entitled to benefits for the same length of time. During periods of heavy unemployment, federal law authorizes extended benefits, in some cases up to 39 weeks; in 1975 extended benefits were payable for up to 65 weeks. Extended benefits are financed in part by federal employer taxes.

32)   Answer: C

The scope of coverage for Workers' Compensation benefits varies by state, with respect to benefits payable in case of death, of total disability, and of partial disability due to specific injuries or continuing during specified periods. Though they vary between states, these benefits generally include the cost of medical bills attendant to treating the illness or injury, as well as some percentage of lost wages. The compensation benefits, set forth by the state, take precedence over the funding source. Employees are entitled to the level of benefits mandated by the state without regard to the financial status or desires of the employer. Therefore, even if the employer is self-funded or self-administered, he is required to offer the full level of benefits required by the state's Workers' Compensation Commission. Self-funded group health insurance plans may be exempt from mandated benefits under ERISA guidelines, but are not exempt under Workers' Compensation regulations.

33)   Answer: A

The scope of coverage for Workers' Compensation benefits varies by state, with respect to benefits payable in case of death, of total disability, and of partial disability due to specific injuries or continuing during specified periods. Though they vary between states, these benefits generally include the cost of medical bills attendant to treating the illness or injury, as well as some percentage of lost wages. The compensation benefits, set forth by the state, take precedence over the funding source. Employees are entitled to the level of benefits mandated by the state without regard to the financial status or desires of the employer. Therefore, even if the employer is self-funded or self-administered, he is required to offer the full level of benefits required by the state's Workers' Compensation Commission. Self-funded group health insurance plans may be exempt from mandated benefits under ERISA guidelines, but are not exempt under Workers' Compensation regulations.

34)   Answer: E

The scope of coverage for Workers' Compensation benefits varies by state, with respect to benefits payable in case of death, of total disability, and of partial disability due to specific injuries or continuing during specified periods. Though they vary between states, these benefits generally include the cost of medical bills attendant to treating the illness or injury, as well as some percentage of lost wages. The compensation benefits, set forth by the state, take precedence over the funding source. Employees are entitled to the level of benefits mandated by the state without regard to the financial status or desires of the employer. Therefore, even if the employer is self-funded or self-administrated, he is required to offer the full level of benefits required by the states Workers' Compensation Commission. Self-funded group health insurance plans may be exempt from mandated benefits under ERISA guidelines, but are not exempt under Workers' Compensation regulations.

35)   Answer: A

The cost of Workers' Compensation insurance premiums are borne by the employer, with no contribution by the employee. The authors of the Workers' Compensation legislation intended that the significant cost of this compulsory insurance would provide an incentive to employers to increase workers' safety programs and result in decreased work related injuries. Stringent safety programs instituted by major corporations have nevertheless failed to stop the rise in industrial accident rates. It is estimated that industrial accidents cost U.S. manufacturers more than $11 billion per year.

36)   Answer: B

The cost of Workers' Compensation insurance premiums are borne by the employer, with no contribution by the employee. The authors of the Workers' Compensation legislation intended that the significant cost of this compulsory insurance would provide an incentive to employers to increase workers' safety programs and result in decreased work-related injuries. Stringent safety programs instituted by major corporations have nevertheless failed to stop the rise in industrial accident rates. It is estimated that industrial accidents cost U.S. manufacturers more than $11 billion per year.

37)   Answer: A

An indemnity health insurance plan is a legal entity, licensed by the state insurance department. It exists to provide health insurance to its enrollees. An indemnity health insurer "indemnifies" or reimburses the enrollee for the costs of health care claims which are medically necessary and appropriate for his care. Indemnity insurers historically had not spent money or time on utilization or quality management. Now, because of savings demonstrated by the managed care companies, some indemnity companies have adopted these cost saving approaches.

38)   Answer: B

An indemnity health insurance plan is a legal entity, licensed by the state insurance department. It exists to provide health insurance to its enrollees. An indemnity health insurer "indemnifies" or reimburses the enrollee for the costs of health care claims which are medically necessary and appropriate for his care. Indemnity insurers historically had not spent money or time on utilization or quality management. Now, because of savings demonstrated by the managed care companies, some indemnity companies have adopted these cost saving approaches.

39)   Answer: B

A well-run self-insurance program can achieve the following benefits for an employer: reduced service costs that are usually incurred by conventional insurers, exemption from providing benefits mandated by ERISA, elimination of the costs of premium taxes, and improved cash flow.

40)   Answer: A

A well-run self-insurance program can achieve the following benefits for an employer: reduced service costs that are usually incurred by conventional insurers, exemption from providing benefits mandated by ERISA, elimination of the costs of premium taxes, and improved cash flow.

41)   Answer: E

Large employers (greater than 500 employees) tend to self-insure. Conversely, employers with less than 500 employees find it difficult to self-insure, because they lack the cash reserves necessary to handle large claims losses. An employer's decision to self-insure should be based on the size of his employee base, cash reserves, group claims experience, employee health status, and ability to find reinsurance for his catastrophic losses.

42)   Answer: B

Large employers (greater than 500 employees) tend to self-insure. Conversely, employers with less than 500 employees find it difficult to self-insure, because they lack the cash reserves necessary to handle large claims losses. An employer's decision to self-insure should be based on the size of his employee base, his cash reserves, group claims experience, employee health status, and ability to find reinsurance for his catastrophic losses.

43)   Answer: E

Third Party Administrators (or TPAs) usually operate in the environment of the self-insured employer. While he may act as an agent of the "insurer," the TPA is not party to the insurance contract between the employer and the employee. The TPA does not incur any risk for employer or employee losses. A TPA's sole function is to perform "insurance type" administrative services for self-insured employers. These services include, but are not limited to, performing claims adjudication and payment, maintaining all records, providing utilization and quality management, Case Management and managing the provider network.

44)   Answer: D

Third Party Administrators (or TPAs) usually operate in the environment of the self-insured employer. While they may act as an agent of the "insurer" the TPA is not party to the insurance contract between the employer and the employee. The TPA does not incur any risk for employer or employee losses. A TPA's sole function is to perform "insurance type" administrative services for self-insured employers. These services include, but are not limited to, performing claims adjudication and payment, maintaining all records, providing utilization and quality management, Case Management and managing the provider network.

45)   Answer: A

Third Party Administrators (or TPAs) usually operate in the environment of the self-insured employer. While they may act as an agent of the "insurer" the TPA is not party to the insurance contract between the employer and the employee. The TPA does not incur any risk for employer or employee losses. A TPA's sole function is to perform "insurance type" administrative services for self-insured employers. These services include, but are not limited to, performing claims adjudication and payment, maintaining all records, providing utilization and quality management, Case Management and managing the provider network.

46)   Answer: C

TPAs are not paid premiums, nor do they traditionally invest money. These activities are more characteristic of indemnity insurers.

47)   Answer: B

TPAs are not paid premiums, nor do they traditionally invest money. These activities are more characteristic of indemnity insurers. TPAs are not licensed to practice medicine or render medical care.

48)   Answer: A

TPAs do not share risk or bear liability in the insurance contract between the employer and employee, nor do they traditionally collect premiums or invest money.

49)   Answer: B

TPAs do not share risk or bear liability in the insurance contract between the employer and employee, nor do they traditionally collect premiums or invest money.

50)   Answer: A

The car owner and his car insurance company are financially responsible for injury and property damage caused by car accidents.

51)   Answer: A

Each state determines what the minimum level of liability insurance will be for drivers in that state. While the costs of car insurance premiums may vary by the cost of the automobile, the community accident experience, or the driving record of the owner, the minimum policy limits for personal injury protection don't.

52)   Answer: B

Each state determines what the minimum level of liability insurance will be for drivers in that state. While the costs of car insurance premiums may vary by the cost of the automobile, the community accident experience, or the driving record of the owner, the minimum policy limits for personal injury protection don't.

53)   Answer: B

Automobile accident victims are characterized by their youth and the seriousness of their injuries, which include closed head trauma, spinal trauma and permanent disability.

54)   Answer: A

Automobile accident victims are characterized by their youth and the seriousness of their injuries, which include closed head trauma, spinal trauma and permanent disability.

55)   Answer: D

56)   Answer: C

PIP refers to that part of an auto insurance policy that covers medical claims for injuries sustained in an auto accident.

57)   Answer: A

PIP refers to that part of an auto insurance policy that covers medical claims for injuries sustained in an auto accident.

58)   Answer: A

PIP refers to that part of an auto insurance policy that covers medical claims for injuries sustained in an auto accident.

59)   Answer: B

PIP refers to that part of an auto insurance policy that covers medical claims for injuries sustained in an auto accident.

60)   Answer: A

The full benefits of Workers' Compensation allowable in that state. Workers' Compensation is a "no-fault" policy that pays the injured or ill employee, no matter who is at fault.

61)   Answer: E

Workers' Compensation entitlements do not change with respect to injuries, but are the same for all workers in an individual state. However, Workers' Compensation benefits are determined by each state's WC commission, and vary substantially from state to state.

62)   Answer: E

Virtually all workers are covered by WC benefits, including full-time, part-time and temporary workers.

63)   Answer: A

WC benefits are set by the individual state's WC Commission. The benefits, therefore, vary from state to state. Entitlement to benefits does not change because of a worker's seniority, injury, or job status.

64)   Answer: D

WC insurance benefits must cover some percentage of lost wages. All types of workers are entitled to WC benefits, and self-administered or self-funded plans cannot claim a federal ERISA pre-emption from WC insurance.

65)   Answer: D

66) **Answer: E**

The employer's refusal to buy WC insurance opens himself up to liability associated with work-related injuries. Federal law bars the employer from using the first three options as a defense of his case.

67) **Answer: A**

The worker is entitled to WC insurance his first day on the job.

68) **Answer: D**

While the limits of treatment for a work-related injury are theoretically endless in most states, they are subject to the determination of medical necessity and appropriateness.

69) **Answer: C**

While the ADA covers discrimination against persons with disabilities as they relate to employment, state and local government programs, and places open to the public, such as theaters, restaurants, stores, banks, and senior centers, it does not cover housing. The disabled are protected from discrimination under the Fair Housing Amendments Act of 1988, as well as the Rehabilitation Act of 1973.

70) **Answer: D**

Small businesses with more than 15 employees are not exempt from the ADA, the rest are.

71) **Answer: A**

The federal government does not expect an employer to change the nature of the job in order to hire the disabled. The ADA exempts the essential functions of the job from "reasonable accommodations."

72) **Answer: B**

Job descriptions are effective for determining the essential job functions when they are written before the job is advertised and the applicant has been interviewed.

73) **Answer: A**

The ADA describes the qualified candidate as "Any individual with a disability who, with or without reasonable modifications rules, policies or practices of the public entity, . . . meets the essentials requirements for eligibility to receive the services offered by the public entity, or to participate in programs or activities provided by the public entity." This includes the appropriate education, training and experience to perform the job.

74) **Answer: C**

The employee's alcoholism is protected under the ADA. The employer is required to make reasonable accommodations to this disability. However, if the employee's alcoholism interferes with his job performance, he can be terminated.

75) **Answer: D**

The ADA does not protect *current illicit drug use*. This employee is involved in a drug treatment program, and his methadone is a prescribed drug. This drug use does not constitute current drug abuse or the current use of drugs illegally. Employers may ask a job applicant about *current illegal use of drugs* before a conditional offer of employment, and can ask about *current illegal use of drugs* at any time during the employment. Further, employers may, under the ADA guidelines, conduct drug tests and obtain information from treatment programs to monitor drug use. A history of illegal drug use is protected under the ADA, and cannot be inquired about at a job interview.

76) **Answer: A**

Returning to work as soon as possible without modifying the job function and by delaying treating the patient in a timely fashion will probably increase disability time and possibly increase costs by reinjuring the patient.

77) **Answer: D**

78) **Answer: C**

PIP is that part of the automobile insurance policy responsible for coverage of bodily injury of drivers, passengers and pedestrians.

79) **Answer: B**

The quality or orderliness of a Case Manager's record has no impact on the policy limits of PIP coverage, nor does the state change reimbursement rates based on this.

80) **Answer: E**

No-fault insurance implies no blame is assigned to participants. All parties injured during the accident are covered, regardless of blame when a no-fault policy is purchased.

81) **Answer: C**

Transfers to a sibling is not exempted by the state, and this asset transfer would be assessed a penalty period. See *Section 1917(c) of the Social Security Act; U.S. Code Reference 42 U.S.C.1396p(c).*

82) **Answer: A**

The penalty period is calculated by using this formula: Fair market value of the asset/average monthly cost for the facility in that state = penalty period in months. In the above example this would be calculated as $100,000/$2,000 per month = 50 months penalty period. See *Section 1917(c) of the Social Security Act; U.S. Code Reference 42 U.S.C.1396p(c).*

83) **Answer: D**

There is no limit to the penalty period imposed during a "look back" on asset transfers. See *Section 1917(c) of the Social Security Act; U.S. Code Reference 42 U.S.C.1396p(c).*

84) **Answer: E**

The look back period is 36 months prior to the date the individual applies for Medicaid or is institutionalized. With certain types of trusts, this period can be extended to 60 months. See *Section 1917(c) of the Social Security Act; U.S. Code Reference 42 U.S.C.1396p(c).*

85) **Answer: C**

An asset transferred at less than the fair market value will prompt the imposition of a penalty period. Some exceptions to this rule are if the transfer was to the spouse, a trust fund set up to care for the individual or for a reason other than to qualify for Medicaid. See *Section 1917(c) of the Social Security Act; U.S. Code Reference 42 U.S.C.1396p(c).*

86) **Answer: C**

Assets put in irrevocable trusts within 60 months of application for Medicaid or admission to nursing facility are considered transfers of assets below fair market value, and are therefore considered available to the individual.

87) **Answer: A**

Assets placed in trusts established by a parent, grandparent, guardian, or court for the benefit of an individual who is disabled and under the age of 65, using the individual's own funds, are not counted as being available by HCFA.

88) **Answer: D**

The MHPA does not require a plan to offer mental health benefits, but if it does, those benefits must have the same financial limitations as medical and surgical care.

89) **Answer: B**

The MHPA exempts employers with 50 or less workers, and those employers or plans that can demonstrate that parity would cause at least a 1% increase in health care benefits. Specific industries are not addressed in the legislation.

90) **Answer: E**

The MHPA does *not* require health plans or employers to offer mental health benefits. It does *not* require that those benefits be the same as medical or surgical benefits, nor does it require parity in copayments, annual number of outpatient visits, or inpatient days. The MHPA does *not* recognize chemical dependency as a mental health issue, and does *not* require employers or group health plans to cover its treatment.

91) **Answer: D**

92) **Answer: E**

The employer is not permitted to "recoup his losses" on maternity care. Exacting higher copayments or larger deductibles for maternity related benefits would constitute discrimination, as would any limitation in quality, access, or cost above those offered for general medical and surgical benefits.

93) **Answer: D**

Abortions are not a mandated benefit under Pregnancy Discrimination Act regulations. This does not prevent employers from offering abortion services as a benefit. Wives of eligible part-time employees are covered under the Pregnancy Discrimination Act.

94) **Answer: A**

The PDA requires "equal treatment" between employees treated for maternity related complications, and those treated for medical and surgical complications. This does not imply that individuals with maternity related complications are given superior benefits. In the extant case, if disability leave is not available for medical problems, it is not available for maternity-related problems. Full-time and part-time workers are covered under PDA as well as independent contractors. Married and unmarried workers are equally covered under PDA. Employers with less than 15 workers are exempt from the PDA regulations.

95) **Answer: C**

A point of service plan. The POS plans evolved from a PPO, which has provider choice and a network but no gatekeeper, and an HMO, which has a network and gatekeeper but limits provider choice. An indemnity plan has provider choice but no network or gatekeeper.

96) **Answer: B**

97) **Answer: D**

The scope of coverage, under Workers' Compensation, varies by state, with respect to benefits payable in case of death, of total disability, and of partial disability due to specific injuries or continuing during specified periods.

98) **Answer: B**

Managed care is comprised of systems and mechanisms striving to control, direct and approve access to a wide range of services and costs within the health care delivery system. Case Management is one of those mechanisms. Workers' Compensation is a benefit program for injured or ill employees.

99) **Answer: B**

COBRA, The Consolidated Omnibus Budget Reconciliation Act of 1986.

100) **Answer: C**

101) **Answer: B**

102) **Answer: D**

103) **Answer: B**

Although Case Managers make recommendations, actual claims processing is done by a claims examiner.

104) **Answer: C**

105) **Answer: D**

106) **Answer: E**

Currently, definitions of medical necessity contained in health insurance contracts are characterized by ambiguity and inconsistency. They do not clearly cover all clinical eventualities.

107) **Answer: E**

In the standard health insurance contract, when medical necessity is defined, it is often defined in terms of what is appropriate, reasonable, and acceptable. These terms are rarely if ever explained. Further, investigational, experimental and custodial care are usually specifically excluded in the definition, however, they also are rarely if ever defined.

108) **Answer: B**

The issue of what is medically necessary is an important issue, and it affects the payment of every claim for health services. A longer and more inclusive wording of the contract does not solve the problem of defining what is medically necessary; rather, a methodological or procedural approach to the definition is necessary. This procedural approach describes the steps that should be taken when determining what is medically necessary.

109) **Answer: D**

When determining what is medically necessary for a particular case, the reviewer should take into account the contents of the patient's medical record, the opinion of the treating physician, the opinion of an objective physician who is a specialist in the field of medicine in question and the reasonable expectation of the patient.

110) **Answer: E**

When determining what is medically necessary for a particular case, it is important that the reviewer take into account the contents of the patient's medical record, the opinion of the treating physician, the opinion of an objective physician who is a specialist in the field of medicine in question, and the reasonable expectations of the patient.

111) **Answer: D**

112) **Answer: B**

The intent of medical necessity determinations is to protect the subscribers from irregular, dangerous, or unnecessary medical procedures. Perverse incentives for lowering medical utilization, such as year-end bonuses linked to medical loss ratios should have no place in medical necessity determinations.

113) **Answer: D**

The decision-making process for medical necessity determinations should be supervised by the Medical Director, and should be characterized by fairness, reproducibility, and utilization of the best available information.

114) **Answer: D**

Only the Medical Director should make a denial of claim payment for lack of medical necessity. While the Case Manager will be involved in the case presentation and subsequent discussion, the responsibility for making the final decision rests with the Medical Director. The claims personnel should have no say in medical decision making.

115) **Answer: E**

Only the Medical Director should be authorized to make claims denials for lack of medical necessity.

116) **Answer: A**

While benefits can vary state to state, in general unemployment benefits are designed to replace about 50% of an average worker's previous wages. The minimum duration of benefits mandated by the federal government is 26 weeks.

117) **Answer: D**

118) **Answer: A**

CHIP is a federal program to provide health coverage to uninsured children. Though individual states set their own eligibility criteria, they must follow federal guidelines. Eligibility guidelines include low income, uninsured, not eligible for Medicaid. There is no lower age limit to eligibility.

119) Answer: D

120) Answer: D

An indemnity health insurance plan is a legal entity licensed by the state insurance department. It exists to provide health insurance to its enrollees. An indemnity health insurer "indemnifies" or reimburses the enrollee for the costs of health care claims. Indemnity insurers historically had not spent money or time on utilization or quality management. Now, because of savings demonstrated by the managed care companies, some indemnity companies have adopted these cost savings approaches. These companies are referred to as "managed indemnity" companies.

121) Answer: E

These activities characterize managed care rather than indemnity insurance companies.

122) Answer: D

123) Answer: D

Large employers (greater than 500 employees) tend to self-insure. Conversely, employers with less than 500 employees find it difficult to self-insure, because they lack the cash reserves necessary to handle large claims losses. An employer's decision to self-insure should be based on the size of its employee base, his cash reserves, group claims experience, employee health status, and ability to find reinsurance for catastrophic losses.

124) Answer: B

The car owner and his car insurance company are financially responsible for injury and property damage caused by car accidents.

125) Answer: C

No-fault insurance asks the insurance company of each of the parties involved to contribute to paying for damages or costs of injuries, regardless of who caused the accident.

126) Answer: C

Each state determines what its minimum allowable insurance policy limits for medical expenses and lost wages will be.

127) Answer: A

COB is a process designed by insurance companies to limit payments made to claimants. The COB process is structured such that payments made to the claimant do not exceed the expenses incurred.

128) Answer: B

COB rules are voluntary; however, compliance is high among insurers. There is no federal mandate for compliance with COB rules.

129) Answer: B

Under the COB rules adopted by the National Association of Insurance Commissioners (NAIC) the insurance plan that covers the individual as an employee pays first.

130) Answer: A

Under the COB rules adopted by the National Association of Insurance Commissioners (NAIC), the insurance plan that covers the individual as a dependent pays second.

131) Answer: B

Under the COB rules adopted by the National Association of Insurance Commissioners (NAIC), the insurance plan that covers the individual as an employee pays first.

132) Answer: A

Under the COB rules adopted by the National Association of Insurance Commissioners (NAIC), the insurance plan that covers the individual as a dependent pays second.

133) Answer: B

The birthday rule is invoked when two married parents have named the same dependent child in their health insurance policies. The rule can only be invoked when both insurance companies have adopted the birthday rule to settle COB disputes.

134) Answer: C

The birthday rule is invoked when there are two or more policies that cover the claimant as a dependent, and the insurance companies have both adopted the birthday rule. The order of payment is based on the order of birthdays of the parents who have the dependent on their policies.

135) Answer: B

In the case of a dependent carried on two or more insurance policies, the birthday rule is invoked first. If one or both of the insurers of the dependent do not ascribe to the birthday rule, then the male/female rule is invoked. The male/female rule states that the insurer of the father (male parent or guardian) pays first.

136) Answer: A

The divorce decree will usually designate a primary insurance carrier for the child from one of the parents' policies. If the court has not determined a primary insurance carrier, the parent with custody of the child will pay first. The birthday rule is not invoked in cases of divorce.

137) Answer: B

According to COB rules adopted by the National Association of Insurance Commissioners, the insurance carrier of the parent with custody pays first.

138) Answer: A

According to COB rules adopted by the National Association of Insurance Commissioners, the insurance carrier of the parent with custody pays first. The insurance carrier of the custodial parent's spouse would pay second. If the custodial parent is not married, the noncustodial parent's carrier would pay second.

139) Answer: A

The insurance plan of the mother will pay first. COB rules state that the plan of the parent with custody pays first.

140) Answer: C

The insurance plan of the mother's spouse would pay second. According to the COB rules, the plan of the spouse of the parent with custody will pay second.

141) Answer: D

The plan of the spouse of the noncustodial parent pays last.

142) Answer: B

According to the COB rules adopted by the National Association of Insurance Commissioners (NAIC), the plan covering the individual as an active employee will pay first. Workers' Compensation insurance would only be primary if the nurse made medical claims stemming from a job-related injury.

143) Answer: B

According to the COB rules adopted by the National Association of Insurance Commissioners (NAIC), the plan covering the individual as an active employee will pay first, the plan covering that individual as an inactive employee (such as a retiree, or laid-off employee) will pay second. Workers' Compensation insurance would only be primary if the employee made medical claims stemming from a job-related injury.

144) Answer: C

According to the COB rules adopted by the National Association of Insurance Commissioners (NAIC), the plan covering the individual as an active employee will pay first, the plan covering that individual as an inactive employee (such as a retiree, or laid-off employee) will pay second. Workers' Compensation insurance would only be primary if the employee made medical claims stemming from a job-related injury. His unemployment insurance benefit pays for salary replacement, and not health care bills.

145) Answer: A

According to the COB rules adopted by the National Association of Insurance Commissioners (NAIC), the plan covering the individual as an active employee will pay first, the plan covering that individual as an inactive employee (such as a retiree, or laid-off employee) will pay second. Workers' Compensation insurance would only be primary if the employee made medical claims stemming from a job-related injury. His unemployment insurance benefit pays for salary replacement, and not health care bills.

146) Answer: A

According to the COB rules adopted by the National Association of Insurance Commissioners (NAIC), the plan covering the individual as an active employee will pay first, the plan covering that individual as an inactive employee (such as a retiree, or laid-off employee) will pay second. Workers' Compensation insurance would only be primary if the nurse made medical claims stemming from a job-related injury.

147) Answer: C

According to the COB rules adopted by the National Association of Insurance Commissioners (NAIC), the plan covering individuals as a COBRA continuee, will be secondary to a plan covering that individual as an employee, a member or dependent. Unemployment insurance benefits only cover salary replacement, not health care costs. When working for an employer who does not pay health insurance benefits, the employee cannot successfully sue for benefits when he gets ill.

148) Answer: B

According to the COB rules adopted by the National Association of Insurance Commissioners (NAIC), the plan covering individuals as a COBRA continuee, will be secondary to a plan covering that individual as an employee, a member or dependent. Unemployment insurance benefits only cover salary replacement, not health care costs. When working for an employer who does not pay health insurance benefits, the employee cannot successfully sue for benefits when he gets ill.

149) Answer: D

Automobile accidents victims are characterized by their youth and the seriousness of their injuries, which include closed head trauma, spinal trauma and permanent disability.

150) Answer: B

PIP policy minimums are set by the state insurance department. These minimums may not be sufficient to cover the medical costs of more severe injuries.

151) Answer: C

Medical bill review and review for reasonable and customary charges are components of retrospective review, not utilization review.

152) Answer: C

In order to formulate a Case Management plan it is necessary to have an understanding of the patient's medical history, treatment thus far and job expectations.

153) Answer: A

HCFA defines inappropriate utilization as "Utilization of services that are in excess of a beneficiary's medical needs and condition (overutilization) or receiving a capitated Medicare payment and failing to provide services to meet a beneficiary's medical needs and condition (underutilization)."

154) Answer: D

HCFA defines fraud as "The intentional deception or misrepresentation that an individual knows, or should know, to be false, or does not believe to be true, and makes, knowing the deception could result in some unauthorized benefit to himself or some other person(s)."

155) Answer: C

The Medicare program was created by Title XVIII of the Social Security Act. The program, which went into effect in 1966, was first administered by the Social Security Administration; in 1977 the Medicare program was transferred to the newly created Health Care Financing Administration (HCFA). Medicare was created to help the elderly and disabled, not underutilized physicians, though that may seem the case today.

156) Answer: D

Medicare is divided into two parts, Part A, and Part B. Part A, the hospital insurance program, is funded by Social Security taxes and is provided to eligible individuals at no personal expense. As one might suspect, Part A provides a basic hospital insurance plan covering hospital care, extended care, home health services, and hospice care for terminally ill patients.

157) Answer: C

Medicare provides health insurance to persons 65 years old; generally, people over the age of 65 and older are eligible for Medicare benefits on their own or their spouse's employment. Any one of the following must be true: the patient must receive benefits under the Social Security or Railroad Retirement Systems, or must be eligible for benefits under Social Security or Railroad Retirement System, but has not filed for them; or the patient's spouse has Medicare-covered government employment.

158) Answer: C

Medicare was enacted under Title XIX of the Social Security Act and is divided into two parts, Part A and Part B. Part A, the hospital insurance program, is funded by Social Security taxes and is provided to eligible individuals at no personal expense. As one might suspect, Part A provides a basic hospital insurance plan covering hospital care, extended care, home health services, and hospice care for terminally ill patients.

159) Answer: E

Medicare provides health insurance to persons 65 years old; generally, people over the age of 65 are eligible for Medicare benefits on their own or through their spouse's employment. Any one of the following must be true: the patient must receive benefits under the Social Security or Railroad Retirement Systems, or must be eligible for benefits under Social Security or Railroad Retirement System, but has not filed for them; or the patient's spouse has Medicare-covered government employment.

160) Answer: B

The Medicare program was created by Title XVIII of the Social Security Act. The program, which went into effect in 1966, was first administered by the Social Security Administration; in 1977 the Medicare program was transferred to the newly created Health Care Financing Administration (HCFA). Medicare was created to help the elderly and disabled, not underutilized physicians, though that may seem the case today.

161) Answer: A

A person becomes entitled to Medicare on the basis of disability after he has been entitled to Social Security disability benefits for 24 months. An individual has a five-month waiting period before receiving Social Security disability payments, which means that, in most instances, there will be a 29-month period before the individual becomes entitled to Medicare. Those who have served active duty in the armed forces are entitled to Veteran's benefits, which includes care in Veteran's Administration hospitals.

162) Answer: C

A person is considered to have end-stage renal disease if he has irreparable kidney damage that requires a transplant or dialysis to maintain life. A person becomes eligible for Medicare if he requires regular dialysis, or has a kidney transplant, and meets the following requirements: Has worked the required amount of time under Social Security, the Railroad Retirement Board or is a government employee, or the beneficiary is receiving or is eligible for Social Security or Railroad Retirement case benefits, or the patient is a spouse or a dependent child of a person who has worked the required amount of time, or who is receiving Social Security or Railroad cash benefits.

163) **Answer: A**

A person is considered to have end-stage renal disease if he has irreparable kidney damage that requires a transplant or dialysis to maintain life. A person becomes eligible for Medicare if he requires regular dialysis, or has a kidney transplant, and meets the following requirements: He has worked the required amount of time under Social Security, the Railroad Retirement Board or is a government employee, or the beneficiary is receiving or is eligible for Social Security or Railroad Retirement case benefits, or the patient is a spouse or a dependent child of a person who has worked the required amount of time, or who is receiving Social Security or Railroad cash benefits.

164) **Answer: C**

A person becomes entitled to Medicare on the basis of disability after he has been entitled to Social Security disability benefits for 24 months. An individual has a 5-month waiting period before receiving Social Security disability payments, which means that, in most instances, there will be a 29-month period before the individual becomes entitled to Medicare. Those who have served active duty in the armed forces are entitled to Veteran's benefits, which includes care in Veteran's Administration hospitals.

165) **Answer: C**

If a person becomes entitled to Medicare solely because of end-stage renal disease, he has a 3-month wait until he is covered (or the third month after the month in which a regular course of dialysis starts).

166) **Answer: D**

167) **Answer: B**

For those beneficiaries entitled to Medicare solely because of end-stage renal disease, Medicare protection ends 12 months after the month the patient no longer requires maintenance dialysis treatments, or 36 months after a successful kidney transplant.

168) **Answer: B**

If a person becomes entitled to Medicare solely because of end-stage renal disease, he has a 3-month wait until he is covered (or the third month after the month in which a regular course of dialysis starts). For those beneficiaries entitled to Medicare solely because of end-stage renal disease, Medicare protection ends 12 months after the month the patient no longer requires maintenance dialysis treatments, or 36 months after a successful kidney transplant.

169) **Answer: D**

170) **Answer: A**

Medicare Part A. This benefit provides coverage for the following: inpatient hospital services, skilled nursing facilities, home health services and hospice care. Physician fees and outpatient care are covered under Medicare Part B.

171) **Answer: A**

Medicare Part A. This benefit provides coverage for the following: inpatient hospital services, skilled nursing facilities, home health services and hospice care. Hemodialysis and ambulatory surgery are outpatient procedures and are covered under Medicare Part B.

172) **Answer: B**

Medicare Part A provides coverage for the following: inpatient hospital services, skilled nursing facilities, home health services and hospice care. Hemodialysis and ambulatory surgery are outpatient procedures and are covered under Medicare Part B.

173) **Answer: A**

174) **Answer: C**

175) **Answer: D**

176) **Answer: C**

Only medically necessary care is covered in the Medicare program.

177) **Answer: B**

Medicare will help to pay for 100 days of care in a skilled nursing facility. Only medically necessary care is covered in the Medicare program.

178) **Answer: C**

Medicare Part B helps pay for the cost of: physician services, outpatient hospital services, medical equipment and supplies and other health services and supplies. Inpatient hospital stays are covered under the Part A program.

179) **Answer: B**

Medicare Part B helps pay for the cost of: physician services, outpatient hospital services, medical equipment and supplies and other health services and supplies. Inpatient hospital stays and hospice care are covered under the Part A program.

180) **Answer: A**

If a person less than 65 years old becomes eligible for Medicare due to end-stage renal disease, the benefits extended to the patient by Medicare will only cover those medical expenses that are attendant to the treatment of the end-stage renal disease. Arthroscopic and retinal surgery are not treatments for end-stage renal disease, and are therefore not covered.

181) **Answer: B**

If a person less than 65 years old becomes eligible for Medicare due to end-stage renal disease, the benefits extended to the patient by Medicare will only cover those medical expenses that are attendant to the treatment of the end-stage renal disease. Speech therapy and neurosurgery are not treatments for end-stage renal disease, and are therefore not covered.

182) **Answer: D**

A reserve day is one of sixty "extra days" of hospital care that Medicare will pay for during the lifetime of a beneficiary. Medicare Part A includes an extra 60 hospital days that can be used if the patient has a prolonged illness necessitating a hospital stay of longer than 90 days. A Medicare beneficiary has only 60 nonrenewable reserve days in a lifetime. The beneficiary has the right to choose when to use these "reserve days."

183) **Answer: A**

A "reserve day" is one of sixty "extra days" of hospital care that Medicare will pay for during the lifetime of a beneficiary. Medicare Part A includes an extra 60 hospital days that can be used if the patient has a prolonged illness necessitating a hospital stay of longer than 90 days. A Medicare beneficiary has only 60 nonrenewable reserve days in a lifetime. The beneficiary has the right to choose when to use these "reserve days."

184) **Answer: C**

Medicare defines a benefit period as that period of time that begins the first day of a patient's admission to a hospital, skilled nursing facility or hospice, and ends after he has been discharged for sixty contiguous days. There is no limit to the number of benefit periods a beneficiary may have for hospital and skilled nursing care, but there is a limit to the number of days of care a beneficiary may claim payment for.

185) **Answer: B**

Medicare defines a benefit period as that period of time that begins the first day of a patient's admission to a hospital, skilled nursing facility or hospice, and ends after he has been discharged for sixty contiguous days. There is no limit to the number of benefit periods a beneficiary may have for hospital and skilled nursing care, but there is a limit to the number of days of care a beneficiary may claim payment for.

186) **Answer: A**

Medicare defines a benefit period as that period of time that begins the first day of a patient's admission to a hospital, skilled nursing facility or hospice, and ends after he has been discharged for sixty contiguous days. There is no limit to the number of benefit periods a beneficiary may have for hospital and skilled nursing care, but there is a limit to the number of days of care a beneficiary may claim payment for.

187) **Answer: A**

Medicare recipients are responsible for Medicare coinsurance and deductibles.

188) **Answer: B**

Medicare recipients are responsible for Medicare coinsurance and deductibles. Age does not change a member's financial obligations.

189) **Answer: A**

Though Medicare covers many health care costs, recipients will still have to pay Medicare's coinsurance and deductibles. There are also many medical services that Medicare does not cover; because of this, Medicare recipients sometimes buy a Medicare supplemental insurance (Medigap) policy.

190) **Answer: B**

Though Medicare covers many health care costs, recipients will still have to pay Medicare's coinsurance and deductibles. There are also many medical services that Medicare does not cover; because of this, Medicare recipients sometimes buy a Medicare supplemental insurance (Medigap) policy.

191) **Answer: D**

Medigap is private insurance that is designed to help pay for Medicare cost-sharing amounts. There are 10 standard Medigap policies, and each offers a different combination of benefits. The best time to buy a policy is during your Medigap open enrollment period. For a period of 6 months from the date the patient is first enrolled in Medicare Part B and is age 65 or older, he has a right to buy the Medigap policy of his choice. That is the open enrollment period. Patients cannot be turned down or charged higher premiums because of poor health if they buy a policy during this period. Once the Medigap open enrollment period ends, patients may not be able to buy the policy of their choice. Patients may have to accept whatever Medigap policy an insurance company is willing to sell them.

192) **Answer: A**

Medigap is private insurance that is designed to help pay for Medicare cost-sharing amounts. There are 10 standard Medigap policies, and each offers a different combination of benefits. The best time to buy a policy is during your Medigap open enrollment period. For a period of 6 months from the date the patient is first enrolled in Medicare Part B and is age 65 or older, he has a right to buy the Medigap policy of his choice. That is the open enrollment period. Patients cannot be turned down or charged higher premiums because of poor health if they buy a policy during this period. Once the Medigap open enrollment period ends, patients may not be able to buy the policy of their choice. Patients may have to accept whatever Medigap policy an insurance company is willing to sell them.

193) **Answer: D**

The best time to buy a policy is during your Medigap open enrollment period. For a period of 6 months from the date the patient is first enrolled in Medicare Part B and is age 65 or older, he has a right to buy the Medigap policy of his choice. That is the open enrollment period. Patients cannot be turned down or charged higher premiums because of poor health if they buy a policy during this period. Once the Medigap open enrollment period ends, patients may not be able to buy the policy of their choice. Patients may have to accept whatever Medigap policy an insurance company is willing to sell them.

194) **Answer: A**

The best time to buy a policy is during your Medigap open enrollment period. For a period of 6 months from the date the patient is first enrolled in Medicare Part B and is age 65 or older, he has a right to buy the Medigap policy of his choice. That is the open enrollment period. Patients cannot be turned down or charged higher premiums because of poor health if they buy a policy during this period. Once the Medigap open enrollment period ends, patients may not be able to buy the policy of their choice. Patients may have to accept whatever Medigap policy an insurance company is willing to sell them.

195) Answer: B

The best time to buy a policy is during your Medigap open enrollment period. For a period of 6 months from the date the patient is first enrolled in Medicare Part B and is age 65 or older, he has a right to buy the Medigap policy of his choice. That is the open enrollment period. Patients cannot be turned down or charged higher premiums because of poor health if they buy a policy during this period. Once the Medigap open enrollment period ends, patients may not be able to buy the policy of their choice. Patients may have to accept whatever Medigap policy an insurance company is willing to sell them.

196) Answer: A

The open enrollment period is a period of 6 months from the date the patient is first enrolled in Medicare Part B and is age 65 or older.

197) Answer: C

The open enrollment period is a period of 6 months from the date the patient is first enrolled in Medicare Part B and is age 65 or older. Geography does not affect the Medicare open enrollment period.

198) Answer: B

The open enrollment period is a period of 6 months from the date the patient is first enrolled in Medicare Part B and is age 65 or older. Geography does not affect the Medicare open enrollment period.

199) Answer: D

Medicare Select is another type of Medicare supplemental health insurance sold by insurance companies and HMOs throughout most of the country. Medicare Select is the same as standard Medigap insurance in nearly all respects. The only difference between Medicare Select and standard Medigap insurance is that each insurer has specific hospitals, and in some cases specific doctors, that a patient must use, except in an emergency, in order to be eligible for full benefits. Medicare Select policies generally have lower premiums than other Medigap policies because of this requirement.

200) Answer: A

Medicare Select is another type of Medicare supplemental health insurance sold by insurance companies and HMOs throughout most of the country. Medicare Select is the same as standard Medigap insurance in nearly all respects. The only difference between Medicare Select and standard Medigap insurance is that each insurer has specific hospitals, and in some cases specific doctors, that a patient must use, except in an emergency, in order to be eligible for full benefits. Medicare Select policies generally have lower premiums than other Medigap policies because of this requirement.

201) Answer: B

Medicare Select is another type of Medicare supplemental health insurance sold by insurance companies and HMOs throughout most of the country. Medicare Select is the same as standard Medigap insurance in nearly all respects. The only difference between Medicare Select and standard Medigap insurance is that each insurer has specific hospitals, and in some cases specific doctors, that a patient must use, except in an emergency, in order to be eligible for full benefits. Medicare Select policies generally have lower premiums than other Medigap policies because of this requirement.

202) Answer: D

Other health insurance policies may have to pay, before Medicare pays its share of an individual's bill. For those individuals who have other health insurance policies and are eligible for Medicare (not including Medigap policies), the other insurance will pay first if: the individual is 65 or older; he or his spouse is currently working at an employer with 20 or more employees, and he has group health insurance based on that employment, the individual is under age 65 and is disabled; he or any member of his family is currently working at an employer with 100 or more employees; and he has group health insurance based on that employment; he has Medicare because of permanent kidney failure, or he has an illness or injury that is covered under Workers' Compensation, the federal black lung program, no-fault insurance, or any liability insurance.

203) **Answer: D**

For individuals who have a low income and limited resources, the state may pay for Medicare costs, including premiums, deductibles, and coinsurance. To qualify, the individual must be entitled to Medicare hospital insurance (Part A), his annual income level must be at or below the national poverty guidelines and he cannot have resources such as bank accounts or stocks and bonds worth more than $4,000 for one person or $6,000 for a couple (his home and first car don't count).

204) **Answer: B**

For individuals who have a low income and limited resources, the state may pay for Medicare costs, including premiums, deductibles, and coinsurance. To qualify, the individual must be entitled to Medicare hospital insurance (Part A), his annual income level must be at or below the national poverty guidelines and he cannot have resources such as bank accounts or stocks and bonds worth more than $4,000 for one person or $6,000 for a couple (his home and first car don't count).

205) **Answer: D**

An awareness of the cost-efficiency of preventative care over restorative treatments has prompted the federal government to add to the Medicare benefits package. The following changes in Medicare coverage have been made by the Balanced Budget Act of 1997:
Vaccine Outreach: Currently Medicare pays for one influenza vaccination per year, and one pneumococcal vaccine per lifetime. This program will be extended into the year 2002.
Breast Cancer Screening: Medicare will pay for yearly screening mammograms for women over age 40. The Part B deductible will be waived for this procedure.
Cervical Cancer Screening: Medicare will pay for screening PAP smears every 3 years, and will cover screening pelvic exams every 3 years or yearly for women at high risk. The Part B deductible will be waived.
Colorectal Cancer Screening: Medicare will pay for yearly colorectal screening for people over age 50.
Diabetic Education: Medicare will cover educational programs aimed at outpatient self-management.
Glucose Test Strips: Medicare will pay for glucose test strips for diabetics who are not insulin dependent.
Osteoporosis Screening: Medicare will cover the costs of bone mass tests for beneficiaries who are at clinical risk for osteoporosis.
Prostate Cancer Screening: Medicare will pay for yearly prostate cancer screening for men over age 50.

206) **Answer: D**

An awareness of the cost-efficiency of preventative care over restorative treatments has prompted the federal government to add to the Medicare benefits package. The following changes in Medicare coverage have been made by the Balanced Budget Act of 1997:
- **Vaccine Outreach:** Currently Medicare pays for one influenza vaccination per year, and one pneumococcal vaccine per lifetime. This program will be extended into the year 2002.
- **Breast Cancer Screening:** Medicare will pay for yearly screening mammograms for women over age 40. The Part B deductible will be waived for this procedure.
- **Cervical Cancer Screening:** Medicare will pay for screening PAP smears every 3 years, and will cover screening pelvic exams every 3 years or yearly for women at high risk. The Part B deductible will be waived.
- **Colorectal Cancer Screening:** Medicare will pay for yearly colorectal screening for people over age 50.
- **Diabetic Education:** Medicare will cover educational programs aimed at outpatient self-management.

- **Glucose Test Strips:** Medicare will pay for glucose test strips for diabetics who are not insulin dependent.
- **Osteoporosis Screening:** Medicare will cover the costs of bone mass tests for beneficiaries who are at clinical risk for osteoporosis.
- **Prostate Cancer Screening:** Medicare will pay for yearly prostate cancer screening for men over the age of 50.

207) Answer: B

An awareness of the cost-efficiency of preventative care over restorative treatments has prompted the federal government to add to the Medicare benefits package. The following changes in Medicare coverage have been made by the Balanced Budget Act of 1997:

- **Vaccine Outreach:** Currently Medicare pays for one influenza vaccination per year, and one pneumococcal vaccine per lifetime. This program will be extended into the year 2002.
- **Breast Cancer Screening:** Medicare will pay for yearly screening mammograms for women over age 40. The Part B deductible will be waived for this procedure.
- **Cervical Cancer Screening:** Medicare will pay for screening PAP smears every 3 years, and will cover screening pelvic exams every 3 years or yearly for women at high risk. The Part B deductible will be waived.
- **Colorectal Cancer Screening:** Medicare will pay for yearly colorectal screening for people over age 50.
- **Diabetic Education:** Medicare will cover educational programs aimed at outpatient self-management.
- **Glucose Test Strips:** Medicare will pay for glucose test strips for diabetics who are not insulin dependent.
- **Osteoporosis Screening:** Medicare will cover the costs of bone mass tests for beneficiaries who are at clinical risk for osteoporosis.
- **Prostate Cancer Screening:** Medicare will pay for yearly prostate cancer screening for men over the age of 50.

208) Answer: A

An awareness of the cost-efficiency of preventative care over restorative treatments has prompted the federal government to add to the Medicare benefits package. The following changes in Medicare coverage have been made by the Balanced Budget Act of 1997:

- **Vaccine Outreach:** Currently Medicare pays for one influenza vaccination per year, and one pneumococcal vaccine per lifetime. This program will be extended into the year 2002.
- **Breast Cancer Screening:** Medicare will pay for yearly screening mammograms for women over age 40. The Part B deductible will be waived for this procedure.
- **Cervical Cancer Screening:** Medicare will pay for screening PAP smears every 3 years, and will cover screening pelvic exams every 3 years or yearly for women at high risk. The Part B deductible will be waived.
- **Colorectal Cancer Screening:** Medicare will pay for yearly colorectal screening for people over age 50.
- **Diabetic Education:** Medicare will cover educational programs aimed at outpatient self-management.
- **Glucose Test Strips:** Medicare will pay for glucose test strips for diabetics who are not insulin dependent.
- **Osteoporosis Screening:** Medicare will cover the costs of bone mass tests for beneficiaries who are at clinical risk for osteoporosis.
- **Prostate Cancer Screening:** Medicare will pay for yearly prostate cancer screening for men over the age of 50.

209) Answer: D

The Health Care Financing Administration (HCFA) is a federal agency within the U.S. Department of Health and Human Services. HCFA runs the Medicare and Medicaid programs—two national health care programs that benefit about 75 million Americans. And with the Health Resources and Services Administration, HCFA runs the Children's Health Insurance Program, a program that is expected to cover many of the approximately 10 million uninsured children in the United States. HCFA also regulates all laboratory testing (except research) performed on humans in the United States. Approximately 158,000 laboratory entities fall within HCFA's regulatory responsibility. And HCFA, with the Departments of Labor and Treasury, helps millions of Americans and small companies get and keep health insurance coverage and helps eliminate discrimination based on health status for people buying health insurance.

210) Answer: C

The Health Care Financing Administration (HCFA) is a federal agency within the U.S. Department of Health and Human Services. HCFA runs the Medicare and Medicaid programs—two national health care programs that benefit about 75 million Americans. And with the Health Resources and Services Administration, HCFA runs the Children's Health Insurance Program, a program that is expected to cover many of the approximately 10 million uninsured children in the United States. HCFA also regulates all laboratory testing (except research) performed on humans in the United States. Approximately 158,000 laboratory entities fall within HCFA's regulatory responsibility. And HCFA, with the Departments of Labor and Treasury, helps millions of Americans and small companies get and keep health insurance coverage and helps eliminate discrimination based on health status for people buying health insurance.

211) Answer: B

The Health Care Financing Administration (HCFA) is a federal agency within the U.S. Department of Health and Human Services. HCFA runs the Medicare and Medicaid programs—two national health care programs that benefit about 75 million Americans. And with the Health Resources and Services Administration, HCFA runs the Children's Health Insurance Program, a program that is expected to cover many of the approximately 10 million uninsured children in the United States. HCFA also regulates all laboratory testing (except research) performed on humans in the United States. Approximately 158,000 laboratory entities fall within HCFA's regulatory responsibility. And HCFA, with the Departments of Labor and Treasury, helps millions of Americans and small companies get and keep health insurance coverage and helps eliminate discrimination based on health status for people buying health insurance.

212) Answer: A

The Health Care Financing Administration (HCFA) is a federal agency within the U.S. Department of Health and Human Services. HCFA runs the Medicare and Medicaid programs—two national health care programs that benefit about 75 million Americans. And with the Health Resources and Services Administration, HCFA runs the Children's Health Insurance Program, a program that is expected to cover many of the approximately 10 million uninsured children in the United States. HCFA also regulates all laboratory testing (except research) performed on humans in the United States. Approximately 158,000 laboratory entities fall within HCFA's regulatory responsibility. And HCFA, with the Departments of Labor and Treasury, helps millions of Americans and small companies get and keep health insurance coverage and helps eliminate discrimination based on health status for people buying health insurance.

213) Answer: D

A claims edit is logic within the Standard Claims Processing System (or program safeguard contractor Supplemental Edit Software) that selects certain claims, evaluates or compares information on the selected claims or other accessible source, and depending on the evaluation, takes action on the claims, such as pay in full, pay in part or suspend for manual review.

214) Answer: A

A claims edit is logic within the Standard Claims Processing System (or Program Safeguard Contractor Supplemental Edit Software) that selects certain claims, evaluates or compares information on the selected claims or other accessible source, and depending on the evaluation, takes action on the claims, such as pay in full, pay in part or suspend for manual review.

215) Answer: B

A claims edit is logic within the Standard Claims Processing System (or Program Safeguard Contractor Supplemental Edit Software) that selects certain claims, evaluates or compares information on the selected claims or other accessible source, and depending on the evaluation, takes action on the claims, such as pay in full, pay in part, or suspend for manual review.

216) Answer: D

Authoritative evidence is written medical or scientific conclusions demonstrating the medical effectiveness of a service. It is produced by at least one of the following:

- Controlled clinical trials, published in peer-reviewed medical or scientific journals
- Controlled clinical trials completed and accepted for publication in peer-reviewed medical or scientific journals
- Assessments initiated by HCFA
- Evaluations or studies initiated by Medicare contractors
- Case studies published in peer-reviewed medical or scientific journals that present treatment protocols

217) Answer: C

This monthly benefit is available in the first month that the patient meets the above criteria.

218) Answer: B

The patient does not have to have permanent work restrictions, just diagnosed physical and functional deficits, and be medically clear to participate and willing.

219) Answer: D

220) Answer: D

221) Answer: A

Health insurance does not have COB with Workers' Compensation. COB assures insurers that benefit payment will not exceed 100% of the charges billed.

222) Answer: D

Medicaid is a national insurance program aimed at serving the poor and the "needy." All fifty states, the District of Columbia, Guam, Puerto Rico, and the Virgin Islands operate Medicaid plans. It was created by Title XIX of the Social Security Act, and is part of the federal and state welfare system. State welfare or health departments usually operate the Medicaid program, within the guidelines issued by the HCFA, and are funded by the general tax revenues of the federal and state governments. Persons covered by the Medicaid program have no "out of pocket" expense for coverage.

223) Answer: D

Medicaid is a national insurance program aimed at serving the poor and the "needy." All fifty states, the District of Columbia, Guam, Puerto Rico, and the Virgin Islands operate Medicaid plans. It was created by Title XIX of the Social Security Act, and is part of the federal and state welfare system. State welfare or health departments usually operate the Medicaid program, within the guidelines issued by the HCFA, and are funded by the general tax revenues of the federal and state governments. Persons covered by the Medicaid program have no "out-of-pocket" expense for coverage. Providing medical insurance for the aged is the purpose of the Medicare Program.

224) Answer: A

Medicaid is a national insurance program aimed at serving the poor and the "needy." All fifty states, the District of Columbia, Guam, Puerto Rico, and the Virgin Islands operate Medicaid plans. It was created by Title XIX of the Social Security Act, and is part of the federal and state welfare system. State welfare or health departments usually operate the Medicaid program, within the guidelines issued by the HCFA, and are funded by the general tax revenues of the federal and state governments. Persons covered by the Medicaid program have no "out-of-pocket" expense for coverage. Providing medical insurance for the aged is the purpose of the Medicare Program.

225) **Answer: B**

Medicaid is a national insurance program aimed at serving the poor and the "needy." All fifty states, the District of Columbia, Guam, Puerto Rico, and the Virgin Islands operate Medicaid plans. It was created by Title XIX of the Social Security Act, and is part of the federal and state welfare system. State welfare or health departments usually operate the Medicaid program, within the guidelines issued by the HCFA, and are funded by the general tax revenues of the federal and state governments. Persons covered by the Medicaid program have no "out of pocket" expense for coverage. Providing medical insurance for the aged is the aim of the Medicare Program.

226) **Answer: B**

Medicaid is a national insurance program aimed at serving the poor and the "needy." All fifty states, the District of Columbia, Guam, Puerto Rico, and the Virgin Islands operate Medicaid plans. It was created by Title XIX of the Social Security Act, and is part of the federal and state welfare system. State welfare or health departments usually operate the Medicaid program, within the guidelines issued by the HCFA, and are funded by the general tax revenues of the federal and state governments. Persons covered by the Medicaid program have no "out of pocket" expense for coverage.

227) **Answer: A**

Medicaid is a national insurance program aimed at serving the poor and the "needy." All fifty states, the District of Columbia, Guam, Puerto Rico, and the Virgin Islands operate Medicaid plans. It was created by Title XIX of the Social Security Act, and is part of the federal and state welfare system. State welfare or health departments usually operate the Medicaid program, within the guidelines issued by the HCFA, and are funded by the general tax revenues of the federal and state governments. Persons covered by the Medicaid program have no "out of pocket" expense for coverage.

228) **Answer: D**

Though Medicaid benefits can vary from state to state, the program must furnish the federally mandated services that include: Inpatient Hospital Care, and Outpatient Services, Physicians' Services, Skilled Nursing Home Services for Adults, Laboratory and X-Ray Services, Family Planning Services, Early and Periodic Screening, Diagnosis and Treatment for children under age 21 (EPSDT).

229) **Answer: A**

Though Medicaid benefits can vary from state to state, the program must furnish the federally mandated services that include: Inpatient Hospital Care, and Outpatient Services, Physicians' Services, Skilled Nursing Home Services for Adults, Laboratory and X-Ray Services, Family Planning Services, Early and Periodic Screening, Diagnosis and Treatment for children under age 21 (EPSDT).

230) **Answer: B**

Though Medicaid benefits can vary from state to state, the program must furnish the federally mandated services that include: Inpatient Hospital Care, and Outpatient Services, Physicians' Services, Skilled Nursing Home Services for Adults, Laboratory and X-Ray Services, Family Planning Services, Early and Periodic Screening, Diagnosis and Treatment for children under age 21 (EPSDT).

231) **Answer: A**

Eligibility requirements for Medicaid benefits are set by each state. HCFA has set some minimum standards though. The people who are eligible under these standards include:
- Categorically needy: Families and certain children who qualify for public assistance; that is, they are eligible for Aid to Families with Dependent Children (AFDC) or Supplemental Security Income (SSI). Examples are the aged, blind, and physically disabled adults and children.
- Medically needy: Those people who earn enough to meet their basic needs but have inadequate resources to pay health care bills; for example, TB-infected persons who would

be financially eligible for Medicaid at the SSI level (only for TB-related ambulatory services and TB drugs).

232) Answer: B

Eligibility requirements for Medicaid benefits are set by each state. HCFA has set some minimum standards though. The people who are eligible under these standards include:

- Categorically needy: Families and certain children who qualify for public assistance; that is, they are eligible for Aid to Families with Dependent Children (AFDC) or Supplemental Security Income (SSI). Examples are the aged, blind, and physically disabled adults and children.
- Medically needy: Those people who earn enough to meet their basic needs but have inadequate resources to pay health care bills; for example, TB-infected persons who would be financially eligible for Medicaid at the SSI level (only for TB-related ambulatory services and TB drugs).

233) Answer: D

Eligibility requirements for Medicaid benefits are set by each state. HCFA has set some minimum standards though. The people who are eligible under these standards include:

- Categorically needy: Families and certain children who qualify for public assistance; that is, they are eligible for Aid to Families with Dependent Children (AFDC) or Supplemental Security Income (SSI). Examples are the aged, blind, and physically disabled adults and children.
- Medically needy: Those people who earn enough to meet their basic needs but have inadequate resources to pay health care bills; for example, TB-infected persons who would be financially eligible for Medicaid at the SSI level (only for TB-related ambulatory services and TB drugs).

234) Answer: C

Eligibility requirements for Medicaid benefits are set by each state, HCFA has set some minimum standards though. The people who are eligible under these standards include:

- Categorically needy: Families and certain children who qualify for public assistance; that is, they are eligible for Aid to Families with Dependent Children (AFDC) or Supplemental Security Income (SSI). Examples are the aged, blind, and physically disabled adults and children.
- Medically needy: Those people who earn enough to meet their basic needs but have inadequate resources to pay health care bills; for example, TB-infected persons who would be financially eligible for Medicaid at the SSI level (only for TB-related ambulatory services and TB drugs).

235) Answer: B

Eligibility requirements for Medicaid benefits are set by each state, HCFA has set some minimum standards though. The people who are eligible under these standards include:

- Categorically needy: Families and certain children who qualify for public assistance; that is, they are eligible for Aid to Families with Dependent Children (AFDC) or Supplemental Security Income (SSI). Examples are the aged, blind, and physically disabled adults and children.
- Medically needy: Those people who earn enough to meet their basic needs but have inadequate resources to pay health care bills; for example, TB-infected persons who would be financially eligible for Medicaid at the SSI level (only for TB-related ambulatory services and TB drugs).

236) Answer: D

To be eligible for federal funds, states are required to provide Medicaid coverage for most individuals who receive federally assisted income maintenance payments, as well as for related groups not receiving cash payments. Some examples of the mandatory Medicaid eligibility groups are:

- Recipients of Aid to Families with Dependent Children (AFDC)

- Supplemental Security Income (SSI) recipients (or in States using more restrictive criteria—aged, blind, and disabled individuals who meet criteria that are more restrictive than those of the SSI program and that were in place in the state's approved Medicaid plan as of January 1, 1972)
- Infants born to Medicaid-eligible pregnant women
- Children under age 6 and pregnant women who meet the state's AFDC financial requirements or whose family income is at or below 133% of the federal poverty level (The minimum mandatory income level for pregnant women and infants in certain states may be higher than 133%, if as of certain dates the state had established a higher percentage for covering those groups.)
- Recipients of adoption assistance and foster care under Title IV-E of the Social Security Act

237) Answer: A

To be eligible for federal funds, states are required to provide Medicaid coverage for most individuals who receive federally assisted income maintenance payments, as well as for related groups not receiving cash payments. Some examples of the mandatory Medicaid eligibility groups are:

- Recipients of Aid to Families with Dependent Children (AFDC)
- Supplemental Security Income (SSI) recipients (or in states using more restrictive criteria—aged, blind, and disabled individuals who meet criteria that are more restrictive than those of the SSI program and that were in place in the state's approved Medicaid plan as of January 1, 1972)
- Infants born to Medicaid-eligible pregnant women
- Children under age 6 and pregnant women who meet the state's AFDC financial requirements or whose family income is at or below 133% of the federal poverty level (The minimum mandatory income level for pregnant women and infants in certain states may be higher than 133%, if as of certain dates the state had established a higher percentage for covering those groups.)
- Recipients of adoption assistance and foster care under Title IV-E of the Social Security Act

238) Answer: B

To be eligible for federal funds, states are required to provide Medicaid coverage for most individuals who receive federally assisted income maintenance payments, as well as for related groups not receiving cash payments. Some examples of the mandatory Medicaid eligibility groups are:

- Recipients of Aid to Families with Dependent Children (AFDC)
- Supplemental Security Income (SSI) recipients (or in states using more restrictive criteria—aged, blind, and disabled individuals who meet criteria that are more restrictive than those of the SSI program and that were in place in the state's approved Medicaid plan as of January 1, 1972)
- Infants born to Medicaid-eligible pregnant women
- Children under age 6 and pregnant women who meet the state's AFDC financial requirements or whose family income is at or below 133% of the federal poverty level (The minimum mandatory income level for pregnant women and infants in certain states may be higher than 133%, if as of certain dates the state had established a higher percentage for covering those groups.)
- Recipients of adoption assistance and foster care under Title IV-E of the Social Security Act

239) Answer: C

Transfers to a sibling are not exempted by the state, and this asset-transfer would be assessed a penalty period. See *Section 1917(c) of the Social Security Act; U.S. Code Reference 42 U.S.C.1396p(c).*

240) Answer: B

Transfers to a sibling or a friend are not exempted by the state, and this asset-transfer would be assessed a penalty period. See *Section 1917(c) of the Social Security Act; U.S. Code Reference 42 U.S.C.1396p(c).*

241) Answer: A

Transfers to a sibling or a friend are not exempted by the state, and this asset-transfer would be assessed a penalty period. See *Section 1917(c) of the Social Security Act; U.S. Code Reference 42 U.S.C.1396p(c).*

242) Answer: D

A *penalty period* is that amount of time that a state will withhold payment for a nursing facility, and certain other long-term care services. There is no limit to the length of the penalty period. The penalty period is calculated by determining the fair market value of the transferred asset, and dividing the value of the asset by the average monthly private pay rate of a nursing facility in that state. For example, if an asset worth $120,000 has been transferred, and the average cost of a nursing facility in that state is $2,000 per month, then the penalty period would be calculated as: $120,000/$2,000 per month = 60 months penalty period.

243) Answer: A

A *penalty period* is that amount of time that a state will withhold payment for a nursing facility, and certain other long-term care services. There is no limit to the length of the penalty period. The penalty period is calculated by determining the fair market value of the transferred asset, and dividing the value of the asset by the average monthly private pay rate of a nursing facility in that state. For example, if an asset worth $120,000 has been transferred, and the average cost of a nursing facility in that state is $2,000 per month, then the penalty period would be calculated as: $120,000/$2,000 per month = 60 months penalty period.

244) Answer: B

A *penalty period* is that amount of time that a state will withhold payment for a nursing facility and certain other long-term care services. There is no limit to the length of the penalty period. The penalty period is calculated by determining the fair market value of the transferred asset, and dividing the value of the asset by the average monthly private pay rate of a nursing facility in that state. For example, if an asset worth $120,000 has been transferred, and the average cost of a nursing facility in that state is $2,000 per month, then the penalty period would be calculated as: $120,000/$2,000 per month = 60 months penalty period.

245) Answer: D

States "look back" into an individual's financial records during the evaluation of eligibility for Medicaid. The state looks to find transfers of assets for 36 months prior to the date the individual is institutionalized or, if later, the date he or she applied for Medicaid. For certain trusts, this look back period extends to 60 months. If a transfer of assets for less than fair market value is found, the state will impose a penalty period.

246) Answer: B

States "look back" into an individual's financial records during the evaluation of eligibility for Medicaid. Employment status, rather than financial status, determines Workers' Compensation eligibility. The state looks to find transfers of assets for 36 months prior to the date the individual is institutionalized or, if later, the date he or she applied for Medicaid. For certain trusts, this look back period extends to 60 months. If a transfer of assets for less than fair market value is found, the state will impose a penalty period.

247) Answer: A

States "look back" into an individual's financial records during the evaluation of eligibility for Medicaid. Employment status, rather than financial status, determine Workers' Compensation eligibility. The state looks to find transfers of assets for 36 months prior to the date the individual is institutionalized or, if later, the date he or she applied for Medicaid. For certain trusts, this look back period extends to 60 months. If a transfer of assets for less than fair market value is found, the state will impose a penalty period.

248) Answer: A

The penalty period is calculated by determining the fair market value of the transferred asset, and dividing the value of the asset by the average monthly private pay rate of a nursing facility in that state. For example, if an asset worth $120,000 has been transferred, and the average cost of a nursing facility in that state is $2,000 per month, then the penalty period would be calculated as: $120,000/$2,000 per month = 60 months penalty period.

249) Answer: A

Placing a spouse in a nursing home can be a very expensive proposition. With monthly expenses running $2,000 to $3,000, these bills can quickly wipe out a lifetime of savings, leaving the community-based spouse (community spouse) destitute. This situation is referred to as "spousal impoverishment." In an attempt to prevent this spousal impoverishment, Congress enacted provisions in 1988 that allow a couple to have Medicaid benefits without "spending down" their resources. These provisions help ensure that this spousal impoverishment will not occur and that community spouses are able to live out their lives with independence and dignity. *(Section 1924 of the Social Security Act; U.S. Code Reference 42 U.S.C.1396r-5.)* Medicare eligibility is not necessary for Medicaid benefits.

250) Answer: B

Placing a spouse in a nursing home can be a very expensive proposition. With monthly expenses running $2,000 to $3,000, these bills can quickly wipe out a lifetime of savings, leaving the community-based spouse (community spouse) destitute. This situation is referred to as "spousal impoverishment." In an attempt to prevent this spousal impoverishment, Congress enacted provisions in 1988 that allow a couple to have Medicaid benefits without "spending down" their resources. These provisions help ensure that this spousal impoverishment will not occur and that community spouses are able to live out their lives with independence and dignity. (*Section 1924 of the Social Security Act; U.S. Code Reference 42 U.S.C.1396r-5.*) Medicare eligibility is not necessary for Medicaid benefits.

251) Answer: D

In order to be eligible for Medicaid under this provision, the member of the couple who is in a nursing facility or medical institution must be expected to remain there for at least 30 days. The state then evaluates the couple's resources. After the state's evaluation, it determines the spousal resource amount or SRA. The SRA is the number the state measures against its minimum resource standard for an institutionalized patient to receive Medicaid. An institutionalized spouse who has less than this amount is eligible for Medicaid. The SRA is equal to the following: the combined spousal assets, minus the house, car, household goods, and burial costs, divided by two. It is described in the following formula: SRA = ½ × (couple's combined assets) – (house, car, etc.).

In order to determine whether the spouse residing in a medical facility is eligible for Medicaid, the SRA must be less than the state's minimum resource standard. This number was $76,740 in 1996. If the SRA is greater than the State's minimum resource standard, the remainder becomes attributable to the spouse who is residing in a medical institution as countable or depletable resources.

252) Answer: B

In order to be eligible for Medicaid under this provision, the member of the couple who is in a nursing facility or medical institution must be expected to remain there for at least 30 days. The state then evaluates the couple's resources. After the state's evaluation, it determines the spousal resource amount or SRA. The SRA is the number the state measures against its minimum resource standard for an institutionalized patient to receive Medicaid. An institutionalized spouse who has less than this amount is eligible for Medicaid. The SRA is equal to the following: the combined spousal assets, minus the house, car, household goods, and burial costs, divided by two. It is described in the following formula: SRA = ½ × (couple's combined assets) – (house, car, etc.).

In order to determine whether the spouse residing in a medical facility is eligible for Medicaid, the SRA must be less than the state's minimum resource standard. This number was $76,740 in 1996. If the SRA is greater than the state's minimum resource standard, the remainder becomes attributable to the spouse that is residing in a medical institution as countable or depletable resources. There is no Spousal Poverty Depletion Rate (SPDR).

253) Answer: A

In order to be eligible for Medicaid under this provision, the member of the couple who is in a nursing facility or medical institution must be expected to remain there for at least 30 days. The state then evaluates the couple's resources. After the state's evaluation, it determines the spousal resource amount or SRA. The SRA is the number the state measures against its minimum resource standard for an institutionalized patient to receive Medicaid. An institutionalized spouse who has less than this amount is eligible for Medicaid. The SRA is equal to the following: the combined spousal assets, minus the house, car, household goods, and burial costs, divided by two. It is described in the following formula: SRA = ½ × (couple's combined assets) – (house, car, etc.).

In order to determine whether the spouse residing in a medical facility is eligible for Medicaid, the SRA must be less than the state's minimum resource standard. This number was $76,740 in 1996. If the SRA is greater than the State's minimum resource standard, the remainder becomes attributable to the spouse that is residing in a medical institution as countable or depletable resources. There is no Spousal Poverty Depletion Rate (SPDR).

254) Answer: C

The community spouse's income is not considered available to the spouse who is in the medical facility, and the two individuals are not considered a couple for these purposes. The state is to use the income eligibility standards for one person rather than two. Therefore, the standard income eligibility process for Medicaid is used.

255) Answer: A

The community spouse's income is not considered available to the spouse who is in the medical facility, and the two individuals are not considered a couple for these purposes. The state is to use the income eligibility standards for one person rather than two. Therefore, the standard income eligibility process for Medicaid is used.

256) Answer: B

The community spouse's income is not considered available to the spouse who is in the medical facility, and the two individuals are not considered a couple for these purposes. The state is to use the income eligibility standards for one person rather than two. Therefore, the standard income eligibility process for Medicaid is used.

257) Answer: D

A trust is a legal title to property, held by one party, for the benefit of another. There are usually three parties involved in a Trust. The first is the *grantor*. The grantor is the person or entity who establishes the trust, and donates the assets. A *trustee* is a person or qualified trust company who holds and manages the assets for the benefit of another. The *beneficiary* is the recipient of some or all of the Trust's assets. The assets held by a Trust can exist in many forms, for example, money, real estate, art, businesses, stocks, bonds, and many other tangible assets. Trusts usually come in two varieties: revocable trusts, those trusts whose terms or beneficiaries can be changed, and irrevocable trusts, those trusts whose terms and beneficiaries are unchangeable. Putting an asset in a trust transfers that asset from the individual's ownership to that of the trustee, who holds the property for the beneficiary(s).

258) Answer: A

A trust is a legal title to property, held by one party, for the benefit of another. There are usually three parties involved in a Trust. The first is the *grantor*. The grantor is the person or entity who establishes the trust, and donates the assets. A *trustee* is a person or qualified trust company who holds and manages the assets for the benefit of another. The *beneficiary* is the recipient of some or all of the Trust's assets. The assets held by a Trust can exist in many forms, for example, money, real estate, art, businesses, stocks, bonds, and many other tangible assets. Trusts usually come in two varieties: revocable trusts, those trusts whose terms or beneficiaries can be changed, and irrevocable trusts, those trusts whose terms and beneficiaries are unchangeable. Putting an asset in a trust transfers that asset from the individual's ownership to that of the trustee, who holds the property for the beneficiary(s).

259) Answer: D

A trust is a legal title to property, held by one party, for the benefit of another. There are usually three parties involved in a Trust. The first is the *grantor*. The grantor is the person or entity who establishes the trust and donates the assets. A *trustee* is a person or qualified trust company, who holds and manages the assets for the benefit of another. The *beneficiary* is the recipient of some or all of the Trust's assets. The assets held by a Trust can exist in many forms, for example, money, real estate, art, businesses, stocks, bonds, and many other tangible assets. Trusts usually come in two varieties: revocable trusts, those trusts whose terms or beneficiaries can be changed, and irrevocable trusts, those trusts whose terms and beneficiaries are unchangeable. Putting an asset in a trust transfers that asset from the individual's ownership to that of the trustee, who holds the property for the beneficiary(s).

260) Answer: B

A trust is a legal title to property, held by one party for the benefit of another. There are usually three parties involved in a Trust. The first is the *grantor*. The grantor is the person or entity who establishes the trust and donates the assets. A *trustee* is a person or qualified trust company, who holds and manages the assets for the benefit of another. The *beneficiary* is the recipient of some or all of the Trust's assets. The assets held by a Trust can exist in many forms, for example, money, real estate, art, businesses, stocks, bonds, and many other tangible assets. Trusts usually come in two varieties: revocable trusts, those trusts whose terms or beneficiaries can be changed, and irrevocable trusts, those trusts whose terms and beneficiaries are unchangeable. Putting an asset in a trust transfers that asset from the individual's ownership to that of the trustee, who holds the property for the beneficiary(s).

261) Answer: D

A trust is a legal title to property, held by one party for the benefit of another. There are usually three parties involved in a Trust. The first is the *grantor*. The grantor is the person or entity who establishes the trust and donates the assets. A *trustee* is a person or qualified trust company, who holds and manages the assets for the benefit of another. The *beneficiary* is the recipient of some or all of the Trust's assets. The assets held by a Trust can exist in many forms, for example, money, real estate, art, businesses, stocks, bonds, and many other tangible assets. Trusts usually come in two varieties: revocable trusts, those trusts whose terms or beneficiaries can be changed, and irrevocable trusts, those trusts whose terms and beneficiaries are unchangeable. Putting an asset in a trust transfers that asset from the individual's ownership to that of the trustee, who holds the property for the beneficiary(s).

262) Answer: A

A trust is a legal title to property, held by one party for the benefit of another. There are usually three parties involved in a Trust. The first is the *grantor*. The grantor is the person or entity who establishes the trust and donates the assets. A *trustee* is a person or qualified trust company, who holds and manages the assets for the benefit of another. The *beneficiary* is the recipient of some or all of the Trust's assets. The assets held by a Trust can exist in many forms, for example, money, real estate, art, businesses, stocks, bonds, and many other tangible assets. Trusts usually come in two varieties: revocable trusts, those trusts whose terms or beneficiaries can be changed, and irrevocable trusts, those trusts whose terms and beneficiaries are unchangeable. Putting an asset in a trust transfers that asset from the individual's ownership to that of the trustee, who holds the property for the beneficiary(s).

263) Answer: D

How a trust is treated by HCFA depends to some extent on the type of trust it is; for example, whether it is revocable or irrevocable, and what specific requirements and conditions the trust contains. In general, payments from a trust actually made to or for the benefit of the individual are treated as income to the individual. HCFA considers monies that could be paid to an individual or for the benefit of the individual, but are not, as available resources. Further, amounts that could be paid to or for the benefit of the individual, but are paid to someone else are treated as transfers of assets for less than fair market value. Amounts transferred into a trust, which cannot, in any way, be paid to or for the benefit of the individual, are also treated as transfers of assets for less than fair market value.

264) Answer: B

How a trust is treated by HCFA depends to some extent on the type of trust it is; for example, whether it is revocable or irrevocable, and what specific requirements and conditions the trust contains. In general, payments from a trust actually made to or for the benefit of the individual are treated as income to the individual. HCFA considers monies that could be paid to an individual or for the benefit of the individual, but are not, as available resources. Further, amounts that could be paid to or for the benefit of the individual, but are paid to someone else are treated as transfers of assets for less than fair market value. Amounts transferred into a trust, which cannot, in any way, be paid to or for the benefit of the individual, are also treated as transfers of assets for less than fair market value.

265) Answer: A

How a trust is treated by HCFA depends to some extent on the type of trust it is; for example, whether it is revocable or irrevocable, and what specific requirements and conditions the trust contains. In general, payments from a trust actually made to or for the benefit of the individual are treated as income to the individual. HCFA considers monies that could be paid to an individual or for the benefit of the individual, but are not, as available resources. Further, amounts that could be paid to or for the benefit of the individual, but are paid to someone else are treated as transfers of assets for less than fair market value. Amounts transferred into a trust, which cannot, in any way, be paid to or for the benefit of the individual, are also treated as transfers of assets for less than fair market value.

266) Answer: A

Assets placed in trusts established by a parent, grandparent, guardian, or court for the benefit of an individual who is disabled and under the age of 65, using the individual's own funds, are not counted as being available by HCFA. The Social Security Benefits are counted as an individual's own contribution to the trust.

267) Answer: A

Currently, definitions of medical necessity contained in health insurance contracts are characterized by ambiguity and inconsistency. They do not clearly cover all clinical eventualities.

268) Answer: B

Currently, definitions of medical necessity contained in health insurance contracts are characterized by ambiguity and inconsistency. They do not clearly cover all clinical eventualities.

269) Answer: D

In the standard health insurance contract, when medical necessity is defined, it is often defined in terms of what is appropriate, reasonable, and acceptable. These terms are rarely if ever explained. Further, the terms investigational, experimental treatments as well as custodial care are usually mentioned as specific exclusions in the definition, however, they also are rarely if ever defined themselves.

270) Answer: A

The issue of what is medically necessary is an important issue, and it affects the payment of every claim for health services. A longer and more inclusive wording of the contract does not solve the problem of defining what is medically necessary, rather a methodological or procedural approach to the definition. This procedural approach describes the steps that should be taken when determining what is medically necessary.

271) Answer: B

When determining what is medically necessary for a particular case, the reviewer should take into account the contents of the patient's medical record, the opinion of the treating physician, the opinion of an objective physician who is a specialist in the field of medicine in question.

272) Answer: C

The decision making process for medical necessity determinations should be supervised by the medical director, and should be characterized by fairness, reproducibility, and utilization of the best available information. Arbitrary and capricious behavior is a violation of legal and ethical standards.

273) Answer: B

When cases of medical necessity are litigated, the courts place significant weight on the reasonable expectations of a layperson in the position of a patient. The court implies that if "reasonable laypersons" could expect a certain medical benefit under their contract, then they may be entitled to it. This expectation principle is used by the courts to justify granting a wide range of benefits to the subscriber that the insurer's policy language appear to exclude. In the *Ponder* case, the insurer denied treatment for temporomandibular joint syndrome, because it was excluded by the contract. The fairness of the contract was questioned, since the purchaser of the insurance did not understand the meaning of the exclusionary criteria in the contract. As the court stated, subscribers "could only discover what they had bought with their premiums as their diseases were diagnosed, and they found out to their sorrow, the true meaning of those mysterious words in their insurance contracts."

274) Answer: A

When cases of medical necessity are litigated, the courts place significant weight on the reasonable expectations of a layperson in the position of a patient. The court implies that if "reasonable laypersons" could expect a certain medical benefit under their contract, then they may be entitled to it. This expectation principle is used by the courts to justify granting a wide range of benefits to the subscriber that the insurer's policy language appear to exclude. In the *Ponder* case, the insurer denied treatment for temporomandibular joint syndrome, because it was excluded by the contract. The fairness of the contract was questioned, since the purchaser of the insurance did not understand the meaning of the exclusionary criteria in the contract. As the court stated, subscribers "could only discover what they had bought with their premiums as their diseases were diagnosed, and they found out to their sorrow, the true meaning of those mysterious words in their insurance contracts."

275) Answer: C

When cases of medical necessity are litigated, the courts place significant weight on the reasonable expectations of a layperson in the position of a patient. The court implies that if "reasonable laypersons" could expect a certain medical benefit under their contract, then they may be entitled to it. This expectation principle is used by the courts to justify granting a wide range of benefits to the subscriber that the insurer's policy language appear to exclude. In the *Ponder* case, the insurer denied treatment for temporomandibular joint syndrome, because it was excluded by the contract. The fairness of the contract was questioned, since the purchaser of the insurance did not understand the meaning of the exclusionary criteria in the contract. As the court stated, subscribers "could only discover what they had bought with their premiums as their diseases were diagnosed, and they found out to their sorrow, the true meaning of those mysterious words in their insurance contracts."

276) Answer: B

Whenever possible, the best outcome for everyone involved is to return the patient to his same job. This should be tried prior to considering any other plan.

277) Answer: D

The MHPA of 1996 is a federal law that protects individuals with mental health problems against discrimination, by prohibiting lifetime or annual dollar limits on mental health care, unless comparable limits apply to medical or surgical treatment. Enforcement began during plan years beginning on or after January 1, 1998, and will sunset on September 30, 2001. The MHPA's definition of mental health excludes chemical dependency. Therefore, plans will be able to have separate limits for the treatment of substance abuse.

278) Answer: B

The MHPA of 1996 is a federal law that protects individuals with mental health problems against discrimination, by prohibiting lifetime or annual dollar limits on mental health care, unless comparable limits apply to medical or surgical treatment. Enforcement began during plan years beginning on or after January 1, 1998, and will sunset on September 30, 2001. The MHPA's definition of mental health excludes chemical dependency. Therefore, plans will be able to have separate limits for the treatment of substance abuse.

279) Answer: C

The MHPA of 1996 is a federal law that protects individuals with mental health problems against discrimination, by prohibiting lifetime or annual dollar limits on mental health care, unless comparable limits apply to medical or surgical treatment. Enforcement began during plan years beginning on or after January 1, 1998, and will sunset on September 30, 2001. The MHPA's definition of mental health excludes chemical dependency. Therefore, plans will be able to have separate limits for the treatment of substance abuse. Under the MHPA, plans are *not* required to cover mental health treatment. However, if a plan does have mental health coverage, it cannot set a separate dollar limit from medical care.

280) Answer: A

The MHPA exempts employers with 50 or less workers and those employers or plans who can demonstrate that parity would cause at least a 1% increase in health care benefits. Specific industries are not addressed in the legislation.

281) Answer: B

The MHPA exempts employers with 50 or less workers and those employers or plans that can demonstrate that parity would cause at least a 1% increase in health care benefits. Employers in specific industries are not addressed in the legislation.

282) Answer: D

While annual or lifetime dollar limits cannot be set under the provisions of the Mental Health Parity Act, other limits are allowed. Examples of other allowable limits are:
- Limited number of annual outpatient visits
- Limited number of inpatient days annually
- Per-visit fee limit
- Higher deductibles and copayments, without parity in medical and surgical benefits

283) Answer: D

While annual or lifetime dollar limits cannot be set under the provisions of the Mental Health Parity Act, other limits are allowed. Examples of other allowable limits are:
- Limited number of annual outpatient visits
- Limited number of inpatient days annually
- Per-visit fee limit
- Higher deductibles and copayments, without parity in medical and surgical benefits

If an employer does not offer medical benefits, he does not have to offer mental health benefits; said differently, if an employer chooses not to offer mental health benefits, he must also choose not to offer medical benefits.

284) Answer: B

While annual or lifetime dollar limits cannot be set under the provisions of the Mental Health Parity Act, other limits are allowed. Examples of other allowable limits are:
- Limited number of annual outpatient visits
- Limited number of inpatient days annually
- Per-visit fee limit
- Higher deductibles and copayments, without parity in medical and surgical benefits

If an employer does not offer medical benefits, he does not have to offer mental health benefits; said differently, if an employer chooses not to offer mental health benefits, he must also choose not to offer medical benefits.

285) Answer: A

While annual or lifetime dollar limits cannot be set under the provisions of the Mental Health Parity Act, other limits are allowed. Examples of other allowable limits are:
- Limited number of annual outpatient visits
- Limited number of inpatient days annually
- Per-visit fee limit
- Higher deductibles and copayments, without parity in medical and surgical benefits

If an employer does not offer medical benefits, he does not have to offer mental health benefits; said differently, if an employer chooses not to offer mental health benefits, he must also choose not to offer medical benefits.

286) Answer: D

The Pregnancy Discrimination Act is a federal law that extends to employees with disabilities associated with pregnancies and childbirth, the same rights and benefits offered to employees with other medical disabilities. This federal law was created as an amendment to Title VII of the Civil Rights Act of 1964.

287) Answer: B

The Pregnancy Discrimination Act is a federal law that extends to employees with disabilities associated with pregnancies and childbirth, the same rights and benefits offered to employees with other medical disabilities. This federal law was created as an amendment to Title VII of the Civil Rights Act of 1964.

288) Answer: A

The Pregnancy Discrimination Act is a federal law that extends to employees with disabilities associated with pregnancies and childbirth, the same rights and benefits offered to employees with other medical disabilities. This federal law was created as an amendment to Title VII of the Civil Rights Act of 1964.

289) Answer: D

The Pregnancy Discrimination Act expects employers to treat equally individuals with disabilities attendant to medical and surgical conditions as they do employees with disabilities associated with pregnancy and childbirth. This *same treatment* includes the following categories: health insurance benefits, short-term sick leave, disability benefits and employment policies (such as seniority, leave extensions, and reinstatement).

290) Answer: A

The Pregnancy Discrimination Act expects employers to treat equally individuals with disabilities attendant to medical and surgical conditions as they do employees with disabilities associated with pregnancy and childbirth. This *same treatment* includes the following categories: health insurance benefits, short-term sick leave, disability benefits and employment policies (such as seniority, leave extensions, and reinstatement).

291) Answer: D

The "same treatment" in the Pregnancy Discrimination Act means that in regards to choice, access, cost, and quality, maternity benefits will be the equal of medical benefits.

292) Answer: B

Under the Terms of the Pregnancy Discrimination Act, all of the following are prohibited:
- Limiting the number of physicians or hospitals who provide maternity care, when medical and surgical care providers are not limited
- Limiting the number of plans that offer maternity care, without corresponding limits on medical and surgical care
- Limiting the reimbursement for maternity care, when there are no corresponding limits on medical and surgical care
- Exacting higher deductibles, copayments or out of pocket maximums for maternity care, than medical and surgical care

293) Answer: D

294) Answer: A

Under the Terms of the Pregnancy Discrimination Act, all of the following are prohibited:
- Limiting the number of physicians or hospitals who provide maternity care, when medical and surgical care providers are not limited
- Limiting the number of plans that offer maternity care, without corresponding limits on medical and surgical care
- Limiting the reimbursement for maternity care, when there are no corresponding limits on medical and surgical care
- Exacting higher deductibles, copayments or out of pocket maximums for maternity care, than medical and surgical care

295) Answer: E

All the individuals are covered under the Pregnancy Discrimination Act.

296) Answer: B

Though its scope is large, the Pregnancy Discrimination Act does exclude some benefits. Those benefits are abortions and mandatory maternity leave.

297) Answer: A

Though its scope is large, the Pregnancy Discrimination Act does exclude some benefits. Those benefits are abortions and mandatory maternity leave. When home health and home physical therapy are allowed under medical benefits, they are included under maternity benefits also.

298) Answer: D

Under TEFRA the following was established:

- The "Diagnosis Related Groups" or DRGs, a case-based reimbursement system. This prospective payment system determined the cost of care for selected diagnoses, while also placing limits on rate increases in hospital revenues.
- Exempted medical rehabilitation from DRGs. Rehabilitation would continue as a cost-based reimbursement system, subject to certain limits.
- Amended the Social Security Act, and made Medicare secondary to employer group health plans for active employees 65 to 69 years old and their spouses in the same age group.
- It also revised the Age Discrimination in Employment Act (ADEA) of 1967 by requiring employers to offer active employees age 65 to 69 and their spouses the same health benefits as those made available to younger employees.
- Established peer review organizations (PROs). A PRO is an entity that is selected by HCFA to *reduce costs* associated with the hospital stays of Medicare and Medicaid patients. Further they are charged with conducting reviews of hospital-based care on these patients to *assure quality of care and appropriateness of admissions*, readmissions and discharges. Through this review procedure PROs can maintain and/or lower admission rates, reduce lengths of stay while insuring against inadequate treatment.

299) Answer: C

Under TEFRA the following was established:

- The "Diagnosis Related Groups" or DRGs, a case-based reimbursement system. This prospective payment system determined the cost of care for selected diagnoses, while also placing limits on rate increases in hospital revenues.
- Exempted medical rehabilitation from DRGs. Rehabilitation would continue as a cost-based reimbursement system, subject to certain limits.
- Amended the Social Security Act, and made Medicare secondary to employer group health plans for active employees 65 to 69 years old and their spouses in the same age group.
- It also revised the Age Discrimination in Employment Act (ADEA) of 1967 by requiring employers to offer active employees age 65 to 69 and their spouses the same health benefits as those made available to younger employees.
- Established peer review organizations (PROs). A PRO is an entity that is selected by HCFA to *reduce costs* associated with the hospital stays of Medicare and Medicaid patients. Further they are charged with conducting reviews of hospital based care on these patients to *assure quality of care and appropriateness of admissions*, readmissions and discharges. Through this review procedure PROs can maintain and/or lower admission rates, reduce lengths of stay while insuring against inadequate treatment.

300) Answer: B

Under TEFRA the following was established:

- The "Diagnosis Related Groups" or DRGs, a case-based reimbursement system. This prospective payment system determined the cost of care for selected diagnoses, while also placing limits on rate increases in hospital revenues.
- Exempted medical rehabilitation from DRGs. Rehabilitation would continue as a cost-based reimbursement system, subject to certain limits.

- Amended the Social Security Act, and made Medicare secondary to employer group health plans for active employees 65 to 69 years old and their spouses in the same age group.
- It also revised the Age Discrimination in Employment Act (ADEA) of 1967 by requiring employers to offer active employees age 65 to 69 and their spouses the same health benefits as those made available to younger employees.
- Established peer review organizations (PROs). A PRO is an entity that is selected by HCFA to *reduce costs* associated with the hospital stays of Medicare and Medicaid patients. Further they are charged with conducting reviews of hospital based care on these patients to *assure quality of care and appropriateness of admissions*, readmissions and discharges. Through this review procedure PROs can maintain and/or lower admission rates, reduce lengths of stay while insuring against inadequate treatment.

301) Answer: D

The TEFRA legislation of 1982 was designed to provide incentives for cost containment. Under TEFRA the Diagnosis Related Groups or DRGs program was established. A case-based reimbursement system, this prospective payment system determined the cost of care for selected diagnoses, while also placing limits on rate increases in hospital revenues.

302) Answer: A

The TEFRA legislation of 1982 was designed to provide incentives for cost containment. Under TEFRA the Diagnosis Related Groups or DRGs program was established. A case-based reimbursement system, this prospective payment system determined the cost of care for selected diagnoses, while also placing limits on rate increases in hospital revenues.

303) Answer: B

The TEFRA legislation of 1982 was designed to provide incentives for cost containment. Under TEFRA the Diagnosis Related Groups or DRGs program was established. A case-based reimbursement system, this prospective payment system determined the cost of care for selected diagnoses, while also placing limits on rate increases in hospital revenues.

304) Answer: C

Under TEFRA, medical rehabilitation was exempted from the DRGs. Rehabilitation would continue to be a cost based reimbursement system, subject to certain limits.

305) Answer: B

TEFRA amended the Social Security Act, and made Medicare secondary to employer group health plans for active employees 65 to 69 years old and their spouses in the same age group. It also revised the Age Discrimination in Employment Act (ADEA) of 1967 by requiring employers to offer active employees age 65 to 69 and their spouses the same health benefits as those made available to younger employees.

306) Answer: A

TEFRA amended the Social Security Act, and made Medicare secondary to employer group health plans for active employees 65 to 69 years old and their spouses in the same age group. It also revised the Age Discrimination in Employment Act (ADEA) of 1967 by requiring employers to offer active employees age 65 to 69 and their spouses the same health benefits as those made available to younger employees.

307) Answer: A

Under the terms of TEFRA, Diagnosis Related Groups and Peer Review Organizations were created. Diagnosis Related Groups, or DRGs, are a prospective payment system determined by the cost of care for selected diagnoses, while also placing limits on rate increases in hospital revenues. A PRO is an entity that is selected by HCFA to *reduce costs* associated with the hospital stays of Medicare and Medicaid patients. Further, they are charged with conducting reviews of hospital-based care on these patients to *assure quality of care and appropriateness of admissions*, readmissions and discharges. Through this review procedure PROs can maintain and/or lower admission rates and reduce lengths of stay while insuring against inadequate treatment.

308) Answer: B

Under the terms of TEFRA, Diagnosis Related Groups and Peer Review Organizations were created. Diagnosis Related Groups, or DRGs, are a prospective payment system determined by the cost of care for selected diagnoses, while also placing limits on rate increases in hospital revenues. A PRO is an entity that is selected by HCFA to *reduce costs* associated with the hospital stays of Medicare and Medicaid patients. Further, they are charged with conducting reviews of hospital-based care on these patients to *assure quality of care and appropriateness of admissions*, readmissions and discharges. Through this review procedure PROs can maintain and/or lower admission rates, reduce lengths of stay while insuring against inadequate treatment. HMOs and IPA developed independent of federal legislation.

309) Answer: D

Under TEFRA, Peer Review Organizations (PROs) were established. A PRO is an entity that is selected by HCFA to *reduce costs* associated with the hospital stays of Medicare and Medicaid patients. Further they are charged with conducting reviews of hospital-based care on these patients to *assure quality of care and appropriateness of admissions*, readmissions and discharges. Through this review procedure PROs can maintain and/or lower admission rates and reduce lengths of stay while insuring against inadequate treatment.

310) Answer: B

Under TEFRA, Peer Review Organizations (PROs) were established. A PRO is an entity that is selected by HCFA to *reduce costs* associated with the hospital stays of Medicare and Medicaid patients. Further they are charged with conducting reviews of hospital-based care on these patients to *assure quality of care and appropriateness of admissions*, readmissions and discharges. Through this review procedure PROs can maintain and/or lower admission rates and reduce lengths of stay while insuring against inadequate treatment.

311) Answer: A

Under TEFRA, Peer Review Organizations (PROs) were established. A PRO is an entity that is selected by HCFA to *reduce costs* associated with the hospital stays of Medicare and Medicaid patients. Further they are charged with conducting reviews of hospital based care on these patients to *assure quality of care and appropriateness of admissions*, readmissions and discharges. Through this review procedure PROs can maintain and/or lower admission rates and reduce lengths of stay while insuring against inadequate treatment.

312) Answer: B

Utilization review reviews services for medical necessity, appropriateness and efficiency. It includes review for medical necessity of an admission, length of stay review, discharge planning and all services ordered. It can be done prospectively, concurrently and retrospectively. While dollar amounts may be used to establish the types of services that are reviewed, care is not denied based on cost but on lack of medical necessity, appropriateness or a contractual exclusion. Utilization review compares treatment rendered with nationally recognized and accepted standards of care and protocols.

313) Answer: B

The ADA offers protection for "qualified disabled" individuals. In this case the candidate for the job is not qualified for the job. The ADA does not consider a change in the essential functions of the job to be a "reasonable accommodation."

314) Answer: C

This is the best possible solution for all concerned and should be explored first.

315) Answer: D

316) Answer: C

317) Answer: C

318) **Answer: A**

In order for the Case Manager to arrange as early a return to work as possible, it is necessary for everyone involved in the care plan to understand the job requirements.

319) **Answer: A**

PIP policy minimums are set by the state insurance department. These minimums may not be sufficient to cover the medical costs of more severe injuries.

320) **Answer: E**

No-fault insurance implies no blame is assigned to accidents. All parties injured during the accident are covered regardless of blame when a no-fault policy is purchased.

321) **Answer: A**

The patient usually signs a form, prior to care being rendered, directing Medicare to pay the provider of services directly, and the provider must accept Medicare's allowable charge as payment in full.

322) **Answer: C**

Workers' Compensation is generally the payer for the above listed benefits.

Chapter 6

Community Resources

INTERVIEW TECHNIQUES

The case management process begins with gathering and assessing information. The information gathered will become the basis for the case management plan. The more relevant information known prior to planning, the more appropriate the plan and subsequent outcome will be. It is essential, therefore, that the information collected is complete and accurate. Toward that end, the Case Manager needs to utilize good interview and communications skills. The following steps are applicable regardless of whom you are interviewing.[1]

Introduce yourself and explain the reason why you will be asking so many questions. Ask if it is a good time for the person to talk. Explain the Case Manager's role in the case, and assure the patient that the information collected will remain confidential. Ask permission to proceed.

Empowerment is important. Let the patient do most of the talking. Let him or her use their own words and expressions, so that you can get a clear understanding of the comprehension of the disease process and treatment plan. Allow the patient to speak at his or her own pace and to finish thoughts.

Trust is defined as a firm reliance on the integrity, ability, or character of a person. It is difficult to establish such a relationship over the phone. However, there are a few techniques that can improve a Case Manager's chances of succeeding. For example:

- Be sensitive to the emotional content of the issues being discussed.
- Always use layman's terms when discussing medical problems. It helps to establish a rapport with the patient. Remember that confusing medical terminology may be a barrier to effective communication and trust.
- Offer reassurance to the patient that you are experienced in handling this type of case.
- Explain that you are available to the patient for any questions or concerns he or she may have.

Maintain a respectful demeanor when speaking with the patient. This is especially important when the patient's value system is different than yours. You are acting as the patient's advocate, and many times the patient's idea of what is appropriate and the Case Manager's idea of what is appropriate may not be congruent. A perceived lack of respect for the patient's beliefs or decisions can be another barrier to effective communication and interviewing. Empathy can further your rapport and encourage the patient or family to call the Case Manager, in the future, early enough to make timely interventions, perhaps avoiding costly hospitalizations or complex treatments.

If the Case Manager is interviewing the patient in person (rather than by telephone), he or she should watch their own body language. Nonverbal body language can reveal a judgmental attitude to the patient. If the interview is telephonic, take note of the tone of your voice. During the in-person interview, the Case Manager also should observe the patient's general appearance and body language. Does the patient's body language suggest he or she is tired or in pain? Does your body language confirm your attentiveness?

Listening as opposed to hearing is an active cognitive process requiring sensitivity and focused attention. Active listening requires real participation and uses attending behaviors such as facial gestures, head nodding, note taking and reflecting back what is said. This is also the most important communication skill a Case Manager can have (see under Communication Skills).

Use a pad and pencil to take notes during the interview to prevent omissions. Try to keep the note taking to a minimum during the interview, as it is distracting and can be suspicious to the patient. As soon as the interview is over, complete your notes while the interview is fresh in your mind.

Ask about the major problem first. The details may be filled in as the patient talks about other topics, without you having to ask the delicate questions. Use open-ended questions—those that require more than a one-word answer. Try to avoid "why" questions as they often sound accusatory. Ask combination questions so the patient isn't always answering rapid fire type questions. For example, "Tell me about your family, employment, and what you like to do to relax and enjoy yourself."

Test discrepancies. Sometimes a patient's words and body language do not match. In general, words are easier to change than the way they are expressed. If the words are positive but the expression is not, consider the message negative and vice versa.

Close the interview by sharing your summary with the patient. Your summary should capture the essence of the interview and explain the care plan. After this review, encourage the patient to add information or correct any misunderstandings. This act demonstrates to the patient that you were actively listening and develops consensus on the plan goals.

Initial Assessment

The initial assessment interview should cover the following categories:[2]

- cognitive function
- diagnosis/medical conditions
- medications
- care access
- functional status
- social situation
- nutritional status
- emotional function

Cognitive Function

Cognitive deficits are associated with many diseases of the neurological system such as dementias, infections, tumors, and cerebral vascular accidents. They are also frequently seen in traumatic brain injuries. If, during the interview, the Case Manager notices the patient is cognitively impaired, the Case Manager should seek a proxy, such as a family member or caregiver, to answer questions. The cognitive deficit should be addressed in the ultimate care plan that is developed.

Diagnosis/Medical Condition

The Case Manager should elicit the patient's understanding of the disease process or injury. Questions should bring to light areas of concern for the patient that may require the Case Manager's intervention.

Medications

Medications are a large area of discussion often overlooked when a patient is cared for by multiple providers. Case Managers are in the unique position to detect potential problems with drug administration, such as pharmacy misunderstandings, prescription duplications, and drug-drug interactions. The Case Manager is also able to improve drug compliance by explaining drug side effects, by instructing the patient about how the drug works to improve health, and by eliminating financial barriers.

Care Access

The Case Manager evaluates the health services the patient is using, looking for appropriateness of service type, service location, and provider. Based on these findings, the Case Manager can assist in filling gaps, eliminating duplicate services, arranging for credentialled providers, and negotiating appropriate costs on behalf of the patient.

Functional Status

The evaluation of functional status is an important part of the assessment process. This evaluation includes several areas. Activities of daily living (ADLs) include items such as whether the patient can bathe, feed, dress, toilet and feed himself. Can he do these activities within certain parameters? For instance, can he dress himself if he has assistive devices? Is he mobile? If so, how? Does he need assistance, does he need equipment to be mobile, is he independent on flat surfaces but not able to climb stairs safely, etc.?

Instrumental activities of daily living (IADL) include whether the patient can do housework, shopping and meal preparation. Is the patient subsisting on "tea and toast" because he cannot carry heavier groceries home? Is the environment a barrier to effective wound healing due to the inability to clean house?

Is there a potential for falls? Does the patient have a history of falls? Do new medical circumstances put the patient at risk for falls? For example, the following have been associated with an increased risk for falls; blindness, vestibular problems, syncope, leg or arm weakness, new bandages and casts, and medications such as benzodiazepines or barbiturates. Does the patient need an assessment and assistance in creating a barrier-free environment to prevent falls? Common household improvements include pulling up slippery carpets, marking the edges of steps, improving lighting, and installing hand rails in the bath. Does the patient require a quad cane, a walker, or other assistive device for safety?

The above areas may not always be covered under insurance, but the Case Manager has the option of presenting alternative benefit plans to the referral source and of utilizing community resources.

Social Situation

This area of assessment involves an evaluation of the patient's support system. This is where the Case Manager determines who is available and willing to participate in the patient's care plan. If the family is having difficulty coping with the patient's illness or dependent status, the Case Manager can arrange for social work intervention.

Nutritional Status

Nutritional deficits can be the cause of, or exacerbate, many health problems. In particular, they delay wound healing and adversely affect cognitive function and many disease states such as diabetes mellitus. Poor nutrition also impairs the effectiveness of medication. A Case Manager should assess the nutritional status of patients in their care and incorporate improvement of nutrition into the care plan when appropriate.

Emotional Function

The Case Manager can recognize depression and other emotional disorders during the assessment or in subsequent patient interactions. Emotional disorders negatively impact the well being of the patient, the care plan, and the desired outcomes. The Case Manager is in a position to observe emotional changes in the patient and to have them assessed by the primary care physician. She can also arrange for psychological interventions if necessary.

Remember the three basic goals of an interview are to establish a **R**apport, collect **I**nformation, and formulate a care **P**lan (RIP).[3] Close the interview with a summary that captures the essence of the interview and agreed-upon plan. This allows the patient to correct any misunderstandings and it shows that you were actively listening and that the plan goals are mutual.

COMMUNICATION SKILLS

The effective Case Manager possesses excellent communication skills that are required to coordinate the care plan with the providers of care, the patient and the referral source. Educating the patient, care givers, and referral source is a vital case management function. Explaining the full picture, especially when requesting extra contractual benefits, allows the referral source to make the best possible decision. Do not assume because they are the case management liaison that they have the medical understanding necessary to make the appropriate decision. If there is an attorney involved on a case, the Case Manager should get his or her permission prior to contacting the patient. The Case Manager should assure the patient and family that all communications are confidential and that certain information will not be communicated to the employer. All communications (verbal and written) should be documented.

An effective communication has four components:[4]

1. Sender: The person sending the communication.
2. Message: This includes all information transferred, including verbal and nonverbal content.
3. Receiver: The person to whom the message is sent.
4. Context: The surroundings in which the communication takes place. The environment is identified by factors such as the patient's condition (Is he concentrating on his pain and not you?), cultural background, health beliefs, and values. When you call him do you commit to continuous time to the patient or do you keep answering your phone and handling other cases? All of this sends a message in addition to the intended message.

The method of sending a message is also important to the communication process. Some messages are better communicated in person than by letter or telephone. Some are better communicated in groups or by specific individuals. Certain types of information require written communication. For example, an exercise plan explained to the patient by a physical therapist is reinforced in between physical therapy visits, when a written description and pictures of the exercises are left with the patient. In the same way, a complex medication regimen explained to the patient is enhanced when a written schedule of administration is left with the patient.

Barriers to Communication

There are several areas in which communication is hindered by barriers.[4] These include:

- physical interference
- psychological noise
- information processing barriers
- perceptual barriers
- structural barriers

Physical Interference

Communication must take place in a quiet space and during a time when the patient is not distracted. For example, if the patient is being served lunch, watching a favorite television show, or surrounded by visitors, the ability to effectively communicate is diminished.

Psychological Noise

Is the patient thinking about something else? Is the patient in pain, hungry, angry, etc.? If you can address the patient's psychological barrier, you then have increased the likelihood that effective communication can take place. Sometimes the issue is as simple as who is paying for your services. Many patients refuse case management services because they believe it is an additional cost to them. Explaining that it is already a part of their benefit package, provided at no additional cost, can free the way to effective communication and a commitment to the case management process.

Information Processing Barriers

This occurs when too much information is being sent and the patient cannot process it all. Communication overload occurs and the receiver, being overwhelmed, shuts down. This is also a problem when the patient suffers from cognitive deficits. Information needs to be sent at a rate that the patient can process effectively. By observing the patient's eye contact, the Case Manager can determine the level of attention to the message delivered. A good technique to assess a patient's understanding is to ask the patient for frequent feedback in his own words. Another key issue here is not to use words the patient doesn't understand. This is especially true of medical terminology. Nothing impairs communication like using a vocabulary the patient doesn't understand.

Perceptual Barriers

Perceived barriers are based on each patient's unique experience, cultural background, educational level, and value system. Everything we interpret is subject to this experience, good or bad. If the patient has had negative experiences with Case Managers, everything the Case Manager does or says will be filtered through this perception. If the patient comes from a cultural background where it is not okay to admit to requiring assistance, this will impact communication.

Structural Barriers

If a patient must pass through several layers of bureaucracy, before communicating with the Case Manager, the chance of frustration and anger is high. In a similar vein, Case Managers who communicate important information for the patient through one or more intermediaries risks a miscommunication, like the results in playing the children's game of telephone. This is true whether the communication is with the patient, family, caregivers or your peers. The best way to avoid this is to have team conferences when possible and when not, to personally communicate the message to each individual concerned. Speaking to each team member does not guarantee the message sent is the message received; you still must test for feedback.

The most important aspect in communication is the Case Manager's ability to listen. A rule of thumb for the Case Manager when communicating with patients is to do less talking and more listening. This sends the message that the Case Manager places the needs of the patient above his or her own needs.

SERVICES AND AVAILABLE RESOURCES

Levels of Care

The Case Manager needs to have a comprehensive understanding of the various types of resources and levels of health care services available in the community. This allows him or her to communicate the full range of options available to the patient who requires these services. Following are some of the different levels of care, other than acute care hospital admission.

Long-term care (LTC)[1] is (1) for patients who require complex care and extensive convalescence such as major trauma victims, and (2) for patients with chronic and multiple medical, mental health, and social problems who are unable to take care of themselves. When the proposed care is medically necessary and not custodial, private health insurance will bear the costs. When insurance limits are reached, or the care required is custodial, the primary payer for long-term care is Medicaid. Medicare will pick up a limited amount of long-term care costs if the care is medically necessary and not considered custodial. Medicare will pay 100% of the first 20 days in a skilled nursing facility (SNF) and then 80% up to a total of 100 inpatient days.

Custodial care is defined by the Health Care Finance Administration (HCFA) as care that is primarily for the purpose of helping clients with their home personal care needs such as ADLs; this care could safely and reasonably be supplied by persons without professional skills or training. This type of care can be rendered at home, in an SNF, in a group home, in a foster home, in a convalescence home, in a health-related facility, or in an assisted living or senior complex.

The patient requiring intermediate care needs slightly more assistance than the patient requiring custodial care. They often need moderate assistance with ADLs and some restorative nursing supervision. Most facilities and insurers make little distinction between this and custodial care unless true skilled care is required.

Skilled nursing and subacute care[1] is one step down from acute hospital care. The patient needs to be medically stable and the care required is subacute rather than acute. For an insurer to pay for care at this level the care required must:

- need to be performed by a skilled licensed professional,
- be required on a daily basis, and
- take place at the SNF for reasons of patient safety and economy. In other words if the care can be provided at a lesser level (i.e., the patient's home) safely and at a lesser cost, that is where the services should be provided.

Some of the most frequent reasons for this level of care to be the most appropriate are frequent or complex wound care, rehabilitation where the patient cannot participate long enough to qualify for an acute program, complex intravenous therapy, ventilator weaning, and combination therapies.

Nursing homes (NH), intermediate care facilities (ICF), extended care facilities (ECF), and SNFs all offer a level of care below acute care hospitalization, in which the patient requires daily skilled care from licensed personnel. These facilities all are known as ECFs. It is important for the Case Manager to know the specific policy benefit the patient may have. Many insurance policies will not coordinate benefits with Medicare. That is, if the patient is in an ECF where Medicare is the primary payer, the private health care insurance will not cover the 20% that Medicare does not cover.

Inpatient rehabilitation is an intense inpatient program for a patient who has a recent functional loss such as an amputation. The patient needs to have been independent in performing that function prior to the accident or illness; there also is a reasonable expectation of significant improvement in the functional deficit in a reasonable time frame. The patient also needs to have enough functionality and stamina to participate in the rehabilitation program. This means he must be able to participate in various therapies at least 3 hours per day, 5 days per week, and he must be medically stable. Cognitively the patient must be able to follow 1-2 step commands.

Medicare has strict admission criteria to an inpatient rehabilitation center, and many insurers model their criteria after the Medicare guidelines. There are four main criteria for Medicare:[1]

1. Admitting diagnosis must include one of the following:
   - amputation
   - arthritis
   - cardiac conditions
   - chronic pain
   - congenital disorder
   - cerebral vascular disorder
   - diabetes mellitus
   - fracture
   - head trauma/brain injury
   - multiple trauma
   - musculoskeletal disorder
   - neurological disorder
   - orthopedic condition
   - pulmonary condition
   - spinal cord injury
2. The primary reason for admission must be a recent functional loss. The patient has to have been independent in that function prior to the injury or illness and dependent on someone else to carry out that function. If a patient had a cerebral vascular accident (CVA) 5 years ago and was totally dependent on others for his ADLs and had a second CVA now, he would not qualify for inpatient rehabilitation at this time. Assuming he had been independent prior to the first CVA, he would have met the criteria for inpatient rehabilitation 5 years ago subsequent to the CVA.
3. The physician must document the expectation of significant improvement in the functional deficit in a reasonable time frame.

4. If a patient was previously in a rehabilitative program with an unsuccessful outcome, the patient must have some change in his condition that would indicate that progress is now possible.

It is important to note that some patients will not go directly from the acute care setting to the rehabilitation center. They may not be able to endure the intensity of the program. These patients may go to a subacute or SNF setting, beginning with a half-hour of therapy three times a day and increasing their participation as their stamina increases. Depending on the amount of therapy available at the subacute facility they may continue there, or, if a more intense program is required, they can be transferred to an inpatient rehabilitation center. Often, unless special programs are necessary, patients such as elderly patients who have suffered a stroke will remain in the subacute setting until they are ready for discharge home. Generally, patients with brain trauma, spinal cord injuries, and multiple traumatic injuries will need to slowly progress to an intense rehabilitation program. However, each patient needs to be individually assessed and monitored for progress.

Transitional hospitals[1] are acute care facilities for medically stable patients with long rehabilitation needs and care that is too complex for ECFs. Since these hospitals have only basic or disease-specific equipment and specialists, they are able to provide medically complex care at a lower cost than traditional hospitals. Examples of the types of care delivered are:

- burn care
- extensive wound care
- hemodialysis
- hospice
- infectious disease management
- intravenous (IV) medication therapies
- neurobehavioral rehabilitation
- pain control therapies
- rehabilitation
- total parenteral nutrition
- ventilator care/weaning from ventilators

Home Care

Home care has been the fastest growing component of health care in the 1990s, and returning home, is by far, the preference of most patients. The Case Manager must assess the medical, financial, and social aspects of the patient's home situation to determine if home care is a viable option. While nurses, home health aides, and physical, occupational, and speech therapists as well as durable medical equipment have been available through home care agencies for many years, such therapies as infusion care, ventilators, respiratory equipment, total parenteral nutrition (TPN), complex wound care, etc., are now regularly available. Much of this newer availability has its impetus in managed care, which has encouraged great strides in discharging stable patients from hospital to home. Because of its manifest success in maintaining quality and decreasing costs, even Medicare has entered this arena through Medicare risk contracts with HMOs (health maintenance organizations). Medicare patients enrolled in HMOs may have different benefits than those under the traditional Medicare model. HMOs frequently cover IV therapies at home, hearing aides, and prescription medications differently than traditional Medicare. Each policy needs to be investigated when planning a patient's care. The traditional Medicare model allows for home health visits only if all four of the following criteria are met:[1]

1. The patient is homebound, which means that he or she is confined to the home or that it would be a great hardship to go to an outpatient treatment facility such as a laboratory.
2. The care required includes intermittent skilled nursing services and possibly physical, occupational, and speech therapies.
3. A licensed physician, who reviews the patient's care plan at least every 60 days, oversees the patient's care. The plan also has to be reasonable and medically necessary.
4. The home health care agency is Medicare-certified, which means that the strictest federal standards are met.

Home Care Services

If the above criteria are met, Medicare will cover the following home care services:

- Skilled nursing care: This will only be covered on a very limited basis. The Case Manager must stress to the patient that an average skilled nursing visit is 45 minutes to 1 hour. Only in very rare situations are 8 hours deemed medically necessary. The services performed by the nurse must be skilled.
- Physical therapy or speech therapy: If skilled nursing is deemed to be medically necessary, physical therapy or speech therapy will be allowed if medically necessary. If these services are deemed medically necessary, then Medicare may also authorize occupational therapy.
- Home health aides: Intermittent home health aides may be authorized if medically necessary and skilled services such as nursing or therapies are in place. They are generally allowed up to three times per week for assistance in ADLs.
- Home social services: If skilled services are deemed medically necessary and the patient has social service needs, an assessment and subsequent visits may be authorized.
- Medical supplies: These are covered if the patient's nurse requires them to perform the patient's care (i.e., dressings for wound care or foley catheters for incontinent patients).
- Durable medical equipment: All durable medical equipment must be authorized, as not all equipment is a covered benefit and some equipment such as oxygen has strict criteria for approval. The patient also has a 20% coinsurance on the equipment.

The following are the Medicare parameters for home oxygen use:[5] Arterial gases must be drawn on room air. The PO_2 must be 55 or below or with an arterial saturation of 88% or below, or if the PO_2 is between 56 and 59 or the arterial saturation is 89% or lower, there must also be evidence of one of the following: dependent edema suggesting congestive heart failure, P pulmonale on electrocardiogram (P wave above 3mm), or erythrocythemia with a hematocrit over 56%.

If the PO_2 is between 56 and 59 or the arterial saturation is 89%, the patient must be retested between the 61st and 90th day of oxygen therapy. A renewal prescription with the qualifying test result will be required in the fourth month for further home oxygen therapy.

Home Medications

In 1993 traditional Medicare approved a limited number of IV medications to be administered in the home.[1] This change occurred because otherwise independent patients were being admitted to nursing homes for IV administration. The criteria for home IV medications include the use of an infusion pump and a prolonged infusion of at least 8 hours or infusion of the drug at a controlled rate in order to avoid toxicity. Under the above criteria, here is a list of some of the approved medications:

- Acyclovir
- Foscarnet
- Amphotericin B
- Vancomycin
- Ganciclovir
- Selected analgesics such as morphine sulfate
- Some chemotherapeutic agents when administered by continuous infusion over at least 24 hours.

Medicare-certified home health agencies will have the latest list of approved medications.

Psychological Nurse Assistance

Under certain specific criteria this may be a covered benefit under Medicare.

Hospice

Hospice is a health care program whose goal is to provide supportive care and comfort to terminally ill patients and their families during the final stages of their life. Ideally this care is provided with dignity, at home, with the patient surrounded by his family and friends. In order for Medicare to pay a hospice benefit all of these three criteria must be met:[1]

1. A physician certifies that the patient is terminally ill.
2. The patient or family elects the hospice benefit.
3. The hospice provider must be Medicare certified.

A hospice referral can be made from home or the hospital setting; however, it requires a physician's referral. A representative will call upon the patient and their family to answer questions. The hospice patient is waiving standard Medicare benefits in lieu of the hospice benefit. The patient can receive standard Medicare benefits for unrelated medical problems. Medicare pays this benefit out of Part A. Part A pays for two 90-day benefit periods and one 30-day benefit period (210 days/7 months). In cases with a long duration of a terminal illness, indefinite extensions are available to the patient.

The differences between the Medicare hospice benefit and the standard benefit can be seen in Table 6–1.

Transportation

When patients are so infirm that transportation to and from health care facilities is impossible without assistance, the Case Manager must arrange for their transportation. The successful Case Manager will be informed about all the issues involved in the highly contentious area of patient transportation. The first issue is whether transportation is a benefit under the patient's insurance plan. Many plans exclude air ambulance as a benefit. However, when medically necessary transportation is arranged for and negotiated by a Case Manager, it may be approved. Scenarios where an air ambulance may be approved when the benefit does not exist include a patient with a traumatic injury in an inaccessible region (such as a mountaintop) or for speeding an approved hospitalized transplant candidate to the hospital where the transplant organ awaits.

An air ambulance provides cardiac monitoring, a medication box, and advanced cardiac life support (ACLS) trained personnel, including a registered nurse.

Table 6-1 Standard Medicare Benefit v. Hospice Benefit

Service	Standard Benefit	Hospice
Skilled nursing services	Covered on an intermittent basis	Covered on a 24-hour, 7-day a week, on-call basis
Unskilled services	Nurses aides—maximum of two to three 1-hour visits per week	Personal care aides can be provided for 12 to 16 hours per day; also some homemaking services are included
Physician's services	A physician must order services	A physician must order services
Bereavement counseling	Not covered	Available during the terminal stages and for several months afterward
Social services and volunteers	Social services are very limited	These services are part of the hospice agencies' multidisciplinary staff
Homebound requirement	Mandatory	Not mandatory
Prescription drugs for symptom management and pain control	Rarely paid for	A covered benefit, with a 5% or $5 fee per prescription, whichever is less
Durable medical equipment and oxygen	Covered under strict criteria	Criteria are more lax under hospice and can be for the comfort of the patient
Respite care	Not covered	Limited respite (5 consecutive days per quarter) is allowed in an ECF
Physical, occupational, and speech therapies	Covered	Covered
Continuous care during periods of medical crisis	Not covered	Covered
Deductibles	20% for durable medical equipment	No deductibles

A ground ambulance is of two general types: (1) basic life support (BLS), which includes a BLS paramedic and limited monitoring; and (2) advanced life support (ALS), which includes an ACLS paramedic, cardiac monitoring, and a drug box. Patients requiring oxygen must use ALS or BLS ambulances.

There are other issues involved in transporting patients. A Case Manager arranging for transportation of critically ill patients should be aware of these.

One such issue is intravenous lines and peripheral tubes. When arranging transportation for patients with IV lines, call for ALS transportation. If the patient has tubes (such as gastrostomy or percutaneous endoscopic gastronomy [PEG] tubes) and lines that can be capped off, they should be capped and a lesser mode of transportation can be utilized.

When transportation is a covered benefit, the criteria for authorization include only medically necessary transportation and only transportation to a health care facility. This commonly means transportation between two hospitals, or a hospital and an acute care rehabilitation facility or after a traumatic injury from the site of the injury to the hospital. Transportation home is generally *not* a covered benefit.

Wheelchair vans[5] or ambulette service is generally utilized for stable patients and for routine needs such as doctors' appointments. Wheelchair vans will accommodate a person with his or her own oxygen tank, but the personnel are not licensed to regulate it in any way. Because wheelchair vans, by their very nature, do not transport the critically ill, the medical necessity for their use is often difficult to establish. Without medical necessity, wheelchair vans are not a covered benefit under most insurance plans.

Durable Medical Equipment

There is an ever-increasing range of products available today to meet the patient's needs at home. These products effectively treat and maintain a patient in the home environment. A piece of equipment is considered durable medical equipment if:

- It can withstand repeated use.
- It can be sterilized/disinfected between patient use.
- It has a medical/therapeutic purpose.
- It is not useful to a person in the absence of illness or injury.
- It is appropriate for use in the home.

Durable medical equipment can be divided into the following categories:

- Basic mobility devices: walkers, crutches, canes;
- Assistive devices for activities of daily living: bathroom equipment, ostomy, incontinence, wound care, dressing, feeding, and kitchen aids;
- Extensive mobility equipment: wheelchairs, motorized scooters, hospital beds; and
- Advanced high-tech equipment: oxygen, ventilators, infusion pumps, apnea and sleep monitors, etc.

The Case Manager needs to have a thorough understanding of the basic equipment available. A working relationship with multiple providers is essential for several reasons. One supplier cannot meet the need for all the types of equipment available. Also, the patient should be offered a choice in setting up his or her care plan of which vendor to use. In addition, a reliable vendor can be invaluable when special needs arise. A good vendor should work closely with the Case Manager, the patient, family, physician, and other health care professionals to:

- Perform an assessment when equipment is ordered and delivered.
- Select and set up appropriate equipment.
- Educate patients and their caregivers in the proper use of the equipment.
- Inform the case manager if the equipment ordered by the physician is unsafe or not suitable and the reason why.
- Recommend more suitable equipment when necessary.
- Service and maintain the equipment as needed.[5]
- Loan equipment or replace equipment when lengthy repairs are required.
- Clean and disinfect equipment between patient use.
- Complete insurance paperwork for the patient.
- Be included in team conferences when planning for the patient's needs.

The Case Manager has a responsibility to his or her patients to evaluate the vendors used. Ask the patient, family, or care givers the following questions:

- Was the equipment delivered at the planned time? If not, was a telephone call made to alert them the delivery would be late?
- Were they instructed in the use of the equipment? Did they understand the instructions? Were they asked to demonstrate their proficiency in using the equipment?
- Were the delivery personnel friendly, courteous, and knowledgeable about the equipment?
- Was the equipment clean and in good repair?
- Was the right equipment delivered?
- Were the office personnel friendly, courteous, and knowledgeable?
- Were the finances (insurance forms) taken care of by the vendor?
- Have they had any problems with the equipment?
- Have they had any service interruptions?
- Is the company responsive when a problem arises?

The Case Manager should also determine whether the patient is using the equipment appropriately or at all. More than one Case Manager has been surprised to find the equipment collecting dust somewhere in the house while the insurer pays monthly rental fees. Many times equipment is not utilized, as it does not meet the needs of the patient once it is in the home. For instance, does it fit in the room where it is intended for use? For example, the patient requires a Hoyer lift. Does the patient exceed the safe weight limit? When ordering many pieces of equipment, such as hospital beds or walkers, it is important to note the patient's height, girth, and weight. Special equipment will be needed in the case of tall patients, obese patients, or small children. When arranging for equipment, the anticipated length of use needs to be taken into consideration. Children are still growing and this should be taken into consideration when making the decision to rent or purchase equipment, especially on a long-term basis. Chronic or long-term disabilities will require purchase of equipment while hip replacement or fracture patients will require short-term rentals of equipment. If the patient has a degenerative musculoskeletal condition, this will affect the equipment ordered. The Case Manager should look for equipment that is easily modified as the disease process progresses. For example, a patient with amyotrophic lateral sclerosis (ALS) may require a basic electric wheelchair. We know the condition will progress and should anticipate that the chair purchased can be modified with a high back, neck support, trunk stabilizers, alternate controls, etc., as the condition progresses. When dealing with children's needs their growth must be taken into account to prevent them from outgrowing expensive equipment without their really utilizing it. Most equipment for children has built-in growth modules for expansion as the child grows. If this is not possible, the option to rent is preferable, compared to purchase, for equipment the patient will use for a limited time. In all cases the patient should be encouraged to call the Case Manager if any problems occur with the equipment or the patient's needs change. The Case Manager should work with vendors who are agreeable to rent for 2 to 3 months with the rental fees applied to an agreed-upon purchase price, if the patient still requires or utilizes the equipment past the rental time frame. This arrangement is cost effective, takes into account the fact that equipment needs aren't always matched on the first delivery, and that sometimes perceived needs are different than actual needs.

In addition to the previously mentioned resources there are a variety of other community resources available to assist in filling gaps in needed services for patients. Two excellent resources are the *Case Management Resource Guide*[6] and The National Association for Rare Diseases and Orphan Drugs in Washington, DC. Appendix F has some helpful community resources that could be utilized to assist patients and their families.

Orthoses, Prostheses, and Assistive Devices

Orthoses

An orthosis is a device that is added to a person's body to achieve one or more of the following ends:

- support
- position
- immobilize
- correct deformities
- assist weak muscles
- restore muscle function
- modify muscle tone

The term orthosis generally encompasses such devices as slings, braces, and splints. Orthoses are used to support, or aid in the functioning of, the upper and lower extremities, hands and feet, as well as the trunk and spine. These devices can be relatively simple affairs, made of cotton and plastic, or can be complex electromechanical appliances replete with steel alloys, cantilevered joints, and servomotors.

Prostheses

A prosthesis is a device that restores all or part of a missing body part. The science of prosthetics addresses the mechanical, physiologic and cosmetic functions of restorations. While the orthoses are aimed at assisting the body to restore function, prostheses restore or replace those parts of the human body that are absent or no longer function. The need for replacement and cosmesis rather than a simple increase in functionality stems from a person's need for "wholeness" and a "positive body image." With this in mind, the professional prosthetist has goals of increasing both functionality and cosmesis.

While most lay persons associate the term prosthesis with artificial arms and legs, the field is much larger, encompassing many specialties. Prostheses run the gamut from highly functional devices, such as a lens implant after cataracts surgery or an artificial hip for a hip fracture, to highly cosmetic devices such as breast implants after a mastectomy, wigs (a cranial prosthesis) after chemotherapy, and an artificial eye after an enucleation. Choosing a successful prosthetic device for a patient is not like choosing a good suit of clothes "off the rack" as it were, but, following this metaphor, is more like a formal fitting for a custom tailored suit. The prosthesis is individualized both for its looks and functionality. It takes into account not only such superficialities as size and color, but seeks to meet the individual's needs within the limitations of technology and the individual's ability to compensate. For example, the properties of a prosthetic leg of a 24-year-old athlete will be markedly different from that of the 75-year-old sedentary individual. The athlete will require a leg whose materials can tolerate the impacts of running and jumping, and will include biomechanical devices that add "spring" to the ankle flexion and extension by conserving energy during weight bearing, and allow for a variable swing speeds during the gait. The sedentary individual would benefit from lighter weight materials (which may be less impact resistant) and biomechanical devices in the prosthesis that trade flexibility and energy conservation for increased stability.

Complexities of a prosthesis "fitting": It is instructive for the Case Manager to review the complex process for fitting one of the more common types of prosthesis called a transtibial prosthesis. The transtibial prosthesis is created for individuals who have suffered a below-the-knee amputation.

The Fitting Process: Soon after the patient's "stump" or "residual limb" has matured, it is casted with plaster bandages. While the plaster is drying, the prosthetist hand-molds the cast, by pushing in on those softer prominences composed of skin and muscle tissue, while avoiding the bony prominences. When the cast has dried completely, it is removed from the patient and filled with plaster. When the plaster is dry, the cast is removed, and the model of the residual limb is left.

The Model: The prosthetist marks all the bony prominences at the distal end of the model, and may modify the model by building up plaster over the sensitive bony areas and shaving off plaster over the more tolerant soft tissue prominences. This allows a transfer of weight from those sensitive bony prominences to those tissues that can tolerate weight bearing. The residual limb does not bear weight on its distal end, but rather on those soft tissue areas around the distal end.

The Interface: The interface is that part of the prosthesis that touches the residual limb. A good interface is critical to the prosthesis. It should perform the following functions.

- Helps to hold and stabilize the prosthesis to the residual limb
- Comfortably bears the body weight
- Protects the residual limb from damage associated with friction and weight bearing

To begin the process of creating the interface, an "evaluation interface" is made. The evaluation interface is made by vacuum sealing a layer of clear plastic around the plaster mold. The clear plastic interface is then tried on the residual limb. Clear plastic allows the prosthetist to see how the residual limb "seats" within the interface. With the evaluation interface inserted into a temporary prosthetic leg, the patient is asked to sit, stand and walk; during these exercises interface is evaluated by the patient and the prosthetist. The plastic interface has the additional properties of being heat malleable. If the interface is not an exact fit, it can be heated in warm water and hand-molded to a more comfortable fit.

Alignment: The alignment of the prosthesis with the interface is also vitally important. With the patient wearing the temporary prosthesis, the prosthetist makes careful measurements and adjustments of the prosthesis in relation to the interface, and in relation to its parts (e.g., leg to ankle, foot to toe, etc.). Such measurements as height, degree of "toe-in or toe-out," and walking dynamics are inspected. The alignment of the interface and the prosthesis, as well as the various moving parts of the prosthesis to each other, may be adjusted to allow better walking.

Definitive Prosthesis: After the fitting of the interface and the aligning of the prosthesis are finished, the definitive prosthesis may be made. An average amputee can be fully functional with his prosthesis within a year of amputation.

Repair and Replacement: Complex prostheses require ongoing adjustment and maintenance. Replacement of the prosthesis is a common and predictable event. Many factors influence replacement frequency, for example, lower extremity prostheses bear weight, sustain high impact, and are exposed to the elements. Damage to the prostheses acquired by these activities demands maintenance, repair, and replacement. Replacement frequency depends on the activity level of the patient and the demands put on the prosthesis as well as the complexity of the prosthesis and the properties of the materials used. Further, an individual's prosthetic needs may change. For example, a sedentary individual may become more active, requiring a new prosthesis with more features and flexibility. Conversely, an active individual, with advancing age or disease, may become more sedentary, requiring a replacement prosthesis that is lighter and more stable. Finally, the younger patient will require successively larger prostheses to compensate for growth.

It should be noted that those individuals that fit and produce prosthetics and orthotics are highly trained and certified professionals. Case Managers should ensure proper training and certification of the prosthetist before a referral is made.

Assistive Devices

Assistive or adaptive devices are products that substitute for an impaired function and allow the individual to perform an activity more independently. Adaptive devices should be used only if other methods of performing the task are not available or cannot be learned. A reasonable effort should be made to teach the patient a method of performing the task in question, before an adaptive device is suggested. Mastery of a task, for example, walking, allows the patient greater independence and flexibility in that he or she does not need a wheelchair to move around and is not limited by lack of ramps, etc. The device may serve as a useful supplement, however, or permit a function to be performed if the adapted method cannot be learned or requires too much effort.

The type of assistive device is determined by the needs of the individual patient, his or her abilities and functional limitations, and his or her environment. The Case Manager should be aware of all these parameters before authorizing an assistive device. Such common mistakes as a walker being too heavy for a frail elderly woman, a room being too small for a hospital bed, or doorways too narrow for a wheelchair, plague the inexperienced Case Manager.

The device should have proven reliability and safety. A Case Manager should be aware of a product's safety and efficacy record before recommending it to a client. Simple devices such as crutches and walkers have resulted in injuries due to falls; improperly fitted wheelchairs have resulted in decubiti. The Case Manager should make sure the patient and, when appropriate, family and caregivers receive the appropriate training. This training is often offered by the equipment vendor or by physical or occupational rehabilitation specialists.

The patient and family or caregivers should be involved in the selection of adaptive devices and should be trained in their use. A Case Manager who attends to these issues will increase the likelihood that the device is wanted, meets the patient's needs, and will be fully used. Exhibit 6–1 lists some examples of assistive devices.

Exhibit 6–1
EXAMPLES OF ASSISTIVE DEVICES

Visual Aids

- Glasses
- Contact lenses
- Inplantable lenses
- Magnifying glasses
- Large print books
- Audio books
- Braille books
- Seeing-eye dogs
- Text to speech synthesizers
- Text to Braille translation devices
- Optical character recognition (OCR) computer software

Hearing

- Hearing aids
- Phone receiver with volume control
- TDD telephone services

Speaking/Communicating

- Picture boards
- Text to voice synthesizer
- Computer-augmented speech systems

Orientation to time, place and person

- Memory books
- Cue cards
- Orientation black boards
- Calendars
- Clocks/watches/alarms

Memory

Treatment of memory deficits focuses on compensatory aids:

- Memory books
- To do lists
- Cue cards

Ambulation/Locomotion

- Cane
- Quad cane
- Folding cane chair
- Crutches
- Walker
- Rolling walker
- Wheelchair (nonmotorized)
- Wheelchair (motorized)

Eating Devices

- Built-up handles on eating utensils for weak or incompetent grasp
- Handles on cups and glasses
- Non-skid mats to stabilize plate for eating with one hand
- Rocker knife for one-handed cutting
- Partitions in plates and bowls for eating one-handed

Dressing Devices

- Button hook for buttoning clothes
- Velcro closures on clothes and shoes/boots
- Long-handled shoe horn when reach is limited

Toileting Aids

- Bedside commode, urinal, bedpan
- Built-up toilet and commode seat
- Grab bars next to toilet
- Toilet seat with rails

Shower and Tub Aids

- Long-handled sponge for patients with limited reach
- Washcloth or sponge mitt for patients with weak grasp
- Grab bars in tub
- Tub bench or tub chair
- Hand-held shower nozzle

Transfer Devices

- Plastic or wooden transfer board for sliding transfers
- Gait/transfer belt for use by caregiver, if indicated
- Hydraulic lifts for bed, chair, tub, or car transfers
- Hydraulic or electric stair lifts for patients unable to climb stairs
- Chairs modified with higher seats for patients unable to lift out of chair

Recreation

- Large print playing cards
- Large print books
- Books on audio tape
- Video games
- Specialized wheelchairs (e.g., racing wheelchairs)
- Swimming flotation devices
- Fishing pole harnesses
- Gardening tools with built-up handles
- Specially-designed golf clubs

REFERENCES

1. Powell SK. *Nursing Case Management, A Practical Guide to Success in Managed Care.* New York: Lippincott; 1996.
2. Aliotta, Clarke, Paulwan. Case management assessment and planning for high risk Medicare members. *J Case Manage.* 1998; 4:89–92.
3. Mullahy C. *The Case Manager's Handbook.* Gaithersburg, MD: Aspen; 1995.
4. Cesta T., Tahan H., Fink L. *The Case Manager's Survival Guide.* St. Louis: Mosby; 1998.
5. Health Care Financing Administration. *The Medicare 1994 Handbook.* Washington, DC: US Government Printing Office; 1994; DHHS Publication No. HCFA10050.
6. *Case Management Resource Guide.* Newport Beach, CA: Center for Healthcare Information; 1998.

1) **Which of the following is true regarding the purposes of an orthosis?**

1. It can be used to support body parts.
2. It can be used to position body parts.
3. It can be used to immobilize body parts.
4. It can be used to modify muscle tone.
   A. 1, 3
   B. 2, 4
   C. 1, 2, 3
   D. All of the above
   E. None of the above

2) **Which of the following is true regarding the purposes of an orthosis?**

1. It can be used to replace body parts.
2. It can be used to position body parts.
3. It can be used to amputate body parts.
4. It can be used to modify muscle tone.
   A. 1, 3
   B. 2, 4
   C. 1, 2, 3
   D. All of the above
   E. None of the above

3) **Which of the following is *not* true regarding the purposes of an orthosis?**

1. It can be used to replace body parts.
2. It can be used to position body parts.
3. It can be used to amputate body parts.
4. It can be used to modify muscle tone.
   A. 1, 3
   B. 2, 4
   C. 1, 2, 3
   D. All of the above
   E. None of the above

4) **Which of the following is true regarding a prosthesis?**

1. It may restore or replace all or part of a missing body part.
2. It may improve a person's sense of wholeness or body image.
3. It has as its goals increased function and cosmesis.
4. It may result in injury or illness if improperly fitted.
   A. 1, 3
   B. 2, 4
   C. 1, 2, 3
   D. All of the above
   E. None of the above

5)   Which of the following is true regarding a prosthesis?

1. The term *prosthesis* refers only to artificial arms and legs.
2. It may improve a person's sense of wholeness or body image.
3. Cosmesis is not an issue when fitting a prosthesis.
4. It may result in injury or illness if improperly fitted.
    A. 1, 3
    B. 2, 4
    C. 1, 2, 3
    D. All of the above
    E. None of the above

6)   Which of the following is *not* true regarding a prosthesis?

1. The term *prosthesis* refers only to artificial arms and legs.
2. It may improve a person's sense of wholeness or body image.
3. Cosmesis is not an issue when fitting a prosthesis.
4. It may result in injury or illness if improperly fitted.
    A. 1, 3
    B. 2, 3, 4
    C. 1, 2, 3
    D. All of the above
    E. None of the above

7)   Which of the following is true regarding assistive devices?

1. They are products that substitute for an impaired function.
2. They are a substitute for rehabilitation services.
3. They allow an individual to perform an activity more independently.
4. When prescribing one, little input is needed from the patient or patient's family.
    A. 1, 3
    B. 2, 4
    C. 1, 2, 3
    D. All of the above
    E. None of the above

8)   Which of the following is true regarding the prescribing of an assistive device?

1. An evaluation of the patient's interest and abilities is important.
2. An evaluation of the patient's home and work environment is important.
3. Training the patient on the device is important.
4. Training family members on the device is sometimes important.
    A. 1, 3
    B. 2, 4
    C. 1, 2, 3
    D. All of the above
    E. None of the above

9)   Which of the following is *not* true regarding the prescribing of an assistive device?

1. An evaluation of the patient's home and work environment is important.
2. An evaluation of the patient's interest and abilities is unnecessary.
3. Training the patient on the device is important.
4. Training family members on the device is always unnecessary.
    A. 1, 3
    B. 2, 4
    C. 1, 2, 3
    D. All of the above
    E. None of the above

10) **Which of the following statements are true regarding repair and replacements of prosthetic devices?**

   1. Well-made prostheses should not require replacement. A request for replacement is an indication of shoddy workmanship.
   2. Complex prostheses require ongoing adjustment and maintenance.
   3. Good prostheses are strong and durable, and require no repair or maintenance.
   4. Prostheses may need to be replaced frequently.
      A. 1, 3
      B. 2, 4
      C. 1, 2, 3
      D. All of the above
      E. None of the above

11) **Which of the following statements are *not* true, regarding repair and replacements of prosthetic devices?**

   1. Well-made prostheses should not require replacement. A request for replacement is an indication of shoddy workmanship.
   2. Complex prostheses require ongoing adjustment and maintenance.
   3. Good prostheses are strong and durable, and require no repair or maintenance.
   4. Prostheses may need to be replaced frequently.
      A. 1, 3
      B. 2, 4
      C. 1, 2, 3
      D. All of the above
      E. None of the above

12) **Which of the following factors may influence the rate of prosthesis replacement?**

   1. Activity level
   2. Age of user
   3. Type of prosthesis
   4. Impact resistance of materials used
      A. 1, 3
      B. 2, 4
      C. 1, 2, 3
      D. All of the above
      E. None of the above

13) **Which of the following factors do *not* influence the rate of prosthesis replacement?**

   1. Activity level
   2. Educational achievements of the user
   3. Type of prosthesis
   4. Patient's social status
      A. 1, 3
      B. 2, 4
      C. 1, 2, 3
      D. All of the above
      E. None of the above

14) **Which of the following factors may influence the rate of prosthesis replacement?**

   1. Activity level
   2. Educational achievements of the user
   3. Type of prosthesis
   4. Patient's social status
      A. 1, 3
      B. 2, 4
      C. 1, 2, 3
      D. All of the above
      E. None of the above

15) **Which of the following statements is (are) true regarding prostheses, orthoses and assistive devices?**

1. They require individual customization to the patient's needs and likes as well as his dimensions.
2. Successful and safe use requires patient training.
3. Their successful implementation depends on a thorough evaluation of the patient's interests, abilities and goals.
4. Patient adaptation time is short, and requires little patient effort.
   A. 1, 3
   B. 2, 4
   C. 1, 2, 3
   D. All of the above
   E. None of the above

16) **Which of the following statements is (are) *not* true regarding prostheses, orthoses and assistive devices.**

1. They require individual customization to the patient's needs and likes as well as his dimensions.
2. Even patients who are disinterested in using these devices should be fitted for them.
3. Their successful implementation depends on a thorough evaluation of the patient's interests, abilities and goals.
4. Patient adaptation time is short, and requires little patient effort.
   A. 1, 3
   B. 2, 4
   C. 1, 2, 3
   D. All of the above
   E. None of the above

17) **Which of the following are (is) considered an assistive device?**

1. Text to speech synthesizer
2. Phone receiver volume control
3. Quad cane
4. Grab bars in the tub
   A. 1, 3
   B. 2, 4
   C. 1, 2, 3
   D. All of the above
   E. None of the above

18) **Which of the following are (is) considered an assistive device?**

1. A "cock-up" splint for the wrist
2. Phone receiver volume control
3. A sling to hold a plegic and atrophied arm in place
4. Grab bars in the tub
   A. 1, 3
   B. 2, 4
   C. 1, 2, 3
   D. All of the above
   E. None of the above

19) **Which of the following are (is) *not* considered an assistive device?**

1. A "cock-up" splint for the wrist
2. Phone receiver volume control
3. A sling to hold a plegic and atrophied arm in place
4. Grab bars in the tub

A. 1, 3
B. 2, 4
C. 1, 2, 3
D. All of the above
E. None of the above

20) **Which of the following is (are) considered a prosthetic device?**
1. A wig for a person suffering from alopecia totalis
2. A lens implant after a cataract removal
3. An artificial hip after a hip fracture
4. Dentures
   A. 1, 3
   B. 2, 4
   C. 1, 2, 3
   D. All of the above
   E. None of the above

21) **Which of the following is (are) considered a prosthetic device?**
1. A built-up shoe to accommodate contralateral leg shortening
2. A lens implant after a cataract removal
3. Leg braces to assist walking after a spinal injury
4. Artificial knee joint for severe osteoarthritis
   A. 1, 3
   B. 2, 4
   C. 1, 2, 3
   D. All of the above
   E. None of the above

22) **Which of the following is (are) *not* considered a prosthetic device?**
1. A built-up shoe to accommodate leg shortening
2. A lens implant after a cataract removal
3. Leg braces to assist walking after a spinal injury
4. Artificial knee joint for severe osteoarthritis
   A. 1, 3
   B. 2, 4
   C. 1, 2, 3
   D. All of the above
   E. None of the above

23) **Introductions, empowerment, trust, active listening, questioning and testing discrepancies are all part of:**
A. Determining functional status
B. Interviewing
C. Communication process
D. None of the above

24) **When the Case Manager is arranging for discharge to a TBI rehabilitation facility she should:**
1. Confirm that the facility can provide the therapies, by credentialed providers, that the patient requires.
2. Verify that there is a board-certified medical director at the facility.
3. Ensure that the facility is accredited by the Joint Commission (or JCAHO) and CARF.
4. Certify an unlimited length of stay to ensure the patient gets the care he needs.
   A. 1, 2, 3
   B. 2, 3 ,4
   C. All of the above
   D. None of the above

25) **Assistive devices include which of the following?**

1. Rolling walker, bedside commode, transfer board
2. Chinstick, prosthetic arm, hearing aid
3. Quad cane, grab bars, hoyer lift
4. Knee brace, long-handled shoehorn, built-up utensil handles
   A. 1, 2
   B. 2, 3
   C. 1, 3
   D. 2, 4

26) **The Case Manager will find which of the following services difficult to arrange at home?**

A. Homemaker services
B. Durable medical equipment
C. Personal care
D. All of the above
E. None of the above

27) **The Case Manager will find which of the following services difficult to arrange at home?**

1. Tocolytic therapy
2. Respiratory therapy
3. Infusion therapy
4. Blood transfusions
5. Dialysis
   A. 1, 2, 3
   B. 2, 3, 4
   C. 1, 4
   D. 4, 5
   E. None of the above

28) **When the Case Manager is arranging for transfer from the acute care setting to a traumatic brain injury (TBI)/rehabilitation facility she needs to verify that the facility:**

A. Can provide the therapies required by the patient
B. Has a medical director who is board certified
C. Is accredited by the Joint Commission (or JCAHO) and CARF
D. 1, 3
E. All of the above

29) **The three basic goals of a patient interview are to:**

1. Provide information.
2. Establish rapport.
3. Provide a care plan.
4. Collect information.
5. Formulate a care plan.
   A. 1, 2, 3
   B. 2, 3, 4
   C. 1, 4, 5
   D. 2, 4, 5

30) **When conducting an interview, it is important that the Case Manager ask about the medical history of the patient. In order to get the most from the interview questions should be of what type?**

A. Open-ended
B. Who, what, where, when, why and how
C. Direct
D. Leading

31) **An example of a volunteer or charity organization is:**

   A. American Diabetes Association
   B. Veteran's Administration
   C. Muscular Dystrophy Association
   D. A & B
   E. A & C

32) **Case Managers should follow up on arrangements they have made for durable medical equipment to:**

   A. Determine if it is being used.
   B. Determine if it was delivered.
   C. Determine if the patient and caregiver are satisfied with the equipment.
   D. Determine if it meets the current needs of the patient.
   E. All of the above

33) **_____ are facilities that provide lower-cost alternatives for complex cases that do not require the services of an acute care facility or specialized care center but require more care than can be provided at home.**

   A. Subacute care centers
   B. Long-term care facilities
   C. Rehabilitation hospitals
   D. Convalescent hospitals

34) **A thorough interview and assessment enables the Case Manager to assist the patient and family to:**

   A. Make informed health care decisions.
   B. Make informed financial decisions.
   C. Cope with the complex health care system.
   D. All of the above

35) **_____ are facilities for medically stable patients. They offer services to patients requiring extended or respite care such as wound management, pain management, dialysis, respiratory care, infusion therapy, physical therapy, occupational therapy and speech therapy.**

   A. Convalescent hospitals
   B. Subacute care centers
   C. Rehabilitation centers
   D. Acute care hospitals

36) **When conducting an interview with the patient it is important to encourage the patient to use his own _____. This will assist the Case Manager to discern the patient's level of understanding or denial of his situation.**

   A. Goals
   B. Values
   C. Words
   D. Beliefs

37) **The Case Manager should maintain her own referral file of facilities and providers that:**

   1. Have accredited expertise
   2. Have specialized programs
   3. Have subacute hospitals
   4. Have experimental protocols
      A. 1, 2
      B. 3, 4
      C. All of the above
      D. None of the above

38) **The Case Manager has the roles of communicator and liaison. This requires that she be familiar with certain components within:**

A. Insurance
B. Legislation
C. Vocational rehabilitation
D. All of the above
E. None of the above

39) **The Case Manager is informed the rehabilitation facility she is presently negotiating with has CARF accreditation. CARF is:**

A. Mandatory accreditation body
B. A non-profit organization established to adopt and apply standards
C. A federally funded program
D. A for-profit accreditation organization which produces rehabilitation guidelines

40) **Which statement(s) describes good negotiating skill?**

1. Be brief and precise as you state your main point.
2. Be aware of male and female communication styles and match your style to that of the vendor.
3. Speak tentatively and communicate to build friendship and agreement.

   A. 1, 2
   B. 2, 3
   C. All of the above
   D. None of the above

41) **Which statement(s) does *not* describe good negotiating skill?**

1. Be brief and precise as you state your main point.
2. Be aware of male and female communication styles and match your style to that of the vendor.
3. Speak tentatively and communicate to build friendship and agreement.

   A. 1
   B. 2
   C. 3
   D. All of the above
   E. None of the above

42) **The Case Manager needs to consider which of the following when placing a patient, needing assistive devices due to a knowledge deficit, in an alternate care setting?**

A. Whether the patient can self-feed
B. Patient safety
C. Location in relation to family
D. Whether the facility has activities the patient likes

43) **Which of the following is important in considering vocational training for an injured worker?**

1. Previous work history
2. Transferable work skills
3. Physical capabilities
4. Physical limitations

   A. 1, 2, 3
   B. 2, 3, 4
   C. All of the above
   D. None of the above

44) **Which of the following statements is (are) *not* true when negotiating for durable medical equipment?**

   A. The deeper the discount agreed upon, the later the vendor should be paid.
   B. Payer authorization and approval is required.
   C. Comparison of rental fees and purchase fees should be done.
   D. The needs of the patient is the first consideration.

45) **A Case Manager has selected a DME vendor for the equipment the patient needs. Which of the following should the Case Manager consider in determining whether a purchase or rental is more cost effective?**

   A. The costs of both the purchase and the rental
   B. The length of time the equipment will be required
   C. Availability and costs of maintenance and service
   D. All of the above
   E. None of the above

46) **A Case Manager is planning rehabilitation for a spinal cord injured patient. When choosing a facility, she should evaluate it in regards to which of the following?**

   1. Peer support for the patient
   2. Specialization of the program and staff in spinal cord injury
   3. Credentials of the rehabilitation staff, are there physical and occupational therapists, rehabilitation nurses, social workers, etc.
   4. Speech therapy
      A. 1, 2, 3
      B. 2, 3, 4
      C. All of the above
      D. None of the above

47) **Ancillary services can include which of the following?**

   1. Laboratory medicine
   2. Diagnostic radiology
   3. Services that are adjuncts to the diagnosis and treatment of the patient's condition
   4. Therapeutic radiology
      A. 1, 2, 3
      B. 2, 3, 4
      C. 1, 2, 4
      D. All of the above
      E. None of the above

1) **Answer: D**

An orthosis is a device that is added to a person's body to achieve one or more of the following ends: support, position, immobilize, correct deformities, assist weak muscles, restore muscle function, and modify muscle tone.

The term *orthosis* generally encompasses such devices as slings, braces, and splints. Orthoses are used to support, or aid in the functioning of, the upper and lower extremities, hands and feet, as well as the trunk and spine. These devices can be relatively simple affairs, made of cotton belts and plastic splints or they can be complex electromechanical appliances replete with steel alloys, cantilevered joints, and servomotors.

2) **Answer: B**

An orthosis is a device that is added to a person's body to achieve one or more of the following ends: support, position, immobilize, correct deformities, assist weak muscles, restore muscle function, and modify muscle tone.

The term *orthosis* generally encompasses such devices as slings, braces, and splints. Orthoses are used to support, or aid in the functioning of, the upper and lower extremities, hands and feet, as well as the trunk and spine. These devices can be relatively simple affairs, made of cotton belts and plastic splints or they can be complex electromechanical appliances replete with steel alloys, cantilevered joints, and servomotors.

3) **Answer: A**

An orthosis is a device that is added to a person's body to achieve one or more of the following ends: support, position, immobilize, correct deformities, assist weak muscles, restore muscle function, and modify muscle tone.

The term *orthosis* generally encompasses such devices as slings, braces, and splints. Orthoses are used to support, or aid in the functioning of, the upper and lower extremities, hands and feet, as well as the trunk and spine. These devices can be relatively simple affairs, made of cotton belts and plastic splints or they can be complex electromechanical appliances replete with steel alloys, cantilevered joints, and servomotors.

4) **Answer: D**

A prosthesis is a device that restores or replaces all or part of a missing body part. The science of prosthetics addresses the mechanical, physiologic and cosmetic functions of restorations. While the orthoses are aimed at *assisting* the body to restore function, prostheses restore or *replace* those parts of the human body that are absent or no longer function. The need for replacement and cosmesis rather than a simple increase in functionality stems from a person's need for "wholeness" and a "positive body image." With this in mind, the professional prosthetist has as his goals increasing both functionality and cosmesis. Poorly fitted prostheses can cause injury or illness.

5)   **Answer: B**

A prosthesis is a device that restores or replaces all or part of a missing body part. The science of prosthetics addresses the mechanical, physiologic and cosmetic functions of restorations. While the orthoses are aimed at *assisting* the body to restore function, prostheses restore or *replace* those parts of the human body that are absent or no longer function. The need for replacement and cosmesis rather than a simple increase in functionality stems from a person's need for "wholeness" and a "positive body image." With this in mind, the professional prosthetist has as his goals increasing both functionality and cosmesis. Poorly fitted prostheses can cause injury or illness. While most laypersons associate the term *prosthesis* with artificial arms and legs, the field is much larger, encompassing many specialties. Prostheses run the gamut from highly functional devices, such as a lens implant for cataracts, an artificial hip for a hip fracture, to highly cosmetic devices such as breast implants after a mastectomy, wigs (a cranial prosthesis) after chemotherapy and an artificial eye after an enucleation.

6)   **Answer: A**

A prosthesis is a device that restores or replaces all or part of a missing body part. The science of prosthetics addresses the mechanical, physiologic and cosmetic functions of restorations. While the orthoses are aimed at *assisting* the body to restore function, prostheses restore or *replace* those parts of the human body that are absent or no longer function. The need for replacement and cosmesis rather than a simple increase in functionality stems from a person's need for "wholeness" and a "positive body image." With this in mind, the professional prosthetist has as his goals increasing both functionality and cosmesis. Poorly fitted prostheses can cause injury or illness. While most laypersons associate the term prosthesis with artificial arms and legs, the field is much larger, encompassing many specialties. Prostheses run the gamut from highly functional devices, such as a lens implant for cataracts, an artificial hip for a hip fracture, to highly cosmetic devices such as breast implants after a mastectomy, wigs (a cranial prosthesis) after chemotherapy and an artificial eye after an enucleation.

7)   **Answer: A**

Assistive or adaptive devices are products that substitute for an impaired function, and allow the individual to perform an activity more independently. Adaptive devices should be used only if other methods of performing the task are not available or cannot be learned. A reasonable effort should be made to teach the patient a method of performing the task in question, before an adaptive device is suggested. Mastery of a task, for example, walking, allows the patient greater independence and flexibility in that he does not need a wheelchair to move around and is not limited by lack of ramps, etc. The device may serve as a useful supplement, however, or permit a function to be performed if the adapted method cannot be learned or requires too much effort. The type of assistive device is determined by the needs of the individual patient, his abilities and functional limitations, and his environment.

8)   **Answer: D**

The type of assistive device is determined by the needs of the individual patient, his abilities and functional limitations, and his environment. Such common mistakes as a walker being too heavy for a frail elderly patient, or a room being too small for a hospital bed, or doorways too narrow for a wheelchair plague the inexperienced Case Manager. Even simple devices such as crutches and walkers have resulted in injuries caused by falls and improperly fitted wheelchairs have resulted in decubiti. The Case Manager should make sure the patient is properly fitted to the equipment and trained in its use. When appropriate, family and caregivers should also receive the appropriate training. The patient and family or caregivers should be involved in the selection of adaptive devices and should be trained in their use. A Case Manager who attends to these issues will increase the likelihood that the device is wanted, meets the patient's needs, and will be fully used.

9)   **Answer: B**

The type of assistive device is determined by the needs of the individual patient, his abilities and functional limitations, and his environment. Such common mistakes as a walker being too heavy for a frail elderly patient, or a room being too small for a hospital bed, or doorways too narrow for a wheelchair plague the inexperienced Case Manager. Even simple devices such as crutches and walkers have resulted in injuries caused by falls and improperly fitted wheelchairs have resulted in decubiti. The Case Manager should make sure the patient is properly fitted to the equipment and trained in its use. When appropriate, family and caregivers should also receive the appropriate training. The patient and family or caregivers should be involved in the selection of adaptive devices, and should be trained in their use. A Case Manager who attends to these issues will increase the likelihood that the device is wanted, meets the patient's needs, and will be fully used.

10)   Answer: B

Complex prostheses require ongoing adjustment and maintenance. Prostheses may even need to be replaced with frequency. Many factors influence replacement frequency. For example, lower extremity prostheses bear weight, sustain high impact and are exposed to the elements. Damage to the prostheses acquired by these activities demands maintenance, repair and replacement. Further, an individual's prosthetic needs may change. For example, a sedentary individual may become more active. Conversely, an active individual with advancing age or disease may become more sedentary. Each of these changes may require the individual to acquire a prosthesis with different properties to accommodate these changes. Finally, the younger patient will require successively larger prostheses to compensate for growth.

11)   Answer: A

Complex prostheses require ongoing adjustment and maintenance. Prostheses may even need to be replaced with frequency. Many factors influence replacement frequency. For example, lower extremity prostheses bear weight, sustain high impact and are exposed to the elements. Damage to the prostheses acquired by these activities demands maintenance, repair and replacement. Further, an individual's prosthetic needs may change. For example, a sedentary individual may become more active. Conversely, an active individual with advancing age or disease may become more sedentary. Each of these changes may require the individual to acquire a prosthesis with different properties to accommodate these changes. Finally, the younger patient will require successively larger prosthesis to compensate for growth.

12)   Answer: D

Many factors influence replacement frequency. For example, lower extremity prostheses bear weight, sustain high impact and are exposed to the elements. Damage to the prosthesis acquired by these activities demands maintenance, repair and replacement. Replacement frequency depends on the activity level of the patient and the demands he puts on the prosthesis as well as the complexity of the prosthesis and the properties of the materials used. Further, an individual's prosthetic needs may change. For example, a sedentary individual may become more active, requiring a new prosthesis with more features and flexibility. Conversely, an active individual with advancing age or disease may become more sedentary, requiring a replacement prosthesis that is lighter and more stable. Finally, the younger patient will require successively larger prostheses to compensate for growth.

13)   Answer: B

Many factors influence replacement frequency. For example, lower extremity prostheses bear weight, sustain high impact and are exposed to the elements. Damage to the prosthesis acquired by these activities demands maintenance, repair and replacement. Replacement frequency depends on the activity level of the patient and the demands he puts on the prosthesis as well as the complexity of the prosthesis and the properties of the materials used. Further, an individual's prosthetic needs may change. For example, a sedentary individual may become more active, requiring a new prosthesis with more features and flexibility. Conversely, an active individual with advancing age or disease may become more sedentary, requiring a replacement prosthesis that is lighter and more stable. Finally, the younger patient will require successively larger prostheses to compensate for growth. There is no association between a patient's educational achievements or social status and prosthesis replacement.

14)   **Answer: A**

Many factors influence replacement frequency. For example, lower extremity prostheses bear weight, sustain high impact and are exposed to the elements. Damage to the prosthesis acquired by these activities demands maintenance, repair and replacement. Replacement frequency depends on the activity level of the patient and the demands he puts on the prosthesis as well as the complexity of the prosthesis and the properties of the materials used. Further, an individual's prosthetic needs may change. For example, a sedentary individual may become more active, requiring a new prosthesis with more features and flexibility. Conversely, an active individual with advancing age or disease may become more sedentary, requiring a replacement prosthesis that is lighter and more stable. Finally, the younger patient will require successively larger prostheses to compensate for growth. There is no association between a patient's educational achievements or social status and prosthesis replacement.

15)   **Answer: C**

Prostheses, orthoses, and assistive devices are aimed at increasing a patient's independence and functionality. These devices require attention to the abilities, interests, and goals of the individual, and should be customized to accommodate them. Most of the devices require training of the patient and sometimes the family members. Adaptation to these devices is difficult, and mastery of them takes time and effort.

16)   **Answer: B**

Prostheses, orthoses, and assistive devices are aimed at increasing a patient's independence and functionality. These devices require attention to the abilities, interests, and goals of the individual, and should be customized to accommodate them. Most of the devices require training of the patient and sometimes the family members. Adaptation to these devices is difficult, and mastery of them takes time and effort.

17)   **Answer: D**

18)   **Answer: B**

Assistive devices substitute for impaired function and promote independence; therefore, a volume control device on a phone receiver and grab bars are assistive devices. Orthoses are devices that are added to the body to support, position, immobilize and assist weak muscles. A cock-up splint and an arm sling are considered orthoses.

19)   **Answer: A**

Assistive devices substitute for impaired function and promote independence; therefore, a volume control device on a phone receiver and grab bars are assistive devices. Orthoses are devices that are added to the body to support, position, immobilize and assist weak muscles. A cock-up splint and an arm sling are considered orthoses.

20)   **Answer: D**

Prostheses are devices designed to replace absent body parts and restore functioning and cosmesis to the patient.

21)   **Answer: B**

Prostheses are devices designed to replace absent body parts and restore functioning and cosmesis to the patient. Braces, splints, slings and special shoes are considered orthotic devices.

22)   **Answer: A**

Prostheses are devices designed to replace absent body parts and restore functioning and cosmesis to the patient. Braces, splints, slings and special shoes are considered orthotic devices.

23)   **Answer: B**

24)   **Answer: A**

Certifications should be time-limited and progress reports should be evaluated prior to extending lengths of stay. Verifying the credentials of the facility and providers is important in choosing an appropriate facility for the patient.

25) Answer: C

A prosthetic arm is a prosthesis and a knee brace is an orthosis, not an assistive device.

26) Answer: E

27) Answer: D

Blood transfusions are not usually done at home due to the risk of transfusion reaction. Dialysis may be done at home, but due to the associated risks it is generally not done at home unless the patient is truly homebound.

28) Answer: E

29) Answer: D

Providing information is not one of the basic goals of the interview. Providing a care plan does not allow the patient to be an active participant in the care planning process.

30) Answer: A

All of the other answers do not leave room for the patient to introduce new information, nor do they leave the door open for free communication.

31) Answer: E

The Veteran's Administration is not a volunteer or charity organization.

32) Answer: E

33) Answer: A

34) Answer: D

A thorough interview and assessment allow for the collection of data required to assist the patient in formulating his case management plan.

35) Answer: B

36) Answer: C

The other answers are important in developing a care plan; however, the best answer for the Case Manager to comprehend what the patient understands about his situation is C.

37) Answer: A

38) Answer: D

39) Answer: B

CARF is a voluntary accreditation. The organization is not-for-profit and establishes national standards for rehabilitation facilities.

40) Answer: A

The Case Manager should not speak tentatively but with assurance, businesslike and assertively.

41) Answer: C

The Case Manager should not speak tentatively but with assurance, businesslike and assertively.

42) Answer: B

Patient safety is the most important issue in this case.

43) Answer: C

All of the above can be utilized to identify possible alternatives in finding employment.

44) Answer: A

Generally, deeper discounts can be obtained with prompt payment agreements.

45)   Answer: D

46)   Answer: A

Patients with spinal cord injuries should not require the services of a speech therapist.

47)   Answer: D

These are all charges outside the basic room and board that a hospital charges.

Alternate keyboard: a computer appliance used to input data. It consists of matrix keys, switches that allow easier manipulation than the regular keyboard.

Assistive device: a device that increases a patient's functionality and independence by substituting for an impaired function.

Augmentative and alternative communication devices (AAC): electronic devices, that assist, augment, or supplement a person's ability to communicate. These devices can range from a simple picture board that has pictures of the desired items or activities that can be pointed to, to computerized systems that can change input using a keyboard, alternate keyboard, head stick, or eye gaze switch into synthesized speech.

Chinwand or chinstick: a pointer or extension device that is mounted to a headpiece and extends from the center of the mandible and angles outward. It is usually coupled with a direct selection input device to aid people with good head mobility but poor upper body strength.

Dial scan: a selection or data input device that resembles a clock with one hand. The single hand on the clock face is used to point to pictures or symbols around the perimeter of the clock face. By pointing the hand to one of the symbols or pictures and actuating a switch, a selection can be made.

Direct selection: making a selection with a single action by directly activating a letter, picture, or other item on an input device. Examples of direct selection are pressing a key on a keyboard, touching a symbol or picture on a touch screen, eye gaze selection system, or an optical headpointer system.

Durable medical equipment: a product is considered durable medical equipment if it meets the following characteristics:

- It is reusable (not disposable).
- It is primarily used for a medical or therapeutic purpose.
- It has little or no use to a person in the absence of illness.

Environmental control systems: a device (usually electronic) that allows the user to control other devices in his or her environment. Thus the disabled operator is able to (remotely) control such systems as heating and cooling, lighting, security, opening windows and doors, and turning on televisions without having to be able to perform the tasks physically. The control unit may be mounted on a bed or wheelchair for ease of access.

Ergonomics: (from the Greek word ergon = work) is the study of how humans interact with their working environments. It utilizes the applied science of equipment design for the workplace. The intended object of the study is to maximize productivity by reducing operator fatigue and discomfort. Ergonomics is also called human factors engineering.

Headwand or headstick: A pointer or extension device that is mounted to a headpiece and extends from the center of the forehead and angles downward. It is usually coupled with a direct selection input device to aid people with good head mobility, but poor upper body strength.

Joystick: a moveable control lever. By tilting the joystick in different directions it can be used to control mechanical devices, such as a motorized wheelchair.

Keyboard emulating interface: a piece of either hardware or software that is connected to a computer. It allows the computer to accept the input from a nonstandard input device, as if it were coming from a standard input device (e.g., keyboard).

On-screen keyboard: a virtual keyboard provided on the computer monitor by specific software. The on-screen keyboard can be used with an "alternate input device" such as an alternate keyboard, an optical head pointer, or sip & puff switch to input data.

Screen-reading software: a computer program capable of reading menus, format commands, and punctuation as well as text on the computer monitor.

Speech digitizer or speech recognition system: a device that allows digitally recorded speech to be analyzed and converted into electronic patterns. These patterns can be used as computer commands or to create text.

Speech synthesizer: a computer output device, it has the capacity to translate text characters into the spoken word.

Telecommunications Device for the Deaf (TDD): a device that allows the severely hearing impaired to communicate via the phone. It consists of a small computer monitor or display screen, a modem, a connection to a phone line, and some means of input (keyboard).

Text to speech synthesis: a function of a computer that allows text to be translated into speech sounds.

Touch screen: a special type of computer monitor that acts as an input device. By touching the pictures or symbols on a computer screen monitor, a user is able to make selections.

Voice recognition system (VRS): a method for inputting data or making selections on a computerized system. VRSs translate speech into digital signals. These digital signals can then be used to make selections or operate a computer or other electronic devices.

Chapter 7

Post-Test

1) **Of the following, which are *not* common causes of malpractice litigation?**
   1. Discourteous behavior by the professional
   2. Poor clinical outcomes
   3. Lack of patient understanding
   4. Substandard medical care
      - A. 1, 3
      - B. 2, 4
      - C. 1, 2, 3
      - D. All of the above
      - E. None of the above

2) **Case Managers may decrease the legal liability associated with patient discharges through which of the following activities?**
   1. Decreasing the average length of stay of their clients
   2. Confirming the integrity of the patient's support network
   3. Reducing the per member per month medical costs of their clients
   4. Confirming the adequacy of follow-up outpatient care
      - A. 1, 3
      - B. 2, 4
      - C. 1, 2, 3
      - D. All of the above
      - E. None of the above

3) **Case Managers are committed to informed consent, providing options for the patient to choose from and educating the patient to make independent decisions. This principle is known as:**
   - A. Veracity
   - B. Beneficence
   - C. Autonomy
   - D. Nonmaleficence

4) **In a malpractice suit the plaintiff must prove two points:**
   1. His compliance with the prescribed treatment plan
   2. Negligence on the part of the Case Manager
   3. Injury from the Case Manager's negligence
   4. Intent on the part of the Case Manager
      - A. 1, 4
      - B. 2, 3
      - C. None of the above
      - D. All of the above

5)   **The following listed items are all causes of _____.**

- Communication failures
- Lack of information given to the family
- Lack of patient understanding
- Discourteous behavior
  - A.   Lack of patient compliance
  - B.   Patient injuries
  - C.   Patient complaints
  - D.   Malpractice litigation

6)   **Of the following statements, which are *not* true regarding ethics, as they relate to Case Management?**

1.   They are rules of conduct that govern a person or members of a profession.
2.   They are thoughts that govern a person's conduct.
3.   They are a society's ideal for a person's conduct.
4.   They are the minimum acceptable standards for a person's conduct.
      - A.   1, 3
      - B.   2, 4
      - C.   1, 2, 3
      - D.   All of the above
      - E.   None of the above

7)   **Which of the following should be disclosed to the patient when a provider is obtaining consent for a medical, surgical or psychological intervention?**

1.   The projected or desired outcomes of the proposed treatment and the likelihood of success
2.   Reasonably foreseeable risks or hazards inherent in the proposed treatment or care (This must be done in manner that the patient can understand.)
3.   Alternatives to proposed care or treatment plan
4.   Consequences of foregoing the treatment
      - A.   1, 3
      - B.   2, 4
      - C.   1, 2, 3
      - D.   All of the above
      - E.   None of the above

8)   **Which of the following are requirements for obtaining informed consent?**

1.   The patient may consent voluntarily or may be coerced if uncooperative.
2.   The patient must have the capacity to give consent.
3.   The patient must be an adult; however, emancipated minors must have parents' consent.
4.   In the event that the patient is a minor or adult without capacity to consent, parents, attorneys or legal guardians may give consent.
      - A.   1, 3
      - B.   2, 4
      - C.   1, 2, 3
      - D.   All of the above
      - E.   None of the above

9)   **As a result of the case *Wickline v. the State of California*, the following is true:**

1.   Providers can be held accountable for negative outcomes when they discharge patients solely at the request of the insurer or payer.
2.   Case Managers can be held liable for negative outcomes as a consequence of their denials.
3.   Insurers and Utilization Review firms can be held liable for negative outcomes as a consequence of their denials.
4.   If a provider appeals an adverse determination and a negative outcome occurs, the liability may be passed to the insurer.

A. 1, 2, 3
B. 2, 3, 4
C. All of the above
D. None of the above

10) **Which of the following statements are true regarding the legal term *tort*?**

1. It comes from a Latin word that means "twist."
2. It implies that testimony has been given falsely.
3. It refers to damage or injury that is done willfully or negligently.
4. It refers only to medical malpractice cases.
   A. 1, 3
   B. 2, 4
   C. 1, 2, 3
   D. All of the above
   E. None of the above

11) **A Case Manager is frustrated by her inability to get her patient to agree to occupational therapy. The patient was involved in a high-speed motor vehicle accident and suffered severe head injuries. When encouraged to attend therapy sessions the patient refuses, becomes verbally abusive and hangs up. Likely reason(s) for this patient's reaction is (are):**

A. Head injuries can result in emotional lability.
B. Head injuries can result in cognitive impairments.
C. Head injuries can result in prolonged head pain and mood depression.
D. All of the above
E. None of the above

12) **Of the following diagnoses, which should trigger an inquiry for potential Case Management services?**

1. Blepharitis
2. Varrucus vulgaris
3. Coryza
4. Pedis planus
   A. 1, 3
   B. 2, 4
   C. 1, 2, 3
   D. All of the above
   E. None of the above

13) **Of the following, which utilization figure for an individual's medical claims would make an appropriate financial threshold for Case Management evaluations?**

A. Claims exceeding $500 per year
B. Claims exceeding $1,000 per year
C. Claims exceeding $10,000 per year
D. Claims exceeding $100,000 per year
E. Claims exceeding $1,000,000 per year

14) **A Case Manager is told by a paraplegic "I feel like half a person." The Case Manager's response should be to:**

A. Distract the patient from self-pity.
B. Help the patient explore personal feelings.
C. Ignore the comment.
D. Actively discourage negative comments.

15) **The Case Manager has a patient who continues to focus on his functional loss. Which of the following would be the best response by the Case Manager?**

  1. "You should be making faster progress than this in PT."
  2. "Your last physical therapy report states you have increased your strength and flexibility."
  3. "Other patients with this injury returned to work 2 weeks ago."
    A. 1, 2
    B. 2, 3
    C. 2
    D. All of the above
    E. None of the above

16) **A patient has just had a full diagnostic workup of his condition. The need for surgery has been ruled out and the condition has been diagnosed as chronic. Which of the following is true of the patient's follow-up needs?**

  A. The patient should be followed every 2 months by the surgeon, in case his condition changes and he requires surgery.
  B. Several other opinions should be sought to confirm the first diagnosis.
  C. Follow up with the patient's primary care physician is indicated to obtain any needed treatment, monitoring or medications required for the chronic condition.
  D. All of the above
  E. None of the above

17) **The Case Manager has a patient with a recent amputation. The patient expresses concern that his wife will no longer find him attractive. The Case Manager should realize that:**

  A. The patient is in a grieving stage.
  B. The patient is experiencing self-pity, which will pass.
  C. Many patients have a distorted body image when they have a long-term disorder.
  D. All of the above
  E. None of the above

18) **Case Managers know that motivating a patient with a knowledge deficit can be problematic. As the Case Manager evaluating the duration and progress of occupational services, what questions would you ask if informed that the patient was making little progress and was noncompliant with his instruction?**

  1. Has anyone explored the reasons for his resistance?
  2. Has anyone discussed his lack of progress and cooperation with his family?
  3. What time of day is he receiving teaching?
  4. Is there a time of day when he is more cooperative and compliant?
    A. 1, 2, 3
    B. 2, 3, 4
    C. All of the above
    D. None of the above

19) **Which of the following statements are true regarding the psychological aspects of chronic disease and disability?**

  1. Only catastrophic illnesses, such as cancer and spinal cord injuries, have psychological ramifications.
  2. Even injuries that are usually considered minor can have severe social and psychological ramifications.
  3. Psychological reactions, such as euphoria and mania, are common in catastrophic illnesses.
  4. Psychological reactions, such as depression and dependency, are common in catastrophic illnesses.
    A. 1, 3
    B. 2, 4
    C. 1, 2, 3
    D. All of the above
    E. None of the above

20) **Which of the following organizations must comply with the mandates of the Americans with Disabilities Act?**

1. Small businesses with fewer than 100 employees
2. The federal government
3. Multinational corporations with headquarters in the United States of America
4. Indian tribes
    A. 1, 3
    B. 2, 4
    C. 1, 2, 3
    D. All of the above
    E. None of the above

21) **Which of the following would help to define the "essential functions of the job" under the mandates of the Americans with Disabilities Act?**

1. The job function takes up the majority of the employee's time.
2. The job function is described in the collective bargaining agreement.
3. The job function is recorded in the written job description.
4. The job function in question is considered "essential" to the jobs of others in the same or similar job.
    A. 1, 3
    B. 2, 4
    C. 1, 2, 3
    D. All of the above
    E. None of the above

22) **Which of the following statements are true regarding the Women's Health and Cancer Rights Act?**

1. It assures rehabilitative therapies, such as physical therapy, to postmastectomy patients.
2. It assures coverage for surgery of the contralateral breast to provide a symmetrical appearance after mastectomy.
3. It assures coverage for postsurgical care, such as lymphedema treatment.
4. It assures coverage for breast prostheses after mastectomy.
    A. 1, 3
    B. 2, 4
    C. 1, 2, 3
    D. All of the above
    E. None of the above

23) **Which of the following statements are true regarding unemployment insurance?**

1. Financing of unemployment benefits varies from state to state.
2. Unemployment compensation benefits guarantee a replacement of 50% of salary.
3. Benefits may be extended past the usual maximum length of benefit, during periods of heavy unemployment.
4. All states pay a minimum of 46 weeks of unemployment benefits.
    A. 1, 3
    B. 2, 4
    C. 1, 2, 3
    D. All of the above
    E. None of the above

24) **Which of the following statements about the Workers' Compensation insurance program is (are) true?**

1. The cost of Workers' Compensation insurance is borne by the employer only.
2. The employee is expected to contribute 3% of his earned income toward Workers' Compensation premiums.
3. The Workers' Compensation program was intended to provide an impetus for an increase in employer safety programs.
4. Employer safety programs have dramatically decreased the industrial accident rate.
   A. 1, 3
   B. 2, 4
   C. 1, 2, 3
   D. All of the above
   E. None of the above

25) **Which of the following statements is (are) true regarding Third Party Administrators (TPAs)?**

1. The TPA usually operates in the environment of the self-insured employer.
2. The TPA is an agent of the insurer.
3. The TPA is not party to the insurance contract and is not liable for losses incurred by employees.
4. The TPA's sole function is to provide "insurance-type" administrative services to the employer.
   A. 1, 3
   B. 2, 4
   C. 1, 2, 3
   D. All of the above
   E. None of the above

26) **Which of the following characteristics are common to victims of automobile accidents?**

1. Senescence
2. Seriousness of injuries
3. Low incidence of head injuries
4. High incidence of spinal injuries
   A. 1, 3
   B. 2, 4
   C. 1, 2, 3
   D. All of the above
   E. None of the above

27) **Which of the following is (are) true regarding Peer Review Organizations (PROs)?**

1. They were established under the Tax Equity and Fiscal Responsibility Act.
2. They are entities selected by HCFA to reduce medical costs.
3. They are entities selected by HCFA to assure quality of care and appropriateness of admissions, readmissions and discharges.
4. PROs concern themselves with the care of Medicare and Medicaid patients.
   A. 1, 3
   B. 2, 4
   C. 1, 2, 3
   D. All of the above
   E. None of the above

28) **Which of the following individuals (is) are *not* protected under the Pregnancy Discrimination Act?**

1. A pregnant but unwed employee
2. A part-time employee
3. An independent contractor
4. Employee of a successor corporation

A. 1, 2
B. 3, 4
C. 1, 2, 3
D. All of the above
E. None of the above

29) **Which of the following mental health benefit limitations are allowable under the tenets of the Mental Health Parity Act?**

1. Annual dollar limit for mental health care
2. Limited number of annual outpatient visits
3. Lifetime dollar limit on mental health care
4. Limited number of inpatient days annually
   A. 1, 3
   B. 2, 4
   C. 1, 2, 3
   D. All of the above
   E. None of the above

30) **Arranging for continuity of care upon discharge from the hospital is also known as:**

A. Discharge status
B. Effective utilization review
C. Discharge planning
D. Timeliness

31) **Case Management documentation should:**

1. Be done upon closure of the case.
2. Be done as close to the time of all contacts as possible.
3. Be thorough.
4. Reflect the patient's level of involvement in care planning.
   A. 1, 2, 3
   B. 1, 3, 4
   C. 2, 3, 4
   D. All of the above

32) **Assessment, planning, implementation, coordination, monitoring and evaluation are referred to as:**

A. The nursing process
B. The scientific method
C. The six components of Case Management
D. None of the above

33) **Accurate, thorough Case Management documentation:**

A. Limits or reduces liability
B. Is a legal medical record subject to state record retention laws
C. Is confidential
D. None of the above
E. All of the above

34) **The role of the Case Manager is that of:**

A. Educator, facilitator, insurance advocate
B. Assessor, planner, educator, facilitator, patient advocate
C. Claims adjuster, planner, educator, facilitator
D. Assessor, medical planner, facilitator

35)   Which of the following is *not* true about Case Management?

    A.   It is a new profession.
    B.   It is an area of practice within one's profession.
    C.   It is performed by a variety of health care providers.
    D.   It is performed in a variety of settings.

36)   Case Managers work in a variety of settings. The following are examples of the provider sector:

    1.   Insurance company
    2.   Infusion company
    3.   Rehabilitation center
    4.   Hospital
        A.   1, 2, 3
        B.   2, 3, 4
        C.   None of the above
        D.   All of the above

37)   Although Case Managers work in a variety of settings, they all have a common denominator of patient advocacy, educating patients and facilitating patients' optimal outcomes, but the focal point of their work is:

    A.   Empowering physicians to be gatekeepers
    B.   Empowering patients to be active decision-makers in their health care
    C.   Mandating care plans to patients and their families
    D.   Mandating services to be provided by their physicians

38)   Case Managers deal with vocational activity most often in a:

    A.   Subacute setting
    B.   Acute care facility
    C.   Rehabilitation center
    D.   None of the above

39)   Which of the following are true regarding the practice of Case Management?

    1.   It is a relatively new profession.
    2.   Certification assures appropriate care plans.
    3.   All Case Managers are nurses.
    4.   Case Management is based on the premise that when an individual reaches his optimal level of wellness and functional capability, everyone benefits.
        A.   1
        B.   2
        C.   1, 3
        D.   2, 4
        E.   All of the above

40)   Which of the following is true regarding the purposes of an orthosis?

    1.   It can be used to replace body parts.
    2.   It can be used to position body parts.
    3.   It can be used to amputate body parts.
    4.   It can be used modify muscle tone.
        A.   1, 3
        B.   2, 4
        C.   1, 2, 3
        D.   All of the above
        E.   None of the above

41) **Which of the following is true regarding a prosthesis?**
   1. The term *prosthesis* refers only to artificial arms and legs.
   2. It may improve a person's sense of wholeness or body image.
   3. Cosmesis is not an issue when fitting a prosthesis.
   4. It may result in injury or illness if improperly fitted.
      A. 1, 3
      B. 2, 4
      C. 1, 2, 3
      D. All of the above
      E. None of the above

42) **Which of the following is true regarding the prescribing of an assistive device?**
   1. An evaluation of the patient's interest and abilities is important.
   2. An evaluation of the patient's home and work environment is important.
   3. Training the patient on the device is important.
   4. Training family members on the device is sometimes important.
      A. 1, 3
      B. 2, 4
      C. 1, 2, 3
      D. All of the above
      E. None of the above

43) **Which of the following factors do *not* influence the rate of prosthesis replacement?**
   1. Activity level
   2. Educational achievements of the user
   3. Type of prosthesis
   4. Patient's social status
      A. 1, 3
      B. 2, 4
      C. 1, 2, 3
      D. All of the above
      E. None of the above

44) **Which of the following are considered assistive devices?**
   1. A "cock-up" splint for the wrist
   2. Phone receiver volume control
   3. A sling to hold a plegic and atrophied arm in place
   4. Grab bars in the tub
      A. 1, 3
      B. 2, 4
      C. 1, 2, 3
      D. All of the above
      E. None of the above

45) **Introductions, empowerment, trust, active listening, questioning and testing discrepancies are all part of:**
   A. Determining functional status
   B. Interviewing
   C. Communication process
   D. None of the above

46) **The Case Manager will find which of the following services difficult to arrange at home?**
   1. Tocolytic therapy
   2. Respiratory therapy
   3. Infusion therapy
   4. Blood transfusions
   5. Dialysis

A. 1, 2, 3
B. 2, 3, 4
C. 1, 4
D. 4, 5
E. None of the above

47) **When the Case Manager is arranging for transfer from the acute care setting to a traumatic brain injury (TBI)/rehabilitation facility she needs to verify that the facility:**

A. Can provide the therapies required by the patient
B. Has a medical director who is board certified
C. Is accredited by Joint Commission (or JCAHO) and CARF
D. 1, 3
E. All of the above

48) **_____ are facilities that provide lower cost alternatives for complex cases that do not require the services of an acute care facility or specialized care center but require more care than can be provided at home.**

A. Subacute care centers
B. Long-term care facilities
C. Rehabilitation hospitals
D. Convalescent hospitals

49) **A thorough interview and assessment enables the Case Manager to assist the patient and family to:**

A. Make informed health care decisions.
B. Make informed financial decisions.
C. Cope with the complex health care system.
D. All of the above

50) **Under the terms of the Tax Equity and Fiscal Responsibility Act, which of the following medical specialties were exempted from the Diagnosis Related Groups (DRGs) Program?**

A. Cardiology
B. Endocrinology
C. Rehabilitation medicine
D. Radiation oncology
E. Family medicine

1) **Answer: B**

    For some it is surprising that bad clinical outcomes and negligent medical care are not common causes of malpractice litigation. In fact, studies have demonstrated that patients rarely identify most substandard medical care.

2) **Answer: B**

    The Case Manager has an obligation of "reasonable care" to the patient. Failing to assure that the discharge is "safe" would be negligent on the part of the Case Manager.

3) **Answer: C**

4) **Answer: B**

5) **Answer: D**

    The items on this list are the common causes for malpractice litigation.

6) **Answer: B**

    Ethics are the rules or standards that govern the conduct of a person or members of a profession. Ethical rules describe a society's ideal of how a person or a professional should conduct him- or herself. Thoughts that govern a person's conduct are not necessarily ethical or virtuous.

7) **Answer: D**

8) **Answer: B**

    Emancipated minors are considered adults under most states' laws. Consent must be given freely, without coercion.

9) **Answer: C**

    Therefore, Case Managers should aggressively seek all data necessary to make an informed decision that is in the best interests of their patient.

10) **Answer: A**

    The word *tort* comes from the Latin *torquêre*, to twist, and implies injury. In law, a tort is a damage, injury or wrongful act done willfully, negligently or in circumstances involving strict liability—a legal wrong committed upon the person or property independent of contract. It may be either: A direct invasion of some legal right of the individual; or an infraction of some public duty by which special damage accrues to the individual; or the violation of some private obligation by which like damage accrues to the individual. Torts are not specific to medical malpractice cases.

11) **Answer: D**

12)   Answer: E

Coryza is a common cold, and blepharitis is a minor infection of the eyelid. Pedis planus are flat feet, and varrucus vulgaris are common warts. None of these conditions requires the services of a Case Manager.

13)   Answer: C

Screening all patients with claims over $500 and $1,000 per year would yield too many claims and too few catastrophic illnesses. Those patients with claims of $100,000 and over would no doubt be well known to the insurers and Case Managers long before their patients hit those thresholds. Thresholds of $5,000 to $10,000 are most commonly seen in the industry.

14)   Answer: B

The Case Manager should permit and encourage the patient to explore his or her feelings without judgment, punishment or rejection.

15)   Answer: C

The Case Manager should be motivating the patient by focusing on his progress not lack of progress.

16)   Answer: C

Chronic conditions not requiring surgery can be handled by the primary care physician (PCP). The PCP can then make referrals when the patient's condition changes or he deems referrals medically necessary.

17)   Answer: C

Many patients are embarrassed or ashamed when their body image changes because of illness or injury.

18)   Answer: C

All of the above questions can help shed light on the reason for the patient's resistance and assist the team in formulating a more effective care plan.

19)   Answer: B

The illness need not be as "catastrophic" as a closed head injury, a cervical spine injury or cancer to cause serious changes in a person's life. A carpenter who loses the use of his hand, a dancer who suffers from vertigo, or a professional athlete who injures his knee are examples of patients whose injuries, although not considered catastrophic by most, have serious effects beyond the physical realm, and into the social and psychological spheres. These patients have not just suffered a serious and painful injury, but have lost careers, hopes, dreams, social status and income. As a result of the life changes precipitated by major illness and injury patients commonly experience: loss; anger; fear and anxiety; depression; and dependency.

20)   Answer: A

The exceptions to the ADA are:
- It does not apply to religious organizations, or private membership clubs, except when these organizations sponsor a public event.
- The federal government or corporations owned by the federal government
- Indian tribes
- Compliance with this act can prove a hardship for small employers. Therefore, if an employer has fewer than 15 employees, he is exempt. (Note: Because an accommodation is expensive for an employer, does not automatically make it a "hardship.")

21)   Answer: D

The following are rules of thumb to help determine if a job function is an "essential function" of the job:
- Essential job functions recorded in the written descriptions of job, prepared prior to advertising for the job or interviewing candidates are considered evidential when determining the essential functions of the job.
- The job function in question takes up the majority of the job's time.

- The job function in question is considered "essential" to the jobs of others in the same or similar job.
- The job function is described in a collective bargaining agreement.

22) **Answer: D**

The Women's Health and Cancer Rights Act is a new law that was enacted as part of an Omnibus Appropriation Bill, and became effective for plan years beginning on or after October 21, 1998. This Act amended ERISA to require group health plans, including self-insured plans that provide coverage for mastectomies, to provide certain reconstructive and related services following mastectomies. The services mandated by the Act include:
- Reconstruction of the breast upon which the mastectomy has been performed
- Surgery and reconstruction of the other breast to produce a symmetrical appearance
- Prosthesis and treatment for physical complications attendant to the mastectomy, for example, lymphedema

23) **Answer: A**

State financing and benefit laws vary widely. In general, unemployment compensation benefits under state laws are intended to replace about 50% of an average worker's previous wages. Maximum weekly benefits provisions, however, result in benefits of less than 50% for most higher-earning workers. All states pay benefits to some unemployed persons for 26 weeks. In some states, the duration of benefits depends on the amount earned and the number of weeks worked in a previous year. In others, all recipients are entitled to benefits for the same length of time. During periods of heavy unemployment, federal law authorizes extended benefits, in some cases up to 39 weeks; in 1975 extended benefits were payable for up to 65 weeks. Extended benefits are financed in part by federal employer taxes.

24) **Answer: A**

The cost of Workers' Compensation insurance premiums are borne by the employer, with no contribution by the employee. The authors of the Workers' Compensation legislation intended that the significant cost of this compulsory insurance would provide an incentive to employers to increase workers' safety programs and result in decreased work-related injuries. Stringent safety programs instituted by major corporations have nevertheless failed to stop the rise in industrial accident rates. It is estimated that industrial accidents have cost U.S. manufacturers more than $11 billion per year.

25) **Answer: D**

Third Party Administrators (or TPAs) usually operate in the environment of the self-insured employer. Although they may act as an agent of the "insurer," the TPA is not party to the insurance contract between the employer and the employee. The TPA does not incur any risk for employer or employee losses. A TPA's sole function is to perform "insurance type" administrative services for self-insured employers. These services include, but are not limited to, performing claims adjudication and payment, maintaining all records, providing utilization and quality management, Case Management and managing the provider network.

26) **Answer: B**

Automobile accidents victims are characterized by their youth, the seriousness of their injuries, which include closed head trauma, spinal trauma and permanent disability.

27) **Answer: D**

Under TEFRA, Peer Review Organizations (PROs) were established. A PRO is an entity that is selected by HCFA to reduce costs associated with the hospital stays of Medicare and Medicaid patients. Further, they are charged with conducting reviews of hospital-based care on these patients to assure quality of care and appropriateness of admissions, readmissions and discharges. Through this review procedure PROs can maintain and/or lower admission rates and reduce lengths of stay while insuring against inadequate treatment.

28) **Answer: E**

29) **Answer: B**

Although annual or lifetime dollar limits cannot be set under the provisions of the Mental Health Parity Act, other limits are allowed. Examples of other allowable limits are:

- Limited number of annual outpatient visits
- Limited number of inpatient days annually
- A per-visit fee limit
- Higher deductibles and copayments are allowed in mental health benefits under MHPA, without parity in medical and surgical benefits

If an employer does not offer medical benefits, he does not have to offer mental health benefits; said differently, if an employer chooses not to offer mental health benefits, he must also choose not to offer medical benefits.

30) **Answer: C**

31) **Answer: D**

Proper documentation will minimize a Case Manager's liability risk.

32) **Answer: C**

33) **Answer: E**

34) **Answer: B**

Case Managers are patient advocates, not insurance advocates. They do not adjust claims, nor are they medical planners; that is the physician's role.

35) **Answer: A**

Case Management by itself is not a profession, but an area of practice within one's profession.

36) **Answer: B**

HMOs, insurance companies and Third Party Administrators are examples of the payer sector.

37) **Answer: B**

38) **Answer: C**

39) **Answer: D**

40) **Answer: B**

An orthosis is a device that is added to a person's body to achieve one or more of the following ends: support, position, immobilization, correction of deformities, assistance of weak muscles, restoration of muscle function, and modification of muscle tone. Prostheses are aimed more at replacement of body parts.

The term *orthosis* generally encompasses such devices as slings, braces and splints. Orthoses are used to support or aid in the functioning of the upper and lower extremities, and hands and feet, as well as the trunk and spine. These devices can be relatively simple affairs, made of cotton belts and plastic splints, or they can be complex electromechanical appliances, replete with steel alloys, cantilevered joints and servomotors. The replacement of body parts is a function of prostheses.

41) **Answer: B**

A prosthesis is a device that restores or replaces all or part of a missing body part. The science of prosthetics addresses the mechanical, physiologic and cosmetic functions of restorations. Although the orthoses are aimed at *assisting* the body to restore function, prostheses restore or replace those parts of the human body that are absent or no longer function. The need for replacement and cosmesis rather than a simple increase in functionality stems from a person's need for "wholeness" and a "positive body image." With this in mind, the professional prosthetist has as his goals increasing both functionality and cosmesis. Poorly fitted prostheses can cause injury or illness. Although most laypersons associate the term *prosthesis* with artificial arms and legs, the field is much larger, encompassing many specialties. Prostheses run the gamut from highly functional devices, such as a lens implant for cataracts, an artificial hip for a hip fracture, to highly cosmetic devices such as breast implants after a mastectomy, wigs (a cranial prosthesis) after chemotherapy and an artificial eye after an enucleation.

42) **Answer: D**

The type of assistive device is determined by the needs of the individual patient, his abilities and functional limitations and his environment. Such common mistakes as a walker being too heavy for a frail elderly patient, or a room being too small for a hospital bed, or doorways too narrow for a wheelchair plague the inexperienced Case Manager. Even simple devices such as crutches and walkers have resulted in injuries owing to falls and improperly fitted wheelchairs have resulted in decubiti. The Case Manager should make sure the patient is properly fitted to the equipment and trained in its use. When appropriate, family and caregivers should also receive the appropriate training. The patient and family or caregivers should be involved in the selection of adaptive devices, and should be trained in their use. A Case Manager who attends to these issues will increase the likelihood that the device is wanted, meets the patient's needs and will be fully used.

43) **Answer: B**

Many factors influence replacement frequency. For example, lower extremity prostheses bear weight, sustain high impact and are exposed to the elements. Damage to the prostheses acquired by these activities demands maintenance, repair and replacement. Replacement frequency depends on the activity level of the patient and the demands he puts on the prosthesis as well as the complexity of the prosthesis and the properties of the materials used. Further, an individual's prosthetic needs may change. For example, a sedentary individual may become more active, requiring a new prosthesis with more features and flexibility. Conversely, an active individual with advancing age or disease may become more sedentary, requiring a replacement prosthesis that is lighter and more stable. Finally, the younger patient will require successively larger prostheses to compensate for growth. There is no association between a patient's educational achievements or social status and prosthesis replacement.

44) **Answer: B**

Assistive devices substitute for impaired function and promote independence; therefore, a volume control device on a phone receiver and grab bars are assistive devices. Orthoses are devices that are added to the body to support, position, immobilize and assist weak muscles. A cock-up splint and an arm sling are considered orthoses.

45) **Answer: B**

46) **Answer: D**

Blood transfusions are not usually done at home because of the risk of transfusion reaction. Dialysis may be done at home, but owing to the associated risks it is generally not done at home unless the patient is truly homebound.

47) **Answer: E**

48) **Answer: A**

49) **Answer: D**

A thorough interview and assessment allow for the collection of data required to assist the patient in formulating his Case Management plan.

50) **Answer: C**

Under TEFRA, medical rehabilitation was exempted from the DRGs. Rehabilitation would continue to be a cost based reimbursement system, subject to certain limits.

Case Management Certification Criteria

To be eligible for voluntary certification as a Case Manager, an applicant must be of good moral character, reputation, and fitness for the practice of case management, and must meet ALL of the licensure or certification requirements and employment criteria described below.

An applicant's license or certification must be based on a MINIMUM educational requirement of a post-secondary program in a field that promotes the physical, psychosocial, or vocational well-being of the persons served. The license or certificate that is awarded upon completion of the educational program MUST be obtained by passing an examination in the applicant's area of specialization. In addition, completion of the educational program's licensing or certification process must grant the holder of the license or certificate the ability to legally and independently practice WITHOUT THE SUPERVISION OF ANOTHER LICENSED PROFESSIONAL AND TO PERFORM THE FOLLOWING SIX COMPONENTS OF CASE MANAGEMENT:

1. Assessment
2. Planning
3. Implementation
4. Coordination
5. Monitoring
6. Evaluation

LICENSURE/CERTIFICATION CRITERIA

To satisfy the Commission for Case Manager Certification's credentialing requirements, an applicant must qualify under ONE of the two categories below and meet the criteria for acceptable employment.

1. *Licensure*: The Commission considers licensure to be a process by which a government agency grants permission to an individual to engage in a given occupation, provided that person possesses the minimum degree of competency required to reasonably protect health, safety, and welfare.

    The licenses must be current and the holder classified as being in good standing in the state in which he or she practices.

Courtesy of Commission for Case Manager Certification, Rolling Meadows, Illinois.

2. *Certification*: The Commission considers certification to be a process by which a government or nongovernment agency grants recognition to an individual who has met certain predetermined qualifications set by a credentialing body. The certification must be current and the holder classified as being in good standing by the credentialing body.

EMPLOYMENT EXPERIENCE CRITERIA

In addition to meeting the licensure or certification criteria, applicants must qualify under ONE of the employment experience categories described below.

1. Able to document a minimum of 12 months of acceptable full-time case management experience or its equivalent under the supervision of a Certified Case Manager (CCM).
2. Able to document a minimum of 24 months of acceptable full-time case management employment or its equivalent.
3. Able to document a minimum of 12 months of acceptable full-time experience or its equivalent as a supervisor, supervising the activities of individuals who provide DIRECT case management services within the six components of case management.

An applicant must also document a minimum of 12 months of acceptable full-time case management employment experience as defined below.

ACCEPTABLE EMPLOYMENT

All applicants must hold a professional license or certificate that allows the holder to legally and independently practice WITHOUT THE SUPERVISION OF ANOTHER LICENSED PROFESSIONAL AND TO PERFORM THE SIX COMPONENTS OF CASE MANAGEMENT. In addition, applicants must be able to demonstrate that, as part of their employment, they apply these components in each of the following five core areas:

1. Coordination and services delivery
2. Physical and psychological factors
3. Benefit systems and cost benefit analysis
4. Case management concepts
5. Community resources

As defined, these core areas MUST:

- Be practiced within a continuum of care that addresses the ongoing needs of the individual being served by the case management process (rather than be restricted to services related to a single episode of care); AND
- Encompass multiple environments such as home care, acute care hospital, rehabilitation facility, workplace; AND
- Involve interactions with all relevant components of the health care system such as physicians, family members, third party payers, employers, other health care providers; AND
- Deal with the individual's broad spectrum of needs.

Appendix B

Consent Agreement Form

Re: Patient: _____
          Plan: _____
          Insured: _____
          Social Security #: _____

Case Management Agreement

To assure appropriate medical case management services, I, *patient name*, authorize my physician, hospital or any other health care professional involved with my care or treatment to disclose all medical, hospital, vocational or related information to *Name of Case Management Company*. I further authorize that this information be shared (as necessary) only with professionals, agencies or insurance companies who will be involved in the coordination, provision or payment of services. I understand that this is a benefit provided to all *Insured Group's Name* employees and their dependents by *Insured Group's Name*.

_____   _____
Patient Signature   Date

_____   _____
Witness   Date

Source: Adapted from C.M. Mullahy, Legal and Ethical Responsibilities of the Case Management Profession, *The Case Manager's Handbook,* 2nd ed., p. 68, © 1998, Aspen Publishers, Inc.

Appendix C

Patient Case Report

Employer Group Name
Case Management Status Report
September 1–September 30, 1998

Employee: Employee #1 (Pt. is not identified to maintain confidentiality.)

Relationship: Employee / Spouse / Dependent

Insurance Data: Name of Insurer

Social: 25-year-old male who lived alone prior to accident.
Lives with mother in rural area after accident.

Past Medical History: Unremarkable

Current Status: Paraplegia
Lives at home with home care services.

INTERVENTION

The Case Manager monitored the patient's clinical status while the patient was hospitalized and arranged for him to transfer from the acute care unit to a skilled nursing unit for rehabilitation. On July 17, 1998, the patient was transferred to the skilled nursing facility for physical therapy, occupational therapy, and wound care. The patient was not able to participate in an acute rehabilitation program at this time due to poor endurance and his extensive wounds. Progress at the subacute level was slow, but steady. While the patient was in the skilled nursing facility, the Case Manager worked with the family members, physician, discharge planner, social worker, and other providers to facilitate a discharge to the patient's mother's home. The Case Manager also was contacted by the employer as the employer wanted the Case Manager to be aware of the fact that this employee's job was waiting for the patient and that the plant he worked in was totally handicapped accessible.

On August 14, 1998, the patient was discharged to his mother's home. He refused to be admitted for acute rehabilitation, preferring to receive home care services. The Case Manager arranged for:

- Daily skilled nursing visits for wound care
- Physical therapy three times a week to:
    - strengthen upper extremity and trunk
    - teach transfers

　　　　　　　　– teach dressing and sitting skills
　　　　● Social work counseling
　　　　　　　　– to encourage him to engage in community activities,
　　　　　　　　– to motivate the patient to utilize community resources,
　　　　　　　　– to assist the patient in coping with this traumatic injury,
　　　　　　　　– and to assist in the transition, eventually, for returning to work.

COST SAVINGS ANALYSIS

By transferring the patient to a skilled nursing facility after he was stabilized, the Case Manager was able to shorten the length of stay at the acute care facility. Additionally she was able to provide the appropriate level of care at a subacute facility at negotiated fees. In discharging the patient to his mother's home, she was able to provide quality, therapeutic care while shortening his skilled nursing facility stay and negotiating for the services provided at home. As he was at his mother's home he also did not require as extensive hours of care (shifts) as he would have had he gone home alone.

The difference in cost between this case being case managed and not is as follows:

PROJECTED EXPENSES WITHOUT CASE MANAGEMENT

Hospital stay:	approximately $1,450 / day x 24 days	$34,800
Skilled nursing facility:	approximately $ 700 / day x 7 days	$ 4,900
Total:		$39,700

ACTUAL EXPENDITURES

Hospital stay:	approximately $1450 / day x 6 days	$8,700
Skilled nursing facility:	approximately $ 500 / day x 18 days	$9,000
Home care:	Skilled Nursing	
	$125 / visit negotiated to $80 / visit x 6	$ 480
	Physical Therapy	
	$175 / visit negotiated to $80 / visit x 2	$ 160
	Social Worker	
	$145 / visit negotiated to $100 / visit x 2	$ 200
Durable Medical Equipment:		
	ROHO Mattress Rental	
	$667 / mo. Rental negotiated to $400 / mo.	$ 400
	Hospital Bed	
	$1,500 purchase price negotiated to $1,000	$1,000
Total:		$19,940
Total Savings:		$19,760

CONCLUSION

The patient will continue to be followed by the Case Manager. Skilled nursing visits, physical therapy, and social work counseling will continue at home to prevent him from being readmitted, to heal his wounds, to prepare him to live with his paraplegia, and to return the patient to work as soon as feasible.

Respectfully Submitted,

Denise Maldonado RN, CCM, BS

Appendix D

Vendor Progress Report

VENDOR NAME

Employee: Name
Identification number: 111-22-3333
Employer Group: Name
Report Period: March 1998

This patient has been receiving occupational therapy, cognitive therapy, and speech and language therapy since January 1998.

GOALS FOR LAST REPORTING PERIOD

1. Improve sensory awareness of right upper extremity.
2. Normalize tone throughout right upper extremity.
3. Improve shoulder stability and assisted range of motion (AROM) of right upper extremity.
4. Improve motor planning skills.
5. Improve gross and fine motor coordination of right upper extremity.
6. Increase ADL (activities of daily living) independence
   - To be able to shave with right hand
   - To be able to write more fluently with right hand
7. Improve task tolerance with minimal encouragement.
8. Improve delayed sequential recall with 75% accuracy.
9. Increase selective attention and attention to detail for lengthy or complex material.
10. Complete word finding tasks with 85% accuracy provided with minimal cues.
11. Retell a short paragraph presented verbally in three to five sentences in length.
12. Improve oral reading skills at the short paragraph level.
13. Follow two-step, two-item written directives to 85% accuracy independently.
14. Utilize a strategy per session to compensate for communication deficits.
15. Improve lingual strength, coordination, and proprioception by executing oral motor activities with clinician and at home.
16. Complete reading comprehension skills of three to four sentences in length.
17. Complete simple deductive reasoning tasks with 80% accuracy.

OCCUPATIONAL THERAPY/PHYSICAL STATUS

Static sitting balance	Good
Dynamic sitting balance	Good
Static standing balance	Good
Dynamic standing balance	Good
Status of right upper extremity (RUE):	

Range of motion of RUE has significantly improved. Mr. X does not appear to present with any physical limitations. He continues to have difficulty with shoulder elevation, supination, and opposition to fifth digit. It is probably due to motor planning difficulties. He continues to use his right upper extremity more spontaneously during all functional activities. He does continue to exhibit difficulty with shaving using his right hand. This is most likely due to motor planning difficulties. His handwriting continues to improve; however, he is hesitant to practice writing on a continual basis.

Fine motor coordination was assessed with the Purdue Pegboard test. He was able to place four pegs in the board in 30 seconds with his right hand (severe impairment) and 16 pegs with his left nondominant hand (intact). This is an improvement, for when he first began therapy, he was unable to manipulate the pegs. There has been no change with fine motor coordination on timed tests.

GOALS FOR NEXT REPORTING PERIOD (1 MONTH)

1. Improve sensory awareness of RUE.
2. Normalize tone throughout RUE.
3. Improve motor planning skills to be able to use right hand for shaving.
4. Improve gross and fine motor coordination of RUE as demonstrated by placing six pegs in the board (Purdue Pegboard Test) with his right hand.
5. Increase ADL independence:
   - To be able to shave with right hand
   - To be able to write more fluently with right hand
   - To use right hand during simple meal preparation

COGNITIVE STATUS

A.	Stamina/endurance	NA	1	2	3	4	5
B.	Concentration/attention	NA	1	2	3	4	5
C.	Orientation to person, place, and time	NA	1	2	3	4	5
D.	Memory						
1.	Long-term/remote	NA	1	2	3	4	5
2.	Immediate	NA	1	2	3	4	5
	a) Visual	NA	1	2	3	4	5
	b) Verbal	NA	1	2	3	4	5
3.	Delayed	NA	1	2	3	4	5
	a) Visual	NA	1	2	3	4	5
	b) Verbal	NA	1	2	3	4	5

Note: In the scale above, the value NA should be assigned when a patient cannot complete the assessment or the category does not apply. In all other cases, values 1 through 5 should be assigned, with 5 being most proficient.

4. Use of compensatory strategies   NA   1   2   3   4   5
Comments: Continues to require moderate cues in order to utilize recommended strategies

5. Ability to complete functional memory assignments   NA   1   2   3   4   5

E. Visual processing
1. Scanning   NA   1   2   3   4   5
2. Compensating for visual neglect   NA   1   2   3   4   5
3. Visual-spatial skills   NA   1   2   3   4   5

F. Academic tasks
1. Reading
a) Estimated pre-injury level   NA   1   2   3   4   5
b) Current   NA   1   2   3   4   5
Comments: Aphasia; continues to demonstrate reduced attention to details, moderate cues required. Note: Mr. X perseverates on word read in a previous sentence. Paraphasias noted during oral reading.

2. Math
a) Estimated pre-injury level   NA   1   2   3   4   5
b) Current   NA   1   2   3   4   5
Comments: Mr. X requires minimal cues to complete simple banking task.

3. Writing   NA   1   2   3   4   5
Comments: Severe difficulty secondary to right dominant involvement.

G. Problem solving
1. Verbal problem-solving   NA   1   2   3   4   5
Comments: Aphasia; Mr. X's word finding difficulties have improved, but continue to affect his verbal problem-solving ability as he displays difficulty expressing himself in complete sentences.

2. Visual problem solving   NA   1   2   3   4   5

H. Executive functions
1. Initiation   NA   1   2   3   4   5
2. Planning   NA   1   2   3   4   5
3. Organization   NA   1   2   3   4   5
4. Flexibility   NA   1   2   3   4   5
5. Follow through   NA   1   2   3   4   5

GOALS FOR NEXT REPORTING PERIOD (1 MONTH)

1. Improve reading comprehension of moderate length or complexity by increasing attention to details given minimal cues.
2. Improve task tolerance with minimal encouragement.
3. Improve delayed sequential recall of auditory and visual information with 75% accuracy.
4. Utilize strategies once per session given moderate cues.

SPEECH/LANGUAGE STATUS

A. Receptive Language
1. Follows directions
a) Oral   NA   1   2   3   4   5
b) Written   NA   1   2   3   4   5
Comments: Reduced attention to details continues when directives are more complex. Continues to demonstrate difficulty with reading on a written directional task.

2. Auditory comprehension: words/sentences/
paragraphs   NA 1 2 3 4 5
B. Expressive language
  1. Word
     a) Naming   NA 1 2 3 4 5
Comments: Mr. X presents with aphasia/apraxia. However, confrontational naming tasks continue to improve.
     b) Finding   NA 1 2 3 4 5
Comments: Mr. X presents with aphasia with increased frustration. Continues to require moderate prompts to utilize strategies. Word finding is moderately to severely reduced during conversational discourse.
     c) Fluency   NA 1 2 3 4 5
Comments: Mr. X presents with apraxia/aphasia. He continues to demonstrate decreased oral fluency. Improvement has been noted.
  2. Syntax   NA 1 2 3 4 5
  3. Verbal organization and sequencing   NA 1 2 3 4 5
Comments: Reduced thought organization, word finding difficulties, and mild apraxia compromise verbal organization and sequencing during story telling. In addition, Mr. X has difficulty repairing breakdowns due to reduced verbal organization. Mr. X is able to sequence accurately three to four sentences given moderate cues.
  4. Deductive/abstract reasoning   NA 1 2 3 4 5
C. Motor Speech
  1. Strength/function of oral musculature   NA 1 2 3 4 5
  2. Dysphasia   NA 1 2 3 4 5
  3. Dysarthria   NA 1 2 3 4 5
  4. Apraxia (verbal, oral)   NA 1 2 3 4 5
  5. Speech intelligibility   NA 1 2 3 4 5
D. Pragmatic Language
  1. Body posture/facial expression   NA 1 2 3 4 5
  2. Verbal initiation   NA 1 2 3 4 5
Comments: Verbal initiation has improved.
  3. Lexicon selection   NA 1 2 3 4 5
Comments: Apraxia/aphasia; reduced word finding skills confound lexical selection.
  4. Topic (introduce, maintain, change)   NA 1 2 3 4 5
Comments: Mr. X introduces topics and maintains those introduced by self and others.

GOALS FOR NEXT REPORTING PERIOD (1 MONTH)

1. Increase selective attention and attention to detail for lengthy or complex material.
2. Retell a short paragraph presented verbally in three to five sentences in length.
3. Complete word finding tasks with 90% accuracy provided with minimal cues.
4. Improve oral reading skills at the short paragraph level.
5. Follow two-step, two-item written directives to 85% accuracy independently.
6. Utilize one strategy per session to compensate for communication deficits.
7. Improve lingual strength, coordination, and proprioception by executing oral motor activities with clinician and at home.
8. Increase reading comprehension skills to four sentences in length.
9. Complete moderately difficult deductive reasoning tasks with 90% accuracy.
10. Repair a communication breakdown by revising intended message one time per session.

Appendix E

Alternate Benefit Plan Form

Benefit Agreement

Plan Contact: _____
Plan: _____
Fax Number: _____

Re: Patient: _____
       Insured: _____
       Social Security #: _____
       Plan Number: _____

Dear _Plan Contact_:

This is to confirm our conversation today regarding the above mentioned patient. _Patient's Name_ requires the following:

_____
_____
_____

I would appreciate it if you would sign below, acknowledging your approval of benefit reimbursement for _Specific Services_. My fax number is ___-___-____.

If you have any questions, do not hesitate to contact me at ___-___-____. Thank you for your cooperation.

Sincerely,

_____, RN, CCM
Case Manager

I have reviewed and am in agreement with the above case management plan.

_____   _____
(Plan's HR Representative)   (Date)

Appendix F

Community Resources

Al-Anon Family Groups
1372 Broadway
Midtown Station
New York, NY 10018
800-356-9996
212-302-7240

Alcoholics Anonymous
475 Riverside Drive
New York, NY 10115
212-870-3400

Allergy/Asthma Information Line-American
Academy of Allergy, Asthma and Immunology
611 E. Wells Street
Milwaukee, WI 53202
414-272-6071

ALS Association
21021 Ventura Boulevard #321
Woodland Hills, CA 91364
800-782-4747
818-340-2060 (fax)

Alzheimer's Association
919 N. Michigan Avenue #1000
Chicago, IL 60611
800-272-3900
312-3355-1110 (fax)

American Association of Homes and Services for
the Aging
901 E Street NW #500
Washington, DC 20004
202-783-2242
202-783-2255 (fax)

American Association of Retired Persons
601 E Street NW
Washington, DC 20049
202-434-2277
202-434-6483 (fax)

American Association of Occupational Health
Nurses
50 Lenox Pointe
Atlanta, GA 30324
404-262-1162

American Association of Preferred Provider
Organizations
1101 Connecticut Avenue NW #700
Washington, DC 20036
202-429-5133

American Brain Tumor Association
2720 River Road #146
Des Plaines, IL 60018
800-886-2282
847-827-9918 (fax)

American Burn Association
C/ Cleon W. Goddwyn, MD
Secretary, American Burn Association
New York Hospital
Cornell Medical Center
525 East 68th Street, Room L-706
New York, NY 10021
800-548-2876

American Cancer Society
1599 Clifton Road NE
Atlanta, GA 30329
800-ACS-2345
404-325-0230 (fax)

American Chronic Pain Association
PO Box 850
Rocklin, CA 95677
916-632-0922
916-632-3208

American Diabetes Association
1660 Duke Street
Alexandria, VA 22314
800-232-3472
703-549-1500

American Heart Association
7320 Greenville Avenue
Dallas, TX 75231
214-750-5300

American Hospital Association
840 North Lake Shore Drive
Chicago, IL 60611
312-280-6511

American Lung Association
1740 Broadway
New York, NY 10019
212-315-8700

American Managed Care and Review
  Association
1227 25th Street, NW #610
Washington, DC 20037
202-728-0506

American Medical Society
515 North State Street
Chicago, IL 60610
312-464-4706 (information)

The ARC of the United States
500 E. Border Street #300
Arlington, Texas 76010
800-433-5255
817-277-3491 (fax)

Arthritis Foundation
1330 W. Peachtree Street
Atlanta, GA 30309
800-282-7800
404-872-0457

Association of Rehabilitation Nurses
5700 Old Orchard Road, 1st Floor
Skokie, IL 60077
708-966-3433

Autism Society of America
7910 Woodmont Avenue #650
Bethesda, MD 20814
800-3AU-TISM
301-657-0869 (fax)

Blue Cross and Blue Shield Association
676 North St. Clair Street
Chicago, IL 60611
312-440-6345

Case Management Society of America
1101 17th Street, NW #1200
Washington, DC 20036
202-296-9200

Centers for Disease Control-National
  Immunization Program
1600 Clifton Road NE
Atlanta, GA 30333
404-639-3311

Cleft Palate Foundation
1218 Grandview Avenue
Pittsburgh, PA 15211
800-24C-LEFT
412-481-0847 (fax)

Crohn's & Colitis Foundation of America
386 Park Avenue South, 17th Floor
New York, NY 10016
800-932-2423
212-779-4098

Employee Benefit Research Institute
2121 K Street NW #600
Washington, DC 20037
202-659-0670

Epilepsy Foundation of America
4351 Garden City Drive #406
Landover, MD 20785
800-332-4050
301-577-2684 (fax)

Guide Dog Foundation for the Blind
371 S Jericho Turnpike
Smithtown, NY 11787
800-548-4337
516-361-5192 (fax)

Health Insurance Association of America
1025 Connecticut Avenue NW
Washington, DC 20036
202-223-7836

Individual Case Management Association
10809 Executive Center Drive #105
Little Rock, AR 72211
501-227-5553

Juvenile Diabetes Foundation International
120 Wall Street, 19th Floor
New York, NY 10005
800-223-1138

La Leche League
1400 N. Meacham Road
Schaumburg, IL 60168
800-LAL-ECHE
847-519-0035 (fax)

Lupus Foundation of America
4 Research Pl. #180
Rockville, MD 20850
800-558-0121
301-670-9486 (fax)

Multiple Sclerosis Association of America
706 Haddonfield Road
Cherry Hill, NJ 08002
800-833-4MSA
609-661-9797 (fax)

Muscular Dystrophy Association
3300 E. Sunrise Drive
Tucson, AZ 85718
520-529-2000
520-529-5300

National Adrenal Diseases Foundation
505 Northern Boulevard, #200
Great Neck, NY 11021
516-487-4992

National AIDS Hotline
800-447-AIDS (specific information)
800-342-AIDS (general information, recording)

National Amputation Foundation, Inc.
40 Church Street
Malverne, NY 11565
516-887-3600

National Association for the Deaf
814 Thayer Avenue
Silver Spring, MD 20910
301-587-6282
301-587-1791 (fax)

National Association for Families Caring for their
   Elders-Elder Care America
1141 Loxford Terrace
Silver Spring, MD 20901
301-593-1621

National Association for Home Care
519 C Street NE
Washington, DC 20002
202-547-7424

National Association of Rehabilitation
   Professionals in the Private Sector
313 Washington Street #302
Washington, DC 20002
202-558-5333

National Association of Social Workers
750 First Street
Washington, DC 20002
202-408-8600

National Council on the Aging- National Institute
   on Adult Day Care
409 Third Street SW #200
Washington, DC 20024
800-424-9046
202-479-0735 (fax)

National Chronic Fatigue Syndrome and
   Fibromyalgia Association
9504 E. 63rd Street #211
Kansas City, MO 64133
816-313-2000
816-313-2001 (fax)

National Council on Child Abuse & Family
   Violence
1155 Connecticut Avenue NW #400
Washington, DC 20036
800-222-2000

National Cushings Association
4645 Van Nuys Boulevard #104
Sherman Oaks, CA 91403
818-788-9239
818-788-9235

National Down Syndrome Society
666 Broadway, 8th Floor
New York, NY 10012
800-221-4602
212-979-2873 (fax)

National Easter Seal Society
230 W. Monroe #1800
Chicago, IL 60606
800-221-6827 (out of state)
312-726-6200
312-726-1494 (fax)

National Eating Disorder Organization
6655 S. Yale Avenue
Tulsa, OK 74136
918-481-4044

National Eye Care Project Helpline
PO Box 429098
San Francisico, CA 94124
800-222-EYES

National Federation of the Blind
1800 Johnson Street
Baltimore, MD 21230
410-659-9314
410-685-5653 (fax)

National Head Injury Foundation
1140 Connecticut Avenue NW #812
Washington, DC 20036
202-296-6443

National Hemophilia Foundation
Soho Building
110 Greene Street #303
New York, NY 10012
800-424-2634
212-431-0906 (fax)

National Hospice Organization
1901 N. Moore Street #901
Arlington, VA 22209
800-658-8898
703-525-5762 (fax)

National Institutes of Health
900 Rockville Pike, Building 31
Bethesda, MD 20892
301-496-4000

National Mental Health Association
1021 Prince Street
Alexandria, VA 22314
800-969-6642
703-684-5968 (fax)

National Multiple Sclerosis Society
205 East 42nd Street
New York, NY 10017
212-986-3240

National Organization on Disability
910 16th Street NW
Washington, DC 20006
800-248-ABLE
202-293-7999 (fax)

National Spinal Cord Injury Association
545 Concord Avenue #29
Cambridge, MA 02138
800-962-9629
617-441-3449 (fax)

National Rehabilitation Association
633 South Washington Street
Alexandria, VA 22314
703-836-0850

The Paget Foundation
200 Varick Street #1004
New York, NY 10014
800-237-2438
212-229-1502

Parkinson's Disease Foundation
710 W. 168th Street, 10th Floor
New York, NY 10032
800-456-6676
212-923-4778 (fax)

Spina Bifida Association of America
4590 MacArthur Boulevard NW #250
Washington, DC 20007
800-621-3141
202-944-3295 (fax)

Tough Love International
PO Box 1069
Doylestown, PA 18901
800-333-1069

United Cerebral Palsy Association of
  America
1660 L Street NW #700
Washington, DC 20036
800-USA-5UCP
202-776-0414 (fax)

United Way of America
11211 Prosperity Farms Road
Alexandria, VA 22314
703-836-7100
703-683-7840 (fax)

Access Rehab
www.accessrehab.com
Agency for Health Care Policy and Research
www.ahcpr.gov
AIDS Global Information System
www.aegis.com/main/
American Association of Legal Nurse Consultants
www.aalnc.org
American Association of Retired Persons
www.aarp.org
American Health Lawyers Association
www.healthlawyers.org
American Medical Specialty Organization
www.amso.com
Case Management Society of America
www.cmsa.org
Centers for Disease Control and Prevention
www.cdc.gov
Department of Health and Human Resources
www.os.dhhs.gov
disABILITY Information and Resources
www.eskimo.com/~jlubin/disabled.html
Electronic Policy Network
www.epn.org/idea/hciclink.html
Food and Drug Administration
www.fda.gov
Health Care Financing Administration
www.hcfa.gov
Health Insurance Association of America
www.hiaa.org
Internet Resources for Special Children
www.irsc.org
Joint Commission on Accreditation of Healthcare Organizations
www.jcaho.org

MedWeb
    www.shadow.net/-arb/medweb.html
National Association of Rehabilitation Professionals
    www.narpps.org
National Committee for Quality Assurance
    www.ncqa.org
National Health Information Center
    www.nhicnt.health.org
National Network of Libraries of Medicine
    www.nnim.nim.nih.gov/index.html

Reading List

The Case Manager's Handbook. Author: Catherine Mullahy. Aspen Publishers, Inc., Permissions Department, 200 Orchard Ridge Drive, Suite 200, Gaithersburg, MD 20878.

Nursing Case Management. Author: Suzanne K. Powell. Lippincott-Raven Publishers, 227 East Washington Square, Philadelphia, PA 19106.

Rehabilitation Nursing (second edition). Author: Shirley O. Holman. Mosby- Yearbook, Inc., 11830 Westline Industrial Dr., St. Louis, MO 63146-3318.

The Americans with Disabilities Act. Editors: Nancy Hablutzel and Brian T. McMahon. GR Press/St. Lucie Press, 100 E. Linton Blvd., Suite 403B, Delray Beach, FL 33483.

Outcome-Oriented Rehabilitation. Editors: Pat Kitchell Landrum, Nancy D. Schmidt, and Alvin McLean, Jr. Aspen Publishers, Inc., Permissions Department, 200 Orchard Ridge Drive, Suite 200, Gaithersburg, MD 20878.

Nurse Case Management in the 21st Century. Author: Elaine L. Cohen. Mosby-Yearbook, Inc., 11830 Westline Industrial Dr., St. Louis, MO 63146-3318.

Inside Case Management. Editor: Rufus Howe. Aspen Publishers, Inc., Permissions Department, 200 Orchard Ridge Drive, Suite 200, Gaithersburg, MD 20878.

Standards of Practice for Case Management. Case Management Society of America. Member: $10; non-member: $12 (call for bulk rate). (501) 225-2229. Fax: (501) 221-9068.

The Singer Report. Managed Care Systems & Technology, 401 Edgewater Place, Suite 508, Wakefield, MA 01880. (617) 246-7585, ext. 228, Fax: (617) 246-7737.

The Journal of Care Management (official bimonthly journal of CMSA). Mason Medical Communications, 1905 Post Road, Fairfield, CT 06430, (800) 313-2002.

Courtesy of Commission for Case Manager Certification, Rolling Meadows, Illinois.

The Case Manager. Mosby-Yearbook, Inc., 11830 Westline Industrial Dr., St. Louis, MO 63146-3318, (800) 453-4351.

Journal of Case Management/LT Care Management. Case Management Institute of Connecticut Community Care, Springer Publishing Company, 536 Broadway, New York, NY 10012-3955, (212) 431-4370.

Case Management Practice Guidelines. Mosby-Yearbook, Inc., Cost: $49.99. Order#: 29088 (800) 426-4525.

Appendix I

CMSA 1996 Statement Regarding Ethical Case Management Practice

INTRODUCTION

This statement is intended to provide guidance to the individual case manager in the development and maintenance of an environment in which case management practice is conducted ethically. Such an environment is one in which morality prevails and there is support for right (good) decisions and actions.

The statement sets forth ethical principles for case management practice. When applied in practice, these principles underlie right decisions and actions. Thus, they can be utilized by individuals or peers to judge the morality of particular decisions and/or actions.

Ethics is inherently intertwined with morality. In the practice of the healthcare professions, ethics traditionally has dealt with the interpersonal level between provider (e.g. case manager) and client, rather than the policy level which emphasized the good of society. Ethics deals with ferreting out what is appropriate in situations which are labeled "dilemmas" because there are no really good alternatives and/or where none of the alternatives is particularly desirable. Thus, ethics addresses the judgement of right and wrong or good and bad.

Ethical Principles in Case Management Practice

As professionals emanating from a variety of healthcare disciplines, case managers adhere to the code of ethics for their profession of origin. In all healthcare practices certain principles of ethics apply. Case management is guided by the principles of autonomy, beneficence, nonmaleficence, justice and veracity.

Autonomy is defined as "a form of personal liberty or action when the individual determines his or her own course in accordance with a plan chosen by himself or herself." This is the fundamental ethical principle of case management practice. The role of case manager as client advocate arises from a commitment to the concept of client autonomy. The needs of the client, as perceived by the client, are preeminent. Thus the client is primary relative to decision making. The case manager collaborates with the autonomous client with the goal of fostering and encouraging the client's independence and self determination. This leads the case manager to educate and empower the client/family to promote growth and development of the individual and family so that self-advocacy and self-direction is achieved. This implies informing and supporting the client in their options and decisions related to their healthcare.

Courtesy of Case Management Society of America, Little Rock, Arkansas.

From application of the principle of autonomy, the practice of case management is concerned with preservation of the dignity of the client and family. The Case Manager is knowledgeable about and respects the rights of the individual and family which arise from human dignity and worth, including consent and privacy. The case management plan is individualized and constantly changing based on the needs of the specific client and family. The Case Manager does not discriminate based on social or economic status, personal attributes, or the nature of the health problems of the client.

Beneficence is "the obligation or duty to promote good, to further a person's legitimate interests, and to actively prevent or remove from harm." In ethical case management practice, the application of beneficence is balanced with the interests of autonomy in order to prevent paternalism and promote self-determination. The definition of the principle of nonmaleficence is related to beneficence. Nonmaleficence means refraining from doing harm to others. The realization of this principle in case management practice involves emphasis on quality outcomes.

Although uniformity of thought about the practical application of the principle within our society does not exist, Frankens defines justice as maintenance of what is right and fair. The concept of distributive justice deals with the moral basis for dissemination of goods and evils, burdens and benefits. The concept of justice raises public health care policy questions as: Who should receive services? Based on what criteria? Who should pay for services for the poor? What services should benefit from government funding? Case management practice brings the issue of comparative treatment of individuals into sharp focus because on a daily basis it deals with allocation of health care resources on an individual level. Case Managers know firsthand the dilemmas related to relative access to care based on such factors as geography and ability to pay.

Decisions regarding such goods and benefits as access to health care services within a society with limited resources are initially analyzed based on individual need. Where a fundamental need exists; that is, in situations when an individual will be harmed if a product or a service is not provided, the Case Manager advocates for the individual to receive it. The Case Manager applies concepts of fairness so as to maximize the individual's ability to carry out reasonable life plans.

Veracity means truth telling. This is an essential operational principle for the Case Manager in order to develop trust. Trust is an essential forerunner of collaborative relationships between Case Managers and client/families and between Case Managers, providers, and payers. Truth telling also is basic to the exercise of self-determination by the autonomous client/family.

CONCLUSION

The professional Case Manager strives for a moral environment and practice in which ethical principles can be actualized. Ethical dilemmas are identified and reasonable solutions sought through appropriate consultation and moral action. The ethical Case Manager is accountable to the client as well as peers, the employer/payer and to him-/herself and to society for the results of his/her decisions and actions.

CMSA Standards of Practice Committee
February 1996

DEFINITIONS

Client: The individual who is ill, injured or disabled who collaborates with the Case Manager to receive services.
Payer: The individual or entity which purchases case management services.
Family: Family members and/or those significant to the client.